PAI

AZMI BISHARA

Palestine

Matters of Truth and Justice

HURST & COMPANY, LONDON

First published in the United Kingdom in 2022 by
C. Hurst & Co. (Publishers) Ltd.,
New Wing, Somerset House, Strand, London, WC2R 1LA
Copyright © Azmi Bishara, 2022
All rights reserved.

The right of Azmi Bishara to be identified as the author of
this publication is asserted by him in accordance with the
Copyright, Designs and Patents Act, 1988.

Distributed in the United States, Canada and Latin America by
Oxford University Press, 198 Madison Avenue, New York, NY 10016,
United States of America.

A Cataloguing-in-Publication data record for this book
is available from the British Library.

ISBN: 9781787387102 *paperback*

9781787387607 *hardback*

This book is printed using paper from registered sustainable
and managed sources.

www.hurstpublishers.com

Printed in Great Britain by Bell and Bain Ltd, Glasgow

CONTENTS

List of Tables, Figures and Maps   vii
List of Abbreviations   ix

Introduction   1

PART ONE
REFLECTIONS ON A JUST CAUSE

1. On Narratives, Myths and Propaganda   15
2. Afterthoughts, Memory and History   57
3. Afterthought 2: The Arab Question and the Jewish
   Question   77
4. On the Arab-Israeli Conflict   107
5. From Liberation Struggle to Border Dispute   137
6. The Road to Nowhere   159

PART TWO
THE TRUMP-NETANYAHU DEAL

7. Zionist Religious-Nationalist Discourse in an Official
   American Text   187
8. Choices and Illusions   227
9. Concluding Remarks   265
Appendix: Arab Public Opinion on the Palestinian Issue   289

Bibliography   305
Index   325

LIST OF TABLES, FIGURES AND MAPS

Tables

Table 1.1:	Jewish Immigrants to the United States and Palestine (1899–1939)	18
Table 1.2:	Distribution of the Settled Population in Palestine (1946)	33
Table 6.1:	UN Resolutions Reflecting PLO Achievements Related to Palestinian Entitativity	160
Table 10.1:	Reasons for Opposing Recognition of Israel (in % of Total Respondents)	297
Table 10.2:	Reasons for Supporting Recognition of Israel (% of Total Respondents)	299
Table 10.3:	Position on Recognition of Israel Cross-Tabulated with Household Income (in %)	302
Table 10.4:	Position on Recognition of Israel Cross-Tabulated with Stated National Priorities (in %)	302
Table 10.5:	Position on Recognition of Israel Cross-Tabulated with Position on Democratic Governance (in %)	303

Figures

Fig. 6.1:	Israel's GDP growth (annual %) 1986–2005	165
Fig. 6.2:	Israel's GDP per capita growth (annual %) 1986–2005	165

LIST OF TABLES, FIGURES AND MAPS

Fig. 6.3:   Israel's GNI per capita growth (annual %) 1986–
            2005   166
Fig. 6.4:   Israel's Foreign Direct Investment (FDI) net
            inflows (% of GDP) 1986–2005   166
Fig. 6.5:   Unemployment Rates in Israel 1983–2005 (% of
            total labour force) (national estimates)   167
Fig. 10.1: Is Palestine a Pan-Arab Issue or an Exclusively
            Palestinian Issue   293
Fig. 10.2: Do You Support Your Country Recognising Israel   296

Maps

Map 6.1a–f: Israeli Settlement Expansion in the West Bank
            (1968–2015)   177
Map 7.1:   The Palestinian Triangle   217
Map 7.2:   Map of Palestine According to "Trump's Vision"
            with Settlement Enclaves Indicated   223
Map 7.3:   Map of Palestine According to Trump's Vision
            Compared to Areas A, B, and C as Delineated in
            the Post-Oslo Cairo Agreement   224

LIST OF ABBREVIATIONS

ACRPS	Arab Center for Research and Policy Studies
ANC	African National Congress
AIPAC	American Israel Public Affairs Committee
AOI	Arab Opinion Index
BLM	Black Lives Matter
DFLP	Democratic Front for the Liberation of Palestine
FDI	Foreign Direct Investment
GDP	Gross Domestic Product
GNI	Gross National Income
IDF	Israeli Defense Forces
IDP	Internally Displaced Person
PLO	Palestine Liberation Organization
PA (PNA)	Palestinian Authority (Palestinian National Authority)
PNC	Palestinian National Congress
UAE	United Arab Emirates
UK	United Kingdom
UN	United Nations
UNCCP	United Nations Conciliation Commission for Palestine
UNESCO	United Nations Educational, Scientific and Cultural Organization
UNRWA	United Nations Relief and Works Agency for Palestine Refugees in the Near East
UNSCOP	United Nations Special Committee on Palestine
US	United States

INTRODUCTION

The story of this book began after a lecture I gave on the Trump-Netanyahu deal, known as "the deal of the century." The lecture had been turned into an Arabic booklet that met with a wide and enthusiastic reception and many encouraged me to then publish it in English. But once it was translated and ready to go to press, I realised it needed some historical background and analysis. This addition gradually expanded to include my thoughts on the Palestine question and a summary of my conclusions from studies and essays I published on this subject in Arabic, Hebrew and English over the past three decades. The result is the present volume in which the lecture occupies just one chapter.

Although I wrote the above-mentioned studies as an academic, I am not a specialist in the sense that innumerable scholars of the history of Palestine, Zionism and the Arab-Israeli conflict, and on whose publications I draw, are. I approach the Palestine issue as a researcher and scholar, but at the same time, as someone to whom this subject is very personal and who has lived with it on a daily basis for years. Palestine is my homeland. However, Israel is not an abstract other for me. I am as familiar with its social, cultural and political life as I am with that of Palestine.

When writing on this question, I bring to bear the greatest possible critical and scientific objectivity, though not necessarily neutrality. You can refer to Israel's control over the West Bank and Jerusalem as an occupation, which is an objective descriptive, but not a neutral one in the eyes of many. Similarly, you can objectively view the

Zionist project in Palestine as primarily a form of settler colonialism, but this is not neutral either. Objectivity concerns using scientific method and available facts. It is also a conscious effort to avoid cherry-picking and letting value judgements and ideological stances influence reasoning processes. If objectivity appears biased to some, it is simply because it is predisposed to truth seeking. Neutrality, on the other hand, is a belief and attitude and not a scientific method; it is a negative moral position of no bias and no alignment, an amoral position. When it comes to an issue of oppression or a consummately humanitarian issue, an amoral position could become an immoral one. I am not neutral towards anything to do with the Palestine question or any other just cause.

It is no coincidence that this book opens with the Nakba (calamity, catastrophe) not just to establish historical context but also to define the subject itself. The Nakba, or "Palestinian Catastrophe," is the term used to refer to the Palestinians' loss of their homeland upon the establishment of the state of Israel in 1948. Chapter 1 discusses this major event: its impact, its various dimensions and the assorted myths that have grown around it. It also discusses its meaning: its ramifications, connotations and symbolic significance. However, my particular concern is to show that the Palestinian cause did not begin in 1967, and that it is not simply about the occupied Gaza Strip and West Bank, despite the current importance of these two chunks of territory as components of the Palestinian cause and their centrality in the international political approach to this question.

The most important reason why I open with the Nakba is that this book, as a whole, is an attempt to show that the question of Palestine is not simply a dilemma awaiting creative policy solutions, but rather a question of injustice that can only be resolved through the application of justice. Justice can take various forms, all of them relative. None of them, however, should involve bargaining with the Palestinians over sovereignty over the West Bank, Gaza and East Jerusalem, as though the problem of Palestine could be resolved by further Palestinian concessions on the territories that, in all events, constitute just 22 per cent of historic Palestine.

As I see it, justice, when applied to the Palestinian question, is primarily founded on a historically shifting equilibrium between the two chief components of justice, equality and freedom. Where the Palestinians as a people are concerned, freedom entails their liberation from occupation and from their status as an occupied people stripped of fundamental rights and as refugees. Equality between the two peoples in the area between Jordan and the Mediterranean can take one of two forms. One is full and equal citizenship within the framework of a single state, either equality in terms of citizenship within a single state based on mutual recognition of each people's identity and communal rights, and on guarantees for equality in the individual rights of both peoples as citizens of this state. The other is equality between them in the framework of two separate and sovereign states, neither subordinate to the other and each one "a state of its citizens," although one has a predominantly Jewish and the other a predominantly Arab character. In the case of Palestine, political programmes (and probably solutions) must also be found to second-order problems that grew out of the principal issue. What is essential, in all cases, is to bear in mind the heart of the matter: that the question began with settler colonialism entailing occupation, expropriation, ethnic cleansing and the forced displacement of the native population to pave the way for the establishment of a Jewish state and for the transformation of the Jewish minority in Palestine to a Jewish majority.

Historical memory is fashioned by the same institutions that shape identity: regimes, myths, historiography, ceremonies, choices of dates and places to commemorate, literature and textbooks that try to pass off manufacturing a collective consciousness. A convergence of diverse interests also plays a part, with some asserting a more dominant influence than others. History is written by the victors, the old adage goes. Certainly, this was true in the past when the victor monopolised the tools of writing history and producing myths. In some cases, collective memory of the oppressed survived to create counter myths that challenged and subverted official history and the dominant collective memory, but only in exceptional cases was the history written from their perspective. In the contemporary world, writing history and forging collective memory are no longer the preserve of the powerful. Even so, new challenges have nonetheless emerged, like disparities in the access to public spaces and the pluralisation of the production and dissemination of information on the internet which levels the status between fact and fiction, and truth and lies.

There remains, of course, the question of ideology, which has always been a modern challenge. However, the end of the Cold War ushered in a new phenomenon: the decline of totalising ideologies and the collapse of the great twentieth century ideologies in favour of the eclectic ideologies of power politics, identity politics and populism. Simultaneously, however, there has been a rise in moral approaches to life. More and more young people in today's world broach social and political issues from a moral perspective (that may be infused with identitarian perspectives, especially in issues involving human dignity) rather than an ideological perspective. Young people from different backgrounds and ways of life (e.g., religious or secular, liberal or leftist or with no definitive worldview) protest together against what they consider unjust. This has opened up new opportunities for the oppressed everywhere. We can easily observe this and even document the resemblance between the poignant scenes and discourses of such movements as the youth solidarity campaigns with Palestine in May 2021, the Black Lives Matter (BLM) movements, the 2019 uprisings of the young generation in Lebanon and Iraq against sectarianism, corruption and armed militias, not to mention the opening phases of the Arab revolutions in 2011.

This historical ethical turn is great news for the struggle for justice; it is to be observed in issues such as the environment, gender and social justice. But here is the place to parenthetically remark that its aversion to politics can also be coupled with scepticism towards political rational considerations of historical social contexts. This approach may magnify its potential to oppose injustices but limits its capability to present alternatives and renders it susceptible to new sorts of populism, such as what one might call "elitist populism," which may appear oxymoronic for now.

When I began preparing this book for publication, it looked as though the Palestinian cause had been thoroughly marginalised. Numerous Arab states were rushing to normalise relations with Israel, arguing that the centrality of the Palestinian cause was a myth and, therefore, not a real priority for Arab states. They were encouraged in this by individuals in the former Trump administration whose pro-Israeli bias was so blind and unconditional that they parroted the positions of the Israeli far right. However, these individuals had conveniently overlooked a number of hard facts, the most salient of which is that the Palestinian people live under a brutal and relentless occupation. It is precisely because individual Palestinians have to endure the perpetual strains and constantly looming cruelties of this reality on a day-to-day basis that their cause is not going to disappear, regardless of the motives of some Arab regimes, whose agendas take no account of their own people's interests, much less those of the Palestinians.

On the other hand, the regional attempts to marginalise the Palestinian cause only de-emphasise the national conflictual aspect of it for the benefit of more emphasis on the democratic struggle for justice in Palestine itself and its interaction with the struggle for democracy and justice in the Arab countries and internationally.

Successive generations of Palestinians have inherited their ongoing cause. For Arab peoples, in general, the importance of this cause stems not just from the fact that it is an Arab cause, but also, and more crucially, from its relation to the still ongoing phenomenon of settler colonialism. As such, the symbolism of injustice in general, and resistance to it, is all the more intensified by the Palestinian plight. Anyone who thinks that Arab public opinion (expressions of which on the Palestinian question are presented in an appendix) has little impact or can be disregarded need only consider the grassroots uprisings in the Arab region in 2011 and, again, in 2019. Whoever thinks that popular opinion is unimportant, or even disregards its existence, should give some thought to the popular uprisings of 2011 and the second wave of 2019.

In light of the foregoing, we should not be surprised that the chain of interrelated events that began in May 2021—the outbreak and spread of waves of mass protests in solidarity with families threatened with expulsion from their homes in Sheikh Jarrah, Silwan and other Jerusalem neighbourhoods to make way for Jewish settlers; the simultaneous protests in defence of the Aqsa Mosque against recurrent incursions by Jewish settlers and the Israeli army; Hamas's claim to expand its concept of deterrence to encompass Israeli abuses in Jerusalem; and the renewed flareup of the war in Gaza—put paid to all the allegations and hype surrounding the "deal of the century." Similarly, these developments burst the bubble of the myth promoted by the far-right circles surrounding former President Donald Trump that held that the US could move its embassy to Jerusalem (in an attempt to legitimise Israel's unilateral annexation of the city in violation of international law) without risking any repercussions.

No analysis of the recent uprising in Jerusalem, which began as the final touches were being placed on this book, is possible without recognising the impact of Washington's decision to proceed with moving its embassy from Tel Aviv to Jerusalem in blatant disregard of Palestinian and Arab feelings. The same applies to the rush on the part of some Arab states to normalise relations or form bilateral alliances with Israel in order to forestall a repetition of what they consider America's abandonment of its allies during the popular Arab revolutions and uprisings of 2011–2. Let us recall, here, that the alliances between some Gulf states and Israel, ostensibly concluded to preserve regional stability, are not as recent as they appear. Strangely enough, alliances preceded the normalisation of relations. They were forged immediately after the uprisings of 2011, and before that in some cases. Their purpose was to avert the democratic transformation in the Arab region. This coincided with the Israeli leadership's concept of security, according to which democratisation in the Arab world would pose an existential threat to Israel.

This is not to deny the existence of other common interests and concerns, most notably the shared fear of Iran. Indeed, Iranian policies trigger alarm not only among authoritarian Arab regimes, but also among democrats and broad sectors of Arab societies due to Tehran's divisive exploitation of sectarian issues and propaganda. This is not to mention its staunch support of the regime in Syria and of sectarian militias in several Arab countries. But this is another matter.

The Palestinian cause is the world's last remaining unresolved instance of settler colonialism. Numerous other instances of this phenomenon have either ended over the course of history, or "normalised," bequeathing residual unsettled issues and grievances among indigenous peoples. Israeli leaders are banking on this latter outcome: that the Palestinian cause will fade into oblivion while Israel maintains the status quo of a state of peace with Arab regimes willing and able

INTRODUCTION

to oppose the popular sentiment on this issue. In most historical cases, settlers have built nations atop the ruins of the cultures and civilisations of other peoples who had inhabited the land for thousands of years, turning them into "indigenous peoples" whose struggle (at least in democratic countries) is limited to pressing demands for reparations, cultural rights and the like. This does not seem to be the case in Palestine where settler colonialism cannot nativise (or indigenise) as it maintains an apartheid regime. On the other hand, the fate of the colonialist settler project in Palestine is bound to differ from, for example, that of the French project in Algeria, for example, where French settlers had the option to return to their own motherland. There is no "motherland" for the present-day generations of Israeli Jews other than Israel itself.

A settler colonial project that began in the twentieth century would inevitably unfold in ways totally unlike its predecessors from the fifteenth to the nineteenth century. This was, after all, the era of the rise and culmination of third-world anti-colonialist and national independence movements. But this is not the main reason why settler colonialism in Palestine cannot be normalised and why the settlers, in this case, cannot be nativised or naturalised. There are two crucial historical factors that prevent this in the absence of a just solution to the Palestinian cause. The first is that as a result of Israel's rejection of the division of Palestine into two states as set forth in the 1947 United Nations Partition Resolution (a resolution the Zionist movement recognised only in order to declare a Jewish state), this colonialist settler venture eventually acquired an apartheid character, especially after Israel "re-unified" the whole of historic Palestine under its rule with its territorial conquests in the 1967 war. The military occupation regime that Israel instituted gradually evolved into a system of ethnic segregation, whereby two peoples living under the same authority and, relatively speaking, in the framework of the same economic system are subject to two entirely different legal systems. Under this binary, civil and human rights are manifestly different for the occupiers and occupied.

Israeli settler colonialism will never be naturalised, no matter how much time passes, unless it first recognises the historic injustice that it has perpetrated against the Palestinian people and acts to redress it.

Half of those currently living in historical Palestine are Arabs and half of them are Jews. All of them live under a government that adopts the Jewishness of the State of Israel as a supreme value, uses its monopoly on violence to ensure religio-ethnic superiority of one ethnic group over the other, and embraces a nationalist ideology with a religious stamp. In short, in addition to the different historical contexts, the evolution of the Zionist settler drive differs from settler drives that founded other countries. Israel did not evolve into a state for all its citizens. It insists on remaining a state fundamentally based on religio-ethnic domination or dedicated to the dominance of a particular ethno-religious affiliation.

The second factor is that by the time a Zionist settler entity established a presence in Palestine, the Palestinians were already in possession of a national consciousness and national aspirations. They simultaneously saw themselves as part of a broader Arab community; an "imagined community" to be more accurate. They had thus developed a sense of national identity long before the colonialist settler movement was powerful enough to subject them to a process of sociocide and/or politicide. Still, despite all attempts to obliterate them as a political and social entity, they have survived as a people aspiring to reclaim their legitimate rights and see their national demands met.

At the same time, an Israeli-Jewish people has emerged in Israel. In this case, of course, the sense of a Jewish national identity originated in the Zionist movement. However, this movement could not have succeeded in creating a nation had it not been for the establishment of the state of Israel. This emergent state, regardless of its illegitimacy in the eyes of most inhabitants of Palestine and the Arab world at the time, proceeded to establish national institutions, build a sophisticated and integrated economy, revive Hebrew as a spoken language, enforce mandatory conscription into a modern army, and weave and market a founding narrative that successfully exploited the historical circumstances of the times. It was such concrete factors that created an Israeli-Jewish people with a claim to both individual and communal rights.

There can be no absolute justice in a situation of this sort, because absolute justice means turning back the clock. The type of justice required here is the eventual achievement of legal and political equality between the two peoples in Palestine in the present day.

INTRODUCTION

I would add a third major obstacle to the naturalisation of Israeli settler colonialism: a regional environment in which Israel is regarded with suspicion and hostility which, in turn, is a source of Israeli fear and antagonism towards Arab peoples' aspirations to liberate themselves from authoritarianism. This deep-seated mutual hostility is both an expression of Israel's alienation from its regional environment and a source of the reproduction of the Arab grassroots rejection of Israel.

As will be discussed in Chapters 2 and 3, what has further complicated the Palestine issue and obstructed Palestinian liberation is its overlap between what I term the "Arab question,"[1] and the issue referred to in Europe since the nineteenth century as the "Jewish question." The particular position of Palestine at the intersection of these two questions has both complicated and aggravated the intractability of the Palestine question.

This book will detail the dimensions of the complexity in conjunction with questions of memory and forgetting. Chapters 4 through 6 will discuss the origin of the Arab-Israeli conflict, a conflict that began at a time when no Arab lands were under occupation except for Palestine, and proceed to discuss the significance of the bilateral or separate processes between certain Arab states and Israel. These chapters will also trace the course of the Palestinian national liberation movement from its formative phase through the period of armed struggle and then to its succumbing to the trap of making peace with Israel in a manner that left all core issues unresolved. The Palestinians gained nothing in return but Israel's recognition of the Palestine Liberation Organization (PLO), and that only came after the movement turned the question issue of Palestine from the unifying Arab cause *par excellence* into an exclusively Israeli-Palestinian conflict.

The upshot of this evolution was the creation of a Palestinian "authority" that possessed neither sovereignty nor a state. Needless to say, this did not resolve the Palestinian question. Instead, it freed Israel from the daily burdens of managing the occupation directly thanks to the introduction of a system of security coordination between Israel

---

[1] Azmi Bishara, *On the Arab Question: An Introduction to an Arab Democratic Manifesto* [Arabic] (Beirut: Center for Arab Unity Studies, 2007).

and the Palestinian Authority (PA).[2] It also marginalised the PLO and triggered a struggle for power in Palestine long before a Palestinian state was even within reach. The current intra-Palestinian rift can only be understood in the context of the decision to abandon the Palestinian national liberation struggle and settle for an "authority" operating under occupation without an ounce of sovereignty.

The second part of the book begins with an analytical reading of the Trump-Netanyahu deal in 2020. This deal may have faded from the political scene despite the din it stirred during the Trump administration. However, it is important to spend some time on it for three reasons. First, the Israeli prime minister who replaced Netanyahu, Naftali Bennett, still thinks in the same terms of the so-called deal: economic incentives instead of justice. Second, Arab states were lured into blaming the victim (the Palestinian people) to justify the alliances they made with Israel partly in order to strengthen their bilateral alliances with the US. There is a long tradition of this type of strategic thinking. It stretches back to the Nakba and involves trading on the Palestinian cause as a means to gain some leverage in the context of diplomatic relations with Western powers. The third reason has to do with the embrace of the nationalist rhetoric of religious Zionism by certain circles in the former Trump administration. This applies in particular to the individuals who arose and acquired influence through the alliance between Zionism and extremist American evangelical churches. These individuals were sometimes more zealous in their advocacy of the ideas and attitudes of religious Zionist rhetoric than the Israeli religious right itself. The official US document laying out Trump's "deal of the century" offers an opportunity to identify the inherent fallacies in this discourse.

The last two chapters are devoted to a discussion of "what is to be done" in the future, and the extent to which this question is related to an analysis of the nature of the currently existing regime in Palestine. In this context, I will address the terms settler colonialism and apartheid. Both can be used as concepts to analyse and gain a clearer understanding of the present-day reality, but surely the choice

---

[2] It is officially known as the Palestinian National Authority (PNA).

of a political programme is contingent on more than analytical models. Should the collective struggle focus on the fight against apartheid and the fight for equal rights in a single state? Or should it aim for the establishment of a separate, democratic and sovereign Palestinian state in the West Bank and Gaza? Ultimately the task is not theoretical and abstract, but practical and quintessentially strategic.

Perhaps another way we could look at this is to ask, should the nature of the existing system of power and control in Palestine be the primary determinant of whether to pursue the "one-state" or the "two-state" solution? Obviously, settler colonialism and the current system of segregation under Israeli rule and apartheid are not mutually exclusive. The colonisers of South Africa did not bring a blueprint for apartheid with them, the system evolved out of a settler colonial regime. The same applies to the apartheid-like system in Palestine. In my view, an analysis and discussion of that system may be helpful to determine the forms of resistance that should (though not necessarily *will*) be adopted, but it is not critical to determining the choice of the solution or political programme. Moreover, the outcome of negotiated solutions, regardless of the choice, have less to do with the structure of the system of control than with the forms, efficacy and tenacity of the resistance; the actions and relative weight of the political actors set on imposing unacceptable conditions, the nature of the international order, the geostrategic situation, and other such concrete factors.

In the last chapter, I discuss ideas related to the strategies of Palestinian struggle, my view being that no academic study can propose a purely theoretical strategy of resistance. After all, resistance strategies do not operate in the abstract; they connect directly with the human actors and concrete circumstances in a specific place and time.

In sum, this book consists of two parts. The first, and longest, is a reading of and reflection on history. I ask for the reader's indulgence here because this part is written in essay form and addresses a number of ideas I believe are essential to a thorough grasp of the history. It thus eschews the chronological unfolding and detailed discussion of historical events that readers might normally expect. Some historical background and details are a must for the proper understanding of the ideas I present, but in order not to contentiously interrupt the flow

11

of the text, I have provided the necessary background in the form of footnotes, long footnotes in some cases. These should be treated as a parallel text to be read in conjunction with the main text. The second part consists of three chapters addressing the Trump-Netanyahu deal, the concepts question of settler colonialism and apartheid, and the question as to what comes next.

This book does not, and cannot, cover all aspects of the Palestinian cause. It is a condensation of decades of personal experience, readings, reflections and writings on the issue.

Acknowledgement: In the task of bringing this book to a rapid conclusion, I was assisted by a team of researchers and assistants who prepared lists of relevant literature, and who reviewed and commented on the text. Hence, I would like to take this occasion to thank Mohammad Almasri, Ayat Hamdan, Dana El Kurd and Hani Awad of the Arab Center for Research and Policy Studies (ACRPS), as well as my assistant Israa Batayneh. I would also like to thank Farah Hawana, Peter Daniel, Mandy McClure and Abby Lewis who helped in editing different versions of the text.

PART ONE

REFLECTIONS ON A JUST CAUSE

1

ON NARRATIVES, MYTHS AND PROPAGANDA

This chapter is specifically intended for readers accustomed to the idea that the Palestine question is the problem of a people under occupation and dates from the Israeli seizure of control over the West Bank and Gaza in 1967. The problem is much older and deeper. In this chapter, I will demonstrate how the origins and the fuller dimensions of the Palestinian cause reside in the Nakba (calamity, catastrophe), an Arabic term, the term denoting the catastrophic consequences of the establishment of a Jewish state in Palestine. During the 1948 War, the majority of the Palestinians, who had until then accounted for the bulk of the population in historic Palestine, were systematically expelled from their homeland. The stark contrast between Israel's independence and the Palestinian Nakba is not only the most appropriate entry point to the topic, but also an opportunity to examine some Zionist myths and the underlying ideological contradictions in dominant political culture in Israel. This chapter starts with the birth of Israel and ends with the birth of the PLO.

Independence

Israel's founding is celebrated in accordance with the Hebrew calendar. This has created a symbolic disjuncture between two dates: the date of Israel's "Independence Day," which the state marks on 5 Iyar,

15

in line with the Hebrew calendar, and the date of the Nakba, which Palestinians commemorate on the day the state of Israel was declared, albeit on 15 May, in accordance with the Gregorian calendar. The resultant temporal gap—the two occasions are usually about a week apart—serves as an appropriate metaphor for the distance between two irreconcilable narratives concerning the same historical event, that of the coloniser and settler, and that of the colonised and the dispossessed refugee.

On "Independence Day," the celebratory fervour in Israel far exceeds that of any other country marking its independence, let alone Arab states where such celebrations are comparatively feeble. In Israel, Independence Day constitutes the main holiday that includes some of the chief rites of the nationalist religion. No religious holiday surpasses it in terms of public participation except perhaps Yom Kippur, which is not festive, but rather a day of fasting, repentance and religious atonement.

Independence Day celebrations are not just official but also social and community events. Families attend local festivities with their children while patriotic songs and films dominate the airwaves. People visit military museums, and listen with rapt attention to accounts of different battles. State-run and commercial television stations air a panoply of documentaries, panel discussions, and personal interviews, reiterating various aspects of the Israeli narrative of the forceful occupation of Palestine and the Zionist project. Parents visit army units in military camps and organise picnics and day trips in the countryside (or what's left of it) and to historic battle sites. All this feeds into the broader construction of an Israeli collective memory centred on the "War of Independence" of 1948.

It is no coincidence that the official Holocaust Memorial Day is also set according to the Hebrew calendar, on 27 Nisan, about a week before "Independence Day." The intended message is clear: the latter is the answer to the former. But the Zionist project to move to Palestine to create a Jewish state was launched long before the Holocaust. In fact, decades after its inception, Zionism was still a marginal phenomenon among European Jews, the primary victims of the Holocaust, and almost non-existent among Mizrahi (Oriental) Jews. Most Jewish Holocaust survivors departed for the US and the majority of those who ended up in Palestine had no other choice, either because of closing immigration doors or due to lack of financial means.

In the late nineteenth century to early twentieth century, an increasingly steady flow of Jewish immigrants made their way from Europe to the US, with numbers peaking in 1905–6. Between 1907–9, Jewish immigration to Palestine increased, but absolute numbers remained very low in comparison. The total number of Jewish immigrants to Palestine from 1905 to 1914 represented only 0.95 to 4.27 per cent of the number of US-bound Jews (a few thousand to Palestine vs tens and hundreds of thousands to the US). Other places, such as Argentina, were also popular destinations for Jewish immigration. After the US recovered from its 1910 economic crisis, the number of immigrants to the US increased and immigration to Palestine and Argentina declined. Between 1911–14, the rate of immigration to both the US and Palestine increased, and continued to rise until World War I.[1]

However, in 1921, the US took measures to limit immigration by imposing quotas based on country of birth.[2] The Immigration Act of 1924 further tightened and codified these limits.[3] In mid-1924, following the establishment of the British Mandate in Palestine and after the US shut its doors, Jews started to immigrate in greater numbers to Palestine. But they also migrated from Palestine. Liebmann Hersch stated that "considering the whole period 1922–29, Jewish emigration carried off from Palestine 30 percent of the immigration. This is all the more striking since the Jews entered Palestine [...] with the intention of staying, and since this enormous rate of return is found in Palestine just when immigration elsewhere was made excessively difficult for the Jews."[4]

---

[1] Gur Alroey, *An Unpromising Land: Jewish Migration to Palestine in the Early Twentieth Century* (Stanford, C A: Stanford University Press, 2014), pp. 109–11.

[2] For the full text of the 1921 Act, see: "Sixty-Seventh Congress: Sec. I. Ch. 8, 1921," *Act*, GovTrack.us, 19 May 1921, accessed at: https://bit.ly/3hUTv1f

[3] For the full text of the 1924 Act, see: "Sixty-Eights Congress: Sec. I. Chs. 185, 190, 1924," *Act*, GovTrack.us, May 1924, accessed at: https://bit.ly/3fgbkWF

[4] Liebmann Hersch, "International Migration of the Jews," in: Walter F. Willcox (ed.), *International Migrations*, vol. 2: Interpretations (Cambridge, M A: National Bureau of Economic Research, 1931), pp. 513–15.

Table 1.1: Jewish Immigrants to the United States and Palestine (1899–1939)

Source:	Liebmann Hersch		Gur Alroey[5]		The American Jewish Year Book	
Year	Jewish Immigrants to the US[6]	Jewish Immigrants to Palestine[7]	Jewish Immigrants to the US	Jewish Immigrants to Palestine	Jewish Immigrants to the US[8]	Jewish Immigrants to Palestine[9]
1881–1898	–	–	–	–	[10]533,478	–
1899	37,000	–	–	–	[11]829,244	–
1900	61,000	–	–	–		–
1901	58,000	–	–	–		–

5 Alroey, p. 110.

6 Hersch, p. 474.

7 Ibid., p. 514.

8 "Statistics of Jews," *The American Jewish Year Book*, vol. 42 (3 October 1940 to 21 September 1941/5701), pp. 617–18, accessed at: https://bit.ly/3c0M0Sj

9 Ibid., p. 632.

10 Net increase. Statistics are only available for the number of Jews admitted to the US at the ports of New York, Philadelphia and Baltimore.

11 Figures for the number of Jews admitted to the US at all ports. Numbers for the years 1881–1907 are an approximate figure for total Jewish immigration to the US.

				656,397							
1902	58,000	—	—	—			
1903	76,000	—	—	—			
1904	106,000	—	—	—			
1905	130,000	—	129,910	1,230			
1906	154,000	—	153,748	3,450			
1907	149,000	—	149,182	1,750			
1908	103,000	—	103,378	2,097			
1909	58,000	—	57,551	2,459			
1910	84,000	—	84,260	1,979			
1911	91,000	—	91,223	2,326			
1912	81,000	—	80,595	2,430			
1913	101,000	—	101,330	3,050			
1914	138,000	—	138,051	2,182			

PALESTINE

Year						
1915	26,000	—	—	—	79,921	—
1916	15,000	—	—	—		—
1917	17,000	—	—	—		18,885[12]
1918	4,000	—	—	—		
1919	3,000	—	—	—		
1920	14,000	—	—	—		
1921	119,000	—	—	—	119,036	
1922	54,000	7,844	—	—	53,524	7,844
1923	50,000	7,421	—	—	49,719	7,421
1924	50,000	12,856	—	—	49,989	12,856
1925	—	33,801	—	—	10,292	33,801
1926	—	13,080	—	—	10,267	13,081

[12] For the period December 1917 to December 1921.

Year	Col 1	Col 2	Col 3	Col 4	Col 5	Col 6
1927	2,713	11,483	—	—	2,713	—
1928	2,178	11,639	—	—	2,178	—
1929	5,249	12,479	—	—	5,249	—
1930	4,944	11,526	—	—	—	—
1931	4,075	5,692	—	—	—	—
1932	9,553	2,755	—	—	—	—
1933	30,327	2,372	—	—	—	—
1934	42,359	4,134	—	—	—	—
1935	61,854	4,837	—	—	—	—
1936	29,727	6,252	—	—	—	—
1937	10,536	11,352	—	—	—	—
1938	12,868	19,736	—	—	—	—
1939	16,405	43,450	—	—	—	—

There is a noticeable correlation between the increase in Jewish immigration and waves of antisemitism in Russia, Eastern Europe and Central Europe. Even before the Holocaust, most Jews seeking refuge during waves of discrimination and persecution or economic hardships immigrated to the US, much like other Europeans at the time. Few Jews chose Palestine as a refuge. As for the relative handful of Zionists that did go to Palestine, they were still akin to a fringe cult. Unlike Jewish religious communities that settled in Palestine over the centuries in order to be in close proximity to the "graves of the ancestors," the new Jewish colonists were motivated by a different zeal. They saw themselves as the vanguard of a national movement intended to establish a Jewish state in Palestine. The early Zionist discourse, in general, disparaged and derided the character and image of "diaspora Jews," and scorned the Jews who chose not to join the settlers in Palestine. Diaspora Jews were expected to at least support the *Yeshuv*)[13] and, later, the state of Israel and to lobby for it abroad.

The national "Independence Day" celebrations and other festive seasons were carefully designed, since 1951, to create rituals filled with symbols, codes and emotive memory triggers, the ultimate aim of which was to construct a nation. By nation, here, I mean not a nation state, but a nation for whom the state must be created; a nation whose diverse histories are re-imagined as an indivisible monolithic history, a single nationalised history that, "necessarily", yes, even teleologically, leads to a Jewish state. This type of creation or foundational myths gives rise to a political culture centred around a proprietorial relationship between an ethnic group (or, in this case, ethno-religious group) and the state and that prioritises ethnic affiliation (or ethno-religious affiliation) as a criterion for the acquisition of rights. It is little wonder, in such cases, that the poorest and most underprivileged tend to stress their ethnic identity, which is identical with that of the state, as a means to demand equality.

Israel's "Independence Day" is an ideal opportunity to reproduce many of the state's founding myths and narratives, starting with the "War of Independence" as a war of the few against the many. Others

---

[13] The *Yeshuv* is the organised Jewish settler society in Palestine before the emergence of the state of Israel.

are the "rebirth" of the Jewish state in Palestine, the narrative of the secular-nationalist construction of the "new Jew" who carries weapons and tills the earth in Eretz Israel, and the "Negation of Exile" (*shlilat hahgula*), the myth of the apolitical existence of diaspora Jews without a nation. This negation, which is essential to Zionism, is performed by turning the Jews into a "nation like all nations"[14] by establishing a Jewish state[15] and by repudiating the "weak" minority status and character of "diaspora Jews" who could not own and cultivate land or protect themselves. This is all to say that, not only were many Jews against Zionism (those willing to participate in European secular society as integrated citizens, and others wanting to preserve their perceived Jewish exilic uniqueness), but also that Zionism was against many Jews. Zionism openly despised the exilic existence, ways of life and general character of diaspora Jews.

Zionist ideology underwent some transformations since it first fused some indispensable religious myths (the eternally promised land and the promise of return) with a secular settler colonialist drive and a militaristic creed in order to found the Jewish nation and establish its link with *Eretz Yisrael* (Land of Israel). Under the combined forces of nation-building nationalist propaganda, ongoing territorial and settler expansion and growing militarisation, the secular myths would

---

[14] This was considered in itself blasphemy by most orthodox religious Jews at that time, and it still is by many as it conflicts with the Jewish religious concept of a divinely elected people. The Zionist project as a whole was perceived as an attempt to interfere in the work of God by in-gathering the Jewish diaspora before the coming of the messiah.

[15] Amnon Raz developed this encapsulation of the essence of Zionism into a moral disquisition against Zionist practices in Palestine. Drawing on critical philosophical (Walter Benjamin) and Jewish theological thought, he argues that exile is a theological concept that defines the foundation of Jewish existence anywhere, including in *Eretz Yisrael* (the land of Israel), since the destruction of the second temple. It contradicts the nationalist concept of exile while it can converge with a critical secular view of reality. Neither Raz's concept of exile or the critical secular view seek redemption in real history (i.e., the return of the Messiah in mundane times, or a realisation of an ideal of progress), but rather consider the act of criticising the present reality and the act of yearning for redemption as redemption itself. Amnon Raz-Krakotzkin, "Exile within Sovereignty: Critique of the 'Negation of Exile' in Israeli Culture," in: Zvi Ben-Dor Benite et al. (eds.), *The Scaffolding of Sovereignty: Global and Aesthetic Perspectives on the History of a Concept* (New York: Columbia University Press, 2017), pp. 393–417.

grow sacred and the sacred (religion) would become more and more politicised and secularised. As Israel transitioned to an advanced industrialised consumer society in the 1970s, a further transformation occurred in Zionist nationalist myths. This was a period characterised by an economic (and partially political) liberalisation and the decline of the value society attaches to manual labour and agriculture,[16] in contrast to early Zionist doctrine and settler culture. Simultaneously, there were growing trends towards individualism and, among sections of the middle class, towards shirking military service. These complex socio-economic changes took place against a backdrop of de facto colonialist practices carried out under the pretence of reviving an ancient people on "their" ancient land, yet could only proceed by ignoring the land's history of 2,000 years and the negation of its recent history: the forced evacuation of most of the native population in 1948, and the reduction of the remaining Palestinians to second-or even third-class citizens in the Israeli state. However, denial of Zionism's expansionist colonising nature, the deception and self-deception of Israelis who did not participate in the transfer project of 1948 and Jewish newcomers (Hebrew: *Olim Hadashim*) through the myth of empty land became impossible after the 1967 war when Israel imposed direct rule over millions of Palestinians under its military occupation.

These secular, militaristic and politicised religious myths and traditions have been institutionalised by annual repetition and adherence to an official schedule commencing with a day of mourning before the actual celebrations. One ritual preceding Israel's Independence Day stands out in this regard. The day before the festivities is marked by a minute of silence to commemorate the millions of victims of the Holocaust. At the sound of a siren, Israeli citizens stop whatever they are doing and stand completely still wherever they may be, in the streets, factories, schools, universities and public spaces; cars also stop, and drivers get out to stand. The shrill of the siren drowns out the sufferings of the native people on whose ruins the Israeli state was built.

---

[16] And the flow of cheap labour from the newly occupied West Bank and Gaza Strip.

Another significant transformation in the Israeli foundational myths was their increasing emphasis on silencing the suffering and on vindicating the expulsion of the majority of Palestinians in 1948. They continued to feature familiar tropes, such as the heroism of the few against the hostile "sea" of many, and increasingly combined them with the notions of "existential threats," wars of no choice and, more and more, the imperative of pre-emptive warfare. The overall thrust was to cast the dispossession as the product of a voluntary flight and an inadvertent consequence of Israeli actions. One gets the impression that there is supposed to be some essential difference between systematic expulsion (which did take place), committing atrocities and war crimes with the intent to generate panic and flight (which did take place), and the displacement provoked by the spread of violence and an advancing enemy army. This myth portrays the Palestinians forced to flee in 1948 as responsible for their own dispossession. Nationalist propaganda[17] simultaneously charged Arab governments with the blame for the Palestinian flight from their homeland during the 1948 war. In all cases, the myths and propaganda covered up the fact that the Palestinians were then systematically prevented from returning to their homes and villages, and that their properties and belongings were looted and/or confiscated by state agencies before being redistributed among the Jewish population. But the biggest cover-up is of the systematic ethnic cleansing of the native population preparatory to the establishment of the Israeli state on terms favouring the Jewish minority mostly comprised of immigrant settlers.[18] It

---

[17] The carefully designed Israeli propaganda acquired an academic appellation in the last decade of the twentieth century, when it was called a "narrative" instead of "history" by post-Zionists with good intentions, i.e., to relativise it *vis-à-vis* the Palestinian narrative, because it probably did become an unquestioned history for the generations raised on it. So, calling it a "narrative" was maybe a sign of progress relative to the hegemonial discourse in the Israeli academia.

[18] See: Walid Khalidi, "Plan Dalet: Master Plan for the Conquest of Palestine," *Journal of Palestine Studies*, vol. 18, no. 1 (1988), pp. 4–33; Walid Khalidi, *All That Remains: The Palestinian Villages Occupied and Depopulated by Israel in 1948* (Beirut: Institute for Palestine Studies, 1992); Nur Masalha, *Expulsion of the Palestinians: The Concept of "Transfer" in Zionist Political Thought 1882–1948* (Washington, D.C.: Institute of Palestinian Studies, 1992); Ilan Pappé, *The Ethnic Cleansing of Palestine* (Oxford: Oneworld Publications, 2006).

is worth mentioning that, of the thirty-seven signatories of the Israeli declaration of independence, only one was born in Palestine. These immigrants unilaterally declared a state that excluded the natives of a country that did not belong to them or they to it. Most of them Hebraised their names afterwards.

Early Zionist ideology and propaganda maintained that the construction of a Jewish nation through the establishment of a modern state outside Europe was the only solution to Europe's "Jewish question." Creating the state was the Zionist project's ultimate aim. The "State for the Jews"[19] was thus both a means and an end, at least according to the founder of the state project, Theodor Herzl, and fellow members of the Central European Jewish intelligentsia who made up the early Zionist movement. From a nation-building perspective in the abstract, such thinking seemed perfectly consistent, at least to its authors from where they stood in turn-of-the-twentieth-century Europe. In application, their state-building project contained two main tensions that would determine its political and cultural development. The first was its permanent tension with its surrounding environment, having been implanted on the ruins of the native people, and in total denial of the injustice of the act. This inherent clash, the conscious and unconscious guilt it has stirred (even in times of peace), and the series of wars, uprisings and acts of resistance generated the militarisation and security-based regimentation of all spheres of life.[20] The second tension resided in how the state and

---

[19] The subtitle of Herzel's book is "The State of the Jews," which in German is: *Der Judenstaat: Versuch einer modernen Lösung der Judenfrage*. "The Jewish State" is therefore an incorrect translation. See: Theodor Herzl, *A Jewish State: An Attempt at a Modern Solution of the Jewish Question*, Sylvie D'Avigdor (trans.), Jacob de Haas (ed.), 3rd ed. (New York: Federation of American Zionists, 1917 [1896]).

[20] In a famous eulogy speech by the Israeli military's erstwhile chief of staff Moshe Dayan for Roi Rotenberg (a 21-year-old security officer from Kibbutz Nahl Oz killed in an ambush by *fedayeen*, or freedom fighters, from Gaza), Dayan, who despised hypocrisy, said it clearly: "Early yesterday morning Roi was murdered [...] Let us not cast the blame on the murderers today. Why should we declare their burning hatred for us? For eight years they have been sitting in the refugee camps in Gaza, and before their eyes we have been transforming the lands and the villages, where they and their fathers dwelt, into our estate. It is not among the Arabs in Gaza, but in our own midst that we must seek Roi's blood. How

society were perpetually caught between contending perceptions of Israeli-ness and Jewishness. This seems almost inevitable given the exclusively religious definitions of "who is a Jew?" used to determine citizenship in an ostensibly modern secular entity built by a purportedly secular nationalist movement. Secular Zionism does not distinguish between religion and nation, which could not be separated in Israel as a Jewish state and a state of the Jews. In fact, the problem predates this. Virtually all the Zionist political terms, symbols, names and codes have their roots in religion, and they were instrumentalised in the colonisation process.[21] The fact that the Zionist ethos secularised them did not stifle their religious connotative force.

The Zionist colonialist settler in Palestine[22] was distinguished by several characteristics from the outset. First, early colonial practices

---

did we shut our eyes and refuse to look squarely at our fate, and see, in all its brutality, the destiny of our generation? Have we forgotten that this group of young people dwelling at Nahal Oz is bearing the heavy gates of Gaza on its shoulders? [...] We will make our reckoning with ourselves today; we are a generation that settles the land and without the steel helmet and the cannon's maw, we will not be able to plant a tree and build a home. Let us not be deterred from seeing the loathing that is inflaming and filling the lives of the hundreds of thousands of Arabs who live around us. Let us not avert our eyes lest our arms weaken. This is the fate of our generation. This is our life's choice—to be prepared and armed, strong and determined, lest the sword be stricken from our fist and our lives cut down." "Moshe Dayan's Eulogy for Roi Rutenberg—April 19, 1956," *Eulogy*, Jewish Virtual Library, accessed at: https://bit.ly/2Q2gvj3

[21] For further discussion of this subject see: Nadim N. Rouhana, "Religious Claims and Nationalism in Zionism: Obscuring Settler Colonialism," in: Nadim N. Rouhana & Nadera Shalhoub-Kevorkian (eds.), *When Politics Are Sacralized: Comparative Perspectives on Religious Claims and Nationalism* (Cambridge: Cambridge University Press, 2021), pp. 54–87. See also: Azmi Bishara, "The Vortex of Religion and State in Israel," [Arabic] *Majallat al-Dirasat al-Filastiniyya*, no. 3 (Summer 1990).

[22] Religious Jewish communities did not settle in Palestine to establish a Jewish state, nor did all the early Jewish settlers of the nineteenth century. Some were Zionists in various interpretations of the word, but some built agricultural communities because they wanted to practise socialist life outside Europe, or for the sake of individual salvation or even because of other Jewish spiritual ideals. Some thought of Palestine as a homeland due to cultural links that cannot be denied. Zionists were a minority even among the Jews in Palestine until the intensive settlement activities of the second *aliyah* (ascending/immigration) in the beginning of the twentieth century, which explicitly declared the goal of building a Jewish state.

included not only building settlements, but also plans to build a separate Jewish economy (conquest of labour) and to engage in "conquest of the land": the religious term *geulat ha-adama* (redemption of the land) was also frequently used. Such practices gradually hardened into an organised national community with armed militias that paraded themselves as a national liberation movement.

This necessarily meant that, first, the existence of an Arab majority was an impediment to be eliminated; second, that the colonial settler project had no mother colonial country;[23] third, that a combination of secular socialist discourses, religious definitions of the nation and religious symbols had to be instrumentalised to justify links to the land of Palestine. Moreover, Zionist settler movements that boasted a socialist, and sometimes even anti-imperialist discourse, were dependent on the Balfour Declaration, the British Mandate and cooperation between the Zionist political leadership and Britain and other imperialist superpowers. Such were the early features of Zionism in Palestine.

Following the creation of the state, the armed militias that were the main tool for ethnic cleansing became the core of the Israeli army. With time, the Jewish religious character of Israeli nationalism became more and more prominent while the socialist trends and discourse receded as Israel liberalised its economy in the 1970s and 1980s. The subsequent emergence of a large middle class and a consumer-driven urban culture, as well as the rising awareness of quality of life issues and the role of individual choice in a globalising economy have not yet succeeded in producing political forces with the ability to counter the militarisation of Israeli society and the drift to religious extremist national chauvinism.

Israel inherited the political and legal structures of British Mandate Palestine, then gradually changed them over time. Democracy in the Zionist nationalist framework—or Jewish democracy as it continues to call itself (or ethnocracy as some researchers[24] have termed it)—

---

[23] As individuals, the settlers before 1948 of course had different mother countries, but the Zionist colonial project was not any specific colonial country's project.

[24] For example: Oren Yiftachel, *Ethnocracy: Land and Identity Politics in Israel/Palestine* (Philadelphia: University of Pennsylvania Press, 2006). See a thin, but accurate, defini-

was the concept Israeli political and cultural elites adopted when envisaging the kind of citizenship and society they wanted to create. It was their key to absorbing the political and ideological diversity of Jewish immigrants. Inheriting the institutions of the British Mandate was also helpful in this regard.

Even if the settler colonial foundation of the state and the occupation were overlooked, as many academics in Israel and elsewhere do, Israel could not be considered a democracy. In its simplest definition, even if we disregard its necessary liberal dimension, modern democracy is not the rule of the ethnic or religious majority over the entire country.[25] The basic component of modern democracy, even in a multi-national or federated state where collective rights are also acknowledged, is citizenship, regardless of religious, ethnic or other affiliation. Were we, purely for the sake of argument, to disregard the settler colonial foundation of the state and the apartheid regime in the West Bank and Gaza, Israel officially defines itself as a Jewish and democratic state.[26] It is a *de jure* ethnocracy with republican rights for Jews and, as Yoav Peled puts it, liberal individual rights for its Arab citizens.[27] However, this too is only theoretical; de facto discrimination policies do not spare individual rights too.

The following five components of Israel's nation-building process have remained constant over time:

1. The declared Jewishness of the state. This precludes all possibility of building a nation for all its citizens and excludes the right of Palestinian refugees to return to their land.

---

tion of ethnocracy according to Nils Butenschon: "a state that allocates citizenship according to specific ethnic criteria (as normally spelled out in a nationality law)." Nils A. Butenschon, "State, Power, and Citizenship in the Middle East: A Theoretical Introduction," in: Nils A. Butenschon, Uri Davis & Manuel Hassassian (eds.), *Citizenship and the State in the Middle East: Approaches and Applications* (Syracuse: Syracuse University Press, 2000), p. 19. Needless to say, this criterion applies for Israeli ethnocracy which is much thicker.

[25] Given that the politicisation of such collective identities in not enshrined in the system.

[26] Written into the introduction of every Israeli basic law.

[27] Yoav Peled, "Ethnic Democracy and the Legal Construction of Citizenship: Arab Citizens of the Jewish state," *American Political Science Review*, vol. 86, no. 2 (1992), pp. 432–43.

2. The official denial of Israeli nationality and insistence that the Jews in Israel and the rest of the world are the nation whose state is Israel.
3. The Judaisation of the land through expropriation, settlement and revisionist Judaisation of the land's history and identity.
4. The "ingathering of the exiles," which translates in legal terms into the right of any Jew (as defined by religious criteria), anywhere in the world, to become an Israeli citizen simply by deciding to go and live in Israel.[28]
5. The renaissance of Hebrew. This process has engaged some progressive cultural aspects, such as breaking free of the restrictions of historically transmitted Biblical and Talmudic Hebrew, and using Hebrew as the language of instruction in schools and universities.
6. Militarisation and security prioritisation: In practice this means physically occupying land, settling it by force while emptying it of its indigenous population, and then protecting the colonial settlements with Zionist militias before 1948 and later with one of the best-equipped armies in the world. It also means maintaining a regional nuclear arms monopoly and qualitative military superiority over the region. In terms of Israeli society, it manifests itself in compulsory military service (the nation's main integration tool, as mentioned above), mandatory reserve duty, and a ubiquitous military ethos.

In sum, after 1948, early Zionist ideology intersected with the founding myths of Israel and the corollary myths regarding the forced displacement of the native population and the destruction of Palestinian society to yield an official Israeli state ideology. It conveniently smooths over the inherent contradictions and tensions that arise when building a state on the ruins of the native people, when

---

[28] The process of the ingathering of exiles included Oriental Jews who became a majority of the Jewish population. In general, this majority which had to give up its culture was alienated, stereotyped and prejudiced against in the context of a European colonial project. This situation was the source of social and cultural tension that complicated the "nation-building" process. Its solution was not integration in a civil framework of Israeli citizenship, nor by producing a civil culture, but in Jewish Israeli Nationalism. Even traditional religiousness was subject to Sionisation.

religion and nationality overlap, when ethnic affiliation becomes the criterion for entitlement to the state and the bond of the individual citizen to the state is marginalised. If these are still existing concrete realities behind the myth, the state-building process also produced a new reality with its own contradictions. It also has its own normality—an unreflective normality. I refer to *sabra* culture, or Jewish Israeli culture, that is reproduced and lives in peace with itself by sustaining the exclusion of the native population and the expropriation and appropriation of their space and their history.

The Nakba

The Zionist movement declared an independent Jewish state in Palestine on 15 May 1948. On 15 May 1947, exactly a year earlier, the UN General Assembly created the United Nations Special Committee on Palestine (UNSCOP) which was tasked with preparing a report to help to resolve the "problem" of Palestine on the eve of the end of the British Mandate. In early September 1947, after extensive investigations, the Committee submitted two plans: 1) A *majority plan*, recommending that Palestine be partitioned into three entities linked together by an economic union to establish an Arab and Jewish state with Jerusalem as a *corpus separatum* placed under the UN's administrative authority; and 2) a *minority plan*, establishing a federal state with Arab and Jewish national "parts" and its capital in Jerusalem.[29]

On 29 November 1947, the UN General Assembly concluded a two-month debate with the adoption of Resolution 181 (II). It approved, with minor changes, the "majority" plan for partition and economic union. Under its terms, the Mandate would end and British armed forces would gradually withdraw. The Arab and Jewish states called for in the plan would be created no later than 1 October 1948. Towards this end, Palestine would be divided into eight parts: three parts would be allocated to the Arab state and three to its Jewish

---

[29] United Nations Special Committee on Palestine, *Question of Palestine/Majority plan (Partition), Minority plan (Federal State)—UN Special Committee on Palestine (UNSCOP)—Report* (New York: 1947), accessed at: https://bit.ly/2QsMPfa

counterpart. The towns of Jaffa and Jerusalem were designated as the seventh and eight parts. The former would become an Arab enclave within Jewish territory and the latter would be administered by the United Nations Trusteeship Council.

The Jewish Agency[30] accepted the resolution, although this was purely in order to seize a historic opportunity to acquire international legitimacy in order to facilitate its project to establish a Jewish state in Palestine beyond the designated borders in the plan. The resolution was rejected by the Palestinian Arab leadership and neighbouring Arab states on the grounds that it violated the right to self-determination in the United Nations Charter.[31] The Palestinians could not agree to partition their country or to the establishment of a settler state on more than half of it. International powers that supported the option of one state in Palestine for both peoples, such as the Soviet Union, eventually concluded that there were no serious political forces on the ground that supported this option.

Resolution 181 (II) failed to acknowledge established demographic facts. In December 1946, the total population of Palestine was 1,972,000; Arab Palestinians accounted for 69 per cent (1,364,000) of this figure and Jews for 31 per cent (608,000).[32] UNSCOP acknowledged that there was Arab majority population of over 1,200,000 and a Jewish minority population of over 600,000,[33] yet it still allocated 55.5 per cent of the total area of Palestine to the Jewish state and 45.5 per cent to the Arab State.[34] The following table shows the offi-

---

[30] The Jewish Agency was created in 1929 to represent the World Zionist Organization to encourage Jews worldwide to assist the Jewish settlement in Palestine and to serve as their political arm and operational executive.

[31] See: UN Department of Public Information, *The Question of Palestine and the United Nations* (New York: 2008), accessed at: https://bit.ly/3dMKkgz

[32] See: Walid Khalidi, "Revisiting the UNGA Partition Resolution," *Journal of Palestine Studies*, vol. 27, no. 1 (1997), p. 11.

[33] *Question of Palestine/Majority plan (Partition), Minority plan (Federal State)—UN Special Committee on Palestine (UNSCOP)—Report.*

[34] Resolution 181 (II), see: Kattan Victor, *From Coexistence to Conquest: International Law and the Origins of the Arab-Israeli Conflict, 1891–1949* (London and New York: Pluto Press, 2009), pp. 146–68; "United Nations partition plan of 1947—Map," *UN Department of Public Information*, accessed at: https://bit.ly/3xmHl6r

cial UNSCOP figures on the distribution of the settled population in the two proposed states, as of the end of 1946.[35]

Table 1.2: Distribution of the Settled Population in Palestine (1946)

Territory	Jewish population		Arabs and other population		Total
Jewish Territory	498,000	55%	407,000	45%	905,000
Arab Territory	10,000	1%	725,000	99%	735,000
City of Jerusalem	100,000	49%	105,000	51%	205,000
Total[36]	**608,000**	**33%**	**1,237,000**	**67%**	**1,845,000**

Source: United Nations Special Committee on Palestine (UNSCOP).

So, according to the proposed UNSCOP plan, Arab residents would constitute 45 per cent of the population in the Jewish state and 99 per cent of the population in the Arab state.[37]

Before the formal declaration of the Israeli state, Zionist militias launched a military campaign of conquest and ethnic cleansing. The Zionist movement had long awaited this moment. It had built national institutions, an exclusively Jewish economy separate from the Arab economy, and the *haganah* armed force,[38] which was not just the core of a future army, but also an entity poised to step into the state institutions bequeathed by the British Mandate. Seizing the opportunity

---

[35] United Nations Special Committee on Palestine, *Official Records of the Second Session of the General Assembly, Supplement No. 11, Report to The General Assembly*, vol. 1 (A/364) (New York: 1947), accessed at: https://bit.ly/3nkDT7H

[36] An additional 90,000 Bedouins, cultivators and stock owners were estimated to be within the Jewish territory in dry seasons.

[37] According to the partition plan, the proposed Palestinian state would have a total of 818,000 Palestinians (if the 71,000 Palestinians of the Jaffa enclave were included) and less than 10,000 Jews. Jerusalem was estimated to have around 105,000 Palestinians and 100,000 Jews. As for the proposed Jewish state, it was estimated to have approximately 499,000 Jews and 438,000 Palestinians, that is "if the Jaffa enclave, totally encapsulated by the Jewish state, had been included, as had originally been proposed by UN-SCOP, the Palestinians would have outnumbered the Jews in the Jewish state as well." Khalidi, "Revisiting the UNGA Partition Resolution," p. 11.

[38] The main armed Zionist organisation before the establishment of the state and its army.

of the hasty withdrawal of the British who had governed Palestine for three decades, the Zionist forces unilaterally declared the establishment of the state of Israel on 15 May 1948. Only then did the Arab states respond by declaring a war that they were not ready for.

By the time the Armistice Agreements were signed in 1949,[39] the newly established state controlled 77 per cent of Mandate Palestine. Only 150,000 Arabs somehow managed to remain in the country. In 1967, Israel occupied the rest of the land, thereby "reuniting" Mandate Palestine under its control. According to the latest statistics reported by the Central Bureau of Statistics (2021), Israel's total population is currently estimated at 9.5 million, of which 6.9 million are Jews (74 per cent) and 1.7 million are Arab (over one-fifth of the population).[40] If we add to this the approximately 4.8 million Palestinians living in the West Bank and Gaza (according to the Palestinian Central Bureau of Statistics figures for 2021),[41]$ we find that about 7 million Jews and more than 6 and a half million Palestinians live under the sovereign rule of the self-designated Jewish state today.

As discussed above, a major part of Israel's post-1948 myth-making and propaganda effort has been dedicated to denial of the Nakba. Israeli officialdom has adamantly refused to acknowledge that the Zionist armies committed ethnic cleansing in the 1948 war, and stuck to the claim that the Palestinians simply fled and/or that Arab governments told them to leave their homes until the war ended. It would take a degree of audacity to pretend that the land had been empty where thousands of Jewish families still live in houses that once belonged to Palestinians who became refugees in 1948. This kind of house even has a name in Hebrew. It is called *Bayet Aravi* (an Arab house) in Israel today. Clearly, the "land without a people" mantra that had been reproduced in Europe during the first half of

---

[39] The 1949 Armistice Agreements were signed between Israel and Egypt on 24 February 1949, then between Israel and Lebanon on 23 March 1949; Jordan on 3 April 1949; and Syria on 20 July 1949.

[40] East Jerusalemites are included in official Israeli statistics.

[41] "Estimated Population in Palestine Mid-Year by Governorate,1997–2021," *Database*, The Palestinian Central Bureau of Statistics, https://bit.ly/2SaWbgE

the twentieth century was no longer sustainable after 1948 when the international community suddenly had to contend with a massive refugee crisis from that heretofore "empty" land. Israeli propagandists had to do some quick PR work and the myth of fleeing Arabs (as Palestinian Arabs were called by the Zionists) during the war (in Hebrew: *h'Aravim barhou*) upon a command blared from Arab capitals suited the bill.

In a 1959 article, the Palestinian historian Walid Khalidi drew on the Arab League's press statements and meeting minutes, as well as Arab and Palestinian newspapers published in the period, to refute the Zionist claim that the Palestinians left their homes because Arab leaders told them to do so.[42] Not only could Khalidi find no evidence of an Arab evacuation order in in the contemporary Arabic sources, he found no reference to such an order in the *haganah* radio and correspondence between the Zionist and British leaderships at the time. He noted that the claim first appeared in 1949, when the refugee issue began to preoccupy Western opinion. He attributed it to the desire of Zionist leaders to acquit themselves from all responsibility for the crisis.[43] There was no evidence of any such order in Arab radio broadcasts, as Khalidi observed: "A day-to-day examination of the broadcasts from the Arab capitals and by secret Arab radio stations in 1948 fails to reveal a single reference, direct or indirect, to an order given to the Arabs of Palestine to leave."[44]$ Indeed, he found evidence to the contrary, namely, that the broadcasts urged Palestinians to stay.[45] In 1961, the Irish journalist Erskine Childers published "The Other Exodus" in *The Spectator* with precisely the same conclusion.[46]

Since the opening of the Israeli archives new Israeli historiographical works have appeared, challenging this Israeli myth, and the official

---

[42] Walid Khalidi, "Why Did the Palestinians Leave, Revisited," *Journal of Palestinian Studies*, vol. 34, no. 2 (Winter 2005), pp. 42–54, 44–54.

[43] Ibid., p. 43.

[44] Ibid, p. 46.

[45] Ibid., pp. 46–7

[46] Erskine B. Childers, "The Other Exodus," *The Spectator*, 12 May 1961, accessed at: https://bit.ly/3u0ty2C

history of 1948, as a whole. Such writings have continued over the past four decades.[47]

Simha Flapan's *The Birth of Israel: Myths and Realities* (1987) undertakes a complete overhaul and meticulous deconstruction of Israeli founding myths. This seminal work refuted "seven myths" created and perpetuated by the official Israeli history of the 1948 war and the establishment of the state of Israel. These were the claims that (1) the Zionists accepted the UN Partition and planned for peace but (2) the Arabs rejected partition and launched war; (3) the Palestinians fled voluntarily, intending reconquest; (4) all the Arab states united to expel the Jews from Palestine; (5) the Arab invasion made war inevitable; (6) a defenceless Israel faced destruction by the Arab Goliath; and (7) Israel has always sought peace, but no Arab leader has reciprocated.[48]$ An objective, i.e., critical, reading of the published diaries of contemporaneous Israeli leaders like David Ben-Gurion, Moshe Sharett and others supports Flapan's conclusions that these seven claims are constructed historical fictions.

Benny Morris acknowledged that Zionist militias expelled Palestinians, but contended there was no "master plan" to ethnically cleanse Palestinians despite the fact that population transfer was a concept intrinsic to Zionist ideology, which aimed to transform Arab lands into a Jewish state. Still, as Morris argues, the displacement of the Arab population of Palestine was a necessary precondition for the existence of the Jewish state.[49]

Many observers, who were thrilled at Morris' detailed and documented "revelations" because they were made by an Israeli historian relying on Israeli archives, have not connected the dots between the refutation of Zionist canards based on archival facts and the need to take a commensurate ethical stance. Morris resembled old Zionist leaders, who were ready to be forthright about the facts while justifying their deeds at the same time, at least in their memoirs and in

---

[47] See: "Silencing: DSDE's Concealment of Documents in Archives," *Report*, Akevot Institute for Israeli-Palestinian Conflict Research, July 2019, accessed at: https://bit.ly/3tnNGw7

[48] Simha Flapan, *The Birth of Israel: Myths and Realities* (New York: Pantheon Books, 1987).

[49] Benny Morris, *The Birth of the Palestinian Refugee Problem Revisited* (Cambridge: Cambridge University Press, 2004), pp. 589–90.

internal discussions. Yes, it was an expulsion, but it was still the right thing to do, they argue, because there was no other way to establish a Jewish state in a country populated by an Arab majority![50] General moral principles or humanitarian values are thereby consciously subordinated to the nationalist value of a Jewish state.

If honest acknowledgement of a crime does not stimulate some form of ethical critique or introspection, then it can only signify brazen shamelessness. This is worse than hypocrisy which at least implies a sense that something wrongful and shameful needs to be concealed. It appears that the dominant contemporary Israeli political culture does not see a need to conceal the truths about ethnic cleansing because it does not consider it, or the plundering and pillaging of Palestinian properties as crimes and moral offenses. Evidently, acknowledgement of historical facts can be motivated by moral critique, as well as by moral impairment.

Khalidi referred to the systematic plan for ethnic cleansing in an article published in 1961: "'Plan Dalet' (Plan D) was the name given by the Zionist High Command to the general plan for military operations within the framework of which the Zionists launched successive offensives in April and early May 1948 in various parts of Palestine. These offensives [...] entailed the destruction of the Palestinian Arab community and the expulsion and pauperization of the bulk of the Palestine Arabs."[51] He quotes Yigal Allon, the head of *Palmach*, the elite unit of the *haganah*: "There were left before us only five days, before the threatening date, the 15th of May. We saw the need to clean out the inner Galilee and to create a Jewish territorial continuity in the entire area of the upper Galilee."[52]

Several historians have challenged Morris, maintaining that there was in fact a master plan for ethnic cleansing and that was implemented.[53]

---

[50] See the examples in Tom Segev's critical writing of Ben-Gurion's biography: Ben-Gurion and Yitzhak Ben-Zvi considered that the transfer of Arabs was a just action, a necessary action. Tom Segev, *A State at all Costs: The Life of David Ben-Gurion* [Hebrew] (Ben Shemen: Keter Sfarim, 2005), p. 430.

[51] Khalidi, "Plan Dalet," p. 8.

[52] Ibid.

[53] Avi Shlaim, "The Debate About 1948," *International Journal of Middle East Studies*, vol. 27, no. 3 (1995), pp. 287–304.

Some argue that the destruction and ethnic cleansing of more than 450 Palestinian villages provide clear *prima facie* evidence of a systemic plan to displace Palestinians from their homes and lands.[54] Israeli historian Ilan Pappé, for example, demonstrated how the Israeli "Plan D" (*Dalet*) was designed as a "masterplan" and carried out by Zionist armed organisations (and later, the Israeli armed forces).[55] Nur Masalha held that the expulsion of Palestinians in order to set up the Jewish state not only followed a master plan, but that forced population transfer has deep roots in Zionist thought.[56]

Ethnic cleansing extended beyond the borders of the proposed partition lines and when the 1949 truce agreements were signed the state of Israel dominated 77 per cent of Mandatory Palestine, far exceeding the 55.5 per cent that the UN partition plan had originally allocated to the Jewish population.

Khalidi referred to the depopulation and destruction of around 420 Palestinian villages, adding that, by the end of 1948, the largest population displacement in Palestine's history had uprooted between 727,700 and 758,300 Palestinians.[57] According to Pappé, the Nakba destroyed 531 villages and emptied 11 urban areas of their inhabitants. In his 2006 book, Pappé observed that by October 1948, almost 800,000 Palestinians had been expelled from what would later become known as the State of Israel.[58]

What became of the people represented by these numbers? In 2019, the UN Relief and Works Agency for Palestinian Refugees in the Near East (UNRWA) observed that 5.5 million registered Palestine refugees currently live in Jordan, Lebanon, Syria, the Gaza Strip and the West Bank (including East Jerusalem).[59] Today, more

---

[54] Masalha, *Expulsion of the Palestinians*.

[55] Pappé, *The Ethnic Cleansing of Palestine*, p. 28.

[56] Masalha, *Expulsion of the Palestinians*, p. 199.

[57] Khalidi, *All That Remains*, p. 582.

[58] Ilan Pappé, "The 1948 Ethnic Cleansing of Palestine," *Journal of Palestine Studies*, vol. 36, no. 1 (2006), p. 7; Pappé, *The Ethnic Cleansing of Palestine*, p. xiii.

[59] "UNRWA Marks 70 Years of Service for Palestine Refugees," *UN Relief and Works Agency for Palestine Refugees (UNRWA)*, 10 December 2019, accessed at: https://bit.ly/3afj1tf. Whereas the BADIL Resource Center for Palestinian Residency and Refugee Rights estimated that there are a further 1,161,812 1948 unregistered refugees in these territories.

than seven decades after the ethnic cleansing of Palestine took place, it has become an established fact and its denial is a fringe idea. Even in Israeli academia, the main facts are acknowledged—either as a result of moral critical thinking, or as a sign of nationalist self-confidence that excuses crimes committed for a "cause".

The Myth of the Few against the Many

Months before war was officially declared and Israel declared independence, *Haganah* armed forces attacked Tiberias, Haifa, Safad and Jaffa and hundreds of villages. In short, ethnic cleansing began on a large scale before the Arab states considered direct intervention. During this "unofficial" phase of the war (December 1947 to 15 May 1948), most of the war effort on the Palestinian side came from volunteer groups of irregular and semi-regular forces that were led by the Arab League Military Committee. The head of the committee, General Ismail Safwat, submitted a report to the Arab League Council on 23 March 1948 estimating that the number of Arab troops in Mandatory Palestine was between 7,700 and 8,000.[60] This included volunteers from Arab countries, as the Arab states themselves refused to participate in the war before 15 May,[61] despite the early ethnic cleansing.[62]

"PHROC Nakba Statement: Stop the Ongoing Nakb a: Protect Palestinian Refugees," *Statement*, BADIL Resource Center for Palestinian Residency and Refugee Rights, May 2019, https://bit.ly/32eMyPm

[60] Government of Iraq, *Report of the Parliamentary Committee of Enquiry into the Palestine Question* [Arabic] (Baghdad: 1949), p. 158.

[61] As the chief of staff of the Iraqi army during that war, Marshal Saleh Aljbouri, put it in his *Memoires*, the Arab governments did not decide to obstruct the Partition plan, they also avoided taking any step that could cause damage to the relations with the British and the Americans. See: Saleh Saeb Aljbouri, *The Plight of Palestine and its Political and Military Secrets* [Arabic] (Beirut: Arab Center for Research and Policy Studies, 2014), pp. 150–1. This book is an important source concerning the history of the war. Except his diaries, it includes correspondence and meetings protocols of the military and political Arab leaderships.

[62] On the fall of Tiberias, see: Mustafa Abbasi, "The War on the Mixed Cities: The Depopulation of Arab Tiberias and the Destruction of its Old, 'Sacred' City (1948–9),"

Ben-Gurion, in his *War Diaries*, stated that the number of Jewish troops on the battlefield on 18 March 1948 was roughly 15,000 (an underestimation).[63] That Jewish forces were nearly double the Arab forces can be partially explained by Kimmerling and Migdal's assertion that the population numbers were deceptive: "Jewish immigration had created a society with a disproportionate share of young men of army age—one and a half times the Arab figure."[64] But a more important reason was that, unlike the native Palestinian society, the Jewish settler society was a highly mobilised one. This was, after all, an intrinsic feature of the nationalist state project. As Avi Shlaim put it: "The Yeshuv was better prepared, better mobilized, and better organized when the struggle for Palestine reached its crucial stage than its local opponents."[65]

It might be true that, at the beginning, there was no major gap between the Arab and Jewish sides in terms of armament or, to a lesser degree, combat experience. However, the latter achieved supe-

---

Journal of Holy Land and Palestine Studies, vol. 7, no. 1 (May 2008), pp. 45–80. On the fall of Haifa, in which British-Zionist collusion played a decisive role, see: Walid Khalidi, "The Fall of Haifa Revisited," *Journal of Palestine Studies*, vol. 37, no. 3 (Spring 2008), pp. 30–58; Motti Golani, "The 'Haifa Turning Point': The British Administration and the Civil War in Palestine, December 1947-May 1948," *Middle Eastern Studies*, vol. 37, no. 2 (April 2001), pp. 93–130; Bilal Shalash, *Jaffa, Blood on Stone: The Jaffa Garrison and its Military Action; Study and Documents* [Arabic], vol. 1 (Beirut: Arab Center for Research and Policy Studies, 2019), pp. 213–59. See also: Itamar Radai, "Jaffa, 1948: The fall of a city," *The Journal of Israeli History*, vol. 30, no. 1 (March 2011), pp. 23–43; Arnon Golan, "The Battle for Jaffa, 1948," *Middle Eastern Studies*, vol. 48, no. 6 (November 2012), pp. 997–1011. On the fall of Safad, see: Mohammad Jamal Barout, "The Fall of Safad: The Beginning of the fall of Galilee," [Arabic] *al-Karmel*, no. 57 (October 1998), pp. 60–74. See also: Mustafa Abbasi, "The Battle for Safad in the War of 1948: A Revised Study," *International Journal of Middle East Studies*, vol. 36, no. 1 (February 2004), pp. 21–47. On the fall of Acre: Mustafa Abbasi, "The Fall of Acre in the 1948 Palestine War," *Journal of Palestine Studies*, vol. XXXIX, no. 4 (Summer 2010), pp. 2–3.

[63] See: David Ben-Gurion, *The War of Independence: Ben-Gurion's Diary 1948–1949* [Hebrew], Gershon Rivlin & Elhana Oren (eds.), vol. 1 ([Tel Aviv]: Ministry of Defence Publication, 1984), p. 310. See also: Abbasi, "The War on the Mixed Cities," pp. 45–80.

[64] Baruch Kimmerling & Joel S. Migdal, *The Palestinian People: A History* (Cambridge, M A: Harvard University Press, 2003), p. 150.

[65] Shlaim, "The debate about 1948," p. 294.

riority over the former, not just in numbers of combatants, but also in the levels of coordination, mobilisation and arms supplies from the socialist bloc in Europe, especially after the declaration of independence.[66] Until early June 1948, the Israeli army's greatest weakness was in firepower and military equipment. The Arab armies were better equipped, especially with artillery and armoured combat vehicles. However, after the first truce in June 1948, Israel received what it needed in machine guns, armoured vehicles, field guns, tanks, airplanes and all kinds of ammunition from Czechoslovakia. The Czech arms and equipment transfer enabled the Israeli army to decisively tip the scales in its favour.[67]

---

[66] Shalash; Haim Levenberg, *The Military Preparations of the Arab Community in Palestine, 1945–1948* (London: Frank Cass, 1993); Moshe Naor, *Social Mobilization in the Arab–Israeli War of 1948 On the Israeli Home Front*, Shaul Vardi (trans.) (New York: Routledge, 2013).

[67] Haggai Frank, Zdeněk Klíma & Yossi Goldstein, "The First Israeli Weapons Procurement Behind the Iron Curtain: The Decisive Impact on the War of Independence," *Israel Studies*, vol. 22, no. 3 (Fall 2017), pp. 125–52; Benny Morris, *1948: A History of the First Arab-Israeli War* (London: Yale University Press, 2008), p. 117. From June 1948, the Israeli army moved on to the offensive, and by the late 1948 Israelis picked off the Arab armies and defeated them one by one. In 1968, Ben-Gurion himself said: "Czechoslovak arms saved the State of Israel, really and absolutely. Without these weapons, we wouldn't have survived." See: "Without these weapons, we wouldn't have survived," [Hebrew] *Youtube*, 12 May 2015, accessed at: https://bit.ly/3vdDyXP. Shimon Peres did not forget to mention this in his book 70 years later. Peres was responsible for weapons procurement and Stalin, as he wrote, ordered Czechoslovakia to purvey the needed weapons when Western countries imposed an arms embargo on all the countries of the region including the Zionist movement. Shimon Peres, *No Room for Small Dreams* [Hebrew] (Rishon LeZion: Yediot Ahronot & Hemed, 2018), p. 50. Rabin acknowledged this fact four decades ago, when the relationship between Israel and the Soviet Union was tense and at its lowest point, emphasising that without those supplies the "independence war" could not have been conducted: "Whatever accounts Israel and the Jewish people have to settle with the Communist bloc, the parallel column must bear an entry in large, clear letters: without the arms from Czechoslovakia—unquestionably provided at the best of the Soviet Union—it is very doubtful that we would have been able to conduct our war for independence." Yitzhak Rabin, *The Rabin Memoirs* (Berkeley and Los Angeles: University of California Press, 1979), p. 34.

After the imposition of a weapons embargo on both sides,[68] the Arab states that depended on Britain and France did not try to purchase weapons from other sources. They had neither the will nor the resources. They also did not want to upset Britain and France. Meanwhile, the Soviet Union broke the embargo through Czechoslovakia, delivering massive arms shipments to the Zionist troops.

Even when the Arab states declared war on 15 May 1948 and started to deploy units of their regular armies, the *Yeshuv* sustained its numerical superiority. Different sources have estimated the total number of both regular and irregular Arab troops operating in Palestine at between 20,000 and 28,000.[69] In contrast, the Zionist militias, especially the *Haganah*—which later became the national army of Israel, or the Israeli Defence Forces (IDF) as it is officially named—deployed between 32,000 and 35,000 troops, with numbers rising to 95,000 by mid-October 1948. The Arab states also reinforced their armies, but they could not match this rate of expansion. By mid-October, the total number of Arab combatants did not exceed 53,000.[70] At each stage of the war, as Shlaim observes, the Israeli army significantly "outnumbered all the Arab forces ranged against it, and by the final stage of the war its superiority was nearly two to one."[71] According to other

---

[68] The United Nations Security Council (UNSC) Resolution 50 on 29 May 1948 called "upon all governments and authorities concerned to order a cessation of all acts of armed force for a period of four weeks; [...] to undertake that they will not introduce fighting personnel into Palestine, Egypt, Iraq, Lebanon, Saudi Arabia, Syria, Transjordan and Yemen during the cease-fire; [...] should men of military age be introduced into countries or territories under their control, to undertake not to mobilize or submit them to military training during the cease-fire; [...] to refrain from importing or exporting war material into or to Palestine, Egypt, Iraq, Lebanon, Saudi Arabia, Syria, Transjordan or Yemen during the cease-fire." United Nations Security Council, *Calling for a cessation of hostilities in Palestine*, Resolution S/RES/50(1948), 29 May 1948, pp. 20–21, accessed at: https://bit.ly/3hb66Ml

[69] Shlaim, "The debate about 1948," p. 294; Amitsur Ilan, "Few versus many, weak versus strong: the case of the War of Independence," in: Alone Kadish & Benjamin Z. Kedar (eds.), *The Few Against the Many, Studies on the Balance of Forces in the Battles of Judas Maccabaeus and Israel's War of Independence* [Hebrew] (Jerusalem: The Hebrew University Magnes Press, 2005), p. 62.

[70] Ilan, "Few versus many."

[71] Shlaim, "The debate about 1948," p. 294.

sources, when the Israeli army was established on 26 May 1948, it counted 42,000 recruits and an additional 10,000 also joined in one month.[72] In the second half of the same year, 25,000 Jewish fighters from European countries arrived and joined the new army.[73] By October 1948, Israeli army recruits already numbered 88,000; by December 1948, they were 108,000.[74]

The *Haganah*'s greatest advantages were a concrete political goal and strong motivation to achieve it, an effective centralised system of command and control and a clear strategy of conquest to establish a Jewish state. In contrast, the Arab armies lacked a coordinated strategy and a unified command structure. Moreover, there is consensus among historians that Arab political leaders, despite their rhetoric, did not order their commanders to prevent the establishment of the Jewish state. They were deployed within the borders of the Arab state as defined by the partition plan and never intended to pass those lines.

It is essential to understand what really happened, not only to refute Zionist myths, which work has been relatively recently done by Israeli and non-Israeli historians, but also to understand the Arab side. For this purpose, we need to distinguish between agency (the power to make decisions, summon resolve and act) and structural aspects so as to address the elephant in the room: the lack of political will and cooperation.

The hesitant intervention in Palestine on the part of the weak governments of newly and nominally independent Arab states was mainly the product of domestic pressures from the prevailing anti-colonial public opinion prevalent, though the inter-Arab connection was also a factor. While the frontline Arab states had formally gained their independence, the independence was still compromised by treaties that allowed the former colonial powers to retain effective control over major policy issues, including military and international affairs.

---

[72] Amitsur Illan, "The Israeli Defence Army and the Arab Armies in 1948," in: Alon Kadish (ed.), *Independence War 1948–1949, Renewed Discussion*, part 1 [Hebrew] (Tel-Aviv: Ministry of Defence, 2004), p. 84.

[73] Yacov Markovitzky, *The Fighting Cinder: Recruitment Abroad during the War of Independence* [Hebrew] ([Tel Aviv]: Ministry of Defence, 1995), p. 13.

[74] Ilan, "The Israeli Defence Army and the Arab Armies in 1948," p. 84.

Examples of such restrictive treaties include the 1946 British-Jordanian agreement, the 1936 Anglo-Egyptian treaty and the 1933 British-Iraqi agreement.

A) Jordan: Transjordan's King Abdullah viewed the invasion as a means to expand his kingdom. Nevertheless, he did so on the basis of informal understandings with the Jewish Agency and Britain that he would be the master of the land assigned to the Arabs of Palestine under the 1947 UN Partition Resolution. Britain, the Jewish Agency and Transjordan shared a common interest in the "abortion of a Palestinian Arab state that would inevitably be headed by their common enemy the mufti of Jerusalem, Hajj Amin al-Husayni."[75] Other accounts indicate that Jordan tried to intervene in Jaffa before 15 May 1948, but was prevented by British colonial authorities.[76]

B) Egypt: In addition to pressure from the vibrant civil society and mobilised public opinion that characterised this era of political pluralism and rising political organisation and trade union activity in Egypt, King Farouq had another motive to participate in the war: his desire to counterbalance Jordan's role in Palestine. However, he was opposed by members of his government, politicians and officers who feared that the Egyptian army was not sufficiently prepared (which was true). The court officials who supported the king's view argued that there would be very little fighting and that military action would be more of a "political demonstration" because, as they incorrectly assumed, the United Nations would quickly intervene.[77] King Farouq refused to coop-

---

[75] Eugene L. Rogan, "Jordan and 1948: the persistence of an official history," in: Avi Shlaim & Eugene L. Rogan (eds.), *The War for Palestine: Rewriting the History of 1948* (Cambridge: Cambridge University Press, 2001), p. 109.

[76] See: Yona Bendman, "British Military Efforts to Prevent the Fall of Jaffa, April 1948," [Hebrew] *Iyunim Bitkumat Israel*, vol. 2 (1992), pp. 302–3.

[77] Morris, *1948: A History of the First Arab-Israeli War*, p. 185. See also: Thomas Mayer, "The Military Force of Islam: The Society of the Muslim Brethren and the Palestine Question, 1945–48," in: Elie Kedourie & Sylvia G. Haim (eds.), *Zionism and Arabism in Palestine and Israel* (London: Frank Cass, 1982), pp. 101–18.; Mohamed Hassanein Heikal, *Thrones and Armies: The Crisis of Thrones, the Shock of Armies* [Arabic] (Cairo: Dar ash-Shurūq lil-Nashr wal-Tawzīʿ, 2009).

erate with King Abdullah in his capacity as commander of the combined Arab forces, even refusing to let him visit Egyptian field positions.[78]

C) Iraq: The Iraqi government was facing internal social and political unrest at the time. So, when it took the decision to intervene, it was already conscious of the fact that the Iraqi army could only intervene in Palestine on terms largely set by King Abdullah of Transjordan.[79]

Finally, both Syria and Lebanon also felt threatened by Abdullah's long-standing ambition to make himself master of Greater Syria. While the Lebanese deployed an effectively symbolic contribution to the Arab war effort, the Syrian government feared that deploying its newly formed army would expose its southern flank with Jordan. Still, in response to heavy public pressure in support of Palestine, Damascus mobilised a limited number of troops.[80] As the combined Arab troops scrambled to do what they could in 1948, the Zionist forces struggled to prevail in what was the deadliest, most demanding war Israel had ever fought in its history.[81]

Refugees

The birth of the refugee problem was the birth of the Palestinian right of return. On 14 May 1948, the UN appointed Count Folke

---

[78] Rogan, p. 115. See also the Iraqi and Syrian positions regarding the leadership of King Abdullah: Saleh Saeb Aljubouri, *The Plight of Palestine and its Political and Military Secrets* [Arabic] (Beirut: Arab Center for Research and Policy Studies, 2014); Taha al-Hashemi, *Diaries of Taha al-Hashemi 1942–1955: Iraq-Syria-the Palestinian Cause* [Arabic], Khaldun Sati' al-Husri (ed. and intro.), vol. 2 (Beirut: Dar aṭ-Ṭali'a lil-Ṭibā'a wal-Nashr, 1978); Adil Arslan, *Prince Adil Arslan: The Recanted Diaries 1948* [Arabic], Youssef Abish (ed.) (al-Mukhtara [Lebanon]: ad-Dar at-Taqadumiyya, 2009).

[79] Charles Tripp, "Iraq and the 1948 War: Mirror of Iraq's disorder," in: Shlaim & Rogan, p. 135; Hanna Batatu, *The Old Social Classes and the Revolutionary Movements of Iraq: A Study of Iraq's Old Landed and Commercial Classes and of its Communists, Ba'thists, and Free Officers* (Princeton: Princeton University Press, 1978), pp. 544–66. See also: Heikal.

[80] Arslan; al-Hashemi.

[81] Compared with it, the 1967 war was a picnic. The element of surprise in the latter war, the technological superiority and conducting the war on the enemies' land dictated the rhythm and outcome of the war, its short duration and the few losses for Israel.

Bernadotte as official mediator for Palestine with the primary mandate of "promoting a peaceful adjustment of the future situation in Palestine."[82] In his September report (A/648), Bernadotte recommended establishing a special UN conciliation commission for Palestine to supervise and assist in implementing the right of return of Arab refugees, with adequate property compensation for those choosing not to return.[83]

On 17 September 1948, Bernadotte was assassinated in Jerusalem by a member of *Lehi*, a Zionist terrorist group. The UN Secretary-General posthumously forwarded his report to the General Assembly and, after several discussions, new amendments were added to a draft resolution, the most important of which came from UK and US representatives. After further discussions from 21 September onwards, UN Resolution 194 (III) was adopted on 11 December 1948.[84] On 21 September 1948, the UN Secretary-General forwarded the report to the General Assembly's First Committee. When discussions resumed in mid-November, the UK submitted a draft resolution that proposed dropping language referring to "Arab refugees," so that its provisions would apply to all individuals displaced in the war. The Committee also accepted a UK amendment proposing that refugees be allowed to return at the earliest "practicable" date, rather than "possible" date.[85]

Syria also submitted a draft resolution (A/C.1/402) which proposed that a commission should "study on the spot and prepare proposals for the establishment of a single state of the whole of Palestine

---

[82] Refer to: United Nations General Assembly, "186 (S-2). Appointment and terms of reference of a United Nations Mediator in Palestine," *Resolution A/RES/186 (S-2)*, 14 May 1948, para. II, accessed at: https://bit.ly/3sQvx8U

[83] See: United Nations General Assembly Official Records, *Progress Report of the UN Mediator for Palestine submitted to the secretary-general for transmission to the members of the United Nations, 16 September 1948*, Third session supplement no. 11 (A/648) (Paris: 1948), accessed at: https://bit.ly/3tRSidZ

[84] For further insight and additional details, see: Terry Rempel, "The Right to Return: Drafting Paragraph 11 of General Assembly Resolution 194 (III), December 11, 1948," *The Palestine Yearbook of International Law Online*, vol. 21, no. 1 (2020), pp. 77–197.

[85] See: Terry Rempel, "Resolution 194 (III), A Retrospective," *al-Majdal*, no. 39–40 (Autumn 2008-Winter 2009).

on a canonisation or federal basis in which all sections of population in Palestine will participate in rights and duties as loyal citizens of a democratic State with wide autonomous privileges in cantons or areas to be assigned to each of them." This suggestion was rejected by the First Committee.[86]

Paragraph 11 of Resolution 194, in its final wording, establishes the right of return and the United Nations Conciliation Commission for Palestine (UNCCP). It *Resolves* that:

> "refugees wishing to return to their homes and live at peace with their neighbours should be permitted to do so at the earliest practicable date, and that compensation should be paid for the property of those choosing not to return and for loss of or damage to property which, under principles of international law or in equity, should be made good by the Governments or authorities responsible; *Instructs* the Conciliation Commission to facilitate the repatriation, resettlement and economic and social rehabilitation of the refugees and the payment of compensation, and to maintain close relations with the Director of the United Nations Relief for Palestine Refugees and, through him, with the appropriate organs and agencies of the United Nations."[87]

Resolution 194 (III) was adopted by a majority of thirty-five countries, with fifteen votes against it and eight abstentions. Israel refused to implement the resolution. In 1950, the Knesset passed the Law of Return granting every Jew in the world the right to settle in Israel. Its 1952 Nationality Law then established automatic Israeli citizenship rights for all Jews.[88] The Knesset also approved the 1950 Absentees' Property Law enabling Israel to directly control, and benefit from, the properties of Palestinian refugees and internally displaced Palestinians.[89] Before that, in 1948, the Israeli army issued an anti-

---

[86] See: United Nations Department of Public Information, Yearbook of the United Nations 1948–49 (New York: 1949), accessed at: https://bit.ly/3sUe6Ep

[87] See: "194 (III). Palestine—Progress Report of the United Nations Mediator A/RES/194 (III)," *Report*, UN General Assembly, 11 December 1948, accessed at: https://bit.ly/3aBHJnZ

[88] "The Law of Return 5710 (1950)," *The Knesset*, accessed at: https://bit.ly/3vCJREt; "Nationality Law, 5712–1952," *The Knesset*, accessed at: https://bit.ly/34wDerl

[89] "Absentees' Property Law, 5710–1950," *The Knesset*, accessed at: https://bit.ly/3uDJJD2

infiltration decree, which 6 years later became the Prevention of Infiltration Law of 1954. The law defines Palestinians who "fled" to neighbouring countries and then tried to return home as "infiltrators" and authorises Israel's security forces to detain and forcibly deport them back.[90]

Many Palestinian refugees tried to go back to their homes. Benny Morris observes that in the period 1949–56, "upward of 2,700 Arab infiltrators, and perhaps as many as 5,000, were killed by the IDF, police, and civilians along Israel's borders." The vast majority of these so-called "infiltrators" were unarmed civilians simply trying to return home for economic and social reasons.[91]

The Nakba gradually evolved from a historical event into a new reality. It marked a rupture in modern Palestinian history; and there is no national Palestinian political history that is not modern.[92]

Before 1948, generations of Palestinians had grown up using the word Nakba for a host of small rural upsets: so-and-so had "been struck by catastrophe" because of the low rainfall that year or due to a sudden death of a son or daughter. The 1948 generation suddenly found itself forced to grasp an actual collective calamity of an unimaginable magnitude: the loss of their homes, their villages and their country. While they might find shelter of sorts in other countries after long, desperate

---

[90] "Forced Population Transfer: The Case of Palestine—Denial of Reparations," *Working Paper no. 22*, BADIL Resource Center for Palestinian Residency and Refugee Rights, October 2018, accessed at: https://bit.ly/32Se9pH. In implementing this order, Israel arrested many infiltrators (both near the borders and deep inside Arab towns) and imposed heavy fines on them. These security actions accounted for 80% of Israel's detainees and prisoners in 1951. Adel Manna', *Nakba and Survival: The Story of the Palestinians who Remained in Haifa and the Galilee (1948–1956)* (Beirut: Institute for Palestine studies, 2016), p. 203.

[91] See: Benny Morris, *Israel's Border Wars, 1949–1956: Arab Infiltration, Israeli Retaliation, and the Countdown to the Suez War* (Oxford: Clarendon Press, 1993), p. 137.

[92] This is also the case in Syria, Lebanon, Iraq and Jordan. National political history is modern. Jewish national history is also as modern as the state of Israel. Some would go back to the establishment of the Zionist movement and the first Zionist congress in Basel (29–31 August 1897). This may be true concerning the nationalist idea, but it should be recalled that the early Zionist movement only represented a small number of European Jews and was only supported by a small minority of Jews elsewhere in the world. In contrast, the Palestinian national movement and the Arab national movement have always been supported by majorities.

and dangerous treks, they would find no new home. For months that became endless years, the simply waited for the storm to clear so that they could go back to their own homes, as they had been promised again and again by successive international resolutions.

The Palestinian Arab community, both urban and rural, was uprooted from the Palestinian littoral. The Palestinian city was destroyed and along with it the dream of modernity that had been cultivated between the two world wars: the dream, shared by the Mandate-era elites and middle classes, of building a future Arab homeland and catching up with the modern world. The Palestinian farmer lost his land, his village and his direct relationship with nature.

The Palestinians were not just dispossessed. They were yanked out of "Place" and thrown into an aspirational future "Time" that only their middle classes and traditional elites had been politically involved in before the Nakba. They were expelled from over 420 places that had been an integral part of the Levant. Before the exile, during the Mandate period, these were places whose different rural "times" had been gradually coalescing into a single Palestinian national "time" under the Mandate's governing institutions and administrative instruments. The refugees were tossed into Arab cities, which accepted the Palestinians when they accepted themselves as Arab urban centres.[93] Displaced economic and educated elites managed to blend into their respective social classes, mostly without giving up their Palestinian affiliation, which grew stronger in exile. However, the bulk of refugees were relegated to clusters of camps that turned into slums that were often shared with rural immigrants from the countryside in the host country, because the new Arab places had yet not merged in one national "time".

The displaced Palestinian was usually welcome in the Arab countries. In Jordan, the country that annexed the West Bank after the 1948 war,[94] Palestinians were welcomed as citizens and participated

---

[93] We will come back to this in the discussion of the "Arab question" in Chapter 3.

[94] The West Bank was annexed by Jordan in 1950; however, this step was widely considered illegal by most countries and was only recognised by the United Kingdom, Iraq and Pakistan. The Arab League decided to consider Jordan's annexation of the areas to be a "trusteeship" until the Palestine case was solved in the interests of its inhabitants. Eyal

actively in building the new state and its economy. Palestinian and Syrian elites helped Abdullah to establish his Emirate in East Jordan since its founding in the 1920s. In Lebanon, problems emerged early on due to sectarian cleavages in the country, and again later because of the price paid by local inhabitants when Israel retaliated against Palestinian armed resistance factions based in the country. In times of political crisis, Palestinians could suddenly be perceived as aliens and rejected by the host society. One is reminded here of how a rape victim might be rejected by a patriarchal community despite the injustice inflicted on her because the value of masculine honour out-weighs human compassion and the will to challenge the original injustice. Politically, solidarity with the Palestinian cause remained a defining component of the pan-Arab identity. The strength of this component dwindled in tandem with the gradual weakening of that identity over time.

The majority of Palestinian refugees were scattered across neigh-bouring countries. By 30 June 1951, the UNRWA had assisted 878,000 refugees in Jordan (including 467,000 in the West Bank), the Gaza Strip (200,000), Lebanon (107,000), Syria (83,000) and 21,000 internally displaced persons inside Israel.[95] Francesca P. Albanese and Lex Takkenberg, who traced the development of the Palestinian refu-gee issue, estimated the total number of refugees in 1948 ranged between 711,000 and 774,000. The distance between the two ends of this scale highlights the challenges involved in collecting and recording historical data.[96]

Benvenisti, *The International Law of Occupation* (Princeton, NJ: Princeton University Press, 2004), p. 108. Joseph Massad said that the Arab League granted the annexation a de facto recognition and that the US had formally recognised the annexation, except for Jerusalem. See: Joseph A. Massad, *Colonial Effects: The Making of National Identity in Jordan* (New York: Columbia University Press, 2001), p. 229.

[95] See: UN General Assembly, *Special report of the Director and Advisory Commission of the United Nations Relief and Works Agency for Palestine Refugees in the Near East*, Official Records: Sixth Session Supplement No. 16 A (A/1905/Add. 1) (Paris: 1951), accessed at: https://bit.ly/2PjX1pN

[96] However, the UNRWA has no mandate in Egypt or Iraq, so caution is advisable in both instances. Iraq refused to allow the UN agency to operate on its territory and said it would

From Refugees to Organised People

Much has been written on the failure of the Arab Palestinian leadership during the British Mandate. The politics of Arab political elites, especially in the 1930s and 1940s, was largely shaped by petty rivalry between two elites, which was sustained and encouraged by the British imperial tradition of divide and conquer. The first group was made up of supporters of the mufti, Hajj Amin al-Husayni, and partisans of the Supreme Muslim Council, an institution invented by the Mandate. The second group of elites, who were evidently subsidised by the Zionist movement, was headed by Raghib al-Nashashibi, whom the British had appointed mayor of Jerusalem in 1920 to replace the mufti's distant cousin, Musa Kazim al-Husayni. The political leadership was so deeply immersed in this rivalry that it was unable to move Palestinian society forward even as Zionist immigration gained momentum.[97] The inter-elite conflict was harmful to the social and political cohesion of Arab Palestinian society at very critical time. It reached the point that some Nashashibi supporters let themselves be organised by the British colonial authorities into so-called peace bands to help British troops repress and assassinate armed rebels in the great 1936–9 revolt.[98]

The mufti, Amin al-Husayni, was the most prominent figure in Palestinian politics and regionally regarded as the most important Palestinian leader in the pre-Nakba period. He was nominated mufti

provide assistance itself. Probably less than 13,000 Palestinians entered Egypt in 1948; most did not remain, despite the fact they were not required to live in camps. Today, the Palestinian community in the country probably has no more than 75,000 members. Francesca P. Albanese & Lex Takkenberg, *Palestinian Refugees in International Law* (Oxford: Oxford University Press, 2020), pp. 35–6, 250; El-Abed Oroub, *Unprotected: Palestinians in Egypt since 1948* (Washington, D.C.: Institute for Palestine Studies/International Development Research Centre, 2009), p. 1. From the late 1970s onwards, Egypt became less welcoming to Palestinians, its supposed commitment to international and regional refugee frameworks notwithstanding. Although it accepts that Palestinians are refugees under the relevant UN resolutions, it does not recognise them as refugees under the 1951 Convention, and nor does it recognise the UNHCR's (the UN refugee agency) mandate over them. This prevents the UNHCR from registering and assisting them, and as a result the vast majority live under the poverty line. Albanese & Takkenberg, p. 244.

[97] Kimmerling & Migdal, p. 93.

[98] Rashid Khalidi, *The Iron Cage: The Story of the Palestinian Struggle for Statehood* (Boston: Beacon Press, 2006), p. 66.

by the British after the death of his brother in 1921 although he lacked the qualifications for the position.[99] According to Rashid Khalidi, he was:

> "far from the archetype of the Arab nationalist leader of the interwar period. He was not a noted public speaker, like Sa'd Zaghlul and Mustafa Nahhas in Egypt, or 'Abd al-Rahman al-Shahbandar and Shukri al-Quwwatli in Syria. Nor was he a self-made man, who had risen to prominence mainly because of his personal qualities and his leadership abilities. [...] Self-consciously a member of the Palestinian notability, the mufti adeptly managed to use the religious institutions he had been placed at the head of to build up a large popular following."[100] His mistakes were numerous, and his political awareness too shallow and traditional, to lead a people facing such complex and urgent challenges. When he was persecuted by the British and fled the country in 1941, he thought that it was right to seek refuge and support from Nazi Germany, the enemy of Britain.

However, the Jerusalemite leadership was not the only institution or elite formation the Palestinians had. There were also new and flourishing political parties and civil associations. It is easy to criticise incumbent Palestinian political leadership in retrospect, but the tremendous challenges of Zionist settler colonialism, the British Mandate and the impacts of the European Jewish question would have been overwhelming for any native political leadership in any imperialist colony in the world at that time.

---

[99] Ilan Pappé narrates that "Directly after his older brother's death, al-Hajj Amin put on the *hamama* (the Hajj's white hat) and began to grow a beard as though he were already the *Mufti*. That day he discarded his European suit for ever. Elections were held on 12 April 1921. Husam Jarallah received most of the votes while al-Hajj Amin only made it to fourth place." He adds that after riots took place in support of al-Hajj Amin, "The British government was now under pressure. On the one hand, there were the results of the preliminary vote for the *mufti*, while on the other, there was clear popular support for al-Hajj Amin's candidacy. The Hight Commissioner was faced with a dilemm a: al-Hajj Amin was inexperienced and had taken part in anti-British activities, but there was no denying his family's prominent position in local politics.[...] Samuel met with al-Hajj Amin the day before the preliminary vote and was favorably impressed, believing that the young man would use his own and his family's influence to bring calm to Jerusalem and the entire country." Ilan Pappé, *The Rise and Fall of a Palestinian Dynasty: The Husaynis, 1700–1948* (Berkeley, C A: University of California Press, 2010), pp. 214, 216.

[100] Khalidi, *The Iron Cage*, pp. 60–1.

Following the Nakba, the ascendant Palestinian urban leadership integrated itself into the wider Arab world. Palestinian elites were instrumental to building up Arab states and capital cities from Amman to Beirut, and Kuwait to other Gulf states. As of yet, there has been no proper, scientific evaluation of this well-known economic, social and professional contribution. It is also the case that, in some of the more conservative states, a patriarchal and narrow local chauvinism has been fostered in which "immigrants" and "refugees" are seen as undesirable and therefore their contributions are unlikely to be acknowledged. Be that as it may, it is crucial to underscore the significant contributions of Palestinian refugees to ensure that the refugee issue is placed in its proper political and national context and to avoid reducing it to a humanitarian issue alone. The Palestinians were not a burden to their host countries. They formed an active, productive and hardworking community that never forgot its homeland.

The PLO was set up by the Palestinian elite and dominated by urban Palestinian nationalist leaders in collaboration with Arab nationalist regimes, thereby tying it to the broader pan-Arab project at the time. The PLO's creation reflected the widespread assumption that the Palestinian issue was not simply a Palestinian, but also an Arab concern. The organisation was established in June 1964, after extensive debates and deliberations between the Arab states on the question of Palestinian representation. These debates unfolded over a four-year period, from 1959–63. The last one took place in the first Arab summit, held at Nasser's request in Cairo from 13–17 January 1964. This summit resolved that "Ahmad al-Shuqayri, the representative of Palestine in the Arab League, will continue his contacts with the member states [in the Arab League] and with the Palestinian people in order to establish the proper foundations for the organisation of the Palestinian people, [and] in order to enable it to fulfil its role in the liberation of its homeland and its self-determination." This was the first operational decision taken both unanimously and at the highest Arab level on the question of a Palestinian entity since Egypt's earlier efforts to tackle this question in March 1959.[101]

---

[101] Moshe Shemesh, "The Founding of the PLO 1964," *Middle Eastern Studies*, vol. 20, no. 4 (1984), p. 121.

The Cairo resolution paved the way for al-Shuqayri to organise the first Palestine National Congress (PNC) in Jerusalem in May 1964. In that meeting, the PNC decreed the establishment of the PLO, approving its national charter and other constituent documents and statutes. However, the majority of the 422 Palestinians invited to attend had been nominated by King Hussein of Jordan whose intelligence agents, moreover, asserted an intrusive presence at the meeting. Furthermore, al-Shuqayri had previously reassured Jordan that the proposed entity would not demand any territorial sovereignty over the West Bank in the Hashemite Kingdom of Jordan. It was only on this condition that Jordan allowed the PNC to convene in Jerusalem where it was officially opened by King Hussein.

The composition of the first PNC reflected al-Shuqayri's reassurances to Jordan. Furthermore, there was a "clear bias towards traditional social leaders and sections of the established families of pre-1948 Palestine and towards the propertied and professional elements of the middle class. Al-Shuqayri also offered seats to nascent Palestinian groups such as Fatah and the Arab Nationalists' Movement, but refused to acknowledge them formally in the PNC."[102] Despite this bias, al-Shuqayri and his colleagues from the educated elite institutionalised the PLO as a complex modern organisation with a national council, an executive committee, national funds and several other agencies, including trade unions, and the organisation's leadership ran it in a professional manner.

A contrasting role was played by other, younger actors who formed militant political organisations, rejected political reliance on the Arab states and advocated armed struggle as the only viable way to liberate Palestine. They approached Palestinian nationalism from the perspective of an independent-minded political leadership in a tense relationship with the governments of neighbouring Arab countries (such as Syria and Jordan), at least when it came to the question of self-representation. They differed in many other ways from the

---

[102] Yezid Sayigh, *Armed Struggle and the Search for State: The Palestinian National Movement, 1949–1993* (New York: Oxford University Press, 1997), pp. 98–9. See also: "The Palestinian National Council," [Arabic] *Encyclopaedia Palestina*, 28 October 2015, accessed at: https://bit.ly/3yt5mcr

older members of the PLO whose founders "had been active in Palestinian nationalist politics before 1948, and many had gained experience of party politics or had held office in the quasigovernmental Arab Higher Committee [...] and other bodies in Palestine."[103] They were from the "strata that had occupied the second echelon in the national leadership under Husayni, and that were effectively denied their chance to govern as a result of the Nakba and of the subsequent marginalisation of the Arab Higher Committee and All Palestine Government."[104]

After 1967—that is, after the defeat suffered by the ruling nationalist bloc of the Arab states which had been involved in the war—the activists who established the various armed factions came to control PLO institutions. These:

> "had been teenagers, or at most in their early twenties, in 1948. Most came from a lower middle-class background, [and] had benefited from the rapid expansion of the education system in the Arab countries in the late 1940s and early 1950s. [...] In brief, the generation that took control of the PLO in 1968–9 and that subsequently staffed its various departments and agencies was strikingly similar in terms of its social origins to the "new elites" that came to power in Egypt, Syria, Algeria, and Iraq between 1952 and 1968."[105]

The emphasis on armed struggle as the only path towards the liberation of Palestine was anchored in a new national charter that revised the founding charter of the PLO. It was infused with Arab nationalist tones, as is evidenced by its name: *al-Mithaq al-Qawmi*.[106]

---

[103] Sayigh, pp. 669–70.

[104] Ibid., p. 95.

[105] Ibid., pp. 669–70.

[106] According to Yezid Sayigh, there was an awareness among the Palestinian armed factions (usually referred to as *fasai'l*) of the domestic, regional and international limitations of the armed struggle against Israel, despite the fact that their military effort never exceeded a limited level in terms of scale and impact. However, the armed struggle was consistently described by the *fasai'l* as the principal, even exclusive, means of liberating Palestine. This is because the armed struggles—Sayigh says—served other primary functions, most importantly: elite formation, political legitimation, nation building and consolidating the Palestinian political "entity". Violence allowed a unique "massing effect" in a segmented society and "the heroic imagery and language of armed struggle gave new

PALESTINE

substance to the imagined community of the Palestinians" who were portrayed as a "revolutionary people waging an active struggle to determine their fate, rather than as a mass of helpless refugees passively awaiting charity handouts." Sayigh, pp. 667–8.

2

AFTERTHOUGHTS, MEMORY AND HISTORY

This chapter deals with several aspects of memory and history after the Nakba. In this context, the instrumentalisation of Zionist biblical archaeology which, in all events, is an ideological construct that does not establish rights, will be discussed, in order to refute the contrived competition of "who was here first?". A second aspect relates to the construction of collective identities and to the specificity of national identity. A third is the political importance of remembering Palestine before the Nakba. This is not just to help define/identify the modern Palestinian polity but also to make it absolutely clear that the Palestinian question did not suddenly arise in 1967 and that the political solutions the Palestinians have accepted or are expected to accept are compromises. In order to explain the historical context of Palestinian national identity, this chapter takes a closer look at the distinction between collective identities and the structures that reproduce them and between the history of the land and national history.

Concerning National Rights: Who Needs Archaeological Nationalism?[1]

Since the Nakba, a whole political culture has developed around the question as to which people have the right to the land of Palestine and

---

[1] Nationalist archaeology attempts to project a contemporary nationalist conception of history onto ancient times, turning back the clock to imagine an ancient pattern underpinning

57

what the nature of such a right might be. This book defends Palestinian rights in the land and to the land of Palestine. It brings to bear a combination of humanist and national modernist approaches, and is based on Palestinians physically being there, uninterruptedly for centuries: going about their daily business, cultivating the land, building the cities, reproducing a culture in interaction with nature and history, and developing national aspirations.

The rights of the native Arab population living in Palestine long before the Crusades are a product of long historical interaction and merging of ethnicities, tribes and communities with a shared Arab Muslim culture in a land without political borders (like all other countries of the Levant and North Africa). The Palestinians are an indigenous native people who had already developed a national consciousness and polity before being exposed to "politicide" and expulsion by a form of settler colonialism. I used the phrase "native indigenous people with national consciousness" and not only indigenous people intentionally, because settler colonialism in different countries acknowledged defeated native populations after a long struggle as indigenous[2] people. This is an achievement of course, but not for a people who were already in the phase of national liberation struggle against colonialism. This is the term usually used to signify/denote natives who had not developed a national movement (in the modern sense) and national aspirations before they were overwhelmed and annihilated as a people (physically and socially) by a strong modern

---

modern nationalism. This is the ahistorical ideological cultural project that I call archaeological nationalism.

[2] Some definitions confuse ethnicity and nationality in order to be more "affirmative" or "politically correct". Take for example the following definition: "Generally, Indigenous refers to those peoples with pre-existing sovereignty who were living together as a community prior to contact with settler populations, most often—though not exclusively—Europeans. Indigenous is the most inclusive term, as there are Indigenous peoples on every continent throughout the world—such as the Sami in Sweden, the First Nations in Canada, Mayas in Mexico and Guatemala, and the Ainu in Japan—fighting to remain culturally intact on their land bases. Indigenous Peoples refers to a group of Indigenous peoples with a shared national identity, such as 'Navajo' or 'Sami,' and is the equivalent of saying 'the American people.' The confusion here reflects noble intentions. See: "Native American and Indigenous Peoples FAQs," *UCLA-EDI*, 14 April 2020, accessed at: https://bit.ly/3nwmknh

settler state, leaving them with, at most, meagre compensations, cultural rights, respect for their memory and identity (at least in democratic countries) and, of course, "narratives" if they wish. What they do not have is a communal right to self-determination and full authority over the land. The proclamation of indigeneity became a very important component specifically in the struggle of the Arab citizens in the state of Israel itself, who are denied the status of indigenous people. This part of the Palestinian people needs the affirmation of indigeneity for its own identity (and pride) and in the struggle for their civil and communal rights in a state that was built in their homeland and in which they became a minority.[3]

The Palestinian national identity and struggle has been a well-documented historical fact since the Third Palestinian Congress. Held in Haifa on 13–19 December 1920, the congress was attended by representatives from different Palestinian cities, towns and villages and by members of various Palestinian Islamic and Christian associations. The participants affirmed national demands and pledged firm support for the establishment of an independent national government. They also elected an executive committee to oversee the development of the national movement in the coming phase. It is clear from the closing statements of the Third Palestinian Congress that its authors had in mind the San Remo conference held earlier that year, in April, and the French colonial occupation's overthrow of the King Faisal government in Damascus in July 1920.[4] Of particular note, the congress resolved

---

[3] See also: Nadim N. Rouhana, "Homeland Nationalism and Guarding Dignity in a Settler Colonial Context: The Palestinian Citizens of Israel Reclaim Their Homeland," *Borderland e-Journal*, vol. 14, no. 1 (Spring 2015), pp. 1–37.

[4] The conference concluded its statement with a national charter, which called for continued Arab opposition to the Zionist policy of establishing a national home on the basis of the Balfour Declaration and for Jewish immigration to Palestine to be halted. It also endorsed the establishment of a national government that would be accountable to a parliament, whose members would be elected by the Arabic-speaking residents of Palestine. See: Abd al-Wahhab al-Kayyali, *Documents on the Palestinian Arab Resistance to the British Mandate and Zionism (1918–1939)* [Arabic], 2nd ed. (Beirut: The Institute for Palestine Studies, 1988), pp. 16–19. The conference endorsed an executive committee (led by Musa Kazem Al-Husseini and his deputy Aref Pasha Al-Dajani) and tasked it with supervising the progress of the national movement. Bayan Nuwayhid Al Hout, *The Political Leadership and*

PALESTINE

to abandon the Greater Syria proposition, which had been one of the most important resolutions adopted by the original twenty-seven members of the First Arab Palestinian Congress in 1919,[5] in favour of the establishment of a Palestinian national government.

Palestinian national identity crystallised under the British Mandate. This is not to say that they had no nationality before that. They were (and still are) Arabs, not just ethnically, but also in their national aspirations.[6] In contrast, the national development of Israelis was

---

Institutions in Palestine (1917—1948) [Arabic] (Beirut: Institute of Palestine Studies, 1986), pp. 139–43.

[5] Held on 27 January to 9 February 1919, the first congress brought together representatives of various cities and regions across Palestine. Arif Dajani, president of the Islamic Christian Association in Jerusalem, was elected as chairman and Ragheb Abu al-Saud al-Dajani, founder and president of the Islamic Christian Association in Jaffa, was elected as his deputy. The conference issued a petition that was then submitted to the Paris Peace Conference. It stated: "We consider Palestine nothing but part of Arabian Syria and it has never been separated from it at any stage. We are tied to it by national (*qawmia*), religious, linguistic, moral, economic, and geographic bonds. We desire that our district Southern Syria, or Palestine, should be not separated from the Independent Arab Syrian Government and be free from all foreign influence and protection. […] [W]e deem every promise or treaty heretofore concluded with respect to our country and its future as null and void." Al Hout, pp. 95–7.

[6] *A Personal Note:* The author experienced an absurd occurrence that had to do with conceptual confusion involving this. In 1989, when I was still a lecturer in Bir-Zeit University in the West Bank, I participated in a debate on Israeli TV on the concept of *umāh* in Hebrew (*ummah* in Arabic). The term "nation" is usually translated to *ummah*, an old term which originally had a different meaning. This is a common enough practice in translation and is considered acceptable as long as the new use of the term gains currency and a new and generally accepted term has not been coined. However, sometimes when an old term is used, the connotations of the term can be a source of many misunderstandings and it can also be misused. In Arabic, the term *ummah* is used to signify the Arab nation, but originally it was used (and is still used) to designate those affiliated with Islam. During that TV programme, I said that there is no Palestinian nation, and that different "Arab nations" are an invention of colonialism; there is an Arab nation, and I am an Arab nationalist, not a Palestinian nationalist. I added, "We do not say Palestinian nation, we say Palestinian People." Thirty years later, an American Zionist right-wing group posted a video clip of that segment of the programme on various social media with the disingenuous comment, "Even Azmi Bishara denies the existence of a Palestinian nation." Thirty-three years later, Arab regimes that were upset (to put it mildly) by my outspoken support of the 2011 Arab revolutions when they erupted discovered that video clip and had their internet trolls circulate it again. I did not respond

mostly state-driven after independence in 1948. The Zionist-organised settler society, the *Yeshuv*, laid the foundation of the state by integrating Jewish emigrants from different countries, nationalities and even different ethnicities into a conscientiously constructed Hebrew culture as part of a colonial venture that conceived of itself as part of a state-building project for a single people.

Palestinian rights to the land are not derived from a claimed genealogical descent from the Canaanites or any other people living in Palestine in ancient times, including the Philistines from whom the land's name was taken. Nor is the Jewish Israelis' right to live in the land of Palestine derived from a purported genealogical or spiritual link to ancient Israelites. Modern Israel was established by force, and not by rights.

---

because their intentions were obvious, and my struggle for Palestine and my writings were too well known to be harmed by the propaganda of authoritarian regimes that have covertly and later overtly allied with Israel. Their cheap propaganda leaped on a single term in translation and took it out of context. They did not bother to consult my writings or recall my well-known positions. Others apparently forgot they, themselves, do not use the expression *ummah falastiniyya* ("Palestinian nation"), but rather *sha'b falastini* (Palestinian people). The same applies in Hebrew by the way: *a'm falstini* and not *umāh falastinit*. When the famous Israeli PM Golda Meir made her notorious statement in which she denied the existence of a Palestinian people, she said: "*ein a'm falstini*" and not *umāh falastinit*. In Arabic, Palestinians, Syrians, Jordanians, Iraqis etc., use the word *sha'b* to describe their country affiliation. So, we say "Palestinian people" and we do not say "Palestinian nation". People who use *ummah* to describe such an affiliation were once accused of collaborating with the colonial attempt to divide or partition the Arab nation. When Palestinians want to express love for Palestine and devotion to their homeland, they usually use the term *watani falasitini* or *wataniyya falstiniyya*, which can be translated to "Palestinian patriot"; they would never say *qawmi faslatini* (Palestinian nationalist). There was nothing out of the ordinary in what I said on that TV programme What was unusual was how my remarks were seized on, distorted by re-translation and cuts, by both right-wing Zionists and right-wing Arab regimes. I returned to this subject 8 years later in the last chapter of my book on civil society (*Civil Society: A Critical Study* [Arabic] (Beirut: Center of Arab Unity Studies, 1996)), in which I argued that we should separate the concept of the nation from ethnic nationalism and strive to build nations of citizens in the Arab countries. I stressed that the Arab affiliation remains a basic cultural identity component of the Arabs and their ethnic nationality, which should be distinguished from state nationality which should designate citizenship and not any other affiliation.

PALESTINE

As members of religions, followers of Islam, Christianity and Judaism, and other religions have inherent religious rights (which is also a modern concept), but this does not confer the political rights to form a state. What is proclaimed as a "right for a state" is a national right. The Palestinians have them by virtue of the two rights mentioned above (a long and continual presence on the land and the right of a people to self-determination). Jewish Israelis achieved these rights by virtue of building a state to host the generations of Jews born in Israel since 1948, and who now have no other homeland.

The national rights of the Jews in Palestine did not exist before the emergence of the Israeli state. The state retroactively accomplished the critical task of building a nation able to claim it possessed national rights but still unable to indigenise itself due to its colonial and apartheid character and unsolved Palestinian issue. Why not take the founding of the Zionist movement and the first Zionist Congress in Basel (29–31 August 1897) as the starting point? This only works in terms of the nationalist vision, not the nation-building dimension, especially when we consider that, in 1897 and for decades afterwards, Zionism was a fringe movement supported by only a small fraction of Jews in Europe, while those in Asia and Africa were not even in the picture.

Until the late nineteenth century, Jewish European secular politics were dominated by the *haskalah*, a political culture that believed in enlightenment and the modern state. It secularised the medieval doctrine of *Dina de-malkhuta dina* ("the law of the kingdom is the law") and "turned it into a historical rationale for the Jews' loyalty to the states in which they lived."[7] The *haskalah* culture entailed the notion and the yearning that the Jews would accept the conditions of modern citizenship.[8] Jewish intellectuals therefore tried to integrate the history of their own communities within the national histories of their European homelands. In Germany, France and Hungary, they were influenced by "the national historical discourse in their countries"[9] and strove to be a part of it. Evidence also indicates that they developed

---

[7] David Biale, *Power & Powerlessness in Jewish History* (New York: Schocken, 1986), p. 103.
[8] Ibid, p. 113.
[9] Guy Miron, *The Waning of Emancipation: Jewish History, Memory, and the Rise of Fascism in Germany, France, and Hungary* (Detroit: Wayne State University Press, 2011), p. 7.

"a homemaking myth that would strengthen their roots in the local motherland."[10] The representation of Jews in European socialist movements and among emancipatory cultural elites was also much higher than their share of the population.

These historical discourses prevailed until the interwar era. The deep contradictions in European societies, ethnic nationalism and political populism continued to produce antisemitism, but the most dominant reactions to it were integrationist egalitarian trends and, antithetically, the religious isolationist trend. But Zionism was there, too. It drew on integration, nationalism and isolationism. It was influenced by European nationalism, not in the direction of integration, but rather towards separation. It sought to establish a nationalism of its own, out of the belief that Jews can only integrate among the civilised nations of the world by constructing a European state, separate from the other European nations. This vision could only be implemented outside Europe.

Until World War II, Zionism was but one of many competing ideological trends among Jews and generally one of the smaller political movements.[11] There were also liberal, socialist and communist assimilationists; Jewish non-assimilationist socialists (Bundists) who were anti-Zionist and yearned for national cultural rights after achieving socialism in their countries; and Orthodox and traditional anti-nationalist Jews. The waning of liberal values in the interwar period and the rise of Fascism and Nazism strengthened Zionists, who preached a solution for the Jews outside of Europe. They reduced Jewish history to a fabled biblical period that was further idealised into a golden age of Jewish sovereignty. On this, they anchored their nationalist claims, while ignoring the nearly 2,000 years since the destruction of the second temple or writing it off as no more than a history of suffering. "Rejecting exilic medieval Judaism as a fundamentally apolitical and subservient culture, the founders of modern Israel sought a synthesis between the image of ancient Israelite power and the lessons of European nationalism."[12]

---

[10] Ibid., p. 8.
[11] Biale, p. 145.
[12] Ibid., p. 150.

However, the narrative that sees Jewish political history through the prism of Zionism only became dominant among Jewish scholars after the state of Israel "achieved a degree of institutional solidity, physical security, and economic well-being unsurpassed in its history,"[13] and after the Jewish state "could monopolize the means of education and implement its views in the official curriculum instructed in its schools."[14] David Myers addresses the role of the founding generation of scholars of the Institute of Jewish Studies of the Hebrew University in Jerusalem in projecting a new and coherent Zionist historical consciousness onto history;[15] a systematisation of the Zionist grand narrative of Jewish History that turned Jewish histories interwoven with the histories of different peoples into one monolithic national history leading from the second temple to the state of Israel.

Zionist archaeological propaganda is an ideological construct that tries, in vain, to prove Jewish continuity in Palestine since before the so-called biblical times. It may serve as a basis for producing a nationalist religious political culture, but it is irrelevant to legitimising modern national rights. The Palestinians are wrong to try compete with it by producing their own ancient histories of Canaanite ancestry. A myriad peoples and ethnicities passed through and lived in this land over the course of millennia. The natural product of this complex and uninterrupted weave of historical, cultural and ethnic interaction was already in Palestine when the Zionist pioneers arrived. It was the Palestinian Arabs. This very presence establishes their right to the land. It makes no sense for them to play along with a contrived archaeological competition.

---

[13] David N. Myers, "Between Diaspora and Zion: History, Memory, and the Jerusalem Scholars," in: David N. Myers & David B. Ruderman (eds.), *The Jewish Past Revisited: Reflections on Modern Jewish Historians* (New Haven and London: Yale University Press, 1998), p. 90.

[14] Uri Ram, "Zionist historiography and the invention of modern Jewish nationhood: The case of Ben Zion Dinur," *History and Memory*, vol. 7, no. 1 (1995), p. 115.

[15] Myers & Ruderman (eds.). See also: Gabriel Piterberg, *The returns of Zionism: Myths, politics and Scholarship in Israel* (London: Verso, 2008), chapter 4.

The Palestinian National Collective as a Modern Identity

The origin of the modern Palestinian identity, according to Baruch Kimmerling and Joel S. Migdal, can be traced to the 1834 revolt against Ibrahim Pasha.[16] Rashid Khalidi argues that, during the period from the start of World War I to the beginning of the British Mandate, Palestine experienced "a strong and growing national identification with Palestine, as the Arab residents of the country increasingly came to 'imagine' themselves as part of a single community." Nevertheless, Khalidi conceded that:

> "this identification was certainly not exclusive—for Arabism, religion, and local loyalties still remained extremely important, and continued to make it possible for Arabs in Palestine to also see themselves simultaneously as part of other communities [...] But it did constitute a new and powerful category of identity that was simply non-existent a generation or two before, and was still novel and limited in its diffusion before World War I."[17]

Yehoshua Porath countered that "the ideology of national self-determination anchored in separate historical and linguistic identity was a revolutionary innovation in Palestine in the twenties, and it is highly doubtful if it could have been grasped by the less educated section of the community."[18]

Although Muhammad Muslih held that Palestinian nationalism was not a priority for the Arab elites in Palestine in the 1920s, he linked the rise of Palestinian nationalism to both local concerns and the unfeasibility of materialising Arab nationalism in a state. "Arab political elites—Palestinian, Syrian, and Iraqi—were confronted with two forces: the push of Arab nationalism and the pull of local nationalism," he observes. "[...] Having failed to translate the 'universalism' of the

---

[16] "The tough rule and the new reforms led to the 1834 revolt's outbreak in the heart of the country, uniting dispersed Bedouins, rural sheikhs, urban notables, mountain fellaheen, and Jerusalem religious figures against a common enemy. It was these groups who would later constitute the Palestinian people." Kimmerling & Migdal, p. 7.

[17] Rashid Khalidi, *Palestinian Identity: The Construction of Modern National Consciousness* (New York: Columbia University Press, 2010), pp. 149–50.

[18] Yehoshua Porath, *The Emergence of the Palestinian-Arab National Movement, 1918–1929* (London: Frank Cass, 1974), p. 307.

pan-Arab doctrine into a concrete reality, they resigned themselves, some painfully and begrudgingly, to the overwhelming pull of local concerns and priorities. Nationalism, which was linked with a specific piece of land and a specific group of people, prevailed."[19]

According to Meir Litvak, the Palestinian historical discourse underwent significant changes over three distinct periods of time. The first period was from the 1920s to 1967, when the discourse favoured a pan-Arab narrative. The second was from 1967 to 1994, which marked the revival and crystallisation of a distinct Palestinian identity within a broader context of Arab nationalism. The third period began with the establishment of the Palestinian National Authority in 1994, which did not deviate from Arabism and Palestinianism but tended to overstress links to the "Canaanite past."[20]

Tarif Khalidi stated that much of the historical work produced by early Palestinian historians was "antiquarian, having no other ostensible purpose than to unearth or record various aspects of Palestinian and Arab history and culture. As the Mandate progressed and was perceived to be dedicating itself to the realization of the Jewish National Home, the 'antiquarian' scholars became more 'nationalist.'" Ever since, history became a "national legacy to be used for reinforcing the on-going debate with the Zionists and the British over the issue of the right to Palestine."[21]

Serious Palestinian research was conducted to demonstrate, not only continuous inhabitance of the land over the centuries, but also to trace the formation of Palestinian collective identity back to historical phases even earlier than the eighteenth century. This is certainly an important research project in terms of the history of the land and the communities that lived on it, but it is irrelevant to national identity, which is a modern political identity. There were several pre-modern

[19] Muhammad Y. Muslih, *The Origins of Palestinian Nationalism* (New York: Columbia University Press, 1988), p. 214.

[20] Meir Litvak, "Constructing a national past: the Palestinian case," in: Meir Litvak (ed.), *Palestinian Collective Memory and National Identity* (New York: Palgrave Macmillan, 2009), pp. 97–133.

[21] Tarif Khalidi, "Palestinian Historiography: 1900–1948," *Journal of Palestine Studies*, vol. 10, no. 3 (1981), p. 64.

religious, sectarian, tribal, regional and other collective identities in Palestine, but the national identity is a modern construct.

My suggestion here is to distinguish between:

1. The history of the land and national history.
2. Collective identity in general, and modern nationalism that seeks political expression of this identity through a state, thereby reproducing it as a national identity.
3. Shifting and mutating constructed "collective identities," on the one hand, and the tangible political, social and cultural structures that reproduce, politicise and consolidate collective identities, on the other. Modern institutional structures, without which discussion of national evolution is impossible, are accessible to empirical research. However, such research must apply this critical distinction between the living collective identities and the macrostructures that enable human agents to reproduce them as national entities (and as national cultures not solely dependent on subjective feelings of affiliation) in order to identify how these factors interplay and theorise their implications.

There have always been collective identities in the land of Palestine, but before the British Mandate there were no political, social and cultural structures that could produce and reproduce a single collective identity, one that united Palestinians and fused their local identities into a people distinct from those in neighbouring countries. That is, Palestinian identities before the Mandate era were not "nationalised," i.e., reshaped by nationalism towards political expression in a sovereign state. These structures arose on a Palestinian national level and in a national territorial framework under the British Mandate and took the form of modern political organisations (political parties and a national leadership), economic associations (banks, business companies), trade unions, Palestinian daily newspapers and cultural and educational institutions. Together they forged the collective Palestinian cultural and political identity in the land of Palestine. The Nakba endangered this collective identity, but a defiant response soon arose in different forms, most notably the PLO.

The history and historical speculations outlined above indicate not only an existing nationalist sentiment, but also the development of a national identity by the people who lived there, whose history permeated the history of the country that shared their name, fully exempting the Palestinians from the need for ideological archaeological competition or for harkening back to imagined ancient ancestries.

Memory and Amnesia

The Nakba represents a rupture not only in Palestinian modern history, but also in modern Arab history because, in the aftermath of defeat, the dialectical relationship with Israel began to displace and, ultimately, serve as the fig leaf for the internal dialectic. The Arabs were staggered by what had happened, but the overwhelming shock became the start of the new partisan ideological pan-Arabism (as opposed to the intellectual and cultural pan-Arabism that spread from the end of the nineteenth century to the first half of the twentieth century).

In general, Arab regimes did not try to analyse and explain the defeat in Palestine. They tended to consider it a historical glitch, a fabrication cut from the same cloth as the "so-called State of Israel" itself. They even avoided saying that name, let alone calling it a state, using instead such terms as "Zionist entity" or "Zionist band" or "the presumed state of Israel," etc.

In the 1950s, military coups in Egypt, Syria and Iraq brought an abrupt end to the so-called liberal era in Egypt and the Levant. The mutinous officers who led the coups had participated in the failed 1948 war[22] and personally experienced the formative shock. The defeat in Palestine was widely perceived as a fiasco that was blamed on unpopular ruling elites dependent on ex-colonial powers and on the myriad of other failures of the former regimes, and it was no surprise that the officers explicitly mentioned the 1948 defeat in their first communiques and promised to liberate Palestine.

The independent Arab countries and states that emerged in the boundaries shaped by colonial partitions did not unite in an Arab state or union. But nor did local national identities replace the wider Arab

---

[22] All the leaders of the first military coups in the Arab world (Husni al-Zaim and Adib Shishakli in Syria, Nasser in Egypt and Abdel Karim Qassem in Iraq) fought as officers in Palestine in 1948.

identity. Moreover, the Palestine cause became an important unifying component of the Arab identity in this fragmented reality. Since then, it has become clear that the rise of local identities in conflict with pan-Arabism casts doubt on the centrality of the Palestinian issue. The question of Palestine fundamentally altered pan-Arab ideology. Heretofore at peace with itself, seeking to bring together peoples with a common language and an imagined shared history, it evolved into an angry political ideology that grew all the more radical as the fragmentation became more obvious in real life. This strident Arab Nationalist movement would quickly acquire enormous impetus under the modernising Arab military regimes of the 1950s and 1960s.

Commemoration and Timing

The Palestinian calamity and cause have remained present in innumerable ways in Arab politics, literature and popular culture; however, for decades, annual commemorations of the Nakba were infrequent in the Arab world, except in refugee camps. Since the 1990s, Palestinian Arab citizens of Israel inside the Green Line[23] held annual commemorations in the form of marches of displaced Palestinians who had been prevented from returning to the villages they fled or were expelled from in 1948.[24] The annual march was launched in the

---

[23] The lines of the armistice between Israel and the Arab countries in 1949, which then became the de facto borders of state of Israel.

[24] Palestinians forced to leave their homes but remained within Israel's borders are categorised as "internally displaced" and were later granted Israeli citizenship by the 1952 Nationality Law. The 1950 Absentees' Property Law categorised these Palestinians as "present absentees" along with others who left the areas by the Zionist Militias even for a short period of time between 29 November 1947 and 15 May 1948, Nimer Sultani, "The Legal Structures of Subordination," in: Nadim Rouhaha (ed.), *Israel and its Palestinian Citizens* (NY: Cambridge University Press, 2017), p. 202, or were not in the Jewish state during the census of 1949, when the truce borders were not clear yet. This euphemism bestowed the legal status of "absentees" on people who had never left the country and who clearly remained physically present. This law also transferred internally displaced Palestinians' properties to the Custodian of Absentees' property, as if they were absent refugees located outside the country. Israeli policies have systematically prevented "absentee" Palestinians from returning to their homes or lands. Writing on IDPs, Hillel Cohen

aftermath of the "1993 Oslo agreements between Israel and the PLO when, according to which it was understood that Palestinians in Israel were left out as an internal Israeli issue."[25]

Then, on the sixtieth anniversary of that formative event, Nakba commemorations were held on a large scale in many Arab countries. They were a manifestation of the increasing concern among large segments of public opinion that something was missing in the relationship between Arab officialdom and Palestine and the growing alarm over the fate of the Palestinian cause and the welfare of

---

estimates the number of internally displaced Palestinians in the early 1950s to be around 25,000 (roughly 1/6 of the total Palestinian population in the country). Although a lack of official statistical data makes it difficult to precisely estimate their current number, the BADIL Resource Center has estimated it at about 420,000, along with about 350,000 in the Occupied Territories. See: Hillel Cohen, "The State of Israel Versus the Palestinian Internal Refugees," in: Nur Masalha (ed.), *Catastrophe Remembered: Palestine, Israel and the Internal Refugees* (London: Zed Books, 2005), pp. 59–60; Nur Masalha, *The Politics of Denial: Israel and the Palestinian Refugee Problem* (London: Pluto Press, 2003), p. 143; Hillel Cohen, "The Internal Refugees in the State of Israel: Israeli Citizens, Palestinian Refugees," *Palestine-Israel Journal*, vol. 9, no. 2 (2002), pp. 43–51; Wakim Wakim, "The Internal Refugees in their Homeland: Present Absentee in Israel," [Arabic] *Palestine Studies Journal*, vol. 45/46 (Winter 2001), p. 93; "Survey of Palestinian Refugees and Internally Displaced Persons 2016–2018: Volume lX," *Survey*, BADIL Resource Center for Palestinian Residency and Refugee Rights, November 2019, accessed at: https://bit.ly/3tn6Kuq. Cohen notes that the UNRWA was mandated to conduct "relief and works programmes" to support the internally displaced in Israel between 1950–2. In this period, UNRWA relief services were managed by the Red Cross. After this, the Israeli government assumed responsibility for taking care of refugees within its borders. Israel viewed the termination of the UNRWA and Red Cross (1949–52) mandate in political terms: allowing UNRWA activity amounted to a recognition of a refugee issue. As a result, the internal refugees were removed from the "UNRWA scroll and were registered in the Israeli population censuses as belonging in their villages and cities of refuge, not of origin." Hillel Cohen, *The Present Absentees: The Palestinian Refugees in Israel since 1948* [Arabic] (Beirut: Institute for Palestine Studies, 2003), pp. 68, 99; Cohen, "The State of Israel Versus the Palestinian Internal Refugees," in: *Catastrophe Remembered*, p. 65.

[25] Nadim N. Rouhana, "Homeland Nationalism and Guarding Dignity in a Settler Colonial Context: The Palestinian Citizens of Israel Reclaim Their Homeland," *Borderland e-Journal*, vol. 14, no. 1 (Spring 2015), p. 22. See also: Nadim N. Rouhana & Areej Sabbagh-Khoury, "Memory and the Return of History in a Settler-colonial Context: The Case of the Palestinians in Israel," *Interventions*, vol. 21, no. 4 (2019), pp. 527–50.

the Palestinian people. The sentiments, which were also expressed in solidarity demonstrations with Gaza against the blockade (2007–present) and against the Israeli bombardment of the heavily populated strip (December 2008–January 2009), also contributed to the build-up of the grassroots rage against repressive police states and their failing social and economic policies which erupted in the Arab uprisings in 2011.

The commemorations were motivated by other factors, as well. One was the Arabs' dawning realisation that they lacked a sense of direction and that fundamental issues were at stake but had been forgotten during the endless backing-and-forthing between regional powers over the "peace process." More troubling was the Palestinian infighting after the 2006 PA legislative elections which degenerated into an armed confrontation between the Fatah and Hamas movements in 2007. A third factor, which may have served as a final straw, was the provocative visits by Western and non-Western heads of state to Jerusalem to take part in Israel's Independence Day celebrations. These leaders needed to be reminded that they were actually celebrating the humanitarian disasters that befell the Palestinian people with the creation of that state.

The 2008 commemorations of the Nakba were thus a kind of "back-to-basics" campaign. It was at once a reassertion of the collective Palestinian/Arab memory and an instance of reminding others of the basics. The Palestinian refugees' right of return, for example, was among the most essential basics that needed to be reiterated at that time. This right had been universally recognised in 1949, long before the emergence of Palestinian militancy, the establishment of Fatah or the PLO, let alone Hamas, which only surfaced officially during the first Intifada in December 1987.[26]

---

[26] Since the early 1980s, the Muslim Brotherhood has played a notable political role in Palestine. However, until the outbreak of the first Palestinian Intifada in December 1987, the group did not play an active role in confronting the Israeli occupation. Rather, its leadership adopted a relatively passive ideology that considered its mission to be purification and re-Islamisation of society, a process that in their view should precede any confrontation with Israel's occupation. This position led to a "generational coup" in the 1980s in the form of establishing "Hamas". The generational coup was partly triggered by the emer-

Many have questioned the insistence on commemorating the Nakba in 2008, the same week that the world's gaze was drawn to the civil war in Iraq—after a devastating occupation that had destroyed the country, with numbers of victims far eclipsing those in Palestine, just as the number of victims in Syria since 2011 exceeds those directly caused by colonising Palestine.

So, what is so unique about Palestine? The Palestinian people are not any more or less unique than other peoples. They are not God's chosen people. On the contrary, they face an occupier who explicitly claims title to a state on their land on the grounds of a divine manifestation to a "chosen people." If the Palestinian question has any similar claim to uniqueness, it is in the dubious honour of being the last true colonial conflict on earth. In the age of decolonisation, Palestinians fell victim to a settler colonial project that has no colonial power to return to, that considers Palestine to be its long lost

---

gence of a new faction, under the name "The Islamic Jihad Movement in Palestine" (*Harakat al-Jihād al-Islāmi fi Filastīn*), from within the ranks of the Muslim Brotherhood. The Islamic Jihad Movement was inspired by the armed struggle of the nationalist factions and by the Iranian revolution (1979). Consequently, the leadership of the Muslim Brotherhood realised on the eve of the outbreak of the first Intifada that if it did not listen to the young generation of activists (especially student activists) and join the national struggle against occupation, then it would lose its political legitimacy and influence within the Palestinian community. Therefore, its leadership agreed on 9 December 1987, after the Intifada broke out, to establish an organisational framework for resistance against occupation. The "Islamic Resistance Movement" (Hamas) was declared on 14 December 1987. The movement distributed its founding statement on 15 December 1987 and its charter was issued on 18 August 1988. See: Glenn E. Robinson, "Hamas as Social Movement," in: Quintan Wiktorowicz (ed.), *Islamic Activism: A Social Movement Theory Approach* (Indian a: Indiana University Press, 2004), pp. 112–39; Khaled Hroub, *Hamas: Political Thought and Practice* (Washington D.C.: Institute for Palestine Studies, 2000); Tareq Baconi, *Hamas Contained: The Rise and Pacification of Palestinian Resistance* (Stanford: Stanford University Press, 2018), pp. 17–28; Helga Baumgarten, "The Three Faces/Phases of Palestinian Nationalism, 1948–2005," *Journal of Palestine Studies*, vol. 34, no. 4 (2005), pp. 25–48; Ziad Abu 'Amr, *The Islamic Movement in the West Bank and Gaza Strip* [Arabic] (Acre: Dār al-Aswār, 1989), pp. 34–5; Iyad Barghouti, *Islamization and Politics in the Palestinian Occupied Territories* [Arabic] (Jerusalem: Al-Zahra' Center for Studies and Research, 1990), p. 61; Hani Awwad, "Understanding Hamas: Remarks on Three Different and Interrelated Theoretical Approaches," [Arabic] *Siyasat Arabiya*, vol. 45 (July 2020), pp. 24–44.

motherland[27] and that monopolises the role of the victim even when it is the victimiser.

There is another crucial reason for remembrance. To forget pre-1948 Palestine is to concede that the conflict suddenly arose in 1967, that it is solely a border conflict and that the Palestinians and Israelis are equivalent sides in this conflict. This historical amnesia was a prerequisite for the Oslo process and its consequences. Forgetting the Zionist occupation of Palestinian territories in 1948 makes it possible to turn the Palestinian and Arab demand of an Israeli withdrawal from 22 per cent of the land (the whole of the West Bank and Gaza)[28] into a starting point for negotiations, rather than what it is: a historic compromise.

Forgetting 1948 also lends itself to erasing the refugee issue from the international (and regional) agenda as some are keen to do, despite the fact that it has always been an international issue, as was Israel's founding. After their expulsion from their homeland, the Palestinians rightfully clung to international resolutions relevant to their plight, such as the acknowledgement of their status as refugees and the (subsequent) recognition of the Palestinians as a people with a right to self-determination. Recall that the Zionist leadership's acceptance of the UN partition plan in 1947 was a ruse. They could not visualise a Jewish state with an Arab population of about 45 per cent and they had their sights set on more territory than allocated to them under the partition plan and on an overwhelming Jewish majority in that territory by expelling the Palestinian majority.

Palestinian refugees continue to live with the loss of homeland, citizenship, basic rights—and suffer the consequences and hope for the future. Keeping the memory of this alive is crucial to the process of seeking proper justice and redress.

---

[27] Many Jewish Israeli individuals who were born in Israel have a second nationality (a foreign passport); Israelis immigrate to the US and to European in search for better life. Some friends of mine emigrated also for political reasons, or because they do not want to be a part of the Israeli reality that they feel they cannot change. But these are individual cases. As a whole, Israeli Jews have a collective national identity that links them to Israel as their homeland.

[28] Historical Palestine is estimated to be 27,000 km², where the West Bank (5,660 km²) and Gaza Strip (365 km²) constitutes 22% of the total land.

Political Memory and Folkloric Memory

Remembering pre-1948 Palestine is not a commemoration of an imaginary lost paradise that existed before the Nakba. Palestine was not a paradise. Creating a myth of a lost paradise is a folkloric memory that also turns the Nakba into a surprise victory of Evil over Good, a natural disaster as a form of divine curse upon this "paradise". This romanticised memory overlooks the historical reality of emerging towns and cities and transforms Palestine into an intimate and cohesive collective of cosy villages. This is the reminiscence of the *fedayeen*[29] fighters, the majority of whom were descendants of peasants. Their memory of Palestine was an idyllic pastoral one: the simple hard-working peasant who had tilled his fields, tended to his flocks, and now, gun in hand, fought for his land. It is no coincidence that his head cover, the *kufiyya*,[30] became the symbol for the struggle. There, in the refugee camps, residents of the same village cultivated the village memory as a link to the homeland and bequeathed it to the next generation, including those who left the camps.

The vast majority of pre-1948 Palestine was rural, it was a simple and underdeveloped or sufficient local economy country and it lacked internal cohesion.[31] But it was waking up to gradual modernisation and modernity. A more modern education system was accompanied by various technological advancements. There was a burgeoning middle class that was partly linked to the educated youth of the traditional aristocratic families, trade in the port cities and new business, employees in the Mandate institutions and the urban Palestinian Christians.[32]

---

[29] From the source *fada* in Arabic which means sacrifice for the sake of a cause, in this case it could mean the readiness of the fighter to sacrifice his life.

[30] Though in different regions of Palestine, different *kuffiyas* and scarfs were worn, and there was no traditional uniform *kufiyya*—but symbols must be uniform to be resonant.

[31] Salim Tamari, "Introduction: Palestine's Conflictual Modernity," in: Salim Tamari, *Mountain against the Sea: Essays on Palestinian Society and Culture* (Berkeley, Los Angeles and London: University of California Press, 2009), pp. 1–21; Issa Khalaf, "The Effect of Socioeconomic Change on Arab Societal Collapse in Mandate Palestine," *International Journal of Middle East Studies*, vol. 29, no. 1 (1997), pp. 93–112.

[32] Al-Hout; Itamar Radai, "The rise and fall of the Palestinian-Arab middle class under the British mandate, 1920–39," *Journal of Contemporary History*, vol. 51, no. 3 (2016), pp. 487–506.

Palestinian cities such as Haifa, Jaffa and Jerusalem were starting to flourish.[33] The idea of a Palestinian people with national aspirations was materialising in tandem with the emergence of an educated elite, some of whom had relocated from the countryside to the cities in order to gain an education.[34] There was also a growing urban labour force accompanied by the growth of a bourgeoisie and a middle class.[35] The flourishing Palestinian cities in the first half of the twentieth century were living testimony to the rising modernity that was interrupted by the mass expulsion and the founding of Israel. Not only was the land not empty, it was rapidly urbanising.[36]

---

[33] On Haifa, see: Maayan Hillel, "Constructing modern identity–new patterns of leisure and recreation in mandatory Palestine," *Contemporary Levant*, vol. 4, no. 1 (2019), pp. 75–90. See also: May Seikaly, *Haifa: Transformation of an Arab Society, 1918–1939*, Walid Khalidi (Foreword) (London: IB Tauris, 2002). On Jerusalem, see: Salim Tamari, "A Musician's Lot: The Jawhariyyeh Memoirs as a Key to Jerusalem's Early Modernity," in: Tamari, *Mountain against the Sea*, pp. 71–92. On Safad, see: Mustafa Abbasi, *Safad During the British Mandate Period, 1917–1948: A Social and Political Study* [Arabic] (Beirut and Ramallah: The Institute for Palestine Studies, 2019).

[34] Kimmerling & Migdal, p. 57.

[35] Rachelle Taqqu, "Peasants into workmen: internal labor migration and the Arab village community under the Mandate," in: Joel S. Migdal (ed.), *Palestinian Society and Politics* (Princeton: Princeton University Press, 2014), pp. 261–86.

[36] Palestinian historians have shown a lot of interest in the pre-1948 cities of Palestine. The motivation of many Palestinian researchers since the 1990s to write about the lost cities and the middle classes is understandable, insofar as these topics have been neglected by the historians of the Palestinian national movement who emphasised the role of the traditional elites of the city, on the one hand, and the peasants on the other. The research on this subject, the preservation of family archives and photo collections, etc., signified a longing for a Palestinian "normal" and the promising modernity that was evolving between the two world wars in Jaffa, Haifa, Jerusalem and other cities. See: Beshara Doumani, *Rediscovering Palestine: Merchants and Peasants in Jabal Nablus, 1700–1900* (Berkeley: University of California Press, 1995); Salim Tamari, "Wasif Jawhariyyeh, Popular Music, and Early Modernity in Jerusalem," in: Rebecca L. Stein & Ted Swedenburg (eds.), *Palestine, Israel, and the politics of popular culture* (Durham, N.C: Duke University Press, 2005), pp. 27–50; Wasif Jawhariyah, Salim Tamari& Issam Nassar (eds.), *The Storyteller of Jerusalem: The Life and Times of Wasif Jawhariyyeh, 1904–1948* (Northampton and Massachusetts: Olive Branch Press, 2014); Mahmoud Yazbek, "Jaffa Before the Nakba," [Arabic] *Journal of Palestine Studies*, vol. 93 (Winter 2013), pp. 36–49; Seikaly; Manar Hasan, "Palestine's Absent Cities: Gender, Memoricide and the Silencing of Urban

PALESTINE

In every rebellion against British colonialism or Zionist settlement, it was the peasants who served as the backbone of the resistance. The peasants became intensively politicised whenever the link with their land was threatened or severed. They then became politicised as refugees, their personal dreams now an issue of international relations, their hopes of returning to their villages subject to the whims of politicians, international decisions and global and regional power dynamics. In the refugee camps, they sustained kinship and identification based on affiliation to their lost villages, but the rhythm of the seasons and popular religious celebrations was replaced by an international conference calendar, endless news broadcasts and interminable speeches by politicians promising liberation. As time passed, their homes in Palestine became the objects of yearning and nostalgia for the second generation of refugees. The first armed operations of the *fedayeen* were "organic" activities of homegrown underground movements whose origins had nothing to do with Arab regimes. At the same time, refugee conferences were held and political institutions evolved based on a national Palestinian identity. Foremost among these was the PLO.

Palestinian Memory," *Journal of Holy Land and Palestine Studies*, vol. 18, no. 1 (2019), pp. 1–20; Beshara Doumani, "Archiving Palestine and the Palestinians: The Patrimony of Ihsan Nimr," *Jerusalem Quarterly*, vol. 36, no. 3–12 (2009).

3

AFTERTHOUGHT 2

THE ARAB QUESTION AND THE JEWISH QUESTION

That the Palestinian cause lies at the intersection of many other issues attracts more international attention, but this has not done it any favours. Quite the opposite, it has been a chronic source of complication and the subordination of this cause to the other issues. In the East, the Palestinian question has become entangled with the complexities of the larger Arab question, and in the West with the Jewish question. This is among the major reasons for the tenacity and persistence of this colonial project at a time when colonialism was abating everywhere else. In this chapter, we deal with the Arab and Jewish questions and their complicating impacts on the Palestinian issue. We also discuss how varying assessments of the causes behind the rise and intractability of the Palestinian question are shaped by divergent ideological approaches to broader Arab issues. The discussion underscores the need not to delay the struggle for democracy and the implementation of justice in the Arab region until the Palestine issue is justly solved, nor to delay the struggle for justice in Palestine until the Arab region is liberated from authoritarianism. The two issues are not separable conceptually, but in the framework of the ongoing struggle for justice, people need to avoid the vicious circle of delaying justice in Palestine until justice in the Arab world is achieved and vice versa.

PALESTINE

Palestine and the Jewish Question

From the 1930s to the end of World War II, antisemitism in Europe assumed unprecedented dimensions, culminating in the Holocaust. The Zionist leadership at the time succeeded in politically utiliing the justified international sympathy with the Jews and integrating it into the Zionist movement's ideological and pragmatic partnership with Western imperialist outlooks and regional policies. Such efforts helped lay the groundwork for immediate international acceptance of the Jewish state when it was declared.

Post-war Arab positions towards antisemitism in Europe varied across the political spectrum between two extremes: from total denial of its existence, dismissing it as a Zionist and imperialist lie (a position heavily influenced by European ultranationalist ideologies), to expressions of full sympathy with Jewish suffering while condemning Zionism. Some Arab positions tended to belittle the magnitude and importance of the Holocaust and make unjustified, unwarranted and even absurd comparisons between it and the Palestinian Nakba. Not only is it inappropriate to compare a heinous European crime to a Zionist one, Palestinians do not need to engage in such futile comparisons, since Palestine is an indirect victim of one and a direct victim of the other. It is neither moral nor in the Arab interest to understate the crimes of antisemitism in Europe. On the contrary, as victims of racism themselves, the Arabs have a moral duty to acknowledge those crimes and to condemn racism in all its forms.

The foregoing are examples of how the prevailing post-war Arab political culture, with all its internal divisions, struggled to respond to the shameful stain of the Holocaust upon Europe and Western civilisation—which the Arabs had absolutely nothing to do with. This is not a gratuitous attack on Europe. Nazism was created in Europe, and it was also fought against and defeated in Europe. However, the reality is that, as atrocious as the Nazis and their allies and facilitators were, Zionism was not the victim. The victims were millions of European Jews, the vast majority of whom were not Zionists.

There was no moral justification for uprooting another people located outside of Europe for the sake of a colonising project that began long before the rise of Nazism. While we may deny the validity

of comparing the Nakba to the Holocaust, there is no denying that
Zionism took skilful tactical and strategic advantage of it afterwards.
Strategies such as instrumentalising the Holocaust in Israeli propaganda, monopolising the role of the victim, invoking the history of
Jewish suffering to justify unjustifiable policies, and levelling charges
of antisemitism against opponents of Zionism or critics of Israeli politics have become the norm.

Of course, European political leaders and probably large segments
of the general Western public were only too happy to rid themselves
of their guilty conscience by shifting it onto the Arab world. Zionism
colluded in this by releasing Europe from any kind of serious reckoning with its brutal past and present in exchange for consistent support
for Israel. This created a situation in which Europe can plausibly deny
a connection between the racism/antisemitism that led to the Jewish
Holocaust of the past and the European xenophobia and Islamophobia
of the present.

Europe and the US also colluded with Israel by accepting its assertion that the Israeli state retroactively represents the victims of the
Holocaust. Of course this is false both historically and logically, but its
effect is to make antisemitism an Arab problem.[1] This helps explain
why some European countries took part in Israel's sixtith Independence
Day celebrations as enthusiastically as they had in the global celebrations for the founding of the United Nations and as enthusiastically as
Theresa May expressed her pride in the Balfour Declaration when she
officially celebrated its centennial anniversary.[2]

Palestinians who fail to understand this context fall victim to it
because they have come to rely on "international concern." They
imagine this concern emanates from a genuine compassion for their

[1] As noted above, Israeli propaganda equates anti-Zionism with antisemitism. But Palestinian
and Arab rejection of Zionism was not a matter of ethnic, religious or social hostility to
Jews, but instead rejection of colonial settlement of their country. See: Azmi Bishara, "Is
Anti-Zionism a Form of Anti-Semitism?," *Case Analysis*, Arab Center for Research and Policy
Studies, 3 March 2019, accessed at: https://bit.ly/3g376AX

[2] "Theresa May says she will celebrate the centenary of Balfour declaration with 'pride'," *The
Independent*, 25 October 2017, accessed at: https://bit.ly/3ni4CBM; "May lauds UK role
in creation of Israel at Balfour centenary dinner," *The Guardian*, 2 November 2017, accessed
at: https://bit.ly/3es2yTX

plight and might lead to the implementation of "international justice."
In reality, American and European concern (officially and among
some segments of the public as well) is not a stance against the injustices of colonialism and apartheid in Palestine; rather, it reflects, for
good or ill, a political interest in Israel and the Jewish question.

During the first Intifada and in the post-Gulf War (1991) era of the
peace process, the Palestinian issue became the subject of an endless
stream of seminars, conferences, dialogues and research projects in
Europe and the US. Countless Americans and Europeans wanted to
hear the Palestinian participants' assurances that they recognised
Israel's right to exist and posed no threat to the Jewish state. They
usually got what they wanted, but it would never be enough, because
how could they be certain? Might this expression of moderation not
just have been a stage in a larger "phased plan" to destroy Israel?
According to the logic underlying this kind of "dialogue," the colonised are supposed to allay the fears of the coloniser; the weak side in
the "dispute" is expected to comfort and reassure the stronger side;
the representatives of the people who lost their homeland and made
a series of concessions that whittled down the demand for the full
liberation of Palestine to the acceptance of a quasi-state on 22 per
cent of their homeland have to reassure the power that is occupying
their land and the territories of other Arab states while maintaining a
regional monopoly on nuclear arms, and while its official discourse
and policies are growing increasingly hard-line (nationalist and more
religious) and expansionist that they, the oppressed, have no "phased
plan" to destroy the Israeli state.

This kind of misdirection, I contend, takes place within the complex historical and political framework of the Western-Jewish relationship. The Palestinians, in this context, are little more than unwitting extras, some of whom are Palestinian and Arab elites coopted
into the peace process industry and content to make their living
(career) on "the cause" or, to be more precise, never ending "dialogues." Though, this peace process industry has weakened over the
respective US presidential terms of Obama (2008–2016) and Trump
(2016–2020), albeit for different reasons.

From the perspective of the Palestinian struggle, Western interest
in Palestine has not been a source of strength. In fact, it is a weakness,

because it reflects Europe's eagerness to rid itself of its Jewish issue—an issue which forms an integral facet of European identity—and to shift its own historical burden of racism and guilt onto the Arabs. Europeans, including European Jews, who are determined to face this legacy rather than project it onto others, are generally opposed to colonialism and other forms of racism.

Zionism, since its inception in the nineteenth century, has consciously tried to exploit explicit and latent sociopolitical and cultural currents in Europe related to the Jewish question and trends to export it to Palestine. These included Protestant streams of thought that confuse religious mythology with history, modern Jews with Biblical Israelites, Palestinians with Canaanites, and religious affiliation with modern nationalism. As carried across the Atlantic by European pilgrims and settlers, the linkages acquired impetus through their heavy use of Old Testament names, terms, codes and the metaphors in the pioneers' pathos narrative and through an American political theology that identified America as a "virgin land" and "promised land." Some streams in Protestantism also gave rise to once marginal eschatological trends that considered the "return" of the Jews to Palestine as a prerequisite for the prophesied second coming of Jesus Christ.

The susceptibility of some Protestant trends to Zionism should not be underestimated,[3] especially given the contemporary role of Evangelical churches in US foreign policymaking. However, the phenomenon long predates this. Due to ubiquitous exposure to Old Testament lore in religious upbringing, literary education and, indeed, many aspects of daily life, some people in Protestant societies could not help but see Palestine and the Jews from a biblical perspective. This outlook played a crucial role in developments in Palestine, from how it inspired the nineteenth-century colonial expeditions to Palestine and how it facilitated lobbying for the Zionist project in Great Britain on the eve of the British Mandate.

---

[3] The religio-cultural susceptibility to Zionism should be understood as a potentiality, not a necessity nor a reductionist generalisation. The solidarity actions and even political stances taken by Protestant charities and organisations, Anglican, Presbyterian, Quakers and others with the oppressed in Palestine and elsewhere manifest the potential of religiously driven humanism too.

PALESTINE

One of the most prominent proponents of the "resettlement" of the Jews in Palestine was Lord Shaftesbury, the seventh Earl of Shaftesbury, who actively devoted most of his life to this cause. As part of his campaign in support of Jewish claim to the Holy Land and further British protection for the Jews of the East, he wrote an article in the January–March 1839 issue of the *Quarterly Review* titled "The State and Prospects of the Jews." The article, which was a review of Lord Lindsay's *Letters on Egypt, Edom and the Holy Land* (1838), marked "the first time a distinguished magazine had treated the problem of Restoration [of the Jews] in all its aspects—religious, political, historical, philosophical."[4] A year later, in 1840, a memorandum on the subject of the "restoration of the Jewish people to the land of Palestine" appeared in *The Times*, the leading British newspaper of the era. This memorandum, which was filled with mystical and biblical allusions, was addressed to the Protestant monarchs of Europe and various governments of Christian territories like Great Britain, Prussia, the Netherlands, Sweden and Norway, Denmark, Hanover, Württemberg (and other parts of Germany), the Protestant cantons of Switzerland and the US.[5] In the 1875 Annual General Meeting of the Palestine Exploration Fund, Lord Shaftesbury said that "We have there [Palestine] a land teeming with fertility and rich in history, but almost without an inhabitant—a country without a people, and look! scattered over the world, a people without a country."[6] Shaftesbury (and not a Jewish Zionist leader) may well be the original copyright holder on the famous colonialist slogan, "A land without a people for a people without a land."

Another forceful advocate of the restoration of the Jews to Palestine with British assistance was Colonel George Gawler. In

[4] Albert M. Hyamson, "British Projects for the Restoration of Jews to Palestine," *Publications of the American Jewish Historical Society*, no. 26 (1918), pp. 135–6; Franz Kobler, *The Vision Was There: A History of the British Movement for the Restoration of the Jews to Palestine* (Published for the World Jewish Congress, British Section; London: Lincolns-Praeger, 1956), p. 50; Paul Charles Merkley, *The Politics of Christian Zionism 1891–1948* (London and New York: Routledge, 1998), p. 40.

[5] Hyamson, pp. 136–7.

[6] "Annual General Meeting of the Palestine Exploration Fund," *Palestine Exploration Fund: Quarterly Statement for 1875*, vol. 7, no. 3 (1875), p. 116.

1853, Gawler published a pamphlet in which he pleaded that Britain was "the divinely appointed agent to secure this end and, in assuring the security of Jewish settlements in Palestine, Britain would at the same time be furthering her own interests."[7] The English clergyman Reverend Samuel Alexander Bradshaw added his voice to those emphasising the duty of the Christian states to restore the Jews to Palestine. In his *Tract for the Times, Being a Plea for the Jews* (1844), Bradshaw even warned against the abandonment of the Jews' "ancestral right to Palestine" and called for a political action to assist the Jews to "return to the land of their fathers."[8] He called on Parliament to allocate 4 million pounds to this end, with a further 1 million to be collected by the churches.[9]

Reverend William Henry Hechler, an Anglican minister assigned to the British Embassy in Vienna, was an active supporter of Herzl, and also contributed a leaflet (probably written in 1882 though it appeared in 1893) titled *The Restoration of the Jews to Palestine according to the Prophets*, exhorting the Jews to return to Palestine. Hechler viewed his duty to help "the secular Herzl" restore the Jews to Palestine as a way of "fulfillingprophecy" of the return of Jesus. He was equally certain that Palestine would be returned to the Jews, a prediction he based on arcane computations.[10]

---

[7] Hyamson, p. 146.

[8] Samuel Alexander Bradshaw, *Tract for the Times, Being a Plea for the Jews* (London: Edwards and Hughes/Ave Marine Lane, 1844), pp. 11, 14.

[9] Ibid., p. 17. Hyamson noted that Bradshaw "was not permanently depressed by the failure of this effort to have any powerful influence upon public opinion." He actually returned to this subject 40 years later by writing a new pamphlet in 1884 titled *The Trumpet Voice; Modus Operandi in Political, Social, and Moral Forecast Concerning the East: Based on Authoritative Bible Testimony*. In this pamphlet, Hyamson noted, Bradshaw stated that "Jews have an inalienable heritage which must eventually return to them, and at the same time, that a fresh field for commercial enterprises was needed to relieve the social misery which prevailed. This would best be done by allowing the Jews to regenerate Palestine." Bradshaw actually proposed that England annex Palestine to Egypt, swearing that he would find more than twenty millionaires ready to donate half a million pounds each for this project as a way to discharge their "responsibilities on earth." See: Hyamson, pp. 142–3, 163.

[10] Merkley, p. 17; Isaiah Friedman, "Theodor Herzl: Political Activity and Achievements," *Israel Studies*, vol. 9, no. 3 (Fall 2004), p. 48.

Henry Grattan Guinness, an Irish Protestant preacher and author, is said to have predicted the great event of 1917 (the Balfour Declaration heralding the occupation of Palestine) in his 1888 book *Light for the Last Days: A Study Historic and Prophetic*.[11] Whether or not he was aware of this "prophecy," the British Foreign Secretary, Arthur Balfour, did issue a declaration in 1917 on behalf of the British government, announcing support for the eventual establishment of a "national home for the Jewish people" in Palestine. The Balfour Declaration came to be seen as "the culmination of a rich tradition of Christian Zionism in British culture" which had a "religious impetus" behind it.[12]

According to Barbara Tuchman, for Balfour,

> the "motive was Biblical rather than imperial. If the Biblical culture of England can be said to have any meaning in England's redemption of Palestine from the rule of Islam, it may be epitomised in Balfour. Though he was the reverse of Shaftesbury, not ardent but a sceptic, not a religious enthusiast but a philosophical pessimist, he was nevertheless strongly infused, like the Evangelicals and the Puritans, with the Hebraism of the Bible. Long before he ever heard of Zionism, Balfour, steeped in the Bible from childhood, had felt a particular interest in the 'people of the Book.'"[13]

According to his niece, companion and biographer, Blanche E. C. Dugdale, it was a "life-long" interest that "originated in the Old Testament training of his mother, and in his Scottish upbringing."[14] As a child, Arthur's Protestant upbringing and exposure to the Old Testament were important socialising factors, but his development was also shaped by the same imperialist motives commonly found in the *Weltanschaung* (worldview) of British politicians in the imperial age (the Suez Canal and the maritime road to India, exploitation of Mosul's oil in Iraq, imperial rivalry with France, etc.).

[11] Henry Grattan Guinness, *Light for the Last Days: A Study Historic and Prophetic*, 2nd ed. (London: Hodder and Stoughton, [1888]), pp. 211–13; 223–4.

[12] Eitan Bar-Yosef, "Christian Zionism and Victorian Culture," *Israeli Studies*, vol. 8, no. 2 (Summer 2003), p. 18.

[13] Barbara W. Tuchman, *Bible and Sword: England and Palestine from the Bronze Age to Balfour* (New York: Ballantine Books, 1984), p. 311.

[14] Blanche E. C. Dugdale, *Arthur James Balfour: First Earl of Balfour, K.G., O.M., F.R.S., Etc.*, vol. 1 (London: Hutchinson & Co., [1936]), p. 433.

The main political religious fundamentalism driving the creation of the Palestinian plight was not Islamic, but Christian. Although the "mainstream" of Protestant churches usually distance themselves from "Christian Zionism", the political mystics of some Evangelical churches are still a problem and source of complication to this very day. After Barack Obama, who was himself raised to believe in a Jewish state and ignore the calamities caused by its establishment, made some remarks about the suffering in occupied West Bank and Gaza, he observed that "a strong majority of white evangelicals—the GOP's most reliable voting bloc—believed that the creation and gradual expansion of Israel fulfilled God's promise to Abraham and heralded Christ's eventual return."[15]

What does being entangled with the Jewish question mean? The Jewish question, or the global Jewish question, if you will (as long as we remain wary of turning the histories of the "West" into "world history," and of its grand narratives), has been outsourced to the Arab region from Europe, and so it remains. The major implications of this include avoiding all framing of the Palestinian question as a colonial issue, allowing Israel to take its place in European society and the "West" in general (as long as it is located outside Europe in the East), and insisting that Israel always be portrayed as the victim, even as it oppresses the Palestinians. This monopolisation of the victim's position by an occupying power is responsible for some of the most hypocritical political culture imaginable. It is exemplified by the Israeli expression "shooting and crying" (Pulling the trigger then crying about it) or by Golda Meir's widely quoted statement allegedly made in London in 1969: "When peace comes, we will perhaps, in time, be able to forgive the Arabs for killing our sons, but it will be harder for us to forgive them for having forced us to kill their sons." Whether she really said this or not, the spread of this assertion of moral superiority combined with the unassailable victimhood of the occupier, even when doing the killing, is the height of hypocrisy.

One of history's great ironies is that antisemitism would only allow Jews to take their place within Europe as long as they left it, or at least pursued "their" political aspirations somewhere else, preferably far

---

[15] Barack Obama, *A Promised Land* (New York: Viking/Penguin Books, 2020), p. 628.

away. The fathers of Zionism themselves expected this when they offered to act as the barrier of Western civilisation against Eastern barbarism,[16] volunteering themselves as colonisers to release Europe from the yoke of both antisemitism and the Jewish question.[17] It is from the combination of the two questions (Arab and Jewish) that the Palestinian question acquires its particular complexity.

It turns out that the Balfour Declaration was also made under the false impression that "the Jews" were politically influential in Russia and that Germany was making "overtures" to Zionism. Such considerations added to Balfour's personal Christian Zionist leanings and Chaim Weizmann's persistent lobbying after his chemical inventions[18] contributed enough to the British war machine to enable him to be accepted as a "respectable gentleman" in British political salons.

---

[16] See: Jacque Hersh, "Inconvenient Truths about 'Real Existing' Zionism," *Monthly Review*, vol. 61, no. 1 (May 2009).

[17] Theodor Herzl argued in his pamphlet *Der Judenstaat* (1896) that it would be in European government interest to help create an independent Jewish state to get rid of antisemitism there, as he wrote: "The creation of a new State is neither ridiculous nor impossible. [...] The Governments of all countries scourged by antisemitism will be keenly interested in assisting us to obtain the sovereignty we want." He argued that this new State in Palestine would be beneficial for the Europeans as it would "form a portion of a rampart of Europe against Asia, an outpost of civilization as opposed to barbarism." Theodor Herzl, *A Jewish State: An Attempt at a Modern Solution of the Jewish Question*, Sylvie D'Avigdor (trans.), Jacob de Haas (ed.), 3rd ed. (New York: Federation of American Zionists, 1917 [1896]), pp. 11–12. Similar statements by other leaders of the World Zionist Organization like Max Nordau and others are too numerous to be quoted in this footnote. In 1896, Reverend William Henry Hechler, a major supporter of Theodor Herzl's Zionist project, wrote to Frederick I, the Grand Duke of Baden, about Herzl's project. He stated that the antisemitic movement had made the Jews realise that they were "Jews first and secondly Germans, Englishmen, etc." Consequently, it reawakened in them a longing to return "as a nation to the Land of Promise [...] Palestine belongs to them by right." Hechler, therefore, urged the Duke to influence his nephew, the Kaiser of Germany, to support Herzl's Jewish State project, since the "Return of the Jews" would be beneficial to the European nations and end antisemitism there. See: Friedman, p. 49; Merkley, pp. 26–34.

[18] Weizmann, a political Zionist leader, who became a British citizen in 1910, and worked as a professor of biochemistry at the university of Manchester during the World War I, discovered how to obtain from starch the acetone much needed by the British arms industry. Weizmann was chosen to be the head of the World Zionist Organization in 1920 and became Israel's first president in 1949.

AFTERTHOUGHT 2

As was documented, "Lloyd George and Balfour, who repeated Weizmann's dubious contention (which was meant to appeal to stereotypes of international Jewry) that if Britain committed itself to Zionism, then Russia's Jews would prevent the Bolsheviks from abandoning the war and American Jews would use their influence in Britain's favour after the war."[19] The imperial struggle with France over the Arab Mashreq was also a factor.[20] Subsequently, British Mandate policies helped the Zionist movement build the autonomous structure of a Zionist para-state and create a separate Jewish-controlled sector of the economy, and frequently benefitted from substantial capital supply as well as the workforce injected by virtue of continued immigration.[21]

---

[19] John B. Judis, *Genesis: Truman, American Jews and the Origins of the Arab/Israeli Conflict* (New York: Farrar, Straus and Giroux, 2014), p. 59. Revisionist historian accounts criticised the declaration's rationalisation by grounding it on interests. Tom Segev asserted that Britain was "not guided by strategic considerations, and there was no orderly decision-making process." The declaration was "the product of neither military nor diplomatic interests but of prejudice, faith, and sleight of hand. The men who sired it were Christian and Zionist and, in many cases, antisemitic. They believed the Jews controlled the world." Tom Segev, *One Palestine, Complete: Jews and Arabs under the British Mandate*, Haim Watzman (trans.) (New York: Metropolitan Books, 2000), p. 33. Compare this with James Renton's account, which stressed the role of propaganda deployed by Zionist activists in Europe. James Renton, *The Zionist Masquerade: The Birth of the Anglo-Zionist Alliance, 1914–1918* (New York: Palgrave Macmillan, 2007), pp. 63–4. See also: Sahar Huneidi, *The Hidden History of the Balfour Declaration* (New York: OR Books, 2019).

[20] The struggle between Britain and France over the Middle East led these two countries to divide the Arab Mashreq between them in the 1916 Sykes-Picot Agreement. Due to British dissatisfaction with the outcome of this secret agreement, the following year they fatefully proclaimed "their support for Zionist ambitions in the Balfour Declaration. And so, the Jews' right to a country of their own became dangerously associated with a cynical imperial manoeuvre that was originally designed to outwit the French." James Barr, *A Line in the Sand: The Anglo-French Struggle for the Middle East, 1914–1948* (London and New York: Simon & Schuster, 2012), p. 375. I mentioned other factors that drove the British to make the declaration. In the words of Mayir Vereté: "had there been no Zionists in those days the British would have had to invent them." Mayir Vereté, "The Balfour Declaration and its makers," *Middle Eastern Studies*, vol. 6, no. 1 (1970), p. 50. See also: William M. Mathew, "The Balfour Declaration and the Palestine Mandate, 1917–1923: British Imperialist Imperatives," *British Journal of Middle Eastern Studies*, vol. 40, no. 3 (2013), pp. 231–50.

[21] Rashid Khalidi, *The Hundred Years' War on Palestine: A History of Settler Colonial Conquest and*

PALESTINE

Palestine and the Arab Question

The Palestine question is the source of the Arab-Israeli conflict. The same colonial partition that generated the Arab question[22] in the Levant (in interaction with local factors and social structures) also produced the question of Palestine.[23]

There are major regional-national tensions between state and nation, and between citizenship and nationality, that create endless complications and conflicts between and within Arab countries. The "Arab question" is rooted in the discrepancy between the failure of modern Arab nationalist aspirations to establish a pan-Arab sovereign nation and the infeasibility of this project, on the one hand, and the failure of the Arab states in building nations based on citizenship on the other. Among the array of factors that are both causes and consequences are: the fragility and legitimacy crisis of postcolonial states, hyper-ideological compensation for the lack of national unity in reality, chronic military interference in politics, the politicising of subnational tribal and sectarian identities, and difficulties in transitioning to democracy. Historically, rivalry between Arab regimes influenced their positions on Palestine. The positions were often determined by international alliances and by the need for Arab regimes to leverage the political legitimacy the Palestinian cause symbolised to the popular consciousness. This cause was most forceful in politics and society

---

Resistance, 1917–2017 (New York: Metropolitan Books, 2020). See also: Sherene Seikaly, *Men of Capital: Scarcity and Economy in Mandate Palestine* (Stanford, C A: Stanford University Press, 2015); Martin Bunton, *Colonial Land Policies in Palestine 1917–1936* (Oxford: Oxford University Press, 2007); Sahar Huneidi, *A Broken Trust: Herbert Samuel, Zionism and the Palestinians, 1920–1925* (New York: I.B. Tauris, 2001).

[22] See: Azmi Bishara, *On the Arab Question: An Introduction to an Arab Democratic Manifesto* [Arabic] (Beirut: Center for Arab Unity Studies, 2007).

[23] The 1920 San Remo resolution, a modified version of the 1916 Sykes-Picot secret agreement between Britain and France, divided the Arab Asian territories of the Ottoman Empire. What would become the states of Syria and Lebanon were supposed to be subjugated to the French Mandate, while Palestine and Iraq fell under the British Mandate. The San Remo resolution also adopted the 1917 Balfour Declaration, which stipulated that the British government favoured the establishment of a national home for the Jewish people in Palestine.

during periods of heightened pan-Arabism and grand political projects, as well as in nationalist responses to defeat.

The PLO, for example, was created during a period of increased regional alignment around pan-Arab objectives. Antagonisms within the PLO were often intertwined with disputes between Arab regimes. In many cases, the Palestinian factional splintering mirrored the patterns of Arab camps, with factions shifting sides between one or another country or bloc according to the shifting patterns. Still, even at the tensest times, during the height of tensions between so-called "Arab-progressive" and "Arab reactionary" camps, the Palestinians have generally managed to maintain unity within the PLO, which eventually became an established and recognised Arab political entity.

As much as Palestine symbolises Arab rejection of colonialism, general postcolonial grievances, Arab identity and injustice to the Arab people, Arab regimes, even those most committed to the cause, cannot resist the temptation to exploit the Palestinian question as a means to an end. Arab regimes tend to exploit the Palestinian cause to promote their own interests in two ways. The first is to elevate the confrontation with the "Zionist enemy" above all internal problems and failures. This allows regimes to accuse critics of treason, sowing divisions in a united front against the enemy and undermining the resistance. The second way is used by some "moderate" regimes which offer concessions on the Palestinian cause in order to improve external relations, strengthen alliances and curb Western criticism of domestic policies in matters related to human rights violations within their own countries, for example.

This latter group of Arab regimes are no less guilty of exploiting the Palestinian issue; in fact, this type of exploitation is currently more widespread. Historically, however, Arab states have adhered to certain general principles regardless of the disputes and tensions between rival camps. For example, there once existed a consensus on common interests related to Palestine in the context of the regional Arab order. It was also generally accepted that the Palestinian issue was a case of unresolved colonialism, and that the national liberation of an Arab people whose land was under occupation was a just and principled cause.

More Repercussions of the Entanglement with the Arab Question

An analysis would almost certainly show that the emergence of Israel in the region, its policies and the conflicts they triggered (and subsequent attempts to shape the region according to Israeli needs) were directly and indirectly related to the rise of military regimes. The first military coups that took place in Syria (1949), Egypt (1952) and Iraq (1958) claimed they were a direct response to the 1948 defeat of the Arab armies and the weakness of liberal-era Arab regimes towards Zionism and its imperial allies. The emergence of Israel in the midst of the Arab region and the question of Palestine changed how the Arabs related to themselves, and how they related to the "West".

No major political or ideological development in the region can be understood in isolation from the gaping wound of Palestine. The Palestine question as a main component of pan-Arabism ideology—despite all the good will of Arab nationalists and their dedication to the Palestinian cause—was turned into a tool of regimes that transformed Arabism from a cultural, national and ethnic identity to an official ideology. As for the regimes that implicitly shrugged off the question as a "problem of the Palestinians," this helped them justify cooperation with Israel, thereby gratifying American decision-makers and safeguarding their tacit tolerance of these regimes' authoritarianism and encroachments on human rights. This grew more difficult as US administrations transitioned from the Cold War era to the more open 1990s, and more so in the post-11 September era and the rise of the neo-conservatives who linked terrorism with the political and social repercussions of despotism, and even more so yet in the current era of widespread grassroots uprisings, pro-democracy movements and their insistence on zero tolerance for autocracy. The geostrategic expansion of Iran also contributed to alignments that shifted the main concern away from the Palestine issue.

The Palestinian issue has been turned into a public relations tool used to enhance the image of a dictatorship or a monarchy in the eyes of Western powers. At least the first type of instrumentalisation by regimes that supported the Palestinian cause was more faithful to historical facts and to the sovereignty of the Arab state. The second type merely trades Palestine for Western acceptance of a regime's own repressive authoritarian rule. It also buys into the Oslo process rhetoric that equates the two sides of a "dispute", to obfuscate the reality of occupying power/coloniser versus occupied people whose land has been colonised. The regime may even resort to blaming the victim in order to justify normalising relations with Israel before the realisation of a just solution for Palestine.

Arab regimes still had to contend with domestic public opinion, a vast majority of which remained strongly pro-Palestinian, in order to gain greater manoeuvrability in foreign policy. Arab regimes could not act as independently from domestic public opinion as impatient Western powers may have imagined. In their bids to distance domestic opinion from the Palestinian question in order to facilitate normalisation with Israel, some Arab regimes initiated campaigns designed to reorder national and public opinion priorities. They focused on persuading their people that it was in their interests to prioritise the strategic interests of their own country, i.e., raising the domestic audience above the Arab nation and the question of Palestine.

The campaigns sometimes went so far as to suggest that serving the interests of the Arab nation and the Palestinian cause detracted from the national interests and the people's welfare, thereby driving a wedge between national and Arab-national/Palestinian causes. This departed sharply from the agenda of the previous regimes. It also presents a naive idea that the pan-Arab national interest and the national security of every Arab country stand in contradiction with each other. In fact, the two are intimately interrelated and mutually dependent even in terms of political interest and benefits.

For example, after coming to power in Egypt, President Anwar Sadat pivoted away from Nasser's Arab nationalist doctrine, citing Egypt's national interests and emphasising Egyptian national identity over Arab identity. This did not imply a construction of an Egyptian civic identity but a new nationalist legitimation ideology of the regime. Sadat had another understanding of where his regime's interests lay, and of Egypt's interests from this perspective. In the years after the 1973 war and prior to the 1979 peace with Israel, Sadat promoted an "Egypt First" trend, with this slogan, echoed by "Egypt First, Second and Last," blazoned across billboards in major cities. In his October Paper of April 1974, Sadat identified Egyptian national-ism as the prime determinant of the "accomplishment of the October War". He added that the Egyptian military had paid heavily in defend-ing the Palestinians and that now, after the 1973 war, it was time for Egypt to consider its own interests as top priority. This was a mere ideological presentation of the interests of the regime, not the state nor the state's nation of citizens.[24] But even in a country such as Egypt with its strong local national identity, the official renouncement of pan-Arabism did not bring the Arab Egyptian people closer to Israel. Meanwhile, the void left by Arabism was filled by the expansion of Islamism, which was encouraged by Sadat's regime at the beginning of his fight against secular Arab nationalism and the left, before he fell victim to the rising radical Islamism. The assassination of Sadat has proven that ideological movement cannot be reduced to a disposable tool. The movement will also use their user and treat them as a dis-posable tool.

In 2002, the newly crowned King of Jordan, Abdullah II, launched the "Jordan First" initiative with the stated goals of "reform and democratization" that were never implemented. The King ordered public and private sector leaders to create a document of principles and methods for domestically modernising Jordan, with a clear shift in focus to "national priorities" and "internal affairs" rather than "com-plicated" international issues. Actually, Jordan's economy and politi-

---

[24] See: Hicham Bou Nassif, *Endgames: Military Response to Protest in Arab Autocracies* (Cambridge: Cambridge University Press, 2021), p. 97; Jason Brownlee, "Peace Before Freedom: Diplomacy and Repression in Sadat's Egypt," *Political Science Quarterly*, vol. 126, no. 4 (Winter 2011–12), p. 650; Ibrahim A. Karawan, "Sadat and the Egyptian-Israeli Peace Revisited," *International Journal of Middle East Studies*, vol. 26, no. 2 (May 1994), p. 252; Amatzia Baram, "Territorial Nationalism in the Middle East," *Middle Eastern Studies*, vol. 26, no. 4 (October 1990), pp. 431–2. Sadat's tone was celebrated by the likes of Fuad Ajami and Rafael Israeli. See: Fouad Ajami, *The Arab Predicament* (Cambridge: Cambridge University Press, 1981), p. 99; Raphael Israeli, "Sadat between Arabism and Africanism," *Middle East Review*, vol. 11, no. 3 (Spring 1979), pp. 39–48. See also: Shlomo Aronson, *Sadat's Initiative and Israel's Response: The Strategy of Peace and the Strategy of Strategy*, n. 14 (Los Angeles, CA: Center for Arms Control and International Security, UCLA, 1978), pp. 1–5; Robert Michael Burrell & Abbas Kelidar, *Egypt: The Dilemmas of a Nation* (Beverly Hills, CA: Sage Publications, 1977), p. 58.

cal system were and still are a major beneficiary of the regional and international "complex issues". The "Jordan First" campaign would become his new working plan for the country, designed to mould citizens in "a unified social fabric that promotes their sense of loyalty to their homeland," he said, stressing that "Jordan First" should become "the common denominator between all Jordanians regardless of their origins, orientations, views, talents, faiths or races." The initiative ignored the fact that, for the majority of Jordanians of Palestinian origins, the term "homeland" is associated with both Palestine and Jordan. Eventually, the "Jordan First" initiative faded into oblivion, leaving only echoes memories of the slogan itself.[25]

Recently, the governments of the United Arab Emirates (UAE) and Bahrain normalised their diplomatic relationships with Israel and aligned themselves more closely with it. Like Egypt and Jordan, they absurdly couched their policies in the rhetoric of "Emirates First" and "Bahrain First," as though these two regimes were in a constant state of war with Israel and had been devoting their resources for such a war at the expense of the interest of their countries and people. Given the UAE's interventionist policies in Yemen, Libya and the Horn of Africa, the sudden normalisation with Israel probably does not reflect a renewed focus on domestic affairs.[26]

---

[25] See: Ahmed Shihab-Eldin, "Jordan First: A King's Modernization Motto Obscures a Palestinian Past and Iraqi Present," *HuffPost*, 6 December 2017, accessed at: https://bit.ly/3dbbk9q; Curtis Ryan, "We Are All Jordan... But Who Is We?" *Middle East Research and Information Project (MERIP)*, 13 July 2010, accessed at: https://bit.ly/3tgYnjT; Marwan Muasher, *A Decade of Struggling Reform Efforts in Jordan: The Resilience of the Rentier System* (Washington, D.C.: Carnegie Endowment for International Peace, 2011), p. 8.

[26] One typical kind of cooperation between Israel and the "normalising" states is manifested in the Pegasus scandal. Pegasus, a blockbuster product of the Israeli NSO hi-tech Group, "a secretive billion-dollar Israeli surveillance company," is sold to various agencies worldwide and is used to target political rivals or opposition figures by infecting phones with Pegasus and hacking them. Patrick Howell O'Neill, "Pegasus Unbound," *MIT Technology Review*, vol. 123, no. 5 (September/October 2020), p. 64. It is a very attractive product for security agencies of authoritarian states. A new partnership between the Citizen Lab at the University of Toronto and Amnesty International resulted in creating a platform developed by Forensic Architecture at Goldsmiths, University of London, with a dataset to unveil violations by the NSO Group. Aaron Schaffer, "The Cybersecurity 202: Group maps alleged victims of NSO Group surveillance tool," *The Washington Post*, 6 July 2021,

PALESTINE

The "country first" slogans touted by Arab authoritarian leaderships in reality mean: the regime first. In the interest of self-perpetuation, promoting their own interests, or improving relations with Washington, these regimes freed themselves from the being accountable and blamed all domestic ills and problems on the Palestinian issue or their country's involvement in it, as a means to free themselves to abandon cardinal principles concerning justice in Palestine, which obviously did not indicate being more attentive for issues of justice in their own countries.

These various steps, coupled with the sidelining of the PLO and formation of the PA, these policy shifts, ideological reorientation and concrete normalisation processes have dramatically altered the international/regional management of the Palestinian question. Unless this is met with a fundamental change in strategy, it will alter the nature of the Palestinian national cause.[27]

---

accessed at: https://wapo.st/2WzmVto. The products are often sold to those agencies which score the worst on these records. Eleven countries were also identified as potential clients of NSO, including: Azerbaijan, Bahrain, Hungary, India, Kazakhstan, Mexico, Morocco, Rwanda, Saudi Arabia, and Togo, in addition to the United Arab Emirates (UAE). Amnesty International, *Uncovering the Iceberg: The Digital Surveillance Crisis Wrought by States and the Private Sector* (London: Amnesty International Ltd, 2021), p. 8. The Group's declared rationale behind its sale of technology to governments and agencies is that it helps them "fight terrorism and serious crime." NSO Group, "NSO Group Statement on Facebook Lawsuit," CISION PR Newswire, 29 October 2019, accessed at: https://prn.to/3jqOkGE. Pegasus impacts the right to privacy in the sense that it is "surreptitious, unauthorized by the rights holder, and has the capacity to collect and deliver an unlimited selection of personal and private data (along with data of any contacts with which a target of surveillance interacts)." Amnesty International issued a report of a detailed conducted investigation, involving more than eighty journalists from seventeen media organisations in ten countries. The report reveals unlawful surveillance and human rights abuses using Pegasus. Many infections that the report deals with date back to the 2016. The spyware has indeed evolved several times since 2016 when it was first publicly disclosed by Citizen Lab. In August 2018, Amnesty International declared the targeting of one of its staff members. (*Uncovering the Iceberg*, pp. 4, 6, 8, 29). Thousands of victims were targeted with NSO's Pegasus. More than 50,000 phone numbers were on a list that included some people targeted by Pegasus. From 34 countries, 600 government officials and politicians were on the list, including three presidents, ten prime ministers, and a king. Craig Timberg et al., "On the list: Ten prime ministers, three presidents and a king," *The Washington Post*, 20 July 2021, accessed at: https://wapo.st/3ztI0DE

[27] This will be discussed further in the second part of this book.

AFTERTHOUGHT 2

The Contemporary Relevance of Understanding the Nakba

It would have been impossible in the aftermath of the Nakba to comprehend this magnitude of this colossal event, let alone its international and European causes. It is therefore an injustice to judge, with the advantage of hindsight, the (quite natural) Palestinian rejection of the UN partition resolution. It should also be borne in mind that at the time the Nakba occurred—that is, when the leadership of the Jewish *Yeshuv* declared the independence of Israel and proceeded to occupy parts of Palestine that had been earmarked for the Arab state—the Palestinians' ability to resist had been already exhausted by the 1936–1939 uprising, although they did resist to the best of their ability. They were also unaware, as were the neighbouring states, of the size and relative strength of the Zionist project, which was far more prepared for battle.[28]

The Arab armies that participated in the 1948 war ended up signing truce agreements with Israel the following year. They did not efficiently mobilise their countries for war materially or logistically; those that took part plunged into battle without planning or preparation and with hastily assembled, ramshackle armies. Despite the sacrifices of volunteers, the Arab states did not wage war against Israel in any real sense. They lacked the necessary will to fight and had to be pushed into battle by a vibrant public opinion at a time of real sociopolitical turbulence. Moreover, Arab political leaderships were divided and the prevailing mutual mistrust prevented any coordina-

---

[28] This issue was already tackled in this text and the historian Walid Khalidi has provided much detail on this subject to the extent of counting armament, supplies and soldiers. See: Walid Khalidi. *Fifty Years since the War of 1948 and the Zionist Arab Wars* [Arabic] (Beirut: Dar al-Nahar, 1998); Walid Khalidi. *Fifty Years since the Partition of Palestine (1947–1997)* [Arabic] (Beirut: Dar al-Nahar, 2002). This is in addition to countless Arab and Palestinian memoirs of those who fought. Although there has been more writing on the subject of expulsion in recent years (including by authors such as Simha Flapan, Nur Masalha, Benny Morris and finally, Ilan Pappé), the Zionist leadership has managed to promote the image of a victim defending itself against enemy armies far surpassing it in number that invaded Palestine—a depiction that contrasts with myriad studies conducted in the Western academia mentioned earlier. This indicates that exposing the truth and refuting myths in the academic sphere does not always shift the extant political and media discourse around those myths.

tion between their armies. Israel won and occupied the Palestinians' land. Like any grand historical event, countless reasons for the Nakba could be cited. The Zionist project was a settler colonial project linked to the British imperialist policy committed to the creation of a "national home for the Jewish people," and British colonial authorities actively empowered the *Yeshuv* and enabled the Zionist movement to implement its programmes. The project was militarily strengthened by the military experience of Jewish officers in the allied armies, especially the British army, during World War II. In 1948, it would be even more concretely strengthened thanks to massive arms shipments to the *Haganah* from the socialist bloc.[29] The Soviets assumed that labour Zionism would be a "progressive" potential ally *vis-à-vis* "reactionary" Arab regimes considered to be allies of the declining British empire and, more generally, they cultivated the notion (when it was expedient to do so) that the Jewish state would be a socialist progressive country. The actions of the radical Zionist armed factions had led the Soviets to imagine that the Zionists were fighting British imperialism in 1948. In fact, in spite of occasional "misunderstandings" between the British and the *Yeshuv* leadership due to the differences in the scope of agendas between considerations of a superpower and a nationalist colonial movement, if Britain was not the real founder of Israel, it surely was a major factor or the chief player in establishing the Jewish state.

The Zionist leadership was state-oriented and had been highly successful in obtaining financial and political support for building political, economic and military institutions during the Mandate period. It consistently strove for the conquest of land (*kibbush ha-adama*) and conquest of labour (*kibbush ha-avuda*). The words "conquest" and "occupation" were not bad words in the Zionist lexicon, but rather sources of pride.[30] The leadership was determined, pragmatic and rational in the sense of being goal-oriented, and it did not balk at using immoral means to reach its goals. It was good both at assessing its own strength and that of its opponents and it knew how to seize the moment.

---

[29] This has been discussed in depth in Chapter 1.

[30] The word *Kibbush* also means conquest and also occupation in Hebrew, and, as mentioned before, the religious term "redemption" was also used.

In the immediate aftermath of the Nakba, Arab elites including Palestinians preferred denial to confronting these harsh realities. Some wrote about the backwardness of Arab societies compared with the European Jewish settler society, an analysis that neglected crucial consideration of international power politics. More immediately, reactions ranged from the claim that Britain had never understood where its true interest lay to nationalist and leftist allegations that the Nakba was a "conspiracy between the British, the Zionists and reactionary Arab regimes".

At least one of these patterns of thought is still alive and guides certain regimes "determined" to bring the US (Great Britain's contemporary equivalent) around to their point of view. They, too, identify themselves as where the US should see its "true interests." But now, instead of translating their alliance with the US into leverage with which to distance the US from Israel, as was the original aim, they ingratiate with Israel as a means to draw closer to the US. This has become the new "golden rule" governing these regimes' alliances with the US. The means have become the end and the end the means.

To some, the Zionist success was nothing but a colonialist lie concocted to advance its imperial agenda in the region. According to this view, internal Zionist Jewish democracy and the institutions that were established by the settlers are written off as fabrications of the propaganda machine that bills Israel as an "oasis of democracy in the Middle East". This underestimation of the state-building and nation-building project in Israel has not been helpful, to say the least. At the other end of the spectrum are those who, in their attempts to "understand" the Nakba, were suddenly overwhelmed with such admiration for the marvels of a Zionist establishment so magnificent that they had little choice apart from abject surrender.

More recently, in the context of normalisation between this or that Arab regime and Israel, a strange argument is advanced, stating that Israel's unity depends on war; therefore, if peace was achieved, even an unjust peace, this unity would quickly unravel and Israel would collapse under the weight of its internal contradictions and divisions. This is no less a fiction than the other two. The peace agreements strengthened Israel.

This pseudo-theory reasons that Israel's existence is temporary and that its demise is inevitable because of its own self-perception as alien in the region. Accordingly, normalisation and peace with Israel is in fact the most powerful weapon against it (some advocates of this idea seem more genuinely convinced of it than others). People may like to quote the famous Israeli saying that "the war in which Israel is defeated will be its last," but the fact is that no one is going to war against Israel. The constant reiteration of such strategically unhelpful statements have an anaesthetising effect in the absence of a strategy for a political struggle that, among other things, takes into consideration Israel's internal contradictions and does not consider either Arab regimes or American foreign policy as immutable givens.

Arab governments that normalised their relationship with Israel do not believe in these ravings or in the wishful thoughts of some of their supporters, but in their own interests. That is their *raison d'état*. Their shared interests with Israel mainly lay in coordinating political and security matters so as to maintain regional stability (by which Arab regime stability in the face of potential recurrent grassroots uprisings is meant) and in coordinating joint lobbying of the West, especially the US, to promote the "strategic importance" of each country for US interests. They seek to persuade the United States and other Western countries to accept their Israeli and Arab allies as they are (i.e., without pressuring them to change domestic policies on democracy, human rights and occupation) and to counter Iran's regional influence and ambitions.

The truth is that Israel can be pressured by coordinated resistance. It can be influenced politically and made to pay a high price for its repressive policies, one that its society is probably unwilling to pay. Sustained pressure can change policy content and orientation. The Israeli withdrawal from Lebanon in the year 2000 was not a result of total military victory and defeat, but of persistent and consistent resistance against occupation. Even the establishment of the PA, considered an achievement by the PLO leadership, was not a result of negotiations but rather of the struggle, especially the first Intifada. It was this that drove Israel to seek an interim solution with the PLO. But Israel is not going to collapse, either through peace or through a single military defeat.

The pluralism that exists in Israel under the umbrella of Zionism is a source of strength rather than weakness. Confident assertions that

Israel is collapsing morally and economically, that emigration is out-stripping immigration, that its internal sectarian conflict is intensify-ing have been made *ad nauseam* since the 1960s and, indeed, they were regular features of internal Arab official propaganda before 1967. Israel does have many social and economic problems, but its economy is strong and knowledge-based,[31] a fact that cannot be understood without the interaction between the military and civil industries, and between military complex organisation skills and cor-porate administration by high-ranking army ex-officers, the American investments, the investment in research in Israeli universities and the

---

[31] In 2019, high-technology exports for Israel were 12,564 million US dollars. Though Israeli high-technology exports fluctuated substantially in recent years, they tended to increase through 2007–2019 period:

	Israel High-Technology Exports (Current USD)	Israel High-Technology Exports (% of manufactured products)
2007	3,121,661,000	7.6
2008	9,662,205,000	17.1
2009	10,540,545,000	23.4
2010	10,584,992,000	19.4
2011	11,681,717,000	18.4
2012	11,565,015,000	19.9
2013	11,744,185,000	19.0
2014	12,408,980,000	19.4
2015	13,753,939,000	22.9
2016	12,199,784,000	21.8
2017	12,057,719,000	21.1
2018	12,971,903,000	22.5
2019	12,564,551,000	23.1

"Israel High-Technology Exports (Current USD)," *World Development Indicators*, accessed at: https://bit.ly/3kfahYe; "Israel High-Technology Exports (% of manufactured prod-ucts)," *World Development Indicators*, accessed at: https://bit.ly/3kfahYe

Israel is also one of the top ten largest exports of arms. It was the eighth largest arms exporter in 2016–20. Pieter D. Wezeman, Alexandra Kuimova & Siemon T. Wezeman, "Trend in International Arms Transfer, 2020," *Fact Sheet*, SIPRI (March 2021), pp. 2, 7, 11, accessed at: https://bit.ly/3DbeDsi

contribution of Jewish scientists who immigrated from developed countries. Israel's institutions are modern and it has a sizeable and vibrant middle class. There remain Sephardi/Ashkenazi tensions and, now, deeper secular/religious tensions, but Israeli pluralism is still able to organise Israeli Jewish society's political, ideological, confessional and cultural diversity within a democratic system under a single national umbrella.

The biggest irony is that the people who came to settle in Palestine from different parts of the world did not all come from one nation, nor even from states sharing democratic political systems. Yet they managed to form a national bond—or whatever you want to call it—and use it for as long as necessary to fortify the nascent civil democratic system for a Jewish collective, without risking collapse into separate tribes, ethnicities and sects. This contrasts starkly with the case of Arab states and peoples, who despite speaking the same language and harbouring aspirations for a united nation before Israel was even founded, are still wary of the concept of democracy for fear it might lead to a disintegration into separate confessional, ethnic or regional communities. That is another challenge to be dealt with.

Israel's conscious nationalist movement attracted people who spoke dozens of languages, came from dozens of different countries and shared only a common religious affiliation to a colonial nation-building project established on land stolen by force from other people. Arab regimes, during the same period of time, prevented peoples who spoke the same language, came from the same cultural background and yearned for a shared destiny from building a nation.

The Arab Question from a Different Perspective

The Palestinian cause attracted widespread support among previously colonised peoples, particularly Arabs. As a result, Palestine became an outlet for their sufferings, at least until the 2011 Arab Spring revolutions and uprisings when they started to face despotism directly. For a long time, Palestine was the only legitimate cause for demonstrations of solidarity and calls for justice that was tolerated by authoritarian regimes in the Arab world.

Arab support for the Palestinian cause was crucial for the continuity of the struggle, but it also imbued Palestine with a symbolic weight that was so heavy as to have a perversive influence. Along with an emergent cottage industry of "cause-building", it generated a growing hubris (not only political, but also literary) that eventually led to the emergence of self-interested elite lobbies that spoiled many Palestinian leaders who began as revolutionaries.

The sheer weight of human suffering experienced by the Palestinian people—robbed of their land and driven into exile only to face a fresh occupation years later—and their ongoing struggle is a key part of the Palestinian question. But it must be emphasised that both the historical and political significance of the Nakba, and its implications for Arab peoples everywhere, go much further than this. In modern Arab history, the occupation of Palestine and the founding of Israel have generated a kind of complex. They inflicted a wound that is still open and inflamed, endlessly providing the Arab world with various pretexts for, on the one hand, a nihilistic and rejectionist ideology or, on the other, capitulation with all its political, cultural, economic and moral ramifications. It is not possible to comprehend this inflamed consciousness without considering Palestine's position in wider Arab culture. The emergence of Israel and the resultant Nakba were the most important embodiment of regional fragmentation and conflict, as well as the greatest obstacle to Arab unity in the Levant and between the Levant and North Africa (Maghreb). There was a time when this dream was considered realistic, a time when Arab states were not as physically entrenched and authoritarian regimes had yet to consolidate themselves.

The above-mentioned preoccupation with interpreting the "meaning" and causes of the 1948 loss of Palestine was reminiscent of the great imponderable of the Arab Enlightenment: "Why is the West advanced and Muslims backward?" An endless list of historical variables might be adduced to answer this question. Since it is so hard to give a satisfactory list of reasons as to *why* a complex social phenomenon emerges, it is impossible to explain why it did not. It is better to focus on the *what*s and the *how*s: what happened, what must we do, how can we understand, how can we move forward towards a defined aim? While asking *why* may stimulate partial scientific answers, it can receive definitive answers only from ethical, moral, normative perspectives. Engagement with the question, just like attempts to answer it, inevitably reflect prevailing values, beliefs and ideologies at any given moment. Whenever political forces tried to come up with a response to the questions "Why did the Nakba happen?" or "Why did the defeat in June 1967 happen?" their answers reflected predominant or emerging ideological trends and assumptions and their political and cultural disagreements were manifested in their disagreements over the assumed reason.

A trend appeared among some parts of the Left that attributed sole responsibility for the Nakba to the "reactionary" nature of Arab societies. For later ex-leftists (some of whom became enthusiastic neo-liberals), this became a cloak for exonerating Zionism. To Arab nationalists the crux of the problem was in the lack of Arab unity, and in the "treason and corruption" of the old elites who ruled the Arab countries after independence. Islamist currents, especially after 1967, have accused both nationalism and leftism, and even the Palestinian national movement itself, of responsibility for the loss of Palestine because of their secularism. The Islamist political current was radicalised in a way that prevented it from integrating itself as one of the many religious currents within a broader national movement, as had seemed possible in the interwar period before the Nakba. It blamed secularism, detachment from Islam and the infidelity of Arab regimes for all the failures.

For so-called "moderate" Arab regimes, surrendering to Israeli dictation of facts on the ground appears to have hardened into something akin to a semi-official ideology. To the people in these countries, "moderation" signifies yielding, in advance, to come what may, regardless of decades of experience with no prospect of justice on the grounds that it is "unrealistic" to aim for justice. To the rulers it is defined as alignment with the US and accepting its Middle East policies, especially concerning peace with Israel. How could despotic regimes be described as "moderate" otherwise? This complicity between "moderate" Arab leaders and Zionism is not new. The "moderate" leaders presumed that Zionism and "the Jews" are very influential (to say the least) in world politics, and Zionist and, later, Israeli leaders nurtured this belief, which outside this context would be considered antisemitic.[32]

---

[32] In truth, some Arab politicians (including independents) were tempted to consider com-

Since events in Palestine are felt not only as a part of a colonial issue, but also as a matter of national dignity and defiance, alternative political and cultural visions have presented themselves as the only path to the liberation of Palestine or to solving the Palestinian question. Even if these remained slogans and never gained traction, it is important not to yield to cynicism on this; people mostly believed in the visions they introduced. Political ideological pan-Arabism was presented, among other things, as a means to liberate Palestine, while the calls for democratisation after the defeat of 1967 grounded themselves in the claim that authoritarianism was the main reason for the defeat. The path of religion-as-political-ideology has portrayed itself as the only escape from an unending series of '48s and '67s. Meanwhile, as "meaning of the Nakba" shifted over time according to the political climate, the fundamental challenge has remained unchanged and inevitable.

Since the outbreak of the Arab Spring revolutions in 2011, questions about citizenship in the nation-building process, democracy, the rule of law and human dignity are back on the public agenda. These questions are being asked for their own sake, not for the sake of Palestine. This is what the Israeli political leadership fears more than

---

ing to an understanding with Zionism as a path to convincing France and Britain to support them against their local and regional rivals. The idea spread during the mandate period in Syria, Lebanon and Palestine that Zionism wielded great influence on the Western powers in policymaking terms. Representatives from the Jewish Agency met with many of these figures and promised to assist them in reaching out to decisionmakers in Paris and London. The researcher Mahmoud Muhareb has dealt extensively with Arab contacts and meetings with representatives of the Jewish agency. See: Mahmoud Muharib, "The Zionist Intelligence: The Beginnings of Spying on Arabs," [Arabic] *Al Mustaqbal al-Arabi*, Year 31, no. 357 (November 2008), pp. 113–29. For information on meetings held between the Syrian nationalist bloc with Jewish Agency representatives, see: Walid al-Mu'allim, *Syria 1916–1946: The Way to Freedom* [Arabic] (Damascus: Dar Tlass, 1988), p. 376; Nizar al-Kayal, *A Study in the Contemporary Political History of Syria 1920–1950* [Arabic] (Damascus: Dar Tlass, 1997), p 122. See also: Mahmoud Muharib, "The Negotiations between the Jewish Agency and the Syrian National Bloc," [Arabic] *Ostour Journal for Historical Studies*, no. 1 (January 2015), pp. 140–59; Mahmoud Muharib, "From Negotiations to Infiltration: The Relationship between the Jewish Agency and the Syrian National Bloc and the Shahbandar," [Arabic] *Ostour Journal for Historical Studies*, no. 5 (January 2017), pp. 165–200.

anything else. Its worst, most uncertain year was 2011, when the Arab people around the region took to the streets chanting some of the answers to these questions.

Neither the need for democracy nor the means to achieve it need be included as part of any reckoning with the defeats of 1948 and 1967. Democracy will be achieved through direct confrontation against despotism and tyranny, the absence of the rule of law, the personalisation of politics, injustice and corruption. This is a national agenda that includes presenting realistic alternatives to the status quo. Unless confronting these societal evils becomes an aim in and of itself, there will be no solutions to these problems. Even if the evolution of authoritarianism is inseparable from the emergence of Israel and the question of Palestine, the struggle for justice, democracy and dignity must bear fruit for their own sake. Palestine will benefit as a result. The instrumentalist approach to these existential issues can be manipulated to work in the opposite direction whenever it suits the arguer who might hold that the pursuit of these moral aims distracts and deviates from the main cause, which is Palestine. Because of the deep conviction that the loss of Palestine and the situation in the Arab countries are connected, nationalists and leftists who organised in the 1950s after the Nakba used to fiercely argue among themselves about whether they should start first with the struggle to change Arab regimes and modernise their countries, or with the armed struggle to liberate Palestine. There was no correct answer to this irresolvable dispute. These issues are still connected, but the struggle against occupation can continue alongside and in parallel with the struggle for democracy in the rest of the Arab world and the struggle for justice in Palestine too—no one has to wait for the other, nor should one's liberation come at the expense of the other's.

While a historical link is undeniable between the problem of Palestine and the issues discussed above, acting as if they are separate is crucial to understanding them and avoiding their exploitation as excuses for inaction, whether in the framework of resistance against the Israeli occupation and attempts to normalise it or in the larger framework of the Arab struggle for democracy and civil rights. Neither one of them is a tool in the service of the other, whereas any achievement in one area will benefit the other as they are all part of the same struggle for justice.

Likewise, an understanding of the direct causes of the Nakba does not necessarily require a profound analysis of the differences between the modern institutions of Zionism and local Palestinian society. The Nakba was not inevitable and did not arise as a predetermined result of a fixed set of circumstances. There are critical junctures in history, such as wars and revolutions, where human agency plays a decisive role and can make a breakthrough that leads to the establishment of new structures, assuming the minimum necessary conditions are present.

This said, the fight for freedom from occupation cannot on principle be put off indefinitely until a comprehensive solution is found to the broader Arab question, hopefully in the form of close cooperation among Arab democratic states in the future (say, for example, along the lines of the European Union model). It is simultaneously obvious that the struggle for democracy in the Arab world took a definitive turn in 2011 and that, in spite of the subsequent setbacks, the grassroots struggle for democracy will also not wait until justice is achieved in Palestine.

4

ON THE ARAB-ISRAELI CONFLICT

Israeli myths on the Arab defeat in June 1967 repeated some of those that emerged after the 1948 war, especially that of the few against the many (or "a sea of enemies"). The results of the June 1967 war changed Israel. For example, Israeli political culture and ideology shifted towards an increasingly intimate fusion of nationalism and religio-political radicalism. The Israeli economy was reinforced with foreign investments, American aid and closer strategic cooperation with the US and Israel found itself ruling directly over an entire society comprised of millions of Palestinians who were not only subjects of military rule, but also a market for Israeli commodities and a source for cheap labour.[1]

---

[1] In 1967, new policy measures were introduced to enable Israel to benefit from a "reservoir of cheap Palestinian labour" without having to face any social or demographic burden of this new force. During the early 1970s, one third of the Palestinian labour force worked in Israel and settlements. See: United Nations Conference on Trade and Development, "UNCTAD assistance to the Palestinian people: Developments in the economy of the Occupied Palestinian Territory," *Report*, Sixty-seventh session (2–3 July, 7–9 September and 28 September–2 October 2020), p. 8, accessed at: https://bit.ly/2Z2PvnT. The Israeli employers benefit from lowering their wages compared to other workers in Israel, with wages paid only in cash accompanied by frequently inaccurate documentation. They deprive the workers of workers' benefits or any comprehensive social protection. Additionally,

Moreover, the post-war dialectic of victory and defeat, epitomised in the arrogance and triumphalism expressed by one side and the humiliation and degradation felt by the other, led to the war of 1973. The losers were driven by a need to restore national dignity while the winners, in their euphoria, could not envision that their defences might not withstand an Arab attack. The shift to a peace strategy in the Arab world occurred only after the October 1973 war. But that was met with the simultaneous shift to the far right in Israel after 1967 and the further consolidation of the bilateral alliance between it and the US. Sadat's separate peace agreement with Israel would mark the beginning of an official Arab disengagement from the Palestinian cause as a source of bilateral conflict between Arab states and Israel. But the Egyptian model—peace with Israel in exchange for Israeli withdrawal from occupied Egyptian territories—could not become a model for the Palestinians.

The June War Syndromes

After the June 1967 war, in which Israel occupied territories of three Arab countries along with the rest of Palestine, Israel added the myth of being caught in a "constant defensive war," which automatically legitimises any "pre-emptive war" or "war of no choice" Israel launches, to its propaganda arsenal. The overwhelming dominance of the Israeli war narrative in the Western media, at least for some time after 1967, proved the thesis of the discursive hegemony of the winner's narrative.[2]

Palestinian workers in Israel also face the abusive permit regime where they get manipulated and abused by both brokers and employers, with no transparency in the criteria for approving permits and quotas, not to mention the long wait and crowded conditions the Palestinian workers have to face on a daily basis at the crossings and the risky and inadequate working conditions, especially at construction sites. See: International Labour Organization, *The situation of workers of the occupied Arab territories*, International Labour Conference: 109th Session, 2021, pp. 6–7, accessed at: https://bit.ly/3hKFfXF; MACRO: The Center for Political Economics, *Work Conditions of the Palestinian Paid-Workers in Israel* [Arabic] ([Tel Aviv]: February 2017), p. 8.

[2] I prefer to use this expression, not the phrase: the winner writes the history.

Palestinians were displaced again.[3] Thousands of refugees became refugees for a second time, in some cases after repetition of the types of war crimes committed in 1948. Three villages, 'Imwas, Yalu and Bayt Nuba,[4] and the city of Qalqilya[5] were ethnically cleansed during the 1967 war. However, Israel did not proceed to full-scale ethnic cleansing, and most of the population continued to live under direct Israeli occupation,[6] a factor that played a decisive role in changing the character of the Palestinian issue. After 1948, the "question of Palestine," internationally, became synonymous with the refugee

---

[3] Between June and August 1967, 200,000 residents of the West Bank found their way to east Jordan, 100,000 of whom were refugees of 1948. Michael Jansen, *The United States and the Palestinian People* (Beirut: The Institute of Palestine Studies, 1970), p. 181.

[4] On 7 June 1967, during the 1967 war, Yitzhak Rabin, the then IDF Chief of the General Staff, ordered the immediate eviction of the three villages of 'Imwas (approximately 2,000 inhabitants as of 1961), Yalu (1,644 inhabitants in 1961) and Bayt Nuba (1,350 inhabitants as of 1961). All these villages are located to the west of Jerusalem near the Green Line. Rabin gave the inhabitants only a few hours to gather their possessions before getting them on their way to Ramallah. To expedite the ethnic cleansing process, as done in 1948 war, the Israeli army shot over the heads of fleeing villagers to make sure they would not come back. Many villagers fled to Ramallah and al-Bira to join relatives, and a few made it on foot across the bombed the Allenby Bridge over the Jordan River to Amman. After being ethnically cleansed, the three villages were bulldozed and dynamited. The area was later declared "public" land. On top of its ruins, the "Canada Recreational Park" was built with Canadian, tax-deductible dollars as it was funded with a $15 million donation by the Jewish National Fund of Canada in 1973.

[5] The town of Qalqilya (population 11,401 in 1961) was also systemically destroyed by the Israeli army during the 1967 war. A third of the houses were razed and its inhabitants were forcefully evicted to Jordan. Benny Morris quoted Moshe Dayan that the houses of Qalqilya have been destroyed "not in battle, but as punishment ... and in order to chase away the inhabitants". Morris also noted that "Altogether, about one-quarter of the population of the West Bank, some 200,000 to 250,000 people, went into exile. Many of them were refugees from 1948 and their descendants who had lived in camps, mostly around Jericho. They simply walked to the Jordan River crossings and made their way on foot to the East Bank." See: Benny Morris, *Righteous Victims: A History of the Zionist-Arab Conflict, 1881–2001* (New York: Vintage Books, 2001), p. 328.

[6] The probability that the population will hold out and remain this time seemed to be the only reason for Ben-Gurion's second thoughts about the war that previously he supported, and that his tutees fought for within Israel's leadership. See: Tom Segev, *A State at All Costs: The Life of David Ben-Gurion* [Hebrew] (Ben Shemen: Keter Sfarim, 2005), pp. 632–4.

issue; after 1967, attempts were made to reduce it to an issue of "occupied territories." Both remain unresolved.

The Palestinians' national cause comprises both the cause of the refugees and the problem of the occupied territories, and more. They are the product of the settler colonial project in Palestine, the origin of these concerns and the Arab-Israeli conflict that, for decades, Israel sought to separate from the Palestinian question.

There was no Arab-Israeli conflict before a Zionist state was declared on the ruins of the Arab people who lived there. At the time the 1967 war broke out, there were no occupied Arab territories except Palestine itself. Neither Egypt's Sinai nor Syria's Golan Heights were under Israeli occupation; both were occupied in 1967. The drive to promote peace agreements with Israel in exchange for Israeli withdrawal from these territories was a drive to distort history. Its success implied that Israel achieved that war's political goals.

Contrary to the claims of many 1967 war historians and analysts, the military conflict was neither "inevitable" nor "pre-emptive" nor "defensive". For Israel, it was a war of choice. Archival evidence indicates that the Americans, Soviets and Israelis were certain that Israel would score a comprehensive victory due to its overwhelming military superiority. As Roland Popp put it, "the initiation of hostilities by Israel itself was certainly not an example of statesmen somehow losing control of the political process but a clear-cut rational decision in a situation where the balance of forces made military defeat virtually impossible."[7]

An increasing amount of evidence belies the claim that there was an impending Arab attack that needed pre-empting. The military escalation between Egypt and Israel lost momentum by the last week of May and neither took any further action that risked restarting the escalation. Documents also show that Egypt's military deployment to the Sinai was limited and merely demonstrative,[8] "amounting to nothing even remotely resembling an invasion force."[9] Nasser's orders to

---

[7] Roland Popp, "Stumbling decidedly into the six-day war," *The Middle East Journal*, vol. 60, no. 2 (2006), p. 238.

[8] It is worth mentioning that up to half of Egypt's compacting forces were still in Yemen at the time, and war-weary after suffering enormous attrition.

[9] Ibid. p. 307.

limit the troop amassment in the Sinai were viewed by some American senior officials as a sign of "peaceful intentions" and that "he would not begin any fight."[10] It was the provocative Egyptian rhetoric that was confusing. As it turns out, this was the product of one-upmanship in the context of the leadership rivalry in Egypt between the President Nasser and his chief of staff Field Marshal Abdul Hakim Amer,[11] and in the context of the pan-Arab nationalist competition between the Egyptian, Syrian and Saudi leaderships. None of them wanted to go to war, but all of them wanted to look firm and resolute while accusing the others of weakness before the enemy.

Israel's leadership was divided between two camps: the hard-line proponents of an immediate strike, mostly including army generals, politicians and ex-commanders such as Moshe Dayan, who became defence minister during the crisis, and the "doves" like then Prime Minister Eshkol and Foreign Minister Eban. The doves were mainly worried about the negative consequences of a potential repeat of the Suez Crisis experience of 1956 (when the superpowers intervened to stop the tripartite invasion of Egypt). However, the US had changed to a more explicit strategic pro-Israeli footing in the past decade in addition to growing animosity towards Arab nationalist regimes. So, the other camp could argue that Washington would support an Israeli war against Arab nationalist regimes considered pro-Soviet and that superpower intervention by either the Americans of the Soviets was unlikely. The hardliners prevailed.[12]

---

[10] Ibid., p. 305. See also: Ersun N. Kurtulus, "The Notion of a 'pre-emptive War:' the Six Day War Revisited," *The Middle East Journal*, vol. 61, no. 2 (2007), p. 229.

[11] Amer's nationalist bravado, personal self-confidence and arrogance turned to panic after the Israel offensive that destroyed the unprepared Egyptian air force in a few hours while the planes were on the ground. He made the catastrophic decision to withdraw from the Sinai immediately, causing a chaotic dispersion of the troops before the war was decided and depriving them of the opportunity to intercept the Israeli attack.

[12] Kurtulus, p. 231. On Ben-Gurion-Eshkol disagreement over the June War, see: S. Ilan Troen & Zaki Shalom, "Ben-Gurion's Diary for the 1967 Six-Day War: [Introduction and Diary Excerpts]," *Israel studies*, vol. 4, no. 2 (1999), pp. 195–220. See also: Yechiam Weitz, "Taking Leave of the 'Founding Father' Ben-Gurion's Resignation as Prime Minister in 1963," *Middle Eastern Studies*, vol. 37, no. 2 (April 2001), pp. 131–52. See also: Eran

While it is true that both Jordan and Iraq joined the Joint Defence Treaty between Syria and Egypt just few days before the Israeli first strike, this treaty was clearly defensive. It essentially pulled treaties signed in the 1950s out of the drawer, and these had never been truly activated and had very little impact. In fact, on the eve of the war, there were no signs of inter-Arab coordination at all. Shortly before the signing of the treaty, Nasser accused King Hussein of Jordan of being "a CIA agent" while Jordan broke off diplomatic relations with Syria. Syria was opposed to the inclusion of Jordan in the treaty to begin with and refused to coordinate its policies with Egypt. When the escalation started, Nasser was at the height of his popularity in Jordan so Hussein joined the treaty with his Egyptian rival for fear public anger might turn against him if he did not. For the very same reasons, he joined the war few days later. As Kurtulus concluded, the treaty was "more or less a faint policy declaration rather than a robust framework for war preparations."[13]

In short, the Arab states on the eve of the war were not preparing to attack Israel. They were busy exchanging accusations and campaigning against each other. Israeli Prime Minister Eshkol knew this. So did the hardline generals who launched a sensationalist media campaign warning that a second Holocaust would happen if Israel did not attack first. In so doing, they effectively executed a public "putsch"[14] against the prime minister.

A parenthetical remark may be in order here. It was at this crucial juncture that the political instrumentalisation of the Holocaust, an integral state strategy today, began in earnest. Menachem Begin, the Likud leader who became the prime minister of Israel in 1977, brought it to a new peak in his public speeches and addresses. Prior to 1967 war, according to David Biale, the Zionist version of Jewish history created a gulf between the diaspora Jews of Europe and the

---

Eldar, "David Ben-Gurion and Golda Meir: from partnership to enmity," *Israel Affairs*, vol. 26, no. 2 (2020), pp. 174–82.

[13] Kurtulus, p. 231.

[14] I call it a putsch because the army generals were directly involved in triggering media incitement against Prime Minister Eshkol due to his hesitation to go to war, and in spreading the atmosphere of fear of a second Holocaust.

"new Hebrews" of Israel. Israeli official commemorations of the Holocaust mainly focused on the few acts of resistance, like the Warsaw Ghetto uprising. It emphasised the "difference between those who took up arms against the Nazis" (often incorrectly alluded to as Zionists in the sub-narrative) and all the other Jews that were led, as the Zionist rhetoric put it, like sheep to the slaughter.[15] The imagery was consistent with how Zionist ideology depicted diaspora Jews as passive and cast Zionism as a revolt against this passivity.[16] After the June 1967 war, however, this ideology was superseded by an "ideology of survival" whereby Zionism no longer constituted a break with Jewish history, but rather its continuation under different conditions.[17] From this perspective, the Jewish state "has led to contradictory feelings of inflated power and exaggerated fear".[18] This ideological shift, which was characterised by a growing use of Holocaust allusions and metaphors in the national discourse, implied that Jews lived in eternal isolation and faced a permanent existential threat to their survival.[19] Such discourse gave rise to two corollaries, at least for right-wing nationalists. The first was that Israel, the exclusive agent of Jewish history, was the consummate victim. The second held that it was futile to make concessions for peace because the threat would always be there. The conclusion: perpetual military empowerment and absolute force superiority is the only way to guarantee of Israel's future security.

As tensions between the Arabs and Israel escalated, there were calls from Israeli society to appoint Ben-Gurion[20] as prime minister and Moshe Dayan as defence minister, and the latter was appointed in the end. However, even Ben-Gurion, who believed in the necessity of a second war with the Arabs because the 1948 war was not sufficient to force them to accept Israel, was among those who urged

---

[15] Biale, p. 158.

[16] Ibid.

[17] Ibid, p. 146.

[18] Ibid.

[19] Ibid, p. 159. See also: Tom Segev, *The Seventh Million: The Israelis and the Holocaust*, Haim Watzman (trans.) (New York: Macmillan, 2000).

[20] The fact that Ben-Gurion himself hesitated and thought that there was no need for such a war was not known to the public.

waiting for commitment from the two superpowers before going to war. He suggested to "dig in" and wait remembering the 1956 intervention of the Soviet Union and the US. Eshkol thought that he had satisfied the generals by giving them the budgets they requested to build a modern army. As Eshkol observed, "You did not receive all of these weapons so that one day you sit and say: now we can annihilate the Egyptian army." Yet, according to Guy Laron, that was exactly their intention, and the intended purpose of building a modern offensive army. The weapons "were purchased to build an offensive army that was capable of expanding Israeli borders."[21]

One could agree with some or most of the technical analysis of Kenneth Pollack concerning the military performance of the Arab armies in 1967[22] (after eliminating the cultural generalisations implicit in the categorisation of "Arab Armies"), but the facts refute his book's initial assertion that, on the eve of the war, "Israel was a goner."[23] This assessment takes at face value the sensationalist propaganda and fear-mongering that were part of the Israeli army leadership's campaign against Eshkol's hesitation to launch an offensive.[24] In his conversation with Israeli Foreign Minister Abba Eban, who was sent by Eshkol to ensure American commitment to support Israel against possible Soviet intervention (without which Eshkol would not go to war despite the pressure from the generals), President Johnson expressed certainty that Israel would win the war.[25]

---

[21] Guy Laron, *The Six-Day War: The Breaking of the Middle East* (New Haven and London: Yale University Press, 2017), p. 261.

[22] Long before Pollack published his book, Egyptian ex-political and military figures wrote critically and in detail regarding the political appointments in the army (including the general commander), false reporting to superiors, false reporting to the public, lack of intelligence information about the Israeli Army and unfeasible war plans due to lack of appropriate training and needed supplies. See: Amin Huweidi, *Lost Chances* [Arabic] (Beirut: Sharikat al-Matbu'at, 1992), pp. 67–83.

[23] Kenneth M. Pollack, *Armies of Sand: The Past, Present and Future of Arab Military Effectiveness* (New York: Oxford University Press, 2019), p. 1.

[24] Segev, *A State at All Costs*, p. 631, in addition to the sensationalist propaganda claiming that the alternative would be a Holocaust (especially considering that Ben-Gurion used to call Nasser Hitler, and some Israelis believed him).

[25] Lorraine Boissoneault, "What the Six-Day War tells us about the Cold War," *Smithsonian*, 6 June 2017, accessed at: https://bit.ly/2wk018D

The Pentagon and the CIA made similar assessments that Israel would easily win, whether it launched an offensive or absorbed a first strike. The Pentagon estimated that Israel would win in seven to ten days in the event of an offensive, and in two to three weeks in the case of a defensive war after an Egyptian first strike. A CIA report, released in April 2004, refuted Israeli claims concerning its relative weakness compared to Nasser's Arab coalition and asserted the counter-claim that Israel had exaggerated Arab strength in order to obtain more aid. The CIA, at the time, estimated that the Israeli air force would prevail in the first twenty-four hours and that Israel would win the war in less than a week.[2]

The June 1967 war was an Israeli war of choice. Israel seized an opportunity to break Nasser's regime and expand its own borders at the same time. Since 1948, Zionist statemen and political leaders, out of the belief that the Arab states would not accept the existence of a Jewish state, held that another war was necessary in order to force the Arab states to at least accept Israel as a fait accompli in the region. A war would simultaneously enable Israel to attain some of the territorial goals the 1948 war left unaccomplished.

In his debate with Shimon Peres after the 1982 Lebanon War, when the Labour Party claimed that Begin and Sharon's Likud government led the country into a war of choice in Lebanon, Ariel Sharon refuted Peres' claims that Israel should only wage wars of "no choice." Sharon, with his typical bluntness, said that only the Jewish rebellion in Auschwitz was a "no choice" action, otherwise all Israel's wars with the Arabs were wars of choice.[27] This implies that, in this respect, the 1967 war was no different from the 1982 war. The apparent differ-

---

[26] David Robarge, "Getting it Right: CIA Analysis of the 1967 Arab-Israeli War," *Studies in Intelligence*, vol. 62, no. 2 (June 2018), pp. 29–35; Bruce Riedel, "The CIA's Overlooked Intelligence Victory in the 1967 War," *Brookings*, 30 May 2017, accessed at: https://brook.gs/30K2NCc. See also: Omar Ashour, "An Inevitable Defeat? The Combat Performance on the Egyptian Front," [Arabic], in; Ahmed Hussein (ed.), *The June 1967 War: Paths and Implications* (Doha/Beirut: The Arab Center for Research and Policy Studies, 2020), pp. 77–8.

[27] Azmi Bishara, *From the Jewishness of the State to Sharon* [Arabic] (Cairo, Dar Al-Shourouk, 2005), pp. 104. See also: Efraim Inbar, "The 'no choice war' debate in Israel," *The Journal of Strategic Studies*, vol. 12, no. 1 (1989), pp. 22–37.

ence is between the self-righteous hypocrisy of labour and leftist Zionists and the unabashed directness of the right-wing nationalists.

In October 1953, in an assessment of the security problems of Israel in the event of the outbreak of a future war, Ben-Gurion stressed that the "factor of time is decisive and fateful." Since Israel lacks any "strategic depth," this means that not only should it assure air dominance by destroying "the enemy air force and to bomb its flight services," but it also should decide the time of the war's outbreak.[28] This point of view subsequently became a national security doctrine that prevailed on the eve of the June 1967 war.[29]

Just as there is a Defeat Syndrome, there is a Victory Syndrome. The war of 1967 ended in a crushing defeat for all the states attacked in the Israeli blitzkrieg. The *Naksa* (setback), as the defeat was named by official Egyptian rhetoric, took a whole Arab generation hostage. It precipitated an outpouring of angry critiques of Arab nationalist regimes as well as the tentative rise of the Arab left and a subsequent surge in Islamist movements.

Since that time, the wrong questions continue to be asked. It is seldom pointed out that the defeat was actually the exception, not the rule. The pro-capitulation camp are not interested in rational analysis because the notion that 1967 is the paradigm for any future war with Israel supports their argument for a peace settlement at any cost, as if the only conceivable form of conflict with a colonial apartheid-like entity is war. Islamist movements clung to the belief that the 1967 defeat was the inevitable result of the commitments of some Arab states to nationalist secular ideologies. They went so far as trying to prove that Israel won because it holds strictly to the principles of Jewish religion![30] In fact, Arab armies have fought much better on

[28] Amir Bar-Or, "The Evolution of the Army's Role in Israeli Strategic Planning: A Documentary Record," *Israel Studies*, vol. 1, no. 2 (1996), pp. 117–18.

[29] See: Yitzhak Rabin, *The Rabin Memoirs* (Berkeley and Los Angeles: University of California Press, 1979), chapter 6; Moshe Dayan, *Moshe Dayan: Story of My Life* (Jerusalem: Steimatzky's, 1976), pp. 243–69. See also: Shlomo Gazit, *At Key Points of Time* [Hebrew] ([Tel Aviv]: Miskal-Yedioth Ahronoth Books/Chemed Books, 2016), pp. 144–66.

[30] See for example: Yusuf al-Qaradawi, *Lesson on the Second Nakba, Why We Were Defeated and How We Can Win* [Arabic] ([n.p.], 1968). See also: Mohammad al-Ghazali, *Jihad Call Home between Internal Deficit and External Conspiracy* [Arabic] (Cairo, Dar al-Sahwa, 1998).

many occasions since 1967, even under the same regimes.[31] For example, just months after the defeat, Jordanian soldiers and Palestinian *fedayeen* supported by a Jordanian artillery battalion proved themselves very capable fighters at the Battle of Karameh.[32] This was followed by the War of Attrition and the 1973 October War, in which the Arab armies acquitted themselves very well despite their different political leaderships. Then there are the many successes of the long resistance period in Lebanon. Yet, none of these observable achievements have been able to erase the deep-seated impressions bequeathed by the June 1967 defeat. This is, in part, due to the ongoing reality of the Israeli occupation created by that war and, in part, because the deep sense of frustration and despair engendered by the defeat cast a long shadow over any later sense of achievement.

The illusion that swift victory was the Israeli army's constant companion asserted a similarly long-lasting effect on the Israeli psyche and created an ideological bent. Also, it quickly proved a formidable handicap. Whenever the Israelis confronted a serious resistance movement (as in Lebanon and in Gaza), they became perplexed, frustrated and, most importantly, lacking in endurance. They could not understand why a similarly quick and low-cost victory eluded them in these contexts. The steadfastness displayed by an Arab resistance movement ran contrary to the dominant expectations of an Israeli political culture and collective consciousness shaped by the successes of the "Six-Day War".

---

[31] Pollack.

[32] A 15-hour battle took place on 21 March 1968 in the town of Karameh in the Jordan Valley between an Israeli force of around 15,000 troops supported by aircraft and the Jordanian army and Palestinian guerrillas after the Israeli forces crossed the Jordan River to destroy the *fedayeen* camps. The Israelis were surprised by the firm strong-willed resistance and had to withdraw without accomplishing their goals. Troops from Jordan's First Infantry Division were the Israeli army's toughest opponents in this battle, fighting in a "highly professional manner, using armour and infantry forces with artillery support." The approximately 300 Palestinian fighters in the battle showed great bravery but "probably did not inflict many Israeli casualties." Despite its limited military significance, the battle became one of the most important confrontations of the Arab-Israeli conflict leading to its "emergence as a central political myth for Palestinian nationalists and their supporters." W. Andrew Terrill, "The political mythology of the Battle of Karameh," *The Middle East Journal*, vol. 55, no. 1 (2001), pp. 91–2.

Until its 1967 victory, Israel was an unstable enterprise in the eyes of its Western allies, including the US. The win pushed Israel fully into the American radar, paving the way for a deep and comprehensive alliance between the two countries.[33] The same applied to Israel's relationship with diaspora Jews to whom the war's outcome meant that Israel was more than just a brief adventure; it was now a guaranteed state project. As a result, the end of the war ushered in intensified Jewish migration to Israel, an exponential increase in investments and an extensive liberalisation of Israel's tactical, settlement-based public sector economy in order to better absorb the investments.

The labour movement that led the colonisation project in Palestine, especially since the second, most politicised, wave of Jewish immigration (1904–14), directed the establishment of the state and orchestrated the building of and pervaded state institutions, started to lose ground to the Jewish nationalist right wing, especially after the war of 1973. In that phase, this trend was supported by a rising urban middle class and the majority of the Sephardi and Mizrahi (Oriental Jewish) population. Holding the European (Ashkenazi) leadership of the country responsible for its misery, this section of the population supported the nationalist populist wing of

---

[33] US government assistance to Israel began in 1949 with a $100 million bank loan. Throughout the 1950s and 1960s, US aid to Israel was far less than it became in later years. France was indeed Israel's main early patron, providing Israel with advanced military equipment and technology, while the US only provided moderate amounts of economic aid (mostly loans). When French President Charles de Gaulle refused to supply Israel with military hardware as a protest against its pre-meditated launch of the 1967 war, the US decided to embrace the role relinquished by France. A year after 1967, the Johnson Administration approved the sale of Phantom aircraft to Israel, establishing the precedent for US support for what later came to be referred to as Israel's qualitative military edge over its neighbours. Average annual US aid increased between 1966 and 1970 to about $102 million, while military loans increased to about 47% of the total. After 1970, the US Congress committed to strengthening Israel's military and economy through large increases in foreign aid. The US provided Israel with $545 million in military loans in 1971, in contrast to the modest amount of $30 million the previous year (1970). In 1974, Israel became the largest recipient of US foreign assistance. Since 1971 and until today, average US aid to Israel was over $2.6 billion per year, two-thirds of which amounted to military assistance. Jeremy M. Sharp, "U.S. Foreign Aid to Israel," *Report*, Congressional Research Service, 22 December 2016, pp. 32–3, accessed at: https://bit.ly/2QUTuiy

the Ashkenazi political elite, who came across less patronising to the mass of Sephardi and Mizrahi (Oriental Jews).

The June war reshaped the image of Israel, just as it reshaped that of the Arab world. The war attracted a great deal of international solidarity with the "victorious victim" against the "vanquished aggressor"— a couple of magic words that people mired in a superficial understanding of either *victimhood* as such or aggression on its own are unable to grasp. Being just a victim is not enough to inspire solidarity and spark the media's imagination, as has been proven time and again. Apparently victory (or winning in general) elicits more sympathy from "international public opinion" than victimhood, real or imagined.

No other occupation beginning in the second half of the twentieth century, during the age of decolonisation, has lasted for more than fifty whole years. The fact that Israel's direct occupation, which the rest of the world also recognises as an occupation, has endured so long raises an important question about the meaning of dealing with Israel as a normal state within the 1967 borders and an occupying state only outside of those borders. Israel is more than 70 years old. Only 19 years of these were spent within the original truce lines up to the war on 5 June 1967. Which, then, is the exception and which the rule? It is neither logical nor natural to consider the "normal" Israel to be Israel as it once was for less than 20 years, rather than as it has been for more than fifty. Moreover, even if we accept this distinction for argument's sake, the Israel of 1948–67 was not a "normal" country that then occupied an area three times its size in June 1967. Even before 1967, it was the product of a settler colonial movement's military occupation.[34]

Perhaps the Israelis themselves were taken by surprise by the swift and overwhelming victory that year. Their natural next step was to rally from the shock and secure political gains from the victory, and their most important object was to secure Arab acquiescence to the existence of the Israeli state without having to compromise on the Palestinian question.

The Eshkol's government was ready to bargain for peace settlement with Egypt and Syria using its territorial spoils of war to barter

---

[34] The issue of normalising settler colonialism will be discussed in Chapter 8.

with. No state could accept such a humiliating trade-off. At the time, the Palestinians and the conflict with Arab states were separated in Israeli political thinking which considered the former a peripheral matter relative to the latter. Two days after the war, Eshkol told the Knesset, "A new situation has been created, which can serve as a starting-point in direct negotiations for a peace settlement with the Arab countries."[35] A week later, on 19 June, the Israeli cabinet adopted a resolution proposing to offer Egypt and Syria the territories they had just lost in exchange for a long-term contractual peace. Cabinet Resolution 563 read, "A. Egypt: Israel proposes signing of a peace agreement with Egypt [and with Syria in point B.] based on the international border and the security needs of Israel."[36] This offer did not address the Palestinian roots of the conflict, but was still labelled a "generous peace offer" and rumours circulated that Cairo and Damascus immediately rejected it.[37] In fact, the offer itself was a fiction created by Israel's foreign minister at the time, Abba Eban. The offer was never presented to the Arabs. The cabinet resolution was mainly a diplomatic ruse to gain American political support in the United Nations against the Soviets, who were about to propose a resolution calling for Israel's immediate and unconditional withdrawal from the territories occupied in the 1967 war.[38]

The Arabs summed up their response to the defeat in what became known as "The Three No's" of the Khartoum Resolution: no negotiations, no reconciliation and no recognition.[39] The resolution, adopted in the summit held in the Sudanese capital on 29 August 1967, stated that the participants agreed:

> "to make a concerted effort to engage in political work internationally and diplomatically in order to eliminate the results of the war and

---

[35] "Statement to the Knesset by Prime Minister Eshkol, 12 June 1967," *Israel Ministry of Foreign Affairs*, accessed at: https://bit.ly/3bFL2eg

[36] Avi Raz, "The Generous Peace Offer that was Never Offered: The Israeli Cabinet Resolution of June 19, 1967," *Diplomatic History*, vol. 37, no. 1 (January 2013), p. 86.

[37] Ibid., p. 87.

[38] Ibid., p. 92.

[39] This is in reference to the Arab League Summit held in the Sudanese capital Khartoum on 29 August 1967, in the wake of the Arab defeat in the 1967 war.

ensure the withdrawal of Israeli forces from Arab lands occupied after 5 June 1967, within the framework of the basic principles to which the Arab countries are committed: no peace with or recognition of 'Israel,' no negotiations with it, and insistence on the Palestinian people's right to their homeland."[40]

This statement defied the defeat and rejected capitulation. However, the Arab countries were still pragmatic in their response to US initiatives. For example, Nasser accepted the Rogers Plan in December 1969.[41]

Israeli post-war thinking encountered a challenge at another level: a surge in Palestinian nationalism and armed resistance factions. This came, moreover, at a time when Arab people throughout the region were searching for a glimmer of hope amidst the darkness of defeat, despair and even cultural shock.

Israel remained dogged in its refusal to comply with the 242 Security Council's resolution and to accept the two basic prerequisites for peace: the right of the Palestinian refugees to return and Israeli withdrawal from East Jerusalem, the Jordan Valley and other parts of the West Bank. In the celebratory government meeting held the day after the war ended, on 11 June, "the status of United Jerusalem" was an item on the agenda. A few weeks after the war, the Knesset adopted three legislative acts to extend its jurisdiction over the occupied Eastern sector of the city. The first act, which was issued on 27 June 1967, stated that "the law, jurisdiction, and administration of the state shall extend to any area of Eretz Israel designed by the government by order." This was in fact an amendment (number 11) to the Law and Administration Ordinance of 1948, and was applied the very next day to a new area of Jerusalem and its vicinity, stretching from Qalandia airport, just South of Ramallah, Southward to the Arab villages of Sour Baher and Beit Safafa, and West to East from the armistice line Eastward to the villages Anata, al-Ram, and al-Tur. The new designation was enacted on 28 June 1967, in accordance with article II-B of the Law and Administration Ordinance, 1948 as

---

[40] "Decisions and recommendations of the Arab Summit," in: Yousef Khoury (ed.), *The Arab Unity Projects 1913–1989*, 2nd ed. (Beirut: Center for Arab Unity Studies, 1990), p. 216.

[41] This will be discussed in Part Two of this book.

amended, and a chart indicated the new boundaries. On the same day, the Knesset passed another amendment extending the municipal jurisdiction of West Jerusalem under the title "Enlargement of the Area of the Jerusalem Municipality."[42] In July 1980, the Israeli Knesset enshrined the annexation constitutionally as it enacted the 'Basic Law: Jerusalem the capital of Israel' by which it proclaimed that "Jerusalem, whole and united, is the capital of Israel" and the city will "remain forever under Israel's sovereignty."[43]

Instead of becoming more flexible after a victory that should have allayed its "existential" fears, Israel hardened its positions towards the Arab countries and continued to ignore the Palestinian issue. The hubris of victory and the experience of dominating another people blinded decision-makers and wider sectors of the public. On the matter of the Egyptian and Syrian occupied in 1967, the leadership of Israel's ruling Labour Party was divided over whether or not to construct and annex settlements (ostensibly to establish "secure borders"). None of the leading figures in the party recognised that there was a Palestinian issue to solve.

Between September 1972 and April 1973, on the eve of the elections to the eighth Knesset, the Labour Party held a lengthy discussion on the future of the West Bank. The "Grand Debate", as it was dubbed, reflected a rift between the leading Labour Party figures. The first group, represented by Yigal Allon, Pinchas Sapir and Abba Eban,[44] advocated what they called territorial compromise (*pshara*

---

[42] Naseer H. Aruri, "Misrepresenting Jerusalem," in: Fouad Moughrabi & Munirakash (eds.), *The Open Veins of Jerusalem* (Maryland: Jusoor Books, 1997/1998), pp. 170–1; United Nations, *The Status of Jerusalem: Prepared for, and under the Guidance of, the Committee on the Exercise of the Inalienable Rights of the Palestinian People* (New York: United Nations, 1997), p. 12, accessed at: https://bit.ly/2UGQFDO; Ofra Friesel, "Israel's 1967 Governmental Debate about the Annexation of East Jerusalem: The Nascent Alliance with the United States, Overshadowed by "United Jerusalem"," *Law and History Review*, vol. 34, no. 2 (May 2016), pp. 376–7.

[43] Aruri, "Misrepresenting Jerusalem," p. 174; United Nations, *The Status of Jerusalem*, pp. 3, 13. See also: Azmi Bishara, "A Brief Note on Jerusalem", *Al-Ahram Weekly*, 22–28 April 2010, https://bit.ly/38ZZ6gS

[44] Yigal Allon (1918–80) joined the *Haganah* in 1931, and later, in 1945, became the Commander in Chief of the *Palmach* (the elite fighting force of the *Haganah* which he co-

teritorialit). The "compromise" entailed splitting the West Bank between Israel and Jordan, whereby the former would annex most of the Jordan Valley from the river to the eastern slopes of the West Bank hill ridge, East Jerusalem and the Etzion bloc, while leaving the remaining parts containing most of the Palestinian population to Jordan. The second group, represented by Yisrael Galili and Moshe Dayan,[45] advocated intensive development, i.e., colonising the occupied areas without changing its official territorial status.[46]

founded in 1941). He occupied different ministerial positions from 1961 to 1977, shortly served as acting Prime Minister of Israel (26 February 1969–17 March 1969) and a deputy prime minister (1968–77). Pinchas Sapir (1909–75) joined the Israel Labour Party after he immigrated to Palestine. He was a member of *Haganah* and became its quartermaster in 1948 with the rank of lieutenant colonel. After the war, he was appointed director general of the Ministry of Defence and later held two ministerial posts including the Ministry of Finance. Sapir became one of the most powerful men in Israeli politics. Abba Eban (1915–2002) was born in South Africa and brought up in England. In 1946, he worked with the Jewish Agency as a political information officer. He served in the British Army in Egypt and Mandate Palestine. In 1949, Eban became Israel's first permanent representative in the UN and served in that post until 1959. He also served concurrently as Israel's ambassador to the US from 1950 to 1959. He was elected to the Knesset in 1959 as a member of the Israel Labour Party and took ministerial roles from 1960 to 1966. He became Israel's Foreign Minister from 1966 to 1974.

[45] Yisrael Galili (1911–86) was a Russian-born political member of the *Haganah* where he was appointed as Chief of Staff of the *Haganah* in 1946. In 1948, he resigned from the *Haganah* and founded the "Unity of Labour–Workers of Zion" party, which he ran until it merged with several other parties to form the Israel Labour Party in 1963. He sat in the Knesset (1949–51 and 1955–77) and also took ministerial roles during that period. Galili was considered one of Golda Meir's top advisers. Moshe Dayan (1915–81) was appointed to the *Haganah's* General Staff in 1947. He also joined the British-organised Jewish Supernumerary Police (Special Night Squads). During the 1948 war, he played a major role on the ground and in negotiations with the Jordanians and Egyptians over the 1949 Armistice Agreements. He was elected as a member of the fourth Knesset on the list of the ruling *Mapai* party and was the Minister of Agriculture (1959–64). On 1 June 1967, shortly before the war broke out, he was appointed Minister of Defence by then Prime Minister Levi Eshkol. Following the death of Eshkol, Dayan remained defence minister in Golda Meir's government in 1969 and was in his position during the 1973 war. After the war, he joined the Likud government headed by Menachem Begin and held the post of Minister of Foreign Affairs (1977–79).

[46] Ronald Ranta, *Political Decision Making and Non-Decisions: The Case of Israel and the Occupied Territories* (New York: Springer, 2015), pp. 121–2.

Eventually, the second group's Galili Plan became de facto Labour party policy in 1973.

Moshe Dayan was the only minister who implicitly advocated turning the newly occupied territories into a "solution" to the Palestinian problem in creating a direct contact with traditional local leaderships. His "Open Bridges" policy opened a civilian passage to Jordan and provided the inhabitants of the occupied West Bank with some much-needed breathing space (these bridges did not connect to Israel and did not allow any passage to or from Israeli areas).[47] He cultivated links with Palestinian mayors and other local leaders in order to construct an alternative leadership to the PLO and transition to some form of self-rule. Note that this was 10 years before the Egyptian-Israeli Camp David Agreement proposed its model for autonomy, or self-rule. Perhaps Dayan's decision to leave the Labour Party in 1977 and subsequently to join the Begin government presented him with

---

[47] Immediately after the 1967 war, the Israeli Minister of Security at the time, Moshe Dayan, established the "open bridges" policy as part of his policy of "indirect rule" in the areas occupied in this war. His strategy was based on maintaining military and security control over the occupied territory while keeping the Arab population separate from Israel. Former Brigadier General Mordechai Gazit, the first military commander of the territories, stated, "We have decided on a policy of opening the bridges and borders because we think it is for the good of Israel now and in the longer range." The "open bridges" policy allowed for the normalisation of the Arab population's life under occupation, maintaining contact with the Arab region, and developing the economic infrastructure in the West Bank in a way that would prevent it from becoming an economic burden on Israel. This policy included relative freedom of movement of people to and from Jordan and allowed exporting specific agricultural and industrial products from the West Bank abroad. In fact, it was a way to dispose of the West Bank agricultural surpluses. The bridges, of course, were open in only one direction; while most of the West Bank's exports to Jordan were exempt from customs, Israel imposed high customs on imports from the East Bank. As for Israel, it protected its farmers by transferring Palestinian agricultural surpluses abroad. The accompanying "privileges" of this policy that were granted to the Palestinians by the military government were subject to revocation if the *quid pro quo* for their continuance, i.e., political calm, was jeopardised. See: Sheila Ryan, "Constructing a New Imperialism: Israel and the West Bank," *MERIP Reports*, no. 9 (May–June 1972), pp. 3–11, 17; Geoffrey Aronson, "Israel's Policy of Military Occupation," *Journal of Palestine Studies*, vol. 7, no. 4 (Summer, 1978), pp. 79–98; Issa Abdul-Hamid, *Six Years of the Open Bridges Policy* [Arabic] (Beirut: PLO Research Centre, 1973).

the perfect opportunity to apply his ideas in partnership with an Arab state—Egypt—which entered into bilateral talks with Israel on Palestinian self-rule in the West Bank and Gaza.

While Arab politicians honed the rhetoric of recovering the territories, Israeli politicians debated the fate of the "territories", turning this issue into just another aspect of Israel's internal political landscape. Meanwhile the Palestinians in the West Bank and Gaza were sucked into the occupation machinery. The Palestinians suffered the hard and brutal realities of the occupation. Through relentless state violence, Israel subjugated the entire population of Palestine to its political sovereignty. Then, on the one hand, it integrated the occupied people into its domestic economic system while keeping total control of the occupied territories' natural resources and skies; on the other, it created the mechanisms and institutions that forcefully imposed ethnic separation, with two systems of rights and two judicial systems. The prolonged occupation of the West Bank and Gaza with its two faces of integration and separation, combined with the inherent contradictions between the Israeli state's Jewish character and criteria for formal citizenship, gradually turned Israel to an apartheid-like state.

In conclusion, the contemporary state of Israel is politically, culturally and economically not just a product of 1948, but also of 1967. The same can also be said about Arab political culture which now had a devastating defeat syndrome to overcome (the October 1973 war and the armed Palestinian resistance movements before and after that war would help to some extent). The sociopolitical impact of the 1967 defeat on the Palestinian cause was revolutionary. Foremost among the repercussions was the rise of the PLO after the defeat of pan-Arab regimes. However, this development simultaneously presented an opportunity to throw the burden of the cause onto the PLO and eventually to reduce the entire Palestinian question to just the West Bank and Gaza.

Can Separate Peace be a Model for the Palestinians?

The 1973 October War was intended, at least as Egypt saw it, to recover national dignity and force Israel to withdraw from the occupied territories in the framework of a political process. After that war, which ended with a partial victory and partial defeat for both sides and after which the military option was abandoned, different kinds of peace talks were initiated. Recuperating "the territories" required American mediation and experience in Israeli affairs (including expertise in Israeli internal politics: parties, coalitions, elections, etc.) in order to discern Israeli plans regarding a possible compromise solution and how willing Israel was to negotiate.

This new direction could only lead to separate peace treaties with each frontline Arab state. There is a fundamental difference between demanding Israeli withdrawal from occupied territories using united threats of force and other collective tactics, and making that same demand at the negotiating table in exchange for political concessions, such as recognising and entering into peace with Israel while ignoring the question of the refugees and the parts of the West Bank that Israel wants to annex. What the new direction also meant was that the Israeli war of 1967 had effectively achieved its aims since, afterwards, Arab states became willing to renounce their pre-1967 demands and aspirations.

The other Arab countries rejected Egypt's bilateral peace treaty with Israel. Algeria, Syria and Iraq led the regional pressure campaign that forced the monarchies to comply as well.

But a key development, just over a decade later, would expose the Arab world to the full ramifications of the Egypt–Israel peace treaty. The Iraqi invasion of Kuwait in 1990 shattered the old Arab regional order and it ultimately swept aside all official Arab objections to Egypt's separate peace with Israel.

The PLO was also influenced by these broader political shifts. It gradually segued into a "Palestinian regime" seeking formal statehood through a separate peace agreement with Israel.

Israel was ready to return the occupied Sinai to Egypt in exchange for long-term peace with the biggest Arab country, without which Syria could not feasibly go to war against Israel. The PLO did not realise that Israel's approach, in which it wanted to drop Egypt from Arab military equations even at the cost of returning the Sinai Peninsula, did not apply to the PLO. The peace with Egypt had brought an end to conventional wars between Arab states and Israel.

Israel's only wars since then have involved non-state actors (Hezbollah and Hamas).

Before President Sadat signed the 1978–9 Camp David peace accords with Israel, an important development took place in the PLO. After the 1973 war, the PLO had begun to acquire unprecedented international recognition as a national liberation movement and as the sole legitimate representative of the Palestinian people, despite a counter-campaign launched by Israel and the US depicting the PLO as a terrorist organisation. During this period, the PLO saw possible Arab-Israeli peace talks aiming to recover "the territories" as a chance to promote the idea of Palestinian control of the West Bank and Gaza. The implicit argument was that if Israel withdraws from the occupied West Bank and Gaza, why should these be territories be handed to Jordan and Egypt? Why not return them to the Palestinians?

The PLO leadership, which had become a symbol of steadfastness after the June 1967 defeat, was engaged in an armed struggle and could not compromise on the principle of the liberation of the whole of Palestine with the goal of establishing a single democratic state, so it encouraged the PLO's leftist factions (mainly the Democratic Front for the Liberation of Palestine, or DFLP) to draft an agenda or a programme or action plan on how to reach statehood. The so-called "ten-point program" called for the establishment of a "fighting national authority" on every inch of occupied land to be liberated from the Israeli occupation.[48] This document represented a discursive step towards the wording of the "two-state solution."

---

[48] According to papers and documents from Fatah's co-founder, Salah Khalaf (which are still being catalogued by the Arab Center for Research and Policy Studies), the Ten-Point Program (1974) was formulated in response to the diplomatic developments that took place shortly after the 1973 October War. President Anwar Sadat told Fatah's delegation that Israel would withdraw from the Occupied Territories in 1967. Therefore, he asked the PLO to join him in the peace talks. Sadat implicitly warned the PLO leadership that their reluctance to participate in the peace conference would allow King Hussein of Jordan to reap the diplomatic benefits, namely annexing the West Bank. Mueen al-Taher, "From Salah Khalaf to Arafat during the October 1973 … The early compromise concerns," [Arabic] *Al-Araby al-Jadeed*, 30 October 2017, accessed at: https://bit.ly/3n8iL4y. According to Salah Khalaf, the first proposal from Fatah that supported the one democratic state in historic Palestine was on 10 October 1968. He stated in a press conference that

Israel, as mentioned above, had its own agenda. It therefore rejected the idea of a Palestinian state in the West Bank and Gaza on the grounds that it would pose a threat to Israel's security. It also insisted that Israeli troops should be deployed along the borders with Jordan (where they remain today) and announced plans to annex existing settlement blocs and the Jordan Valley.

Also in this period, the PLO clashed with Jordan over political representation of the Palestinian people. Egypt and other Arab countries stood by the PLO and, consequently, the 1974 Arab League summit in Rabat declared the PLO to be the sole legitimate representative of the Palestinian people. The PLO did not (and probably could not) grasp that this was the beginning of the separate peace process soon to be launched by Egypt. The exclusive representation decision that the PLO struggled so hard to achieve was later used by Egypt and Jordan to free themselves from their duty to help retrieve Palestinian territories lost in war (i.e., the West Bank and Gaza).

Since the 1991 Madrid Conference, which was actually convened by the US, and the culmination of efforts made by foreign secretary James Baker in the aftermath of the first Gulf war (after the Iraqi occupation of Kuwait), the pursuit of a separate peace (on the basis of the "land for peace" formula) has become the official Arab and Palestinian position. This approach was reiterated in the negotiations that were continued in Washington between a Palestinian-Jordanian delegation and Israel, and between Syria and Israel. In 1993, a secret negotiations track was conducted in Oslo and Israeli and PLO teams agreed on mutual recognition and declaration of principles. This resulted in establishing a separate formal negotiations track between Israel and the PLO.[49] Hence, Jordan negotiated its own peace deal with Israel separately, while the PLO continues to negotiate.

Fatah's strategic objective was to "work toward the creation of a democratic state in which Arabs and Jews would live together harmoniously as fully equal citizens in the whole historic Palestine." Salah Khalaf & Eric Rouleau, *My Home, My Land: A Narrative of the Palestinian Struggle*, Linda Butler Koseoglu (trans.) (New York: Times Books, 1981), p. 139. However, Khalaf said that this proposal "triggered a storm of protest both within the ranks of the Resistance." Ibid.

[49] More about this in Chapter 6.

How Did an Occupation Help the Occupier Evade the Colonial Question?

In general, today, colonialism is squarely framed in the context of *decolonisation* and the internationally recognised right of occupied peoples to resist occupation in pursuit of national *liberation*. However, the case of Palestine is treated as an exception. In Western discourse, including among the mainstream left in Europe (e.g., social democrats), Palestine is a thorny dilemma requiring "creative solutions." It has been disassociated from other cases of national liberation and conflated with border disputes, various contemporary cultural and religious problems, and Europe's own Jewish question. This overly complicated and complicating framing has stood between Palestine and any practical decolonisation project. It has even become a countervailing force against any lasting peace settlement. Rather than help creative solutions replace decolonisation as a framework for a resolution, the passage of time helped the emergence of an apartheid-like system of ethnic discrimination. As "innovative" efforts continued to fail to bridge the gap between Israeli intransigence and a mediated path to any form of genuine justice, the struggle against the occupation continued and the Palestinians introduced creative methods of resistance, most notably the grassroots uprising. Intifada no longer needs translation in many world languages.

The culture of the age of anti-colonial struggle is rooted in the belief that resisting occupation is an intrinsic right enshrined in international law and is also a duty of the occupied people. Modern decolonisation processes were rooted in the international recognition of the inalienable right to self-determination of colonised peoples everywhere. As anti-colonial legal frameworks evolved and independence movements gained momentum, occupying powers scrambled to find ad hoc solutions to the dilemma of maintaining control versus bearing the mounting costs of occupation that prolonged native resistance might imply.

From the Arab perspective, the liberation of Palestine was framed, from the outset, as a struggle between colonialism versus an Arab national independence movement. The fight for liberation was understood to be the task of both the Palestinian and the Arab people, who were exhorted to help "resist a foreign occupation of part of the Arab homeland." In this framework, the Palestinian struggle became not just an Arab issue but the central Arab cause. It became a chief symbol for the broader realm of shared Arab concerns, because it was also a microcosm of other national problems: division, subjugation, foreign domination, Arab fragmentation and the weak legitimacy of ruling regimes. When Arabs demonstrated solidarity with the Palestinians, it was not just at the human level, but also at the political strategic level. Talk of Arab solidarity with Palestine was irrelevant; it was already a common struggle.

Nevertheless, after 1967, when the Arab focus shifted to the recuperation of Arab countries' land occupied by Israel (the Sinai and the Golan), the conflict was reframed as a standard border dispute. There quickly followed attempts to project this framing onto the Palestinian question. The same process that led to bilateral negotiations and separate peace agreements between Arab countries and Israel led to the reduction of the Palestinian cause to a "Palestinian-Israeli dispute" and, before long, to its further reduction to a "border conflict" to be solved ("creatively" of course) through bilateral negotiations, the outcomes of which were determined not by principles of justice, but rather by relative balances of power.

Pan-Arab support for the PLO was initially meant to support independent Palestinian decision-making. Ironically, this would change after a consensus was reached in the 1974 Rabat Summit to cede authority to the PLO as the sole legitimate political representative of the Palestinians. It should be stressed that the PLO's eagerness for autonomy was not entirely motivated by aspirations for prestige, influence or other such whims. It was also necessitated by Arab governments' constant and conflicting meddling in the organisation's internal affairs.

After the 1991 Madrid Conference, Yasser Arafat continued to manifest this trend with his insistence on separating the Palestinian negotiating delegation in Washington from its Jordanian counterpart.[50]

---

[50] On 14 September 1993, one day after signing the Oslo agreement, the Palestinian members of the Jordanian-Palestinian delegation became a separate entity, and each delegation continued to negotiate with Israel in accordance with the Madrid formula.

What was the result? A separate and comprehensive Jordanian-Israeli peace agreement and a muddled and blundering Palestinian-Israeli peace process lacking even a minimum of shared understanding between Israel and the PLO. The process still has not ended, nearly three decades after Jordan and Israel signed their bilateral peace deal in 1994.

The Arab paradigmatic shift has contemporary echoes. Take for instance official Arab regime responses to the ongoing blockade of Gaza. During four Israeli wars on Gaza (2008–9, 2012, 2014, 2021), the Arab regimes were split between those expressing "solidarity" with the Palestinians and those holding them responsible for incurring Israel's wrath. When the Gazan people's anger and frustration at the blockade erupted in 2008 and furious crowds stormed the Rafah crossing between Gaza and the Sinai, Cairo was caught off guard. In order to defend and promote its official position on facilitating the blockade and contributing to its success (which did not enjoy popular support), the government invoked national defence and drummed up Egyptian patriotic sentiments against "Palestinian incursions" into Egyptian territory. PA President Mahmoud Abbas flirted with this rhetoric. In a speech to commemorate Yasser Arafat's death, he used the word "invaders" to describe demonstrators who spontaneously rallied to protest the blockade at one of its harshest levels before the war on Gaza in 2008.[51]

Two kinds of positions or views co-existed in the years after the Madrid Conference. One reflects the myriad interests of Arab regimes that disengaged themselves and their states from collective political identification as Arabs with shared national security concerns, interests and positions. The other reflects the desire of the political leadership of the PLO to itself become an Arab regime. Convergence between the two resulted in the idea of leaving the Palestinian issue to the Palestinians.

Arab governments welcomed the PA as an Arab regime (as they welcomed the PLO in 1974) because they could then shunt respon-

---

[51] "Palestinians Topple Gaza Wall and Cross to Egypt," *The New York Times*, 24 January 2008, accessed at: https://nyti.ms/3dRgBDw; "A Speech by President Mahmoud Abbas on the Fourth Commemoration of the Martyrdom of Yasser Arafat," [Arabic] *Journal of Palestine Studies*, vol. 19, no. 76 (Fall 2008), p. 196.

sibility for "the Palestinian issue" onto the PA and PLO. This made it easy for them to fall in with the political transformation of Palestine from an occupied Arab land to a Palestinian-Israeli border dispute. "The Palestinian problem" became first the *Palestinians' problem*, then the *problem of the Palestinians in the West Bank and Gaza* after its discursive shift from a colonial liberation struggle to a struggle for separate political entity. It thus morphed from solidarity with a resistance drive aimed at national liberation to a half-hearted search, together with the international community and the Israelis, for technocratic solutions to the problem. This search evolved into negotiations between the occupied and an occupier who refuses to accept that the only reasonable subject of negotiation is how to end their occupation. Then the negotiations segued into an "ongoing political process" in which "solutions" and "exit strategies" are defined according to prevailing balances of power. As for the only acceptable negotiating "partner" to the occupier in this process, it is Palestinian political elites who can be extorted into making their people pay the price for preserving the status quo.

In this context, according to the new paradigm, Arab pundits and politicians rely heavily on such notions as "international legitimacy" and "the international community." These terms represent alternate, virtual worlds, separate from the real world. The "international community" is not even an imagined community. It is merely a political term purposed to serve the current balance of powers. The "two-state" option, as a "solution" to be achieved through negotiations, is the result of the altered context which is characterised by the search for technocratic solutions to an unfathomable "dilemma". The irony is that what made the Arab regimes and PLO relinquish the liberation struggle and accept the idea of a two-state solution, which by definition marginalises the right of return, was their willingness to accept mediation rooted in international power balances, which effectively translates into exclusive dependence on US foreign policy. This is precisely what enabled Israel to render this same solution meaningless by refusing to withdraw to the 1967 borders (including east Jerusalem), insisting on maintaining its settlement clusters in the West Bank, and refusing to acknowledge the right of return to the Palestinians. Today, peace process negotiations continue to be obstructed by these three Israeli No's.

If the framework of US-mediated negotiations gave Israel little incentive to show some genuine flexibility, the above-mentioned gradual rightward shift in Israeli society since 1967 towards the ultra-nationalist and religio-nationalist ideologies ensured that Israel would dig in its heels further but that its colonialist/expansionist tendencies would gain impetus. Not only were these growing right-wing segments of Israeli society suffused with the euphoria of power and victory, they grew fearful to the point of hysteria of losing the territories seized in that war and proceeded to found various radical right and religious movements dedicated to the cause of annexing the West Bank. Perhaps the best known is the *Gush Emunim* movement which then splintered off into even more radical settler movements. At the same time, there was a growing perception amongst an increasingly fanaticised public that the "Biblical Land of Israel" was finally, thanks to the war, interlinked with the modern state.[52]

This idea reverberated across Israeli public discourse, causing the secularist and religious dimensions of the Zionist project to interlock, leading to a growing fusion between the state's secularist discourse and politics, and religious frames of reference. The most dangerous aspect of this was the fusion of nationalist and religious extremism in Israel—something which Arabs struggled to understand, since in Arab countries political religious radicalism and nationalism are ideologically antithetical.

It was at this time of the Israeli shift towards the religio-nationalist extreme right and closer Israeli-US bonding that the Arab regimes became caught in the game of American domestic politics. Suddenly, after turning acceptance of American international hegemony into a strategy for peace dependent on US pressure on Israel, they "discovered" that Israel is a domestic issue in America.[53] This generally means that the former exerts pressure on the latter by manipulating its internal politics.

This thesis is disputed, of course. Chomsky, for example, calls it a myth that exonerates American foreign policies, arguing that the

---

[52] Bishara, *From the Jewishness of the State to Sharon*, pp. 69–76.

[53] This "discovery" would drive some Arab countries to the opposite strategy of allying themselves with Israel in order to gain clout in the American administration.

Israeli lobby in the US is strong because of the American policy in the Middle East and not the other way around.[54] Others made an effort, a courageous one (at least in American academia), to demonstrate how influential the Israel lobby is.[55] Before them, some American politicians[56] expressed their disapproval of the Israeli lobby's growing influence on congressional decision-making through financing electoral campaigns, agitation and intimidation.[57]

Former President Barack Obama spoke frankly about the influence exerted by the American Israel Public Affairs Committee (AIPAC) on elected American politicians by either enticing them with votes and fundraising or menacing them with threats of potential accusations of being anti-Israeli or even antisemitic.[58] He said that the tactics used by Israeli Prime Minister Netanyahu to lobby for certain policies exasperated him and put him on the defensive, noting that this actually turned Israel into a domestic issue by "reminding me that normal policy differences with an Israeli Prime Minister [...] exacted a domestic political cost that simply did not exist when I dealt with the United Kingdom, Germany, France, Japan, Canada or any of our closest allies."[59]

It seems that both views are correct. The Israeli lobby is well organised and very influential. Yet, although American alignment with Israel doubled its influence in US domestic politics, Israel would not determine American policies if the underlying strategies behind these policies consciously changed. Seen from their perspective,

---

[54] Noam Chomsky, "The Israeli Lobby?," *The Washington Post*, 24 March 2006, accessed at: https://wapo.st/3yYuPuu

[55] John J. Mearsheimer & Stephen Walt, *The Israel Lobby and U.S. Foreign Policy* (New York: Farrar, Straus and Giroux, 2007).

[56] See, for example: Paul Findley, *They Dare to Speak Out: People and Institutions Confront Israel's Lobby* (New York: Lawrence Hill Books, 1989).

[57] John B. Judis wrote that President Truman knew of the injustice done to the Palestinians and as a "genuine Liberal [...] had moral qualms about Zionism," and tried to press for a return of the Palestinian refugees but failed just like other presidents (like Obama) who had good intentions towards the Palestinians "but under relentless pressure from supporters of Israel and after 1948 from the Israeli government itself, they gave up." Judis, p. 7.

[58] Obama, p. 629.

[59] Ibid., p. 633.

Chomsky is right. It may be very difficult for the White House to ever reach the decision to voluntarily exert real pressure on Israel, but if and when it finally does decide to impose at least a semi-just peace, then the Israeli lobby would not be able to block it. The political pluralism and cultural changes in the American-Jewish community should also be taken into consideration here, particularly in light of how Israeli policies are alienating more and more American youth (including Jewish youth), a trend that acquired impetus from the Trump-Netanyahu alignment and from Israel's alliance with right-wing Evangelical fundamentalists.

From this perspective, those pushing the idea among the Arabs that this or that American administration will never prioritise the Palestinian issue if the PLO and Arab regimes do not make further concessions erroneously assume that American involvement is the only way to pressure Israel. The idea plays to Israel's advantage. During most of the presidential terms that saw a growth in American public interest in the region, pressure on the Arabs and Palestinians to make further concessions to Israel grew in tandem. American involvement is important, but it is not an alternative to Palestinian strength. Only after the first Intifada and (with some Arab pressure) during the 1990 Gulf War was American pressure noticeably exerted on an Israeli government.[60]

The Arab and Palestinian political forces that opted for the "political process" as an exclusive strategy based on the good will of American presidential administrations (while always holding their breath for the next one) sometimes also focused on the internal power-play between the Israeli left and right. The Israeli left has gradually shrunk, while the right has either dismissed peace as unrealistic or supported it cynically as an instrument to increase Israeli power and promote Arab capitulation. But both sides of the Israeli domestic political spectrum have been consistently united on the principle of keeping the most land with the least Arabs on it which, in turn, means giving up the least possible amount of territory and the largest possible number of Arabs. This common principle underpins

---

[60] The Israeli government of Yitzhak Shamir. This case will be discussed in Chapter 7 during the historical review of American peace initiatives.

the current Israeli political consensus, although it is hardly a good basis for peace or even for an unjust settlement. Israeli governmental approval of any peace settlement is contingent on the extent to which it is compatible the prevailing domestic consensus. Should the Palestinians accept this as a condition for peace, they would have to accept the Jewish nature of Israel, renounce the right of return and drop any aspirations to retrieve Jerusalem, in addition to discarding any other lingering "Arab delusions".

In keeping with the plans to keep as much land as it can with as few Palestinians as possible on it, Israel continues to intensify settlement construction and build highways and ring roads to connect the areas it intends to annex to each other and to the urban centres inside the Green Line. In Israel, urban planning and construction policies are still conducted with the mentality of a colonial settler drive and this drive is defended by the Israeli state's security and foreign policies. In Israel, the logic of state does not just contradict the mentality of an expansionist colonial settler movement; the two fully complement each other, existing side by side in the same government and implementing different aspects of the same policy.

To conclude, the separate peace negotiations by each Arab country to restore land occupied in June 1967 signalled that Israel had achieved the goals of that war. The model could not be applied to other Arab countries because once Egypt was out of the military equations, no more Arab wars against Israel were possible and Israel no longer had an incentive to withdraw to its pre-1967 borders. The PLO's attempt to follow suit by turning the Palestinian liberation cause into an Israeli-Palestinian territorial dispute rendered the pursuit of justice dependent on relative balance of power with Israel, and on the complex American-Israeli relationship. It took a long time for the colonial question to reappear with some force in the political discourse. Only after years of peace process dead ends did it once again become clear that the occupation of the West Bank and Gaza could not be reduced to a border dispute because it is an extension of a colonial policy that took the form of a system of ethnic discrimination and separation.

5

FROM LIBERATION STRUGGLE TO
BORDER DISPUTE

From the PLO to the PA

Refugee camps were the home of the Palestinian struggle for liberation and the cradle of resistance organisations. From the 1950s until
the PLO's 1982 departure from Lebanon, the camps in Jordan, Syria
and Lebanon became nationalist training grounds and shaped the
course of the struggle and how it was fought. The return to Palestine,
not just as a wish but as a political demand supported by international
resolutions, and the existence of resistance movements justified staying in refugee camps that would gradually become poor neighbourhoods and shanty towns. With the loss of these two justifications for
their existence, refugee camps were plunged into states of abject
misery and despair. This is especially true of the Lebanese camps that
turned into slums. What is a refugee camp in an Arab state if it is
prevented from participating in the liberation struggle and there is no
hope of return on the horizon?

No attention has been paid to what became of the Palestinian
camps, having once formed the epicentre of the militant struggle,
after the decline of the resistance factions. It is important to mention
here that, with the exodus of the PLO from Jordan in 1970 and
Lebanon in 1982, Palestinian resistance activity was banned in all the

Arab states. The 1982 Israeli war on Lebanon closed off the last avenues open to them.

The official Lebanese justification for perpetuating this misery is its declared opposition to permanent settling/naturalisation of Palestinian refugees (*Tawtien*), in Lebanon, ostensibly to keep the right of return alive. The latter part of that sentence has largely been forgotten. What remains is the firm ban on the naturalisation of Palestinian refugees and their descendants in Lebanon. So, Palestinian emigration from Lebanon is encouraged and the idea of their being naturalised elsewhere is neither rejected nor condemned.

In Syria, the refugee camps did not turn in to ghettos. They were integrated into the nearby cities and towns, yet encouraged to keep Palestinian memory and identity intact. The Palestinians were integrated in the social and economic life of the country and had the same rights as the Syrian citizens except the right to vote to the People's Assembly, which is not a real parliament in any case. The camps became vibrant cultural and political centres under an authoritarian regime that did not discriminate against Palestinians any more than it did against Syrians. Since 2011, the refugee camps, like the rest of the country, suffered the consequences of the regime's violent attempt to suppress the revolution, the degeneration of the revolution into civil war and the atrocities of both the regime and the extremist Islamist factions. During the 1990s, Syria entered peace negotiations with Israel on the basis of the "land for peace" formula. The two sides did not reach an agreement. Damascus demanded the full Israeli withdrawal to the pre-June 1967 borders, but the right of return for Palestinian refugees was not among its demands in the bilateral negotiations.

In Jordan, where Palestinian elites participated in building the kingdom before and after 1948, Palestinians have been granted citizenship and have reached high-ranking political positions including the post of prime minister. But things changed after the regime's military clash with the PLO in 1970. Amman still manoeuvres between maintaining equal rights in practice and constructing a Jordanian identity (which since 1970 became more and more East Jordanian) in that it discriminates against Palestinians in public sector jobs and government positions. The Palestinian citizens who served in the army and the security apparats before 1970 were purged, and since then the Jordanian military and police forces are recruited only from half of the population.

In October 1994, Jordan signed a permanent peace treaty with Israel. The terms did not cover the right of return for the Palestinians who live in Jordan. The matter was not even seriously raised during the negotiations. Nevertheless, Amman must insist on the right of return, both in theory and in domestic political discourse, because the alternative is to capitulate to the implementation of the full and equal citizenship principle, which would reopen issues of Jordanian identity, privileges and discrimination.

Be that as it may, what does the right of return mean in a country where the Palestinians are a nominal majority of its citizens and an integral part of its economy and social fabric? We are speaking of a country that once annexed the West Bank[1] without concern for such demographic issues as Jordanian vs Palestinian, simply because these identities had not existed as distinct, mutually exclusive affiliations. In both doctrine and attitude, this state did not originally consider the Jordanians and the Palestinians to be two peoples. The change occurred after September 1970, when tensions between armed factions of the PLO and the Jordanian army spiralled into a fierce military confrontation, which fell just short of turning into a civil war, and which ended with the PLO's expulsion from Jordan.

After the last front of armed resistance (Lebanon) was closed to the PLO in 1982, the movement's centre of gravity was forced to relocate to the interior. This would eventually lead to the popular uprisings against the Israeli occupation of the territories seized in 1967 (the two Intifadas). This occurred after Israel had crushed the resistance in the Lebanese camps and Arab countries had put an end to cross-border resistance activity. The Palestinian armed struggle could not defeat Israel, but it kept the Palestinian cause alive in the aftermath of the Nakba, and especially after the Arab defeat in 1967. It helped to mould a Palestinian political national entity and heat up the borders between Israel and frontline Arab states, thereby forestalling a peace process

---

[1] The West Bank became part of Jordan after the truce agreement in 1949 and was annexed formally on 24 April 1950.

that did not include the Palestinians. After being forced to relocate to Tunisia, out of reach of a direct avenue for armed resistance, the PLO started to appreciate the value of the political and civil struggle in the occupied territories (the last line of confrontation). It began to allocate much greater financial and organisational resources to those parts of Palestine where a whole society lives under occupation and armed struggle cannot be a main strategy.

The Intifadas were sparked by the occupation power policies of oppression, land confiscation and settlement building in the territories occupied in 1967 including East Jerusalem, but they also aimed to achieve the larger goal of obtaining recognition of the PLO and to counter attempts to sideline it in order to better be able to dictate political conditions. The PLO's position in the Arab world plummeted after Syria, Jordan and Lebanon were closed to Palestinian militant activity. The first Intifada came in time to help in the end of 1987. It did so by preserving the liberation struggle through sustained popular revolt and innovative strategies for grassroots organisation and mobilisation. It shattered the stereotypes of Israeli political culture and disrupted the normality of occupation. For the first time, it caused a de facto freeze in settlement activity. But the first Intifada came to an end after years of struggle with the emergence of epoch-making events, such as the collapse of the Soviet Union and the Iraqi occupation of Kuwait.

At this point the PLO began to seek Israeli and American recognition so that it could harvest some of the political achievements of the Intifada. This inaugurated a new phase in the history of the Palestinian national movement.

But it is crucial to bear in mind that the Palestinian liberation movement began as a refugee movement. This beginning consolidated the foundations of the modern Palestinian national identity and preserved it. The armed struggle was also instrumental in this process. It generated the national identity's patriotic vigour, dynamism and new symbols.

A refugee camp may be treated as a temporary state of limbo until the right of return has been achieved, or as the base, school and community of a resistance movement. If it is treated as neither this or that, it will, as mentioned above, degenerate into a pit of poverty and despair. This was the fate of many camps when horizons closed to the armed liberation struggle and the national project of return after the Oslo Accords. Then, the consequent slum culture gave rise to radical political modes of religiosity heretofore unknown in the camps. Many have left the camps for any country willing to provide a visa.

Avoiding this deterioration requires a plan for national resistance that includes the refugees. Unfortunately, it is all too clear that this subject has been deliberately ignored since the beginning of the "peace process" between the PLO and Israel. The subsequent neglect of the fate of the refugees of Lebanon and Iraq (and, more recently, Syria), as well as the apparent indifference to this on the part of Palestinian leaders and officials, marked a symbolic turning point that revealed the lack of a national Palestinian strategy that includes the camps and pays attention to their humanitarian conditions too. The foregoing helps explain why the refugee camps in Arab countries stand out in the solidarity demonstrations during popular protests and uprisings in Palestine; they insist on somehow belonging to, being affiliated with, the struggle in Palestine.

After the establishment of the PA in the framework of the Oslo Accords, the resultant Palestinian entity was bound by separate peace agreements with Israel that include provisions regulating the economy, civil life and security. The occupation itself and relentless Israeli settlement expansion have been reduced from themes of a liberation struggle to "areas of disagreement" to be settled sometime in an indefinite future by negotiations.

The problem is not that the PLO was recognised by Israel and the US as a representative of Palestinians within the Palestinian territories as a preliminary step towards the Oslo negotiations, but rather that it then turned its back on the refugees. It is impossible to sustain the demand for the right of return unless the refugees are allowed to play an active role in the national movement. Without them, the Palestinian question gets reduced to PA borders, the limits of its authority in the West Bank and Gaza, and the ongoing intra-Palestinian conflict over this fractured authority.

The Palestinian national liberation movement has made three historic mistakes since adopting the idea of establishing a Palestinian state:

1. Treating Israeli recognition of the PLO as a goal to be achieved by making political concessions (recognising Israel, condemning what Israel deems as terrorism, ending the Intifada)[2] before Israel recognises the rights of the Palestinian people or their statehood.
2. Agreeing to become an authority devoid of sovereignty under occupation while continuing negotiations as a hostage (a hostage to the negotiating process and to the occupation, and a hostage to the consequences of dedicating most of its energy at the international level to securing financial support for the PA, and to the vested interests of new social sectors that emerged under the new conditions created by an authority operating under the occupation).
3. Giving up not only the armed struggle, but also the civic and political struggle for the sake of a strategy entirely dependent on peace negotiations under US sponsorship.

Yasser Arafat's late realisation of this predicament led him to mutiny. After the attempt to almost literally hold him hostage in order to dictate the final status agreement to him, he evoked the liberation struggle to trigger the second Intifada in October 2000. He paid for that choice with his life. His successor, Mahmoud Abbas, disagreed with him. He thought that the solution was to proceed with the "peace process," in a consistent manner, to the very end. Unsurprisingly, it quickly became clear that the international system was quite happy to overlook the PA's repressive policies against its opponents, and with regard to administrative matters; as long as it remained politically "moderate," all would be forgiven. A little corruption is forgivable, politically speaking.

Instead of a move towards a unified strategy, a fateful split in the Palestinian ranks occurred under the PA. This was due, in part, to the effective abandonment of the PLO in exchange for limited authority under occupation. The power struggle this precipitated (as contemptible as this was, especially when carried out under the occupation) would not have been as definitive and destructive had it not been for the geographical separation between the West Bank

---

[2] That is how recognition of the PLO by Israel was to be reciprocated, according to Peres, one of the engineers of the Oslo Declaration of Principles. See: Shimon Peres, *No Room for Small Dreams* (Rishon LeZion: Yediot Ahronot & Hemed, 2018), p. 198.

and Gaza. It culminated in an as yet irreconcilable rift and split in governmental authority.

The Palestinian people faced an entirely new and unfamiliar situation after Oslo. They had not been divided during the era of the British Mandate when they lived under one political administrative unit. Nor were they divided after the Nakba thanks to the PLO's swift action to preserve the political unity of the Palestinian people. This PLO's unifying force lasted for decades despite Palestinians' geographical disunity and ideological and political pluralism, and despite the Arab governments' mingling in PLO affairs.

When Netanyahu came to power and decided to escalate settlement building in the occupied territories and actually disregarded the "peace process", and when Trump came to power and supported Israel's unilateral actions to create de facto realities on the ground, the PA, under Abbas, faced a strategic crisis, having abandoned all alternatives to the "peace process."

In the context of the bizarre peace process between occupier and occupied, people were penned into the ghettos of Gaza and the West Bank and walls were erected to hide their presence. It was as though they were a foreign body in their own land. In this peculiar case, however, it is the foreign body that is rejecting the host, not the other way around. Something much more dangerous was emerging than the "Bantustanisation" that some opponents of Oslo (including the author) had predicted.

The Rupture

When Palestinians were allowed to go to the ballot box in the 2006 general elections, it was within the broader context of ongoing American pressure on its regional Arab allies to reform domestic governance. A Hamas government was elected. Although it rejected the Oslo agreements according to which the PA was established and the elections were conducted, this did not stop it from taking part in the polls then assuming power in the Oslo framework, while continuing to project itself as a resistance movement under occupation. The Hamas-led PA government opposed negotiations. But in order to stay in a power structure that was produced in the negotiations framework, they did not object to the PA president, Mahmoud Abbas, continuing to negotiate. The government itself did not negotiate, but nor was it able to make the refusal to negotiate binding on others.

Soon afterwards, Israel imposed a crippling and illegal blockade of Gaza as a means to overturn the 2006 election results. The Hamas-led government then stated that it was willing to negotiate although it would not compromise on certain "non-negotiable principles". This triggered a debate over the difference between "respecting" and "accepting" the agreements the PLO signed with Israel.

The Mecca Agreement (February 2007) between Fatah and Hamas created a national unity government that collapsed after political infighting in June 2007. Hamas seized power in Gaza and Fatah did the same in the West Bank. Egypt joined the Israeli blockade of Gaza, purportedly on the pretext that the Hamas-controlled government is not the legitimate Palestinian authority and accusing it of failing to secure the Gaza side of the border with Egypt.

The various Palestinian-Palestinian reconciliation efforts, proposals and framework agreements that followed posed questions like: how can an armed movement that fights the Israeli occupation be united with a movement that is committed to coordinating with Israel on security matters? How can their respective security apparatuses be united under one authority? Do such different political organisations give up authority for the sake of unity? The split between the political authorities in the West Bank and Gaza still continues with no reconciliation in sight, despite the efforts towards this end since 2007. It sometimes seems as if the never-ending "reconciliation process" has been substituted for the never-ending "peace process".

When Hamas joined the PA without accepting the political accord that established the PA, many assumed that Hamas intended to play the same game with the current negotiator with Israel (the Palestinian president) that Yasser Arafat, as PLO leader, had once played with the official Palestinian delegation in Madrid. Arafat constantly undermined the negotiations until Israel understood that it had to deal with the PLO instead and that it had to recognise Arafat. The result was—as mentioned above—that recognition itself became a subject of negotiation, an Israeli "concession" that required many more concessions from the Palestinian side first. Israeli recognition of the PLO was the sole "achievement" of the shift from Madrid to Oslo. Although PLO leadership got what it wanted, recognition proved to be a poisoned chalice: the conditions attached effectively dismantled the PLO and voided it of all substance. The Palestinian people have paid the price.

Does Hamas also seek recognition by Israel? What political price would it have to pay for this? This may seem far-fetched, but it certainly is seeking American and European recognition and, after the war of May 2021, it seems closer to, at least, de facto international recognition. Hamas, in its bid for power, played both resistance movement and party politics. It seized the opportunity of the 2006 legislative assembly elections and won. Then it demanded its share in power, but without first paying the price of accepting the conditions of the Oslo Accords. It wanted a share of the pie, but none of the costs. The price to be paid to the Israelis had to be borne by Fatah alone. This was an arrangement Fatah had never agreed to. According to Fatah, Hamas should share the costs, which include stopping armed operations and joining coordination with Israel. On the other hand, in taking on its new administrative responsibilities, Hamas has changed, perhaps in spite of itself. The erstwhile militant resistance movement now finds itself in a situation in which just managing to secure essential provisions for the people under its jurisdiction is a major achievement.

The political struggle to end the blockade of Gaza under Hamas rule has taken the place of militant resistance, but this still required occasional armed resistance which always ran the risk of escalating into an Israeli war on Gaza. This was a step backwards. It is the price Hamas paid for agreeing to act as a government under a continuing occupation. The positive outcomes are that Hamas asked to join the PLO, which it had previously refused to recognise; it finally agreed to raise the Palestinian flag, after years of adhering to an Islamist anti-national political ideology and attitude; and it changed its poorly written covenant in 2017 to remove the anti-Jewish language.

The eruption of civil unrest and infighting between the two major political forces, Hamas and Fatah, led to the unravelling of the national unity government and an intensification of the Gaza blockade, which continues today. It also led to lifting of the blockade of the West Bank, albeit with political conditions attached and the constantly looming threat of a reimposition of the blockade should Israel so decide.

At this point, in the media, the internal Palestinian conflict started to overshadow the main conflict. It seemed that national unity and a genuine, unified national project would remain out of reach and that the focus had shifted to a constant "servicing" of talks between the two factions in order to keep the Palestinians from internecine confrontation.

Gaza Is Not Just an Occupied Territory

To exclusively think of Gaza as a territory occupied in 1967 contradicts history and demographics. Nor is it possible to understand the current conflict within Gaza only as a conflict between rival political factions vying for power.

The truth is that Gaza is an enormous refugee camp—a prison; indeed, a concentration camp.[3] Denying its true nature is to agree that the Palestinians are one "side" in a Palestinian-Israeli "conflict," that the Palestinian problem began in 1967 and that this vast refugee camp is no more than an occupied territory that awaited Sharon's unilateral decision to militarily withdraw from it in 2005. Not only does this view hamper a just solution to the question of Palestine, it deliberately avoids one.

Moreover, even according to the wording of UN Security Council Resolution 242, Gaza is not a country that can be considered freed from occupation since 2005. It is a part of the Palestinian territories occupied in 1967 which include East Jerusalem along with the West Bank.

---

[3] The Gaza Strip is a completely walled-in area 27 miles (45 km) long and 3–7 miles (5–12 km) wide. It is one of the most densely populated places on earth, with around 1.9 million Palestinians living there. The overwhelming majority of people in Gaza are refugees from within Palestine. Almost three-quarters of Gazans (nearly 1.4 million) are refugees expelled in the 1948 war from what is now Israel, or their descendants. Today, people in the Gaza Strip are struggling with multiple living and economic difficulties, with 80% of the population dependent on international assistance and an average unemployment rate of over 50%, one of the highest in the world. See: "Where We Work," *UN Relief and Works Agency for Palestine Refugees in the Near East (UNRWA)*, accessed at: https://bit.ly/2QIZN8t

In the last war on Gaza, in May 2021, Hamas reminded the world that it is a part of occupied Palestine. Its actions said that if Jerusalem is occupied then this means that Gaza is not freed from occupation and, therefore, Hamas has the right to participate in the resistance against occupation. One may not accept the movement's rhetoric and its tactics, but this statement is correct in principle.

The Palestinians conduct their daily lives under two governing authorities in addition to the occupation. The incumbents in both authorities see it in their interests to perpetuate their rule. For contingents of the PA in Ramallah, this entails serving the security of Israel. But this did not make the contradictions with Israeli go away. The result is that, in this context in which the PA seeks to use its position to acquire more autonomy and land, and eventually leverage itself into a state, that language of justice is superseded by a rights-based discourse; the right to movement, the right to trade, the right to receive aid and so on. Indeed, protecting the right to basic everyday necessities in Gaza, for example, consumes most of the Hamas political energy.

On 22 May 2021, the PA launched the process to hold Palestinian legislative elections, the first since 2006. The PA then postponed the elections indefinitely. They were supposed to lead to political unity. Under normal circumstances, elections are conducted in the framework of an existing unity embodied in a governing entity that serves as the umbrella under which elections are held. Elections do not *produce* unity. The PA officials, themselves, do not believe in democratic accountability and they actually believe that Palestinian society "isn't ready" for democracy.[4] They needed the 2021 elections to strengthen their relations with Europe and the US under the post-Trump White House, and they hoped that the elections would cement the status quo.

As for the Western nations, they betrayed the hollow nature of their commitment to, or at least "wish" for, the democratisation of the Arab region when not only did they reject the validity of the 2006

---

[4] According to interviews with high-ranking officials of the security apparatus conducted by Dana El Kurd. See: Dana El Kurd, *Polarized and Demobilized: Legacies of Authoritarianism in Palestine* (New York: Oxford University Press, 2020), pp. 53, 64.

election results,[5] they also joined forces with Israel to impose the blockade on Gaza. The Gazans have suffered for 14 years under this siege, during which time Hamas consolidated its grip on power over this narrow, heavily populated strip of land (which was already extremely poor and deprived even before the blockade).

Despite the plans outlined in the Mecca Agreement to achieve national unity and rebuild the PLO, it was clear that national unity was not part of the "peace process" strategy either at the Palestinian or regional level. In the latter context, it did not fit with the growing trend, since 2001, in which "moderate" regional powers demonstrate their readiness to align with Israel against "extremist" counterparts. The "moderate" bloc could barely stomach Yasser Arafat (who was never a part of the radical bloc) in his last days, and one could almost hear a sigh of relief at his death. In like manner, after the Mecca Agreement, the bloc was unable to countenance Palestinian national unity unless it acceded to the "peace process" with Israel and renounced the strategy of resistance. On the other hand, the "moderates" would have been quite happy if the next election results were rigged to ensure the return of the PA to Fatah.

The hardening of this new political reality reflected the drastic realignment that had occurred in the Arab world. Early signs of this new reality appeared in the responses of the authoritarian Arab regimes (aka "the moderates") to the siege of the Mukata'a (Arafat's headquarters in Ramallah) by Israeli troops in 2003–4 and to the Lebanon War in 2006. It is equally visible in their attitudes towards the ongoing blockade of Gaza and towards the successive wars on Gaza in 2008–9, 2012, 2014 and 2021.

The rivalries between the Arab regional axes in the fifties and sixties had never experienced anything of this sort. Even at the height of Egyptian-Saudi tensions in the Nasser era, there existed an unquestioned understanding of Arab solidarity. It was taken for granted that normalisation with Israel was unthinkable in the absence of a just solution to the Palestinian question. Today's blocs have drawn a question mark above these previously inviolable principles. This is a new reality in the Arab world. It is one that has tempted the US and Israel

---

[5] The elections had been internationally supervised and deemed legitimate.

to pursue a strategy based on cooperation with the "moderate" Arab states which are increasingly open to the idea that their real enemies are Iran and the popular resistance movements.

An Arab Peace Initiative

In 2002, the Arab League Beirut Summit endorsed a peace initiative that has been reiterated in several Arab League summits since then. The initiative conveyed the consensus of Arab states on a comprehensive and lasting peace with Israel in exchange for the latter's withdrawal to the pre-June 1967 orders and the establishment of a Palestinian state. Israel rejected it out of hand, and, according to the logic of Israeli and American foreign policymakers, the Arab Peace Initiative was an expression of a non-binding Arab position.

While Saudi Arabia was under intense scrutiny following the 9/11 terrorist attacks in 2001, then Crown Prince Abdullah of Saudi Arabia gave an interview to New York Times journalist Thomas Friedman in which he proposed "full withdrawal from all the occupied territories [...] for full normalisation of relations." Friedman took pride in being the first to bring Crown Prince Abdullah's Arab Peace Initiative to the public.[6]

---

[6] Marwan Mu'asher, who was at the time the Jordanian ambassador to the US, suggested that Friedman got the idea of the Arab Peace Initiative from a conversation they had over breakfast on 28 November 2001, when Mu'asher told Friedman about a similar idea King Hussein of Jordan had developed in 1998. Mu'asher pointed out that he discussed "the king's idea of collective peace and security guarantees for Israel in return for total withdrawal for all Arab occupied land and a solution to the refugee problem" with Friedman. The latter published a column in The New York Times on 6 February 2002, suggesting that "the twenty-two members of the Arab League offer Israel full diplomatic relations, normalized trade, and security guarantees in return for Israel's total withdrawal to the June 4, 1967, lines." Less than a week later, Friedman was in Riyadh talking to Abdullah. On 17 February 2002, The New York Times published Friedman's interview with Crown Prince Abdullah of Saudi Arabia, during which Friedman presented the idea to him. Crown Prince Abdullah was very concerned about his country's image in the US at the time. Marwan Muasher, *The Arab Center: The Promise of Moderation* (New Haven: Yale University Press, 2008), p. 116; Thomas L. Friedman, "Dear Arab League," *The New York Times*, 6 February 2002, accessed at: https://nyti.ms/3g55LcN; Thomas L. Friedman, "An

Two decades later, the same American columnist was overjoyed when Arab states normalised their bilateral relationships with Israel outside the framework of the initiative and in the absence of a just solution for Palestine. Friedman supports whatever he thinks is beneficial for Israel at any given moment. In the grips of his enthusiasm over the normalisation agreement signed between Israel and the UAE, he called on Saudi Arabia to join in.[7]

Instead of holding to UN General Assembly and Security Council resolutions, Crown Prince Abdullah, who aimed at improving his country's image after the 9/11 terrorist attacks, produced a peace initiative with its frame of reference: a non-binding Arab diplomatic initiative. Israel rejected it, but at the same time, because of its non-binding nature, viewed it as "deserving encouragement" and, of course, in need of development by more Arab initiatives with further compromises. Political concessions made free-of-charge invite demands for more concessions. So naturally the US congratulated the Arabs for having come up with such an initiative and then ignored its substance.

Israel, which has no official peace plans of its own and has never agreed to an international resolution or an American peace initiative,[8] snubbed the Arab Peace Initiative that offered it a chance for peace with the whole Arab world. Instead, it wanted more political concessions and more diplomatic initiatives. It would not be disappointed. In the last year of the Trump era (2020), a logic akin to the thinking that originally produced that initiative led certain countries to forsake it and normalise their relationships with Israel without stipulating any conditions. The Arab Peace Initiative thus became non-binding, even for the Arab states that launched it.

The view that the Arab Peace Initiative reflects a non-binding stance concludes that the initiative was not a genuine compromise but

---

Intriguing Signal From the Saudi Crown Prince," *The New York Times*, 17 February 2002, accessed at: https://nyti.ms/3wTR03j

[7] Thomas L. Friedman, "A Geopolitical Earthquake Just Hit the Mideast," *The New York Times*, 13 August 2020, accessed at: https://nyti.ms/3tLLcaW; Thomas L. Friedman, "Jumping Jehoshaphat! Have You Seen How Many Israelis Just Visited the U.A.E.?," *The New York Times*, 2 March 2021, accessed at: https://nyti.ms/32J7Vsr

[8] This will be analysed in depth in Chapter 7.

an Arab "position" that has not been fully formed and needs further discussion and amendment. In fact, the reduction of the Arab Peace Initiative to a "position" that requires further discussion and amendment is the fate of any peace initiative under power balances so skewed against the proposing party that it is constantly forced to retreat. This is why, in most cases, peace initiatives are either mediated through a neutral third party (in which case the adversaries will stick to their positions until a compromise can be negotiated) or initiated by the victor in a conflict (in which case the initiative becomes an avenue to consolidating the winner's political gains). Alternatively, peace initiatives can simply be put forward by actors powerful enough to impose them.

In the event that the party proposing the initiative (i.e., the Arab states) is the weaker party, there is no feasible way for them to enforce a just solution in a negotiated agreement. This is not "structurally" ordained. It has to do with political will, internal rivalries, dependence on external powers like the US and the inability and/or unwillingness to coordinate positions and common interests in the pursuit of other joint concerns (such as the relationship with Iran).

The Arab Peace Initiative was welcomed in American and European circles because it signalled the readiness of all Arab countries to normalise relations with Israel in line with the "land for peace" principle. It was not long before Western congratulations to the Arabs became demands for normalisation to be implemented in various ways before a solution to the Palestinian question could be attained. This, they said, would "encourage" Israel to take the "risk of peace". John Kerry, when he served as the chairman of the Committee for Foreign Affairs, expressed this view in a speech to Congress after his visit to the Arab region in 2009.[9] He blamed the Bush administration for not doing enough to encourage the Arab Initiative or take advantage of it. However, when he became Obama's secretary of state a few years later, neither he nor the president did very much either.

---

[9] Lecture delivered at the Saban Centre for Middle East Policy at the Brookings Institution in Washington on 4 March 2009. John Kerry, "Restoring Leadership in the Middle East: A Regional Approach to Peace," Martin Indyk (intro.), *The Brookings Institution (Washington, DC)*, 4 March 2009, accessed at: https://brook.gs/32d5hd6

Western advisers, ex-politicians and journalists, who come up with ideas to the Arab regimes, some of whom originate from Zionist liberal circles (American or Israeli), tell Arab regimes seeking advice on image enhancement that such gestures towards normalisation would improve their image in the West, and calm "Israeli fears" over Arab intentions.

According to their argument, Israel is not opposed to a just solution; it is simply "afraid" that the Arabs wish to destroy it. The Israeli leadership is not racist, arrogant or power-drunk; it is just anxious and worried. What the Arab regimes need to do, therefore, is to adopt conciliatory attitudes to dispel the Israeli anxieties. So argued the advisors who convinced the Saudis to produce this sort of initiative in order to improve their public image.

Just as we have previously encountered Arab "moderation," we have encountered this Israeli fear before. It is the same fear that led the Zionist leadership to drive the Palestinians into the desert, to oppress the people under its occupation and to pulverise the Beqaa Valley and the villages of southern Lebanon with cluster bombs. The Palestinians are also expected to appreciate Israel's "understandable" fear of the right of return, of returning East Jerusalem and of withdrawing to the pre-1967 borders. Doubtlessly, the fear factor does play a role in current Israeli decision-making, but it is mostly the fear of losing the next elections and the fear that any meaningful concessions would cause Israel's so-called national unity to crumble. In fact, the real problem is Israeli hubris (as discussed earlier). When Israel actually feared war (I do not mean existential fear, but rational fear that facilitates pragmatic calculations), it usually made concessions if the other side was ready to accept them, as was the case of the Sinai withdrawal to avoid another war with Egypt. The withdrawal from Lebanon was also due to strategic calculations in which fear or cost in this case played a role. Even the recognition of the PLO and the Oslo Accords were a result of the fear inspired by the Intifada. Israeli acceptance of the PLO as a "partner for peace" stemmed from the fear of a "worse" alternative.

As noted above, Arab states behind the Saudi-led initiative were ready to modify it or even give it up in favour of other peace initiatives. To this end, they have tripped over themselves to turn reality on its head. Take, for example, the implausible transformation of Ariel Sharon into unwitting peacemaker when Arab leaders at Sharm el-Sheikh[10] informed him that his plan to disengage from Gaza was a huge step forward in the implementation of the George W. Bush roadmap for peace. He was certainly surprised. Earlier, Sharon had publicly stated that that his unilateral withdrawal was intended to scupper the Bush roadmap! He wanted to offload Gaza without having to address the other items on the roadmap that was accepted by Arafat and rejected by Sharon.

It must be acknowledged that, as things stand, the chance of reaching a settlement with Israel that would be acceptable to both Israel and the Arabs has dwindled to the point that only someone with no grip on reality could possibly believe that such a thing remains an option. Israel has even less motivation to reach such a settlement today, after the threat of full-scale war was eliminated by Egypt's separate peace and after some Arab countries (the UAE, Bahrain, Sudan and Morocco), which had never even been at war with Israel, abandoned the Arab Peace Initiative in favour of signing bilateral peace agreements with Israel without exacting any political concessions of any kind. The UAE and Bahrain have long been coordinating with Israel on security matters and regional issues, even lobbying the US together for the same "causes". So, for them, in any case, normalisation just made that pre-existing relationship official.

This is all part of an unfolding trend in which Arab regimes are acting on the advice that a very specific version of "realism" is the ultimate political mode and culture they should strive for. Being "realistic" in this sense means pragmatism in keeping regime interests, people's interests, and state interests separate, and unquestioningly accepting Israel, America's political hegemony in Israel and the myth of Israel's hegemony in America.

There is a strong and unyielding consensus across the Israeli political spectrum on the refusal to withdraw to the pre-1967 borders (including from East Jerusalem) and to dismantle most of the Israeli

---

[10] On 8 February 2005, a summit held in Sharm El-Sheikh, Egypt, was attended by the Egyptian President Hosni Mubarak, King Abdullah II of Jordan, Israeli Prime Minister Ariel Sharon, and President of the Palestinian Authority Mahmoud Abbas.

settlements, which the state is determined to annex. There is no equivalent official Arab consensus mirroring the Israeli consensus, especially after it became clear that the Arab Peace Initiative was not meant for Palestine and became moribund. But Arab governments can only be so flexible. It goes without saying that if they were to go for a proposition that complied with the adamant Israeli No's, it would never be accepted by Palestinian or Arab public opinion. Were they to cite the frequently trumpeted argument that the right of return is the main obstacle to a peace settlement, a formula that excluded the demand for the right of return would still come up against the Israeli refusal to budge. The Israeli red lines were entrenched in the course of the domestic party politics, political manoeuvring and demagoguery of Israeli politicians as Israeli society drifted further and further to the right. The politicians that made them are not willing to deal with them. Indeed, they are unable to deal with them unless considerable external pressure is applied. Effective Arab and Palestinian pressure is the very antithesis of begging for Israeli acceptance of so-called Arab moderation.

To speculate over possible techniques the Arabs could employ to bypass the Israeli No's is another exercise in self-delusion that began with the Oslo process and continues today. Naturally, all Arab attempts to impress Israel will be greeted with Israeli pats on the back. But Israel never accepts any of the substance of the Arab attempts it encourages. It makes deliberately vague commitments to a path towards peace and normalisation, with the understanding that this can only happen through negotiations and that those negotiations must be carried out without preconditions and under American sponsorship.[11]

Despite Israel's flat rejection of the Arab Peace Initiative, the Arab countries continued to push it, going so far as pay for a publicity campaign in the Israeli press to promote it among the Israeli public.[12]

---

[11] The recent normalisation between Israel and the UAE, Bahrain, Morocco and Sudan (the latter two should be distinguished from the first two because they were blackmailed into signing treaties) took place through American mediation (Trump diktats, to be precise) without involving negotiations.

[12] In 2008, a paid publicity campaign was launched, with advertisements in *Yediot Ahronot,*

FROM LIBERATION STRUGGLE TO BORDER DISPUTE

It is unclear what trying to persuade Israel of this initiative could possibly mean after it had categorically rejected its basic components. How can a state be persuaded to give something up that it obtained and kept through sheer force and is unwilling to renounce, despite having no right to it? What does "right" mean when the language of negotiations is the language of balances of power and dictates by force or the "might makes right" principle, which comes under the heading of "political realism"? That the Arabs remained committed to a peace proposal that they had offered to Israel and that Israel turned down is incomprehensible. This behaviour and the aims behind it are totally divorced from reality. The proof of this came later with the next application of the political logic exercised by those eager to shed the "burden" of the Palestinian cause (a burden they had never shouldered to begin with) in order to publicly align with Israel. The four aforementioned states proved that Israel was right (from its perspective, of course) to reject the Arab Initiative and wait. It fully understood the mentality behind the Initiative. It had no fears that needed allaying.

Israel is not afraid and it is not ready to pay a price for peace with Arab states, with whom a de facto peace already exists. The shelf life of the fear thesis expired ages ago. There is no threat of war whether from Arab countries or the PA. It is the Arab regimes that are afraid and seeking American protection; some even seem ready to accept Israeli protection.

If Israel were truly afraid and genuinely seeking Arab recognition (in addition to security, safety and so on), then peace should be one of Israel's top priorities. So why did Israel not seize the opportunity presented by the Arab Peace Initiative? This is the logical approach to

Maariv and *Haaretz*, three major Israeli newspapers, to promote the Arab Peace Initiative and persuade the Israeli public to accept it. The advertisements included a Hebrew text saying, "Fifty-seven Arab and Muslim countries will establish diplomatic relations with Israel in exchange for a full peace accord and the end of the occupation." Additionally, the full text of the Arab Initiative, complete with its seven points, was published in Israeli newspapers. Similar campaigns were carried out in Palestinian and European newspapers. See: "The Advert for the Arab Peace Plan That Appeared in Israel's Hebrew Press," *BBC News*, 20 November 2008, accessed at: https://bbc.in/39OfW12; "Arab Plan Explained in Hebrew Ads," *BBC News*, 20 November 2008, accessed at: https://bbc.in/38Ldh6Z

vindications of Israeli behaviour or ploys to get the Arabs to make more concessions. Is it not strange that Israel has never initiated a serious peace proposal or made the slightest effort to demonstrate good faith? Yet there are dozens of areas where it could do so. It could halt settlement construction and dismantle the ones Israel itself calls illegal settlements, as it promised. It could put an end to targeted political assassinations. It could abide by the Hague's International Court of Justice ruling[13] on the matter of the separation wall, which is only one of the apartheid walls erected in Palestine. It could announce its intention to withdraw to the 1967 borders in exchange for peace. It could rescind the laws annexing the Golan Heights and Jerusalem. Any of these actions would provide evidence that Israel is truly seeking peace.

There is nothing to be negotiated between colonisers and a people under occupation. If there are to be negotiations, they should only occur preparatory to the implementation of an explicit decision on the part of the occupying power to fully withdraw from the occupied territories and recognise the right of self-determination of the people under occupation. Ignoring this principle leads to unbalanced negotiations between "two sides". This is the language used to frame the occupation today that already took an apartheid shape. We constantly hear of "two sides" in a "dispute" in which both "sides" claim "rights of the same land" and of both having their respective "moderates" and

---

[13] An International Court of Justice advisory opinion on the separation wall's construction was issued in 2004 and was subsequently adopted by the UN General Assembly. It called on Israel to cease construction of the separation wall, dismantle sections already completed and repeal related legislative measures. It also obliged Israel to pay reparations for damage caused by the construction of the wall. Israel is, accordingly, obliged to return the land, orchards, olive groves and other immovable property it seized from any natural or legal persons in order to construct the wall in the Occupied Palestinian Territories. If restitution is materially impossible, Israel has an obligation to pay compensation to the affected persons. The Court also maintained that Israel has, in accordance with the applicable rules of international law, an obligation to compensate all natural or legal persons who have suffered any form of material damage as a result of the wall's construction. See: "Advisory opinion of the International Court of Justice on the Legal Consequences of the Construction of a Wall in the Occupied Palestinian Territory," *United Nations*, accessed at: https://bit.ly/32IOVdD

"extremists". This is a gross misrepresentation of the problem. It is for this reason that liberation movements historically tended to state that their purpose is to resist the occupying power, not to negotiate with it. In cases of prolonged occupation, ways had to be found to reconcile the management of the everyday life of the people under occupation with the ongoing struggle which they sustained until the occupying power finally announced its willingness to withdraw. At that point it became legitimate to negotiate over how the withdrawal would be managed (or how an apartheid regime is dismantled).

6

THE ROAD TO NOWHERE

This chapter will discuss the process leading to the PA's establishment and the marginalisation of the liberation movement in favour of the Trump-Netanyahu deal to be discussed in Part Two. It will also include some concluding remarks for Part One.

The PLO's most significant achievement was creating a political body that represents the Palestinian people as a collective—the PLO was the organised expression of the Palestinian entity and entitativity. Against all odds, it was also able to achieve several successes in the international sphere; from formal recognition of the PLO by more countries than had diplomatic relations with Israel at one point, to major UN resolutions in support of the Palestinian people and their cause, to admission to the UN as a non-member observer. Table 6.1 lists important resolutions that strengthened Palestinian entitativity over time.

The achievements of the first Intifada are not easy to evaluate briefly. It forced the Palestinian issue on the international public and official agenda and redrew the image of Israel, putting paid to notion of "victim" and driving home its nature as an occupation power that maltreats the occupied people under its authority. That the Israeli army was turned into a riot police to suppress civil protests split Israeli society during the first Intifada and severely reduced public morale.

PALESTINE

Table 6.1: UN Resolutions Reflecting PLO Achievements Related to Palestinian Entitativity

Item	Resolution Number	Organ	Date
The Palestinian people's right to self-determination is recognised.	2672	General Assembly	8/12/1970
The PLO is invited to participate in General Assembly debates.	3210	General Assembly	14/10/1974
The inalienable rights of the Palestinian people in Palestine are reaffirmed.	3236	General Assembly	22/11/1974
The PLO is granted observer status.	3237	General Assembly	22/11/1974
Zionism is determined a form of racism.	3379	General Assembly	10/11/1975
The PLO is invited to participate in efforts to achieve peace in the Middle East.	3375	General Assembly	10/11/1975
The settlements are determined to have no legal validity, and a Commission is established to examine the situation relating to the settlements.	446	Security Council	22/3/1979
Israel is called upon to dismantle existing settlements and to cease the construction and planning of settlements. (This resolution was passed unanimously.)	465	Security Council	1/3/1980
The Palestinian people's right to self-determination is supported.	38/58	General Assembly	13/12/1983
It is reaffirmed that the Permanent Observer Mission of the PLO to the United Nations is covered by the provisions of the Agreement between the United Nations and the United States of America regarding the Headquarters of the United Nations.	42/229	General Assembly	12/3/1988

The PLO is deemed entitled to have its communications circulated as official documents.	43/160	General Assembly	9/12/1988
It is decided that the designation "Palestine" should be used instead of "Palestine Liberation Organization" in the United Nations system.	43/177	General Assembly	15/12/1988
It is reaffirmed that illegal Israeli actions in the Occupied Territories cannot be recognised.	ES-10/3	General Assembly	15/7/1997
Palestine is accorded the status of non-member observer state in the United Nations.	67/19	General Assembly	29/11/2012
It is decided that the flags of non-member observer states at the United Nations, including the Palestinian flag, shall be raised at Headquarters and United Nations offices.	69/320	General Assembly	10/9/2015

Source: Prepared by the researcher after consulting the United Nations General Assembly and Security Council resolutions on Palestine.

Only some of the damage it caused to the Israeli macro-economy during the first Intifada (1987–93) will be detailed here. The Palestinians carried out several forms of economic resistance activities, including strikes, boycotts of Israeli goods and refusal to pay taxes to military occupation authorities. A high percentage of Palestinian workers from the occupied territories who worked on settlements in the territories or in Israel itself (in construction, agriculture, and factories among other sectors) did not report to work for many reasons, from the general strikes to the curfews. Israeli employers suffered a severe manpower shortage as a result. To compensate for loss of income, the Palestinians revived self-sustenance projects and relied on household economies. Although the economy of the Palestinians in the occupied territories was adversely affected, the main aim was to raise the cost of Israeli occupation. As economic studies show, the Intifada cost Israel millions of dollars a day in increased military expenditure, a decline in investments, losses in trade, increased unemployment, a decrease of the purchasing power of Israelis, and a drop in tourism. The labour-intensive agricultural and construction sectors were the hardest hit. Israeli sources' estimates of the damage to Israel's economy as a result of the Intifada varied, depending on the source, with some trying to underplay the damage to others that assessed it as "traumatic".[1]

According to World Bank data, unemployment rates almost doubled from 6.33 per cent in 1985 to 12.24 per cent in 1990, then increased further to a high of 14.08 per cent in 1992.[2] The foreign direct investment (FDI) rate declined from 0.55 per cent to 0.25 per cent of GDP in 1987–90.[3] Israel's annual GDP per capita growth plunged from 5.42 per cent in 1987 to 1.22 per cent and–1.12 per cent in 1988 and 1989, respectively. In 1990–3, the GDP per capita growth rate fluctuated sharply, with a high of 4.10 per cent in 1992 and a low of 1.39 per cent in 1993.[4] A similar trend applies to Israel's GDP growth rate, gross national income (GNI) growth rate and GNI per capita growth rate in the same period.[5] The slight increase in growth was partially attributed to the large waves of Jewish immigration to Israel at the time, mainly from the former Soviet Union, which contributed to the housing boom and stimulated Israeli eco-

---

[1] See: Andrew Rigby, *The Palestinian Intifada Revisited* (Sparsnäs, Sweden: Irene Publishing, 2015); Judith Gabriel, "The Economic Side of the Intifadah," *Journal of Palestine Studies*, vol. 18, no. 1, Special Issue: Palestine 1948 (Autumn 1988), pp. 198–213; Sébastien Dessus, "A Palestinian Growth History, 1968–2000," *Journal of Economic Integration*, vol. 19, no. 3 (September 2004), pp. 447–69.

[2] "Unemployment, total (% of total labor force) (national estimate)—Israel," *The World Bank*, accessed at: https://bit.ly/3xLDG2q

[3] "Foreign direct investment, net inflows (% of GDP)—Israel," *The World Bank*, accessed at: https://bit.ly/3vEaI2w

[4] "GDP per capita growth (annual %)—Israel," *The World Bank*, accessed at: https://bit.ly/3xAYp8O

[5] "GDP growth (annual %)—Israel," *The World Bank*, accessed at: https://bit.ly/3xG72PB; "GNI growth (annual %)—Israel," *The World Bank*, accessed at: https://bit.ly/3eO7dj7; "GNI per capita growth (annual %)—Israel," *The World Bank*, accessed at: https://bit.ly/3ti1wiC

nomic activity. The total number of Jewish immigrants from the former Soviet Union to Israel increased from 12,900 immigrants in 1989, to 185,200 in 1990 and 147,800 in 1991.[6] However, the "economic" boom created by greater immigration was only "temporary and accompanied with strong inflation" in both Israel and the occupied Palestinian territories.[7]

The second Intifada (2000–3) erupted in a year of high economic growth in Israel. According to the data, the second Intifada, like the first, exacted a high toll on the Israeli economy: billions of dollars of additional security spending, declining investment rates, a drop in tourism and high unemployment. Unemployment in 2003 climbed to 13.51 per cent, the second highest rate since 1969 (the earliest official data available). The highest recorded rate was in 1992 after the first Intifada.[8] After a significant increase in FDI rates in the years characterised by rising hopes for peace after the Oslo accords (from 1.50 per cent in 1998 to 6.08 per cent in 2000), FDI rates plummeted to lows of 1.35 per cent in 2001 and 1.31 per cent in 2002.[9] Israel's GDP growth rates declined from 7.46 per cent in 2000, to only 0.12 percent and –0.01 per cent in 2001 and 2002.[10] Israel's GDP per capita growth rate, GNI growth rate and GNI per capita growth rate experienced the same downward trend in the same period.[11] The Bank of Israel described the 2 years following the breakout of the second Intifada as "the longest in Israel's history" due the heavy economic recession.[12]

Signing the Oslo Accords (1993–5), especially the 1994 economic protocol (the Paris Protocol), benefitted the Israeli economy, which

---

[6] Mark Tolts, "Demography of the Contemporary Russian-Speaking Jewish Diaspora," in: Zvi Gitelman (ed.), *The New Jewish DiasporHead A: Russian-Speaking Immigrants in the United States, Israel, and Germany* (New Brunswick, New Jersey, and London: Rutgers University Press, 2016), pp. 23–4.

[7] Dessus, pp. 453–4.

[8] "Unemployment, total (% of total labor force) (national estimate)—Israel."

[9] "Foreign direct investment, net inflows (% of GDP)—Israel."

[10] "GDP growth (annual %)—Israel."

[11] "GDP per capita growth (annual %)—Israel;" "GNI growth (annual %)—Israel;" "GNI per capita growth (annual %)—Israel."

[12] Shlomo Swirski, "The Cost of Occupation: The Burden of the Israeli–Palestinian Conflict 2010 Report," *Adva Center* (June 2010), p. 13.

witnessed a renewed growth (increasing rates of GDP growth, GDP per capita growth, GNI growth, GNI per capita growth and FDI) and a drop in unemployment rates to 8.46 per cent by 1996.[13] Despite the Paris Protocol's declared aim of boosting Palestinian economic growth, improvements were, of course, less felt by the Palestinians. In the years following Oslo, the Palestinian economy still struggled due, on the one hand, to its structure and its subordinate relationships with the occupying power and with international aid and, on the other, to its chronically dysfunctional and unproductive public sector, which is dependent on the political objectives of international donors and Israeli domestic politics.[14]

The first Intifada, which sustained several years of broad and organised grassroots resistance that included numerous acts of civil disobedience, certainly did not fail. But it gradually subsided against the backdrop of massive geopolitical shifts that shook the world. The most far-reaching changes were the overhaul of the international

---

[13] "GDP growth (annual %)—Israel;" "GDP per capita growth (annual %)—Israel;" "GNI growth (annual %) Israel;" "GNI per capita growth (annual %)—Israel;" "Foreign direct investment, net inflows (% of GDP)—Israel;" "Unemployment, total (% of total labor force) (national estimate)—Israel."

[14] For more on the economic impacts of the Paris Protocol, see: Jeremy Wildeman & Alaa Tartir, "Can Oslo's Failed Aid Model Be Laid to Rest?," *Policy Brief*, al-Shabaka, 18 September 2013, accessed at: https://bit.ly/3yUnBYI; Alaa Tartir, Sam Bahour & Samer Abdelnour, "Defeating Dependency, Creating a Resistance Economy," *Policy Brief*, al-Shabaka, 13 February 2012, accessed at: https://bit.ly/3vKy6M8; Ibrahim Shikaki & Joanna Springer, "Building a Failed State: Palestine's Governance and Economy Delinked," *Policy Brief*, al-Shabaka, 21 April 2015, accessed at: https://bit.ly/2RaGyVT; Nur Arafeh, "Long Overdue: Alternatives to the Paris Protocol," *Policy Brief*, al-Shabaka, 27 February 2018, accessed at: https://bit.ly/3uEptRS; Nur Arafeh, Samia al-Botmeh & Leila Farsakh, "How Israeli Settlements Stifle Palestine's Economy," *Policy Brief*, al-Shabaka, 15 December 2015, accessed at: https://bit.ly/3p8zxS0; Khalil Nakhleh, "Oslo: Replacing Liberation with Economic Neo-Colonialism," *Commentary*, al-Shabaka, 10 April 2014, accessed at: https://bit.ly/3uEGdII; Ahmad El-Atrash, "Israel's Stranglehold on Area C: Development as Resistance," *Commentary*, al-Shabaka, 27 September 2018, accessed at: https://bit.ly/3g3kkgS; Tariq Dana, "The Palestinian Capitalists That Have Gone Too Far," *Policy Brief*, al-Shabaka, 14 January 2014, accessed at: https://bit.ly/3uCz0c3; Yara Hawari, "The Revival of People-to-People Projects: Relinquishing Israeli Accountability," *Policy Brief*, al-Shabaka, 6 April 2021, accessed at: https://bit.ly/3i8fJgb

THE ROAD TO NOWHERE

Figure 6.1

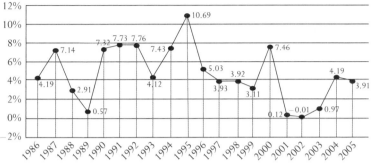

Israel's GDP growth (annual %) 1986–2005

Source: World Bank National Accounts data, and OECD National Accounts data files.

Figure 6.2

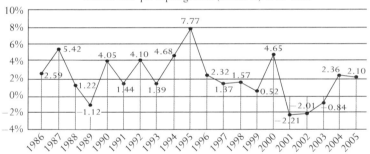

Istrael's GDP per capita growth (annual %) 1986–2005

Source: World Bank National Accounts data, and OECD National Accounts data files.

order that followed with the break-up of the Soviet Union and the collapse of its global system and the collapse of the Arab order, within which the PLO had flourished, after the Iraqi invasion of Kuwait.

It was precisely because of the first uprising's civil character, which had riveted international attention, that former President George H. W. Bush Sr. was compelled to address the Palestinian issue when he called on the Arab world to join an alliance against Iraq and lend Arab legitimacy to a war to liberate Kuwait. The Madrid Peace Conference

165

PALESTINE

Figure 6.3

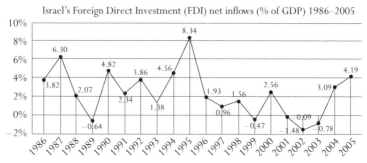

Israel's Foreign Direct Investment (FDI) net inflows (% of GDP) 1986–2005

Source: World Bank National Accounts data, and OECD National Accounts data files.

Figure 6.4

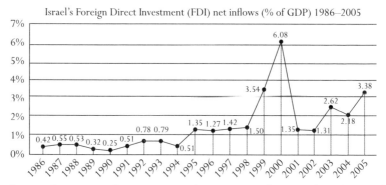

Israel's Foreign Direct Investment (FDI) net inflows (% of GDP) 1986–2005

Source: International Monetary Fund, International Financial Statistics and Balance of Payments database, World Bank, International Debt Statistics, and World Bank and OECD GDP estimates.

was held in 1991, just after the Kuwait war, and was attended by representatives of the West Bank and the Gaza Strip as part of a joint Palestinian-Jordanian delegation, which insisted on the PLO being the formal representative of the Palestinian people. It should be stressed that it was the Intifada that enabled the reinstatement of the PLO nearly a decade after the organisation had been driven from Lebanon and sidelined.

Israel would not have long to celebrate its success in removing the PLO from Lebanon in 1982. After its failure to translate its military

166

Figure 6.5

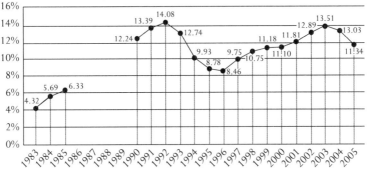

Unemployment Rates in Israel 1983–2005

(% of total labour force) (national estimates)

Source: World Bank, International Labour Organization, ILOSTAT database.

conquest into a separate peace agreement with Beirut, it found itself facing a gruelling war of attrition with the Lebanese resistance against the Israeli occupation of south Lebanon. Largely due to failures of Likud governments in Lebanon, the Israeli Labour Party returned to power in 1984. Labour's comeback was also partially due to a political coalition deal with the Likud, a deal that did not change the steady rightward drift of Israeli society since the 1967 war and Likud's 1977 electoral victory which had ended Labour's uninterrupted streak as Israel's ruling party since the establishment of the state.

Under the premiership of Yitzhak Rabin (1992–5), the Labour Party reached the conclusion that the existing strategy of violent suppression was futile. It realised that it had to deal with the Intifada politically, which meant that it needed to negotiate with the representatives of the Palestinians even if they were supporters of the PLO. Yasser Arafat, for his part, agreed to this formula and allowed a delegation from the Occupied Territories to negotiate with an Israeli delegation under PLO supervision, but insisted that the PLO, rather than that delegation, should be the signatory to any agreement with Israel. The PLO leadership bypassed that track and reached an agreement with Israel in Oslo, a declaration of principles, that included not even one principle of a solution to the Palestinian issue, an agreement that the delegation from the Occupied Territories would have never agreed to. The difference is that the PLO was ready to pay a price for Israeli recognition and accept anything that included such a recognition, because it would save it from the political wilderness it found itself in after the collapse of the socialist block and of the Arab order after the occupation of Kuwait.

This was a grave mistake. The declaration of principles included mutual recognition, procedures, and establishment of a Palestinian Authority, but no solution, not even principles of a possible solution.[15] The practical effect of the Oslo Accords was to reduce the PLO to a constituent body of the PA under Israeli sovereignty whose main function is to safeguard Israeli security.

Before this, the PLO committed another error which was to insist on the dissolution of the joint Palestinian–Jordanian delegation after the Madrid peace negotiations. This was not in the interest of the Palestinian people either. Rather, it served the PLO leadership which had invested in and committed to the issue of representation out of the belief that this was the only way to ensure its political survival. The dissolution allowed Jordan to sign a separate peace treaty with Israel in 1994 without reclaiming the land Israel seized in the 1967 war. The responsibility for this now fell squarely on the PLO. The Jordanian leadership maintained direct secret talks with Israel for a long time,[16] but it could never sign an agreement before the Palestinians did. If the PLO and Jordan had continued to negotiate jointly, neither of them would have dared sign a peace treaty without first regaining East Jerusalem.

As discussed and argued in the previous chapter, this approach gave rise to the term "Palestinian–Israeli conflict," which did not exist prior to the Oslo agreement. International organisations and the Western media had until then used the term Arab–Israeli conflict,

---

[15] The late Syrian President Hafez Assad told the author (in a meeting also attended by foreign minister Farouk Al-Share' that when Arafat updated him about the agreement he told him that, as he sees it, every item in this agreement needs an agreement.

[16] For a detailed account of these contacts, see: Yossi Melamn & Daniel Raviv, *Hostile Partnership: The Secret Contacts between Jordan and Israel* [Hebrew] ([Tel Aviv]: Mitam, 1987). See also: Avi Shlaim, *Lion of Jordan: The Life of King Hussein in War and Peace* (New York: Vintage Books, 2007).

while the Arab world used the term Palestinian cause which, in turn, was viewed as an Arab cause. There had been no such thing as a "Palestinian–Israeli conflict," as if the two sides were both countries or symmetrical sides and on equal footing.

The Oslo Accords initiated a peace process that aimed to achieve a negotiated treaty between Israel and the PLO based on UN Security Council Resolutions 242 and 338 but without first reaching an agreement on the interpretation of these resolutions. The Oslo I Accord (officially called the Declaration of Principles on Interim Self-Government Arrangements or Declaration of Principles) was the reached through secret negotiations in Norway and signed in 1993 in Washington, D.C. It was preceded by Letters of Mutual Recognition, according to which the signatories accepted each other as a partner of negotiation. Thus, the PLO recognised the State of Israel, while Israel recognised the PLO as "the representative of the Palestinian people." The agreement postponed discussion of the most difficult issues between both parties to the "final status" negotiations. The deferred issues are four: the status of Jerusalem, the fate of Palestinian refugees, the Jewish settlements in the occupied territories, and the establishment of the Palestinian state and its borders. The agreement (called Oslo I) codified the results of the Oslo negotiations and laid out a three-phase plan towards peace. The first phase called for the withdrawal of Israeli forces from the Gaza Strip and Jericho in the framework of a special schedule that kept Israel responsible for the external security and internal security of Israeli settlers in these areas. On 29 April 1994, the Protocol on Economic Relations (Paris Protocol) was signed between Israel and the PLO. It reconstituted economic and trade relations between Israel and the PA in a way that tied the Palestinian economy to Israel. In Cairo in May 1994, an agreement was signed regarding the West Bank and Jericho, regulating Israel's partial withdrawal from the Gaza Strip and the city of Jericho in the West Bank and the transfer of local authority to the PA.

The second phase was inaugurated in 1995 with the Interim Agreement on the West Bank and the Gaza Strip. Oslo II (as it was called although it was signed in the Egyptian resort of Taba) provided for the gradual redeployment of Israeli forces in the West Bank and transfer of certain powers to the PA. The Israeli withdrawal from the designated parts of the West Bank was to be completed at least twenty-two days before the eve of the Palestinian National Council elections. Redeployment was to be carried out in phases, the first phase of which covered populated areas. The West Bank, as a whole, was split into three administrative areas—Areas A, B and C—each accorded a different status. Area A (approx. 18 per cent of the total territory of the West Bank) would be exclusively administered by the Palestinian National Authority. Area B (approx. 22 per cent of the total territory of the West Bank) would be jointly administered by the PA and Israel, whereby the PA governs civilian life, but Israel controls security. In Area C (approx. 60 per cent of the total territory of the West Bank), both civil and security affairs are administered by Israel. Oslo II defined the basic terms for the transfer of authority from Israel to the Palestinians, as well as the powers that Israel retains under this agreement. Finally, Oslo II was to culminate in a "Permanent Status Agreement" bringing an end to the interim phase on 4 May 1999. As we know, that never happened, the "taxonomy" of areas A, B and C became a "permanent status" issue, and the Israeli building of settlements continued to change the character of the West Bank, including East Jerusalem.

In May 1997, the Hebron Protocol was signed as a prelude to the beginning of permanent status talks. The protocol divided Hebron into Area H-1 (about 80 per cent), which would come under Palestinian control, and Area H-2, where Israeli settlers reside, which would remain under Israeli control. Since then, Hebron has become a vivid illustration of the Israeli apartheid system produced after the Oslo agreements. Finally, the Wye River Memorandum of October 1998 was signed to help both parties continue to fulfil their obligations under previous treaties with the goal of reaching a final status. The Israeli government of Ehud Barak, elected in 1999, did not implement the agreed upon redeployments, preferring instead to unilaterally dictate his terms for a "permanent status agreement" first. Camp David II (2000) was arranged for this purpose. The attempt backfired, precipitating renewed confrontation in the second Intifada.

After Oslo

Yitzhak Rabin realised that the alternative to the PLO was a growing Hamas. He thought that he would be able to "rescue" the PLO and bring it back to the international arena through an agreement involving the only concession he ever intended to make: recognising the PLO. In exchange, the Intifada would stop, the PLO would recognise Israel and agree to negotiate without any clear shared principles concerning a just solution, and it would become a partner in "maintaining order" and fighting "terrorism" in the occupied territories. The "conflict" would thus end and negotiations would continue until an agreement was reached. This is why the Oslo Declaration of Principles and the subsequent Cairo Agreements had deferred any solution of the so-called "permanent status issues" into which the Palestinian cause was split. Not only was there no consensus on these points per se, but nor was there a consensus on the baseline principles and foundations for resolving these issues. Therefore, autonomy under a new Palestinian Authority was proposed as an interim solution. This was convenient for Israel. It absolved the occupying power of its civil responsibilities towards the local population (creating a luxurious situation for the occupiers, an occupation with costs, that numerous Israeli commentators have called "deluxe occupation") while requiring the PLO wield its authority on behalf of Israel's security interests in the name of counterterrorist security coordination. This was how the PLO was practically marginalised from the moment it was formally recognised. Not only did it become an authority without a state, but it became hostage to the Israeli occupation.

After being rescued by the Oslo Accords, the PLO was soon eclipsed by the institutionalisation of a Palestinian National Authority. The leaders of the PA, who were also the leaders of the PLO, understood that the latter was the source of the legitimacy of the former, so they strove to replace and control what remained (namely its title). They succeeded to the degree of reducing the PLO into an instrument for the PA to utilise or dispense with as necessary. For example, when Hamas won the Palestinian Legislative Council elections in 2006, the PA revived some of the PLO's institutions as a means to supplant the parliament over which it had just lost control.

After Oslo, the PA set about changing official titles without any material effect. The head of the authority, called "chairman" according to Oslo, became "Palestinian president" even though his powers did not change in the slightest. The "Authority Council" became the "Legislative

Council," which now had an increased membership. Israel tolerated these lofty appellations, and why should it not? They were merely pieces in a game of symbols, a slew of ceremonial titles and emblems used to compensate for what was missing on the ground: sovereignty. Sadly, this culture of compensation through symbols spread from politics into literature, art, film and other cultural realms. A form of national narcissism arose to fill the voids in the national reality.

Each time Israel was supposed to implement one of the Oslo steps related to the "redeployment" of Israeli forces pursuant to the Cairo Agreement (1994) or the Oslo II Accord (1995), a political storm would break out in Israel. No Israeli prime minister wanted to be the one to do the redeploying and hand more areas to the PA as stipulated under the agreements.

Naturally, extremist forces did their best to obstruct the process. The indeterminate, hesitant and partial nature of the agreement and the phased arrangement for its implementation, which was intended as a confidence-building measure to test the credibility of both sides, invited attempts to sabotage it. On 25 February 1994, only five months after the Oslo I Accords were signed, an Israeli settler and US immigrant named Baruch Goldstein opened fire on a large congregation of Palestinian Muslim worshippers who had assembled for prayers in the Ibrahimi Mosque in Hebron, killing twenty-nine and wounding 125. In retaliation for this massacre, a spate of suicide attacks were carried out by Palestinian individuals and members of Islamist militant groups. The first of these targeted a bus stop in the city of Afula within the Israeli borders on 6 April 1994, killing eight and injuring fifty-five. Another four more deadly suicide attacks by Palestinians took place the same year.

On 4 November 1995, Prime Minister Rabin was murdered by an Israeli religious nationalist. Shimon Peres, who succeeded him as prime minister, tried to play the strongman because he lacked the military profile that, in Israeli eyes, partially legitimised Rabin's peace with the PLO. Peres escalated the "war against terrorism" and the consequence was another wave of suicide bombings in urban centres carried out by Hamas and Islamic Jihad. On 11 April 1996, Peres initiated the sixteen-day Operation "Grapes of Wrath" against Lebanon, in which Israel launched massive air raids and extensive shelling on southern Lebanon. It killed hundreds of Lebanese civilians, including those who were killed in the shelling of a UN compound at the village of Qana on 18 April 1996. The Israeli public mood shifted in response, swinging from sympathy with Rabin as a victim of extremism, shock at the assassination of an elected prime minister and fear of Jewish radical religious nationalists to anger and vengefulness against the Palestinians. Rather than concluding from the failure of a partial peace that a more just peace was required, people in the centre of the Israeli political spectrum concluded that "moderate Palestinians" were either too weak to control their Islamist rivals, or too devious and elusive to be trusted.

Netanyahu, who became prime minister on 18 June 1996 after Peres lost the elections, tried to avoid ordering redeployment in Hebron. His inaction led to the Tunnel Uprising on 25 September 1996 in protest against the excavations below Al-Aqsa Mosque and to a clash between Palestinian and Israeli security forces. Afterwards, Netanyahu had no choice but to implement deployment in Hebron, which he did in January 1997. The 1996 confrontation was one of the reasons Netanyahu lost the 1999 elections.

Ehud Barak succeeded Netanyahu, serving from 1999 to 2001. Ehud Barak, the prime minister and ex-chief of staff, was in fact a military man of the special commando units who committed assassinations with his own hands and believed in power politics with the elitist military mentality of the fast-acting special units that he once led in the army. No sooner did he take office than a political crisis broke out anew. Initially, he banked on peace talks with Syria, but was unsuccessful. With the support of the American diplomat, Dennis Ross, Barak tried to limit Israel's withdrawal from the Golan Heights in such a way that Israel could continue to control the shores of Lake Galilee. He did not order redeployment in the West Bank because he did not trust Arafat, claiming that he wanted to know where all this was heading. Actually, this should have been a Palestinian demand. What Barak wanted was to reach an agreement on the final status issues on Israeli terms before implementing redeployment and other interim period obligations. Under US pressure and with the collaboration of some of Arafat's minions, Arafat was brought to Camp David to negotiate permanent status issues before Israel met its com-

mitments and without a previously worked out agreement on the
principles of negotiation. Arafat knew this was an attempt to force
him to accept Israel's terms on the final status issues.[17]

The Clinton administration made a serious mistake by going along
with Barak on this. The 2000 Camp David Summit proved a debacle
and not just because of the unequal land swaps put on the table. As
part of the solution to the permanent status issues, the US administration and Israel tried to arm-twist or browbeat Arafat into giving up
any right to sovereignty in Jerusalem, and effectively giving up any
claim to the 1967 borders. Arafat refused, for which he was met with
international censure, especially from the "Western world" which
considered the Clinton–Barak alliance (i.e., the alliance between the
US Democratic Party and the Israeli Labour Party) a "moderate" one
that represented the "enlightened" camp. Arafat's rebuff of its patron-
age was not to be tolerated.

After Camp David

Now that Arafat dared to say no to Washington, his destiny hinged
on his people rallying around him. The second Intifada erupted when
Ariel Sharon acted out the principle of sovereignty in person. With
Barak's go ahead, he paid an unwelcome "visit" to Al-Aqsa Mosque,
which was unquestionably a deliberately provocative intrusion. Later,
the PA and Hamas joined the Intifada, which had been started by
members of Fatah's constituency, turning the Intifada into a military
confrontation between the forces of the Palestinian people, including
security forces, and Israeli forces. At its fiercest peak, the Intifada was
characterised by the suicide operations of Hamas and Islamic Jihad
against Israeli civilians and Ehud Barak's deployment of the Air Force
for the first time since 1967 in the West Bank.

In 2002, Sharon became prime minister. Reverting to military
force to assert control, he ordered the reoccupation of Palestinian
cities, beleaguering Arafat's offices and residence in Ramallah, and
ordered the assassination of Arafat in 2004. Arafat paid with his life
for supporting resistance against occupation, albeit after it became

---

[17] The author regularly met with Arafat and knew his position.

THE ROAD TO NOWHERE

clear to him what the negotiating process meant: accept US-Israeli dictates or face isolation and siege.

The Palestinian leadership that took over the PA faulted Arafat. These are their takeaways from the second Intifada: that Arafat had sometimes treated the negotiations as a tactic rather than approaching them strategically, that resistance was a grave mistake and that negotiations were the only path towards a solution. So when Mahmoud Abbas became PA president, he vowed commitment to negotiations and rejected Arafat's recourse to the second Intifada. Abbas met with Sharon at the 2005 Sharm el-Sheikh Summit where they agreed to a truce. The PA also agreed with the US to retrain and "re-educate" (i.e., re-indoctrinate) Palestinian security forces on the principles of counterterrorism and security cooperation with Israel, the occupying power. This project was ultimately American-run and overseen by General Keith Dayton. General William Ward was initially announced as security coordinator of the project to restructure the Palestinian security forces.[18]

Abbas worked hard to prove he was not Arafat and that the Israelis could trust him, not only in "fighting terrorism" but in all kinds of ways. This was acknowledged by Israel's security apparatus, but it did not convince the Israeli leadership or the Israeli public to accept a just solution. The Israeli public, which was veering more and more to extremist religious nationalism, merely thought, as long as the PA was doing most of the dirty work, why agree to a state now? Why stop settlement expansion? Why not push for annexation? Then, at long last, the Trump-Netanyahu deal gave Abbas his "reward".

Abbas believes that armed resistance is wrong. Yet, he ignores the glaring fact that his own strategy, that of endless peace negotiations in the Oslo framework, has failed. Sometimes, he seems to gloat about his failures just to annoy those who disagree with him. Palestinian fragmentation has contributed to this petty spitefulness.

What does a Palestinian leader who gave the occupying country everything it wanted, only to find himself tricked and his favours unreciprocated, have to be proud of? Mahmoud Abbas is not a "trai-

[18] "Rice appoints a Palestinian security coordinator and praises Abbas' efforts," *Al Jazeera*, 7 February 2005, accessed at: http//bit.ly/38MS5gS

175

tor" or an Israeli agent. The problem is that he genuinely believes what he thinks. However, without a shift to a liberation strategy, his approach may lead to a successor who receives his instructions directly from the occupier.

At no point did this Palestinian leadership manage to convince Israel and the US that negotiations had to be based on clear foundations and basic principles to lead to a just and lasting solution. Israel continued to see negotiations as an open-ended "political project" in which the balance of powers determined the pace and the substance, such as it was. As endless negotiations, held purely for form, dragged on, the "peace process" was abbreviated to "the process." At the same time, the occupying power continued to step up settlement activity and reinforce the reality of Israeli control while the PA continued to lack any approximation of sovereignty even over densely populated areas that Israel wanted to get rid of for demographic reasons.

The Oslo Declaration of Principles and the PA's establishment ushered in an insatiable wave of settlement construction and expansion, which devoured more and more Palestinian land.[19] The longest settlement freeze was during the first Intifada and that was unavoidable. Only the most radical ideological settlers were ready to live in the midst of a rebelling populace. After the PLO became hostage to the occupation, it could no longer resist settlement activity.

Whenever critics contested the belief that Oslo would lead to the establishment of a state, PLO leaders defended their support for it

---

[19] The settler population of the West Bank and Gaza Strip alone (excluding those in East Jerusalem and the Golan Heights) increased from 115,700 in 1993 to 203,000 by the end of 2000 (an increase of approximately 75 per cent). Five years after signing Oslo II, the number of Israeli settlers in occupied East Jerusalem had increased by around 15,000 and was estimated at around 400,000 settlers in 2002. See: Anne Le More, *International Assistance to the Palestinians After Oslo: Political Guilt, Wasted Money* (London and New York: Routledge, 2008), p. 47; Franke Wilmer, *Breaking Cycles of Violence in Israel and Palestine: Empathy and Peacemaking in the Middle* East (Lanham and London: Lexington Books, 2021), p. 38. At the beginning of 2019, the West Bank (including East Jerusalem) contained 131 settlements, 110 outposts and 620,000 settlers. A Human Rights Council report observed that settlement expansion more than doubled in the years after 2016 and predicted its continued rise. See: "Israeli Settlements in the Occupied Palestinian Territory, Including East Jerusalem, and the Occupied Syrian Golan," *Report of the Secretary-General A/HRC/37/43*, UN General Assembly, 6 March 2018, accessed at: https://bit.ly/3gJRAM2

Map 6.1a-f: Israeli Settlement Expansion in the West Bank (1968–2015)

Map 6.1b

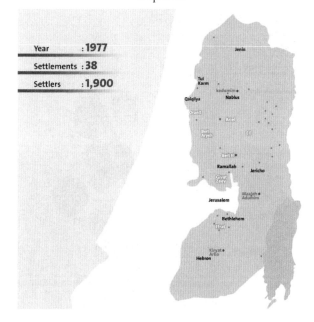

PALESTINE

Map 6.1c

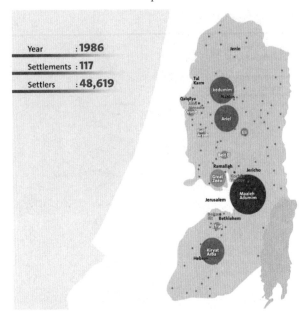

Year : **1986**

Settlements : **117**

Settlers : **48,619**

Map 6.1d

Year : **1997**

Settlements : **126**

Settlers : **152,577**

THE ROAD TO NOWHERE

Map 6.1e

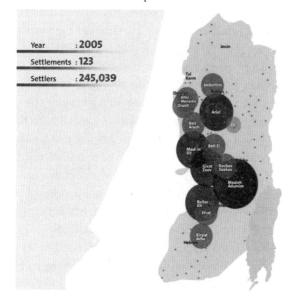

Year	: 2005
Settlements	: 123
Settlers	: 245,039

Map 6.1f

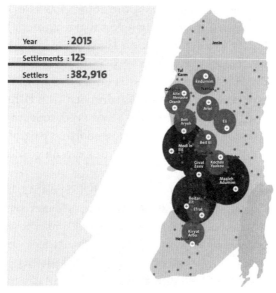

Year	: 2015
Settlements	: 125
Settlers	: 382,916

Source: Adapted from Yotam Berger, "How Many Settlers Really Live in the West Bank?," *Haaretz*, 15 June 2017, accessed at: http://bit.ly/38XuZoN

with the argument that the agreement was needed to counter the threat that settlement expansion posed to the Palestinian cause. The agreement would at least enforce a freeze on the construction of settlements, they said. During the negotiations, settlement expansion witnessed its most spectacular growth since 1967. The PLO could do nothing to stop it, having excluded the option of resistance as long as it wanted to retain any sort of governmental authority. By the Trump era, withdrawing from the Oslo Accords as a reaction to the Trump-Netanyahu deal was no longer option, strategically or tactically. Israel had long since put paid to the Accords in practice. For Israel, the status quo (or a modified version of it) is an acceptable final status, as long as the PA continues to fulfil its main purpose of protecting Israel's security. The PA, which continues to act as though the Oslo process had not ended, remained in a state of denial.

It was under this PA leadership, as characterised by its takeaways from the second Intifada, that the drastic split between Hamas and Fatah occurred in 2006, after Hamas's victory in legislative council elections led to armed clashes in Gaza between forces controlled by the two movements, as discussed in the previous chapter. The intra-Palestinian conflict stemmed from the obligations associated with the Oslo Accords and the security forces that it created. Yet, para-doxically, Hamas was determined to take power using the mecha-nisms of the Accords it refused to recognise, while simultaneously criticising the Palestinian president's commitment to them. The confrontation between Hamas and Fatah ended with Hamas gaining the upper hand in Gaza. This created a new predicament for Hamas: it was now the sole leader of a highly populated part of Palestine that was under a blockade. It now had to focus on governance and survival in this context.

This was a controversial process that included positive dimensions. Hamas had to build or rebuild institutions, whether semi-regular military institutions or civil service institutions similar to those in the West Bank—only under more difficult circumstances. The experi-ence of exercising power and managing the blockade engaged Hamas in political processes more than ever before. Like Fatah in the West Bank, Hamas built up partisan authority and established partisan secu-rity forces. With two partisan authorities in two discontinuous geographical areas, the Palestinian people and their case were in major trouble, especially given growing Israeli power and its extreme right-wing Israeli leadership.

The Palestinian rift, which led to unprecedentedly disparate and contradictory political leadership strategies, favoured the rising power of the Israeli right (because of the marginalisation of pro-peace discourses). It also brought about the decline in official Palestinian influence regionally and internationally—despite a parallel increase in international solidarity with the Palestinian people. Fatah and Hamas poured the majority of their resources into their mutual hostility. Reconciliation efforts were in vain, and this failure further reduced the credibility of both factions and, at a larger level, it tarnished the reputation and image of the Palestinian national movement. Even though both sides recognised how detrimental their split was to the Palestinian people and cause, their desire to retain power and reinforce their own security strength prevailed over higher commitments.

When Obama became president, the US administration began to view a complete freeze on settlement building in the West Bank and East Jerusalem as not only desirable, but as a prerequisite for Israeli–Palestinian peace negotiations to advance.[20] But Obama eventually realised there could be no chance of progress as long as Netanyahu was in power, so he gave up and washed his hands of the peace process. Obama probably could have but did not want to exert any pressure on Netanyahu,[21] whether due to American domestic politics or to foreign policy priorities such as the nuclear deal with Iran which was already a sufficient source of public tension with Netanyahu. So, Israel continued to expand and intensify settlement activity, leaving the PA stuck with security coordination with Israel and no negotiations. Then came the Trump presidency.

---

[20] See the following article, which criticises Obama's position from a right-wing perspective, maintaining that the condition of freezing settlements was unnecessary and novel in American policy, as no previous administration sponsoring the negotiations had placed this condition: Elliot Abrams, "The Settlement Obsession: Both Israel and the United States Miss the Obstacles to Peace," *Foreign Affairs*, vol. 99, no. 2 (July/August 2011), pp. 142–52.

[21] Obama, pp. 634–6.

PART TWO

THE TRUMP-NETANYAHU DEAL[1]

When, after 3 years of fanfare, the administration of President Donald Trump released its proposed plan for peace between the Palestinian people and Israel, its substance came as no surprise, exceeding expectations only in how closely it hewed to the discourse of the Israeli right. The details of the political portion of the plan were announced on 28 January 2020, some eight months after the economic portion was made public at a workshop in the Bahraini capital of Manama in June 2019. These two parts—the political and the economic—together constituted the plan, officially titled "Peace to Prosperity: A Vision to Improve the Lives of the Palestinian and Israeli People." With his typical bombast, Trump called it the "Deal of the Century"—I prefer "the Trump-Netanyahu deal".

The document is merely a political initiative, not an agreement or treaty binding on future US presidents. Even so, it set a dangerous precedent by accepting and legitimising the facts on the ground cre-

---

[1] This chapter builds on a lecture I delivered at the Arab Center for Research and Policy Studies on 3 February 2020 on President Trump and Israeli Prime Minister Netanyahu's plan "to resolve the Palestinian-Israeli conflict." See: Azmi Bishara, "Trump-Netanyahu Deal … The American-Israeli Right-wing Plan to End the Palestinian Cause in a Historical Context," *Arab Center for Research and Policy Studies YouTube channel*, 6 February 2020, accessed at: http://bit.ly/2HOR7Wj

ated by the occupation, taking the status quo as its starting point. Consider, for example, the question of Jerusalem. Without an act of Congress, it may be impossible for any future president to reverse Trump's decision to relocate the US embassy from Tel Aviv to Jerusalem since the move came in pursuance of existing legislation, pressed for by the Israeli lobby, although not previously implemented by the White House.[2]

The Trump administration enthusiastically endorsed, and helped reinforce, the power politics approach that dominates Israeli political culture. It is instructive to compare this to the approach of former President George H. W. Bush (1989–1993). As a way of exerting pressure on then Israeli Prime Minister Yitzhak Shamir, Bush threatened to withhold the guarantees for a $10 billion loan to Israel. Shamir buckled to the pressure, attending the 1991 Madrid Peace Conference before receiving the necessary guarantees, which were not released until Yitzhak Rabin was elected prime minister in 1992.[3]

---

[2] On 23 October 1995, both houses of Congress overwhelmingly passed the Jerusalem Embassy Act mandating that "the United States Embassy in Israel should be established in Jerusalem no later than 31 May 1999." However, the act allowed the president to invoke a six-month, renewable waiver of the application of the law on "national security" grounds, and Presidents Clinton, Bush and Obama repeatedly did so. On 6 December 2017, Trump recognised Jerusalem as Israel's capital and ordered the relocation of the embassy, which was officially completed on 14 May 2018. See: "S.1322—Jerusalem Embassy Act of 1995," *Congress.Gov*, accessed at: http://bit.ly/2HOShRO

[3] Shamir insisted that Israel would not negotiate, directly or indirectly, with the PLO or anyone affiliated with it and further demanded the exclusion of Palestinians residing in East Jerusalem from the negotiations; the PLO agreed to these terms, limiting itself to presenting a list of Palestinians from the Occupied Territories to participate in the negotiations. Before initiating talks, Israel further demanded that the Palestinian delegation formally acknowledge that the scope of negotiations be limited to autonomy in the Palestinian territories. Feeling that this rigid approach would make talks impossible, former Secretary of State James Baker sent a message to the Israeli government essentially telling them to "call us when you are serious about peace." See: Thomas L. Friedman, "Baker Rebukes Israel on Peace Terms," *The New York Times*, 14 June 1990, accessed at: https://nyti.ms/3uQQTE5. President George H.W. Bush subsequently indicated that he would look into other ways to proceed towards a peace plan "because we're not going to sit here and do nothing." George H. W. Bush, "The President's New Conference—June 29, 1990," in: *Public Papers of the President of the United States: George Bush, 1990*, Book I—1 January to 30 June, 1990 (Washington, D.C.: United States Government Printing

The Bush administration's position had an impact on the outcome of the 1992 Israeli elections, contributing to the Likud Party's loss for the first time since 1977.

In contrast, (by comparison), the Trump–Netanyahu deal clearly inhabits an utterly different political context and culture. It cannot be understood apart from developments within American politics and culture in the post-Obama era,[4] or without consideration for the radical right-wing settlers and evangelicals that surrounded Trump, who, despite his right-wing populist inclinations, was himself politically vacuous.

Office, 1991), p. 882. In September 1991, tensions between Bush and Shamir reached a breaking point. Hours before the Israeli ambassador to the US presented a formal request for the loan guarantees, Bush took the unusual step of holding a press conference, during which he asked Congress to hold off on any action on the request for 120 days. He had previously called on Israel to freeze settlements in the Occupied Territories and indicated that he would not consider Israeli requests for loan guarantees until after the Madrid Peace Conference, slated for October 1991. He also threated to exercise his presidential veto if Congress denied his request, but that proved unnecessary. He additionally refused to promise that the loan guarantees would be approved after the 120 days, conditioning them on progress at the Madrid Peace Conference and an end to settlements. Shamir ignored these threats; although he made "conciliatory" gestures to the US and affirmed his support of the proposed peace conference, he asserted that Israel would be ready to fight a bitter battle if it came to that. The loan guarantee issue persisted after the Madrid Conference as Bush continued to make them contingent on an end to settlement construction, which his administration considered "a hindrance to peace." Ultimately, Bush withheld the loan guarantees for a year, until after Rabin's election in the summer of 1992.

[4] These developments include the fraught debate around populism and neoliberalism and their interconnectedness, the consequences of previous US wars abroad and disagreement over what they mean, and the responses to Trump's election, which itself was a reaction to Obama's presidency. Although it is important to understand the Trump-Netanyahu deal within the US context, such consideration is outside the scope of this study. Trump's vision is indeed a result of fractures in US domestic politics, populist and white supremacist reactions to Obama's term, the rising influence of Christian Zionism in American evangelicalism, and the increasing electoral and foreign-policy activism of radical evangelical churches and their links with the Israeli lobby, with significant implications for the Middle East.

185

7

ZIONIST RELIGIOUS-NATIONALIST DISCOURSE IN AN OFFICIAL AMERICAN TEXT

Starting from Scratch

Before delving into "Peace to Prosperity", it may be useful to briefly review US peace initiatives since 1967. Such an overview will show that Trump's vision constituted a crucial shift, from a strategic alliance with Israel and unconditional commitment to its security to outright identification with the Israeli right, the embrace of its language and arguments, and the aspiration to impose its positions on Palestinians and Arab states. With this transformation, the US completely abandoned its role as a "mediator" in negotiations or custodian of the so-called peace process. This overview will spotlight the respective positions of the Arab world and Israel towards these American initiatives, demonstrating that the ostensible Arab rejection of peace is nothing more than a myth; the persistent rejecter has been Israel.

My goal in focusing on Israeli intransigence is to refute the lies that justify support for the so-called "deal of the century." So, for example, "the Arabs" and Palestinians in particular are blamed for their supposedly persistent rejectionist positions, which pro-Trump Arab states sought to deny by eagerly supporting normalisation with the occupying state before it recognised Palestinian rights and accepted a just solution to the Palestinian issue. The truth is that Arab states have consistently signed on to previous peace initiatives. The "problem" with Arab states has never been their implacable rejectionism; quite the contrary, it has been their desire to please. Furthermore, in trying to resolve the cognitive dissonance between their behaviour and their upbringing, proponents of normalising relations with Israel often vilify Palestinians, making unfounded accusations against them (e.g., the oft-repeated claim that "they sold their land!").

It is important to emphasise this point, because in justifying normalisation with Israel, some Arab politicians parrot the typical Israeli lie that Palestinians and Arabs have always rejected peace initiatives while Israel has accepted them.[5] This myth has plagued Arabs since the Zionist movement agreed to the 1947 partition plan (UNGA Resolution 181),[6] which granted it a land and a state, while Arabs (and not just Palestinians) rejected the plan because it entailed the establishment of a settler state on territory overwhelmingly inhabited by Arabs. At that point in time, it was only to be expected that the owner of the land would balk at such a division, especially since the immigrant settler did not just intend to live on the land, but also to establish a state designed to exclude its indigenous inhabitants. By the same token, the Zionist movement naturally accepted that same plan because it helped it accomplish (even if only partially) its primary goal of establishing a Jewish state in Palestine, despite Jews (including new settlers) constituting a minority of Palestine's inhabitants. The Yishuv leadership embraced partition as a provisional solution, actually an expedient, a way to gain international legitimacy for a Jewish state in Palestine, before expanding to occupy the rest of the country and expelling its inhabitants, ostensibly in response to the Arab interven-

---

[5] Echoing Israeli Minister of Foreign Affairs Abba Eban's comment that the Arabs "never miss an opportunity to miss an opportunity," Saudi Prince Bandar bin Sultan told Yasser Arafat a few hours before the latter's meeting with President Clinton on 2 January 2001, in which Arafat would either accept or reject the Clinton Parameters for a final settlement: "Since 1948, every time we've had something on the table we say no. Then we say yes. When we say yes, it's not on the table anymore. Then we have to deal with something less. Isn't it about time we said yes?" Matthew Brodsky, "Mahmoud Abbas and the persistence of Palestinian mythology," *The Guardian*, 19 May 2011, accessed at: https://bit.ly/3gsZY15

[6] See: Chapter 1.

tion, which was itself triggered by ethnic cleansing and the unilateral declaration of a Jewish state prior to the creation of an international mechanism to implement the partition plan.

While the US has always been absolutely partial to Israel, it has tried to mediate the conflict when Egypt moved to alignment with the US and was ready for separate peace with Israel, and when Syria and the PLO proved receptive to the idea, particularly after the fall of the Berlin Wall, the 1989 collapse of the socialist bloc and the rise of unipolarity, and the Iraqi occupation of Kuwait, where the formation of an international alliance to liberate the country included Arab states.

Successive US peace initiatives have assumed an identifiable template, with each one predictably building on its predecessor. In contrast, the Trump-Netanyahu deal started from scratch, effectively wiping the slate clean.

Early US initiatives after the 1967 occupation did not address the Palestinian issue and of course did not deal with the PLO, which was considered a 'terrorist organisation'. The first of these, the Rogers Plan, was proposed in June 1970. Named after Nixon's Secretary of State William Rogers,[7] it reduced the conflict to the June 1967 war and its aftermath—that is, to the issue of the territories occupied in 1967, with reference to a "compromise" on the issue of the 1948 refugees. Based on UN Security Council Resolution 242 (issued on 22 November 1967),[8] it called for Arab recognition of Israel and the return to Jordan, Egypt and Syria of the territories occupied in the 1967 war.[9] Israel rejected the plan, asserting that it did not suffi-

---

[7] Rogers served as Secretary of State under former President Richard Nixon (1969–73) and was followed by Henry Kissinger as Secretary of State (1973–77).

[8] United Nations, *Resolutions and Decisions of the Secretary Council 1967: Security Council Official Records Twenty-Second Year* (New York: 1968), pp. 8–9, accessed at: http://bit.ly/31DlKas

[9] Rogers officially announced the plan at a talk he gave at a conference in Washington D.C. on 9 December 1969. The plan also provided for the establishment of demilitarised zones, guarantees for the security of Israel and Arab countries, Israeli freedom of navigation in the Straits of Tiran and the Suez Canal, and a fair compromise as a solution to the refugee problem, and required the agreement of all parties, especially Jordan and Israel, on decisions concerning Jerusalem, barring unilateral, final decisions by any single party. See: William Rogers, "Address by Secretary of State William Rogers, December 9, 1969," in: *The Quest*

ciently address its security needs and lacked guiding principles for direct negotiations leading to an official peace treaty. Moreover, the plan's demand for withdrawal from occupied territory might include occupied East Jerusalem, which was unacceptable to Israel.[10]

The first US initiative after the 1967 war, which was based on UN Security Council Resolutions 242 and 338, was thus accepted by Egypt and Jordan, but rebuffed by Israel. (As for Palestinians, the Rogers Plan neither addressed nor recognised them). In contrast, Arab states have accepted US peace initiatives, despite the so-called "Three No's of Khartoum" after the 1967 defeat. The Three No's did not, as is often claimed, represent a new position or coherent political program; they simply reiterated the existing positions of Arab states decrying the outcome of a war of aggression—namely, the Israeli military occupation of Arab lands.

Let us now move on to the second US initiative, spearheaded by Zbigniew Brzezinski, who served as national security advisor to President Jimmy Carter from 1977 to 1981. Brzezinski's initiative was, first and foremost, a plan for autonomy in the West Bank and the Gaza Strip. This was the first formal US proposal for establishing Palestinian autonomy, though the autonomous territories were to be linked with Jordan. Israel rejected the plan because Carter did not commit to guarantees for Israel if it made any "concessions" during negotiations.[11]

At the insistence of Egyptian President Sadat,[12] a clause on Palestine was added to the Camp David Accords, allowing him to save face and

___

for Peace: Principal United States Public Statements and Related Documents on the Arab-Israeli Peace Process 1967–1983 (Washington, D.C.: US Department of State, 1984), pp. 23–9.

[10] Jerome Slater, "The Superpowers and an Arab-Israeli Political Settlement: The Cold War Years," *Political Science Quarterly*, vol. 105, no. 4 (Winter 1990–1), pp. 571–3; "Rogers Plan," *The Knesset*, accessed at: https://bit.ly/2SbNTAZ; Naktal 'Abd al-Hadi 'Abd al-Karim Muhammad, *The Positions of the United States towards the Palestinian Issue* [Arabic] (Amman: Dar al-Mu'taz, 2016), pp. 43–6.

[11] Khalid Hammad 'Iyad, *The United States and the Peace Process in the Middle East (1973–2013)* (Amman: Alaan Publishers & Distributors, 2017), pp. 28–31.

[12] The Camp David Accords were concluded after Sadat visited Israel on 19 November 1977, following a meeting between Moshe Dayan and Egyptian Deputy Prime Minister Hassan Tuhami in Morocco. "Israeli-Egyptian Relations: Israel and Egypt Open Peace Talks in Marrakesh, December 1977," *Israel State Archives*, accessed at: https://bit.ly/3cHDsQU

avoid the public appearance of completely abandoning the Palestinian cause, the ostensible crux of the conflict. Pursuant to approval from his counterpart, Israeli Prime Minister Menachem Begin, a proposal was floated for autonomy for the West Bank and the Gaza Strip, with no reference to a Palestinian state.

The peace agreement stated: "Egypt and Israel agree that, in order to ensure a peaceful and orderly transfer of authority, and taking into account the security concerns of all the parties, there should be transitional arrangements for the West Bank and Gaza for a period not exceeding five years [...] To negotiate the details of a transitional arrangement, Jordan will be invited to join the negotiations on the basis of this framework. These new arrangements should give due consideration both to the principle of self-government by the inhabitants of these territories and to the legitimate security concerns of the parties involved."[13] Despite this provision, everyone involved was aware that the idea of Palestinian autonomy had been grafted onto the treaty as a mere formality, and it was notably devoid of any Israeli recognition of the established Palestinian leadership.

The third plan—"an American peace initiative for the longsuffering peoples of the Middle East"—came in 1982 under the administration of Ronald Reagan.[14] Reagan's initiative outlined an executive framework for a solution based on Palestinian autonomy in the West Bank and Gaza Strip, whereby Palestinians would manage their own internal affairs provided they did not pose a threat to Israel; there was no mention of a Palestinian state. The initiative stipulated that Palestinian autonomy be tied to Jordan and that settlement activities be frozen for 5 years. Reagan explicitly affirmed that the US would not support the establishment of a Palestinian state in the West Bank and the Gaza Strip. Even so, Begin rejected the proposal, describing it as "stillborn" and maintaining that Reagan, simply by suggesting Palestinian autonomy, had betrayed the friendship between the US and Israel.[15] The

---

[13] See: "Camp David Accords—17 Sep 1978," *Israel Ministry of Foreign Affairs*, accessed at: https://bit.ly/3eCnvvm

[14] "Address to the Nation on United States Policy for Peace in the Middle East, 1 September 1982," United Nations, accessed at: https://bit.ly/3wXCR5l

[15] Israel's rejection was premised on the idea that Palestinian autonomy would lead to a

initiative came as Israel's wanton militarism, exemplified by Ariel Sharon, and the chauvinism of the Israeli right, embodied by Begin, were at their peak, just a few months after the Israeli army invaded Lebanon and laid siege to the PLO in Beirut, a time when the promise of Israeli victory was still alive.

A sea change occurred in the Arab world and the region following the second Gulf War (7 August 1990–28 February 1991). With that reckless, arrogant action, the Iraqi regime committed a lethal mistake, wronging not only Kuwait but also Iraq itself and putting the final nail in the coffin of "Arab national security" and the prevailing Arab regional order.[16] The international and regional order shifted, allowing regional powers like Turkey, Iran and Israel to step in during the subsequent historical phase and extend their influence across the Arab world absent of any single Arab state with comparable power on the one hand and devoid of any collective national security arrangement on the other.

Palestinian state, which would "pose a serious danger" to Israel's security, though Reagan had clearly indicated that the US "would not support the establishment of an independent Palestinian state in the West Bank and the Gaza Strip." Reagan also affirmed that, from the US perspective, Palestinian autonomy would be realised in cooperation with Jordan, which would provide the best opportunity for a fair and lasting peace. Amman had reacted positively to the initiative, while Israel "issued rejection after rejection of US proposals." Saying that Israel refused to negotiate on the plan, Begin announced that it would not resume talks on Palestinian autonomy unless they were based on the Camp David Accords; the accords contained no provision for the freezing of settlements, which Israel considered an inalienable right and an indispensable part of its national security. Begin equated Reagan's proposal with the 1969 Rogers Plan calling for Israel's withdrawal from almost all of the West Bank and echoing former Prime Minister Golda Meir, he said that anyone who supported the Reagan Plan was a traitor. See: David K. Shipler, "Israel Rejects Reagan Plan for Palestinians' Self-Rule; Terms it 'a Serious Danger'," *The New York Times*, 3 September 1982, accessed at: https://nyti.ms/39O4jqA

[16] I find my attention drawn to five years in particular that saw cataclysmic events that transformed the history of the region and influenced the course of world history as well: 1948 and 1967, with their wars; 1979, which saw major upheavals, including the Iranian Revolution, the escalation of the conflict between the Ba'athist regimes of Syria and Iraq and the separate peace between Egypt and Israel (which was signed in 1979 but had its roots in 1978); and 1990, when Iraq invaded Kuwait. No doubt, the 2011 uprisings deserve to be included in this list, since they, too, heralded major transformations, but we are still living through this stage of history.

On 6 March 1991, having assumed office in what would soon be the world's only superpower—the now-toothless Soviet Union was to collapse a few months later—George H. W. Bush announced a new vision for peace before Congress that would evolve into the fourth US initiative. American efforts to drum up support for a war of liberation against an occupying power had led to accusations of double standards, and Bush had promised Arab states joining the anti-Iraq coalition that he would turn his attention to the Palestine issue as soon as Iraqi forces had been expelled from Kuwait. "A comprehensive peace must be grounded in United Nations Security Council Resolutions 242 and 338 and the principle of territory for peace,"[17] Bush said. Although he presented no concrete proposal, he sent Secretary of State James Baker on shuttle diplomacy trips around the region, which ultimately led to the 1991 Madrid negotiations between Israel, Syria, Jordan and the Palestinians. The PLO did not directly participate in the negotiations due to Israeli "taboos," but directly appointed the Palestinian delegation consisting of public figures from the West Bank and the Gaza Strip. Baker's point man on these shuttle trips was Dennis Ross, who proved extremely adept at undermining peace negotiations over multiple US administrations by working consistently to adjust them to fit the Israeli positions. Indeed, Ross's role exemplifies the impact of the Israeli lobby on successive administrations' decisions regarding Palestine and the Arab-Israeli conflict. Contrary to popular opinion, the Israeli lobby does not limit its efforts to Congress.[18]

---

[17] George H. W. Bush, "After the War: The President; Transcript of President Bush's Address on End of the Gulf War," *The New York Times*, 7 March 1991, accessed at: https://nyti.ms/2V6Ct4S

[18] Working under both Republican and Democratic administrations, from the Carter administration in the 1970s to the first Obama administration in 2011, Ross has had a major hand in shaping US foreign policy in the Middle East, particularly in the so-called peace process. According to John Mearsheimer and Stephen Walt, "Middle East policy was largely shaped by officials with close ties to Israel and to prominent pro-Israel organizations," such as AIPAC and the Washington Institute for Near East Policy (WINEP). Mearsheimer and Walt point to Dennis Ross in particular—the lobby's "man" in Washington, he joined WINEP after leaving government in 2001—as well as Aaron Miller, who has lived in Israel and often visits there. They add, "These men were among President Clinton's closest advi-

The Madrid negotiations ultimately led nowhere, partly due to Israeli refusals to engage with the Palestinian team. Although the PLO was not officially present at the talks, it was common knowledge that it had directly appointed the Palestinian delegation. Menahim Begin's successor, Yitzhak Shamir, subsequently lost the elections and the Labour Party once again assumed power, this time under the leadership of Yitzhak Rabin. With Rabin's reluctant approval, Minister of Foreign Affairs Shimon Peres pursued a new negotiation path in Oslo, opening a direct channel between Israel and the PLO. The Oslo negotiations ran parallel to the Madrid talks and were not attended by the United States, at least not formally. While Rabin had wanted, and failed, to reach a bilateral peace agreement with Syria first, he gave Peres the green light for the Oslo track after realising that the alternative to talks with civil activists and PLO-appointed delegates would be Hamas. The Oslo talks were thus a direct result of the first Intifada, the Palestinian peaceful uprising and civil disobedience movement. Although by this time, the movement was turning towards violence as mass participation caved into fatigue, the severe economic repercussions of lengthy general strikes, and regional and global developments.

As negotiations began in Oslo, the PLO found itself in a double bind. Its 1982 expulsion from Lebanon, the 1991 Palestinian exodus from Kuwait and strained relations with the Gulf countries due to Yasser Arafat's expressed solidarity with Iraq during the Kuwait crisis all coincided with the collapse of the Arab regional order. Moreover, while the 1987 Intifada had made impressive achieve-

---

sors at the Camp David summit in July 2000. Although all three supported the Oslo peace process and favoured creation of a Palestinian state, they did so only within the limits of what would be acceptable to Israel." Ross was described by an unnamed US official in the administration as "far more sensitive to Netanyahu's coalition politics than to US interests." See: John J. Mearsheimer & Stephen M. Walt, "The Israel Lobby and US Foreign Policy," *Working Papers Series No. RWP06–011*, Harvard University: John F. Kennedy School of Government, Faculty Research, 15 March 2006, p. 18, accessed at: https://bit.ly/3xyYVo2; Laura Rozen, "Fierce Debate on Israel Underway Inside Obama Administration," *Politico*, 28 March 2010, accessed at: https://politi.co/3eCYT5F. See also, Marwan Bishara, "What's Special about US-Israeli relations?," *Aljazeera*, 26 July 2016, accessed at: https://bit.ly/3iJEiAm

ments, it had exhausted its potential and was overtaken by historic events, namely, the collapse of the Soviet Union and the 1990–1 Gulf War. The PLO, headquartered in Tunis with no financial support from the Gulf countries or the Soviet Union, was forced to try to salvage its position, particularly in light of the de facto end of the first Intifada. It was now not only ready to make peace with Israel— it had been prepared to accept a two-state solution since the late 1970s—but willing to amend the Palestinian National Covenant and to engage in security coordination with Israel, all in exchange for formal recognition of the PLO and the establishment of a Palestinian authority in the West Bank and Gaza, with no corollary promise of an independent Palestinian state.

Let us now move on to the fifth US initiative, that of US President George W. Bush, Jr., whose "roadmap for peace" provided for the establishment of an independent Palestinian state. Based on this vision, a diplomatic "Quartet" was formed consisting of the US, Russia, the European Union and the United Nations. The roadmap was introduced in October 2002, in the midst of the second Intifada and during Ariel Sharon's tenure as prime minister (2001–6). The Palestinian leadership accepted the roadmap without reservation, while the Israeli government accepted it in principle with fourteen reservations, which in practical terms amounted to rejection.

In order to take the roadmap entirely off the table and seize the initiative from the US, Sharon unilaterally decided in 2005 to withdraw from the Gaza Strip with no prior agreement with the PA. By withdrawing from Gaza, he signalled that Israel—not the US— would set the pace and act as it saw fit. A narrow, densely populated strip of land, Gaza has few resources and no promising future for settlements, and is also a centre of active resistance against the occupation. Consequently, it was in Israel's interest to rid itself of both Gaza and the roadmap.[19] By taking this step, it sought to solve its

---

[19] The statements of Israeli leaders like Ariel Sharon, Ehud Olmert and Shimon Peres justifying the unilateral withdrawal from Gaza to the Israeli public with reference to demographic and strategic concerns are too many to be quoted. Sharon adviser Dov Weissglass summarised this thinking neatly in an interview with *Haaretz* that seemed intended to convince the right-wing Israeli public: "The significance of the disengagement plan is the freez-

own problem in Gaza, but not Gaza's problem nor that of the rest of the Palestinian territories.

As prime minister, Sharon pursued a two-pronged strategy to establish new realities on the ground. First, he waged total war on the Palestinian Authority, invading Ramallah in 2002 and assassinating Yasser Arafat in 2004. Second, he withdrew unilaterally from the Gaza Strip, relieving Israel of the demographic "burden" of a mass of Palestinians resisting the occupation, and then besieged it. Arafat, who agreed to the roadmap with no amendments, was assassinated by Israel; in contrast, Sharon, who rejected the roadmap, received a letter from Bush in 2005 promising Israel security guarantees and expressing support for its unilateral withdrawal from Gaza. The letter contained a key sentence suggesting that it was unrealistic to expect Israel to withdraw from all of the occupied territories and return to the 1949 Armistice Agreement borders under any future peace agreement, implying that the US was committed to a policy of border adjustments.[20]

The sixth round of US diplomatic initiatives was the so-called "road to peace" under President Barack Obama. In a speech delivered at Cairo University a few months after taking office in 2009, he announced that he would dedicate himself to pursuing peace between Palestinians and Israelis "with all the patience [...] that the task requires."[21] His patience soon wore thin. More importantly, he sought to avoid any head-on confrontation with the Israeli lobby on the Palestinian issue, only showing a limited willingness to defy the lobby when negotiating the nuclear agreement with Iran. During

---

ing of the peace process, and when you freeze that process, you prevent the establishment of a Palestinian state, and you prevent a discussion on the refugees, the borders and Jerusalem. Effectively, this whole package called the Palestinian state, with all that it entails, has been removed indefinitely from our agenda. And all this with authority and permission. All with a presidential blessing and the ratification of both houses of Congress." "Top PM Aide: Gaza Plan Aims to Freeze the Peace Process," *Haaretz*, 6 October 2004, accessed at: https://bit.ly/2Rq90n3

[20] "Letter from President Bush to Prime Minister Sharon," *The White House*, 14 April 2004, accessed at: http://bit.ly/37HleK2

[21] "Remarks by the President at Cairo University, 6–04–09," *The White House: Office of the Press Secretary*, 4 June 2009, accessed at: http://bit.ly/39Q7XQy

Obama's second term, Secretary of State John Kerry assumed responsibility for the peace process.

Upon taking office, Kerry arranged a meeting at the White House, led by Obama, between Mahmoud Abbas and Benjamin Netanyahu. The informal talks immediately crumbled because Netanyahu refused to freeze settlements, which up until that point the US had deemed illegal and an obstacle to peace. And that was that: Obama subsequently avoided any direct engagement with "the peace process", turning it entirely over to Kerry with the knowledge that his diplomatic efforts would amount to nothing and that there was no hope of any flexibility from Netanyahu. Obama's plan called for the establishment of a Palestinian state within the 1967 borders and including the West Bank, the Gaza Strip and East Jerusalem, but Netanyahu rejected the proposal. Referring to Bush's letter to Sharon recognising the unfeasibility of a return to the 1967 borders, Netanyahu suggested that Obama was breaking a decades-old American commitment to Israel on this point.[22]

On 23 September 2011, the Quartet released a plan to resuscitate peace talks.[23] Meanwhile, the Palestinian Authority applied to join the United Nations Educational, Scientific and Cultural Organization (UNESCO). Opposed to any attempt by the PA to join any international organisation, including UNESCO, Israel responded by establishing 2,000 new settlement units. In 2013, Kerry made several official visits, but presented no actionable initiatives. A relatively advanced proposal was floated in 2016, just before the conclusion of Obama's presidential term and his own term as secretary of state—in other words, when it was too late. Neither Kerry nor Obama attempted to pressure or impose terms on Israel. On the contrary, Israel was rewarded for its intransigence.[24] In public remarks, Kerry

---

[22] Ethan Bronner, "Netanyahu Responds Icily to Obama Remarks," *The New York Times*, 19 May 2009, accessed at: https://nyti.ms/37QP4M5

[23] "Statement by Middle East Quartet," *United Nations*, 23 September 2011, accessed at: http://bit.ly/2uXJhXT

[24] In 2016, the Obama administration finalised the third Ten-Year Security Assistance Memorandum of Understanding (MOU) with Israel, as part of which the US pledged $38 billion in military aid to Israel over a decade (covering FY2019 to FY2028). This was the

outlined six principles underlying his last proposed programme, including the two-state solution framework with land swaps based on the 1967 borders and previous UN resolutions related to the Palestinian-Israeli conflict, including secure borders for both sides.[25]

Kerry's speech on the 2016 plan contains multiple references to satisfying Israel's security needs. Indeed, the proposal was predicated on the need to protect Israel's Jewish character from the Palestinian "demographic threat". It reflected the weak moral position of a presidential administration on its way out the door, not the sort of definitive negotiating terms that might have emerged at its beginning. In any case, Israel rejected the content of Kerry's speech out of hand, though it was welcomed by the PA and Arab countries—contradicting once more the widespread belief that Palestinians and/or Arabs resist US peace initiatives or plans.

In fact, the Arab League had convened in a show of support for Kerry soon after his appointment as secretary of state, in response to US administration efforts to resume Palestinian-Israeli negotiations after talks came to a standstill in October 2010 over the settlement issue. In its meeting on 30 April 2013, the Arab League amended its 2002 peace initiative—which had received no response from Israel—to recognise the principle of land swaps, thereby allowing for the Israeli annexation of so-called settlement blocs (Ariel, Ma'ale Adumim and Gush Etzion) later included in Kerry's final proposal, though the idea was met with nothing but rejection and disdain in Israel.

In *The Only Language They Understand* (2017), Nathan Thrall concludes that the US has neither the interest nor motivation to exert pressure on its ally, nor to change the status quo and create a Palestinian state, no matter how "small, poor, and strategically incon-

largest military aid package of its kind for Israel, already the largest recipient of American aid. The previous ten-year agreement, signed under the George W. Bush Administration in 2007, provided Israel with a $30 billion military aid package (about $3 billion a year) over a decade (FY2009–18). See: Jeremy M. Sharp, "US Foreign Aid to Israel," *Report*, Congressional Research Service, 16 November 2020, p. 6, accessed at: https://bit.ly/3tTw0II

[25] "Remarks on Middle East Peace," *US Department of State*, 28 December 2016, accessed at: http://bit.ly/2SODUDn

sequential." That is why US policy "remains designed to thwart actions that would raise the cost of the status quo, and so in effect sustains it."[26] At the same time, negotiations will never succeed or produce any meaningful result as long as there are no fixed negotiating terms and agreed-upon principles. Thrall argues that the US should at least support the UN in clearly defining the terms of any future agreement,[27] but the prevailing Israeli consensus irrationally "fears" this prospect, although any terms the US supported would surely be favourable to Israel. Netanyahu clearly expressed this "fear"[28] in his 2016 speech to the AIPAC Policy Conference, stating, "Those terms would undoubtedly be stacked against us. They always are."[29] This quote sums up years of unyielding Israeli rejection of any diplomatic initiative that might later set the terms for serious negotiation, which Israel apparently believes should be defined solely by its own power and explicit dominance.

Act First Agree Later

To kick off the seventh round of US peace initiatives, President Trump created a four-person team responsible for the Palestine issue. The first member of the group was Jared Kushner,[30] his son-in-law, whose credentials were being the son of a real estate developer, a

---

[26] Nathan Thrall, *The Only Language They Understand: Forcing Compromise in Israel and Palestine* (New York: Metropolitan Books, 2017), p. 209.

[27] Ibid., p. 215.

[28] I put the word fear here in quotation marks because unlike Thrall I do not accept the Israeli occupying power's claim to fear at face value.

[29] Ibid.; "PM Netanyahu addresses the 2016 AIPAC Policy Conference," *Israel Ministry of Foreign Affairs*, 22 March 2016, accessed at: https://bit.ly/3x3NC6W

[30] Trump's son-in-law is the son of real estate developer Charles Kushner. A graduate of Harvard University, he secured admittance despite his poor high school grades thanks to a $2.5 million donation from his father to the university in 1998, according to journalist and author Daniel Golden. Kushner obtained a law degree in 2007 from New York University, also a recipient of his father's largesse in the form of a $3 million grant in 2001. Trump appointed him White House senior advisor, a rare instance in which a US president has given a major position to a family member, possibly because the position does not require Senate confirmation. Kushner headed the team of lawyers who wrote Trump's vision for peace and who, like Kushner, do not hide their right-wing Zionist leanings.

donor to Israeli settlements and a strong supporter of Netanyahu who identifies wholly and openly with Israel. To be fair to Kushner, his knowledge of the region and the Palestine issue comes from prodigious reading—by his own estimation, as many as twenty-five books about the Middle East.[31] Even assuming the truth of this assertion, one shudders to imagine which books he read. As Trump's senior advisor and son-in-law, he was received like a king in Arab countries.

The second member of the group was David Friedman, a right-wing Zionist whose close relationship with Trump dates back to his time as a bankruptcy lawyer (despite his reality TV persona, Trump is a terrible businessman who has declared bankruptcy more than once). It is a reasonable assumption that Friedman, appointed by Trump to serve as US ambassador to Israel, played a major role in writing the text of the eventual deal, in cooperation with Netanyahu. The other two members of the group were Jason Greenblatt[32] and Avi Berkowitz.[33]

The Trump administration began the implementation of its peace deal before it had even been announced, a clever strategy concocted by the aforementioned group designed to gauge the reactions of the Arab world and the international community at each step. The administration clearly saw the Arab world through the eyes of cer-

---

[31] Josephine Harvey, "Jared Kushner Says He's 'Read 25 Books' On The Israeli-Palestinian Conflict," *HuffPost*, 29 January 2020, accessed at: http://bit.ly/2VdH6dq

[32] An American lawyer, Greenblatt served as executive vice-president and chief legal officer to Trump and the Trump Organisation, and later as President Trump's adviser on Israel, as well as assistant to the president and special representative for international negotiations. In 2016, Greenblatt stated that the West Bank settlements are "not an obstacle to peace." See: Ruth Eglash, "Top Trump adviser says Israeli settlements are not an obstacle to peace," *The Washington Post*, 10 November 2016, accessed at: https://wapo.st/3pfZkb2. When Greenblatt resigned from his position in late 2019, he was succeeded by lawyer Avi Berkowitz.

[33] Berkowitz's sole credentials appear to be his personal friendship with Kushner. He studied at an Orthodox *yeshiva* in Israel and graduated from Harvard University in 2016, when he worked on Trump's presidential campaign. He was served as logistical manager for a live media broadcast from Trump Tower and an assistant to Kushner. Some called him Kushner's "protégé" while others described him as Kushner's "coffee boy." See: Bess Levin, "Trump's New Mideast Point Man is Jared Kushner's Former Coffee Boy Avi Berkowitz," *Vanity Fair*, 5 September 2019, accessed at: http://bit.ly/2w106AY

tain Gulf state rulers, which led them to underestimate negative reactions. For example, there is more than one indication that the UAE was consulted on the plan ahead of time and expressed enthusiastic support for it.

The first step of the deal, which the US took on 31 August 2018, was to end US financial assistance to UNRWA, cutting a full third of the organisation's $1 billion annual budget.[34] In practical terms, the suspension of aid to the organisation meant that the US no longer recognised the existence of a Palestinian refugee issue. UNRWA is not a non-governmental organisation or a charity, but a UN organisation established, with the support of the US, pursuant to Resolution 194/1948, which calls for the return of Palestinian refugees and was followed by dozens of UN resolutions affirming the right of return for refugees.

The second step, taken on 6 December 2017, was to relocate the US embassy from Tel Aviv to Jerusalem. On the face of it, the move appeared as simply the belated execution of a 1995 congressional act requiring the US to recognise Jerusalem as the capital of the Jewish state no later than May 1999. However, the act also allowed the president to waive implementation every six months, which is what every US president had done since 1995. The waiver provision itself, in a law drafted by pro-Israel members of Congress, and its use by every successive administration reflected a common understanding that implementing the highly controversial act would undermine the US administration's credibility as a mediator on Israel-Palestine.

Trump openly dismissed warnings about the potential consequences of the move, first saying that "the world would not end" then bragging that he had moved the embassy and nothing had happened.

The third step in implementing the Trump-Netanyahu deal was to close the PLO office in Washington, D.C.[35]

When no appropriate Arab or Palestinian reaction followed from the previous actions, the fourth step was taken. On 18 November

[34] "US Ends Aid to Palestinian Refugee Agency UNRWA," *BBC News*, 1 September 2018, accessed at: https://bbc.in/2SOL8Hn

[35] Karen DeYoung & Loveday Morris, "Trump Administration Orders Closure of PLO Office in Washington," *The Washington Post*, 11 September 2018, accessed at: https://wapo.st/37UMdSi

2019, Secretary of State Mike Pompeo declared that the US no longer considered Israeli settlements in the West Bank to be in violation of international law,[36] meaning that as far as the American administration was concerned, the West Bank was not occupied territory. With this declaration, Pompeo—who is no less ideologically extreme than the four group members described above—did away with the permanent status issues that were ostensibly the subject of negotiations, abandoning the negotiation framework in place since the Oslo Declaration of Principles.

This marked a radical shift in the US position on Israeli settlements in the occupied territories. In 1979, the Carter administration abstained from voting on Security Council Resolution 446[37] condemning the establishment of settlements in the Occupied Territories on the grounds that they were "a serious obstacle to peace in the Middle East and had no legal basis," in a departure from the usual US practice of vetoing condemnations of Israeli policy.

The US position nearly shifted under Reagan, whose staunch support for Israel extended to its West Bank settlements. On 2 February 1981, around two weeks after officially taking office, Reagan expressed opposition to the Carter administration's position on settlements, saying that to him, they were "not illegal." Needless to say, Begin's government welcomed Reagan's informal declaration, but the latter's administration warned him of potential repercussions. He subsequently retracted his declaration on the basis of the 1978 Hansell Memorandum,[38] which had concluded that while "Israel may

---

[36] Karen DeYoung, Steve Hendrix & John Hudson, "Trump Administration Says Israel's West Bank Settlements Do Not Violate International Law," *The Washington Post*, 19 November 2019, accessed at: https://wapo.st/37T2Ygy

[37] "Resolution 446 (1979) of 22 March 1979," *UN Security Council*, accessed at: http://bit.ly/2uniqUJ

[38] The Letter of the State Department Legal Adviser Concerning the Legality of Israeli Settlements in the Occupied Territories, which came to be known as the Hansell Memorandum, was issued on 21 April 1978. Herbert Hansell, who served as the legal adviser of the US State Department under Carter, sent the letter to Congress at the request of two House subcommittees; it was also published in *State Magazine*. See: Herbert J. Hansell, "United States Letter of the State Department Legal Adviser Concerning the Legality of Israeli Settlements in the Occupied Territories," *International Legal Materials*, vol. 17, no. 3 (May 1978), pp. 777–9.

undertake, in the occupied territories, actions necessary to meet its military needs [...] the establishment of the civilian settlements in those territories is inconsistent with international law." In addition, Reagan called continued Israeli settlement construction "provocative and unnecessary," and as part of his peace initiative, he called on Israel to halt new settlements in September 1982. Multiple presidential statements affirmed that the settlements posed an obstacle to peace talks, and throughout Reagan's tenure, the State Department's official legal position on settlement expansion was based on the Hansell Memorandum.[39]

The Clinton administration officially supported the principle of land for peace and similarly considered Israeli settlements an "obstacle to peace," though it did make exemptions for "natural growth" needs which allowed Israel to continue settlement construction in the West Bank and occupied East Jerusalem.[40] George W. Bush also expressed concerns about settlement expansion, saying that it impeded efforts towards peace and urging Israel to keep its commitment to "dissolve illegal settlements."[41] At that time, Israel made a formal distinction between legal and illegal settlements. This is an important point: from the perspective of international law and for a colonised people, there is no such thing as a legal settlement, but if the determination of the legality or illegality of settlements rests with the Israeli government, this represents a de facto extension of Israeli law to the occupied territories and, in turn, their effective annexation by stealth.

After Obama took office in 2009, the official American position shifted. The refusal to freeze settlements in the West Bank and East Jerusalem was no longer simply a theoretical obstacle to peace; a freeze was widely understood to be a practical precondition for the success of Israeli-Palestinian peace negotiations.[42] This position,

---

[39] Bernard Gwertzman, "State Department; about the West Bank and the Emperor's Clothes," *The New York Times*, 25 August 1983, accessed at: https://nyti.ms/32gWTtm

[40] Khaled Elgindy, "Trump Can't Kill the Peace Process, it was already Dead," *Slate*, 17 April 2019, accessed at: http://bit.ly/2wy5cVI

[41] Matt Spetalnick, "Bush: Israel settlement expansion 'impediment'," *Reuters*, 3 January 2008, accessed at: https://reut.rs/36SzWgy

[42] Elliott Abrams, "The Settlement Obsession: Both Israel and the United States Miss the Obstacles to Peace," *Foreign Affairs*, vol. 99, no. 2 (July/August 2011).

which made resumption of negotiations contingent on the freezing of settlements, was unprecedented but short-lived. While Abbas clung to it, Obama later abandoned this precondition, and when in 2011, the UN Security Council issued a resolution calling for the cessation of settlement construction, the US vetoed it.[43] Much later, during a 2016 Security Council session, the US representative declined to exercise her veto over a resolution condemning settlement activity,[44] but this was towards the end of Obama's term, when he began to more openly convey his frustration with Netanyahu. In a 2017 interview with Israeli TV, Obama explicitly said that Netanyahu's policy of supporting settlements in the occupied territories made a future Palestinian state impossible.[45] Considering this historical record, Pompeo's 2019 declaration that the settlements were legal obviously reflected a radical shift.

In practical terms, Trump's incremental introduction of his proposal was neither foolish nor accidental. Adopting a right-wing Zionist approach, the four-person team drawing up the plan deliberately sought to take some of the permanent status issues of the Oslo Accords—borders (including settlements), Jerusalem and refugees—off the table, relieving Israel of the burden of pursuing a fair, lasting solution through negotiations and formally nullifying the Oslo Accords. The Palestinian president is right to be angry and correct to say that there is nothing left for him to negotiate. He nevertheless continues to cling improbably to negotiations as an exclusive strategy, even though successful talks hinge on the vicissitudes of domestic elections and politics in Israel and the US. Despite his recognition of the observable negative outcomes of that precarious strategy, Abbas is in complete denial of the relationship between means and ends, strategy and outcomes.

---

[43] "United States Vetoes Security Council Resolution on Israeli Settlements," *UN News*, 18 February 2011, accessed at: https://bit.ly/2Sbhqeb

[44] "Resolution 2334 (2016)," *UN Security Council*, 23 December 2016, accessed at: http://bit.ly/2wGIOtt; "Israel's Settlements Have No Legal Validity, Constitute Flagrant Violation of International Law, Security Council Reaffirms," *UN Security Council*, 23 December 2016, accessed at: http://bit.ly/2T97x0V

[45] "Obama Says Israeli Settlements Making Two-State Solution Impossible," *Reuters*, 10 January 2017, accessed at: https://reut.rs/2GLM60b

In a closed-door meeting with American senators to discuss the Trump administration's Middle East peace plan, Kushner warned the PA that if it did not agree to negotiate on the basis of the Deal of the Century, the Trump administration would support Israel's unilateral annexation of settlements and enclaves in the West Bank.[46] Yet, the end result of the so-called "deal of the century" is annexation. Kushner's ultimatum encapsulated the perverse dilemma facing Palestinians: negotiate based on a plan calling for the annexation of settlements, or the settlements will be annexed.

The Text: No Need to Read Between the Lines

In the title of this chapter, I used the term "Trump-Netanyahu deal" to refer to Trump's self-professed "vision."[47] I chose that description not only because the content of the plan reflects Netanyahu's thinking, and not only because Netanyahu and the Israeli right sought to take advantage of Trump's presence in the White House to achieve important political gains. I chose it as well because this was a partisan deal intended to help both Trump and Netanyahu in their respective domestic elections. Trump burnished Netanyahu's image among the Israeli right and mainstream by granting his ideas cachet in the White House and, by extension, some Arab capitals; similarly, by flattering Netanyahu, Trump courted his own electoral base, especially its extreme evangelical, Christian Zionist core.

In this respect, the Trump-Netanyahu deal is instructive, illustrating how the transnational populist right operates on the level of international relations and showing how the capitalist logic of real estate development underlies the actions of the government of a superpower with no commitment to international legitimacy. First, the deal exemplifies a power-based approach, in which power means the ability to impose one's will, even if it means trampling international laws prohibiting the forceful annexation of others' land or violating previ-

---

[46] Barak Ravid, "What Jared Kushner Told Senators about Trump's Middle East Peace Plan," *Axios*, 4 March 2020, accessed at: http://bit.ly/2vWYxoe

[47] The White House, *Peace to Prosperity: A Vision to Improve the Lives of the Palestinian and Israeli People* (January 2020), accessed at: https://bit.ly/2S6c3Rt

ous agreements and commitments. Second, the deal fully embraces the Israeli narrative, espousing all the absurdities inherent in the contemporary politicisation of the biblical narrative. Third, the language of the deal is a throwback to the colonial rhetoric of the nineteenth century, communicating its misbegotten proposals in egregiously paternalistic and condescending terms.

The deal gives Israel complete custodianship of the occupied territories, allowing it continued control over security in the state of Palestine, while simultaneously "aspiring" to give Palestinians responsibility for "as much of their internal security as possible." In other words, the state of Palestine's full sovereign responsibility for even its own internal security remains uncertain—a mere potentiality, and even if it were realised, it would not include control of crossings and borders; according to the deal,

> "the State of Israel will maintain overriding security responsibility for the State of Palestine, with the aspiration that the Palestinians will be responsible for as much of their internal security as possible, subject to the provisions of this Vision. The State of Israel will work diligently to minimise its security footprint in the State of Palestine according to the principle that the more the State of Palestine does, the less the State of Israel will have to do."[48]

It goes on to suggest that Jordan assist the PA to combat "terrorism". The deal subsequently elaborates:

> "Should the State of Palestine fail to meet all or any of the Security Criteria at any time, the State of Israel will have the right to reverse the process outlined above. The State of Israel's security footprint in all or parts of the State of Palestine will then increase as a result of the State of Israel's determination of its expanded security needs and the time needed to address them."[49]

This means that Israel will unilaterally determine its security needs, and how and when it will act on them—a succinct description of the current status quo. In short, the deal nominally recognises the Palestinian Authority as a "state," but gives it no sovereignty, as Israel

---

[48] "Part A: Political Framework," in: Ibid., p. 21.

[49] Ibid., p. 23.

can decide when and how to cross the "borders" of this state and conduct security operations on its territory.

The document's overall language is the most abysmal sort of colonial-speak one could possibly find in the present day, promising rewards for Palestinians if they meet Israel's subjective standards and punishing them by reversing the entire process if they meet with Israeli disapproval. Such language can no longer be legitimately uttered in any other context, inextricably linked as it is to fallacious ideas of racial supremacy and the "civilising missions" of the nineteenth century that asserted that only white men were qualified to judge the interests of colonised people. The colonised people were treated according to similar perceptions of how children should be raised or socialised, where they must be punished and rewarded until they learned to submit, in the hope that they would eventually become qualified to govern themselves "as much as possible."

This paternalism extends to culture and education. The document attributes Israeli bromides about violence and terrorism to Trump, quoting him as though he were an intellectual or philosopher:

> "As President Trump has said: 'Peace can never take root in an environment where violence is tolerated, funded and even rewarded.' Therefore, it is very important that education focuses on peace to ensure that future generations are committed to peace and to ensure that the Israeli-Palestinian Peace Agreement can endure. Promoting a culture of peace will be an important element of the Israeli-Palestinian Peace Agreement with the goal of creating an environment that embraces the values of coexistence and mutual respect throughout the region."[50]

The necessity of education for peace is thus emphasised, but only Palestinian educational curricula are spotlighted as a source of concern. No similar pressure is brought to bear on Israel to purge its educational curricula of racism and hostility towards Arabs and Palestinians or of the Zionist religious narrative about the history of the land, although numerous Israeli polls indicate that racism is widespread among Israeli Jewish youth. The aChord Center, for example, recently conducted a comprehensive study, published by the Hebrew

---

[50] Ibid., p. 35.

University, assessing youth public opinion in Israel ("The 2021 Index for Shared Society Progress in Youth") based on a survey in May and July 2020 of 1,091 teenage boys and girls aged 16–18 from secular Jewish, religious Jewish, ultra-Orthodox (Haredi) and Arab backgrounds. The survey found that two-thirds (66 percent) of ultra-Orthodox youth (Haredi youth), 42 per cent of religious Jewish youth and a quarter (24 per cent) of secular Jewish youth expressed feelings of fear and hatred towards Arabs. Similarly, a majority of ultra-Orthodox youth and nearly half of religious Jewish youth hold negative stereotypes of Arabs (58.2 per cent of Haredi youth, 41.3 per cent of the religious Jewish youth and 19.4 per cent of the secular Jewish youth expressed this view). Moreover, a high percentage (49 per cent) of religious Jewish youth and 23 per cent of secular Jewish youth expressed support for denying Arabs the right to vote (Haredim were not asked this question).[51] These findings are consistent with general Jewish public opinion in Israeli society. For example, the results of the 2021 Israeli Pluralism Index conducted by the Jewish People Policy Institute reveal a preference among a majority of religious Jews for Israel to be more Jewish (Haredi: 92 per cent; religious: 89 percent; national religious: 87 per cent). The survey reports, "Only a tiny minority of Jews in Israel (one percent) would prefer that Israel cease to be a Jewish state" and become a state of equal citizens. The findings also show that almost two-thirds (61 percent) and more than half (51 per cent) of right and centre-right Jews, respectively, agree that the Jewish state must give legal preference to Jews over non-Jews.[52]

The Trump-Netanyahu document espouses the right-wing national-religious Israeli narrative that casts the Torah as some combination of international law, contemporary political document and official title deed—as if God, like Trump, were a real estate broker.

---

[51] See: Tal Orian Harel et al., "The Partnership Index among Youth in Israel in 2020," *Index*, aChord, the Hebrew University of Jerusalem, April 2021, pp. 76, 78–9, 82, accessed at: https://bit.ly/3teHpSm (in Hebrew).

[52] See: Shmuel Rosner, Noah Slepkov & Camil Fuchs, "The 2021 Israel Pluralism Index: Consensus and Disagreements," *The Jewish People Policy Institute*, 8 April 2021, accessed at: https://bit.ly/2PHLYH9

In contrast, it contains not a single word reflecting the Palestinian narrative. The Israeli narrative is not distinguished or identified as such, since for the authors of this document, it is the default narrative, the rule to which everything else is an exception. A national-religious Jewish fundamentalism pervades the entire text:

> For Judaism, Jerusalem is where Mount Moriah [or the Temple Mount, as it later came to be called] is located. According to Jewish tradition, it was there that Abraham nearly sacrificed his son, Isaac, until God intervened. Centuries later, Jerusalem became the political centre of the Jewish people when King David united the twelve tribes of Israel, making the city the capital and spiritual centre of the Jewish people, which it has remained for nearly 3,000 years. King David's son, King Solomon, built the First Temple on Mount Moriah. According to Jewish tradition, inside the Temple, within the Holy of Holies, were stored the original Ten Commandments, revealed by God to Moses at Mount Sinai. The First Temple was destroyed by the Babylonians in 586 B.C. The Second Temple was built atop the same mountain and stood until it was destroyed by the Romans in 70 A.D. However, Jerusalem never lost its holiness to the Jewish People: It remains the direction to which Jews throughout the world turn in prayer and the destination of Jewish pilgrimage. Every year, on the 9th day of the Jewish month of Av, Jews fast, mourn and commemorate the destruction of the two Temples. Although Jews pray today at the Western Wall [the Wailing Wall], which was a retaining wall of the Second Temple, the Temple Mount itself is the holiest site in Judaism. There are nearly 700 separate references to Jerusalem in the Hebrew Bible. For 100 generations the hopes and dreams of the Jewish people have been encapsulated by the words 'Next Year in Jerusalem.'[53]

This lengthy quote had to be cited in its entirety to demonstrate the absurdity of a text that is ostensibly an international policy document serving as the basis for a future Palestinian-Israeli peace treaty. It is more akin to a Knesset speech by the head of the nationalist-religious party, its language reminiscent of the Israeli propaganda found in pamphlets passed out to Evangelical tourists in Jerusalem.

The document does not fail to remind us that the Torah includes 700 references to Jerusalem whereas the Qur'an makes no mention

---

[53] "Part A: Political Framework," in: *Peace to Prosperity*, p. 15.

of it, referring only to the Al-Aqsa Mosque in the context of the Prophet Muhammad's nocturnal journey from Mecca to Jerusalem (*al-Isrā*); it was only the later Umayyad Caliphate that showed interest in Jerusalem, it notes.[54] For this trivial reason, Jerusalem must remain the undivided capital of Israel—the only thing missing is the lofty label *eternal*, so beloved by the Israeli right.

Yet, contemporary Jerusalem is neither the Biblical nor the Qur'anic city. The fact that Jews consider it a spiritual centre does not make it the capital of Israel, just as the presence of Muslim and Christian holy sites does not turn it into a Muslim or Christian capital; Jerusalem could be the capital of two states created by a political solution and still include holy places for Jews, Christians and Muslims. Religious matters are beyond our scope here, but it must be stressed that with this document, the Trump administration not only embraced a fundamentalist religious discourse based on the Torah (which is not exactly a pacifist text), but effectively aligned itself with the extreme position of a specific—and decidedly modern—religious strand of Judaism to the exclusion of all others.[55]

It is imprudent, to say the least, for a global superpower to approach relations between modern states based on politicised inter-

---

[54] Ibid., pp. 15–16.

[55] The main strand of Orthodox Judaism forbids ascending the Temple Mount before there are any signs of the Messiah's coming. Before it was Zionised intellectually (and, in some cases, pragmatically, since it found itself part of and in need of certain institutions of the Jewish state), it did not even recognise the state of Israel on the grounds that it was a secular, messianic state interfering with the work of God. The secular Zionism underlying the establishment of Israel did not initially adopt this biblical discourse and prior to 1967, its discourse was not focused on Jerusalem or the Temple Mount. Though Zionism was never free of religious symbols or references (e.g., to define who is a Jew), it eventually incorporated aspects of religious political discourse, through a process of the Zionisation of Orthodox Jews and the religionisation of the Zionist discourse on Jerusalem and the West Bank following their occupation. While only a minority of Israeli society is interested in praying on the Temple Mount, this sector, small though it is, constituted an important part of Netanyahu's coalition with outsized influence on his and other right-wing governments. Under the influence of Kushner's team, as well as that of American Evangelical Christian Zionism, the Trump administration adopted this national-religious discourse wholesale.

pretations of religious texts. *States, sovereignty, legitimacy, international law, colonialism, the right to self-determination* and related terms and phrases describe and are grounded in modern human endeavours and thought, not Biblical. If the text of the Torah were taken as a reference for contemporary politics, genocide would be legitimate and even divinely ordained.

A superpower whose constitution enshrines the separation of church and state invoked scripture as a political argument in an official diplomatic text, and this deployment of religious text for colonial purposes passed unremarked by the international community. Even from a religious Jewish perspective, this "vision" constitutes a partisan abuse of religion. What is new and noteworthy in this case is the US president's endorsement, thanks to the presence of someone like Trump in the White House.

The document similarly appropriates Israel's secular narrative of its connection to the region and views security through the Israeli lens. Israel (which occupies the land of others) is cast as a victim throughout the document, which makes repeated references to the plight of Israelis with nary a word about the ongoing suffering of Palestinians since the Nakba. If it gestures to Palestinian suffering, it is in the context of mistakes made by their leaders and always with the implication that they brought suffering on themselves. At the same time, the text refers repeatedly to Israeli "concessions" to Palestinians over the past decades. Of particular note is the following passage:

> "No government should be asked to compromise the safety and security of its citizens. This is especially true for the State of Israel, a country that since its establishment has faced, and continues to face, enemies that call for its annihilation. Israel has also had the bitter experience of withdrawing from territories that were then used to launch attacks against it."[56]

The document thus adopts the narrative of overriding Israeli victimhood, even though it is in fact the victimiser in this context, occupying the land of others and engaging in decades of aggressive warfare, from the 1956 war against Egypt to the 1967 war (which

---

[56] "Part A: Political Framework," in: *Peace to Prosperity*, p. 7.

Israel deceptively portrays as a "defensive war") and the assault and invasion of Lebanon in 1982 and 2006. Arab states did wage a war in 1948, but only after the Zionist movement unilaterally declared a state in Palestine and began seizing land and "cleansing" it of its indigenous inhabitants, in areas of both the future Arab and Jewish states as designated by the UN partition plan. The only offensive Arab war was the 1973 war. Scholar and public intellectual Noam Chomsky did not consider this an aggressive war against Israel, however,[57] but rather an offensive to recover occupied Arab territory after Israel had rejected all international initiatives and resolutions calling for its withdrawal.

The word 'occupation', in the sense of seizing a territory by force,[58] does not appear in the text. What are we talking about, then? The document refers to the occupied territories as "territory captured in a defensive war,"[59] in reference to the 1967 war. This echoes Israeli terminology from the early years of the occupation, when the Israeli government called the occupied territories *shtahim muhzakim* (captured or seized territories). The Hebrew was officially translated into Arabic as *al-manatiq al-mudara* ("administered regions") before the Israelis authorities began using the Biblical designation of Judea and Samaria. As the terms suggest, the intention was for Israel to administer these regions until peace negotiations were initiated; the occupied territories were "held hostage" and the ransom was peace with the Arab states (on Israeli terms, of course). In referring to the occupied territories as "captured"—a term used by no other country—the document's authors thus borrowed the original Hebrew wording. This is a particularly apt illustration of the way the document deliberately distorts language with the aim of distorting reality.

Reading the document through from beginning to end transports the reader from the realm of international politics and conflict reso-

---

[57] Noam Chomsky, *Fateful Triangle: The United States, Israel, and the Palestinians*, Edward W. Said (Foreword), 3rd ed. (Cambridge, M A: South End Press, 1999), pp. 99–100.

[58] It is used in the text, but only in the sense of "work," as in: "This project will increase job placement rates for Palestinian youth and women by providing them with career counseling, specialized training, and job placement services in a concentrated effort to employ them in higher-wage, high-growth occupations" [author's emphasis].

[59] "Part A: Political Framework," in: *Peace to Prosperity*, p. 8.

lution to a different world entirely—that of real estate development, which the plan's authors apparently believe is a vocation, a higher calling and political panacea, capable of truly improving people's lives and delivering the kind of real, practical solutions that politicians can only dream of. The text is shot through with the kind of jargon Trump might use to hype his latest project: "To support this new development, the economic development program will identify financing for the construction of restaurants, shops, hotels, cultural centres, and other tourism facilities within this zone." Would that differ from the existing settlement economic zones that already employ Palestinians? Israel exploits the impoverished Palestinian workforce, who are paid salaries that range from 30–40 per cent of the legal minimum wage a day, not only by importing workers to Israel but also in the West Bank itself. Twenty settlement industrial zones were established along with hundreds of Israeli factories and dozens of agricultural settlements that cultivate over 9,000 hectares of occupied West Bank land.[60]

"Fast-track accessibility to the Muslim Holy Shrines should be developed and maintained. The specific details of this area, including, without limitation, taxation, and zoning should be negotiated between the parties."[61] The document that begins with invocations of the Torah wraps up with details about tourism, recreation, restaurants and hotels. The idea of a contemporary international diplomatic text citing scripture is no less ridiculous than a peace initiative that promises the construction of restaurants. They may as well have taken the farce to its logical conclusion and provided menu suggestions.

Fallacies

The text articulating the Trump-Netanyahu "vision" is riddled with gross fallacies that insult the reader's intelligence.

First: "It must be recognized that the State of Israel has already withdrawn from at least 88% of the territory it captured in 1967."[62]

---

[60] Matthew Vickery, *Employing the Enemy: The Story of Palestinian Labourers on Israeli Settlements* (London: Zed Books, 2017), p. 3, 82, 89.

[61] Ibid., p. 18.

[62] Ibid., p. 8.

Here, the authors are referring to the withdrawal from Sinai, implemented within the framework of the peace treaty with Egypt. The remaining 12 per cent comprises the occupied Palestinian territories and the Golan Heights. In order to emphasise the significance of Israeli "concessions", the text lumps all Arabs together—something the authors seem to do when it suits their purposes. But is Israel ready to negotiate over the occupied territories with all Arab countries combined? Of course not. Israel rejected the Arab Peace Initiative unanimously supported by the Arab League at the March 2002 Beirut Summit. Later amended by the Arab League to further accommodate the US administration, the plan proposed peace, normalising relations with Israel and the principle of land swaps.

Second: "[T]he State of Palestine will benefit from special access to certain designated facilities at the State of Israel's Haifa and Ashdod ports, with an efficient means of exporting and importing goods into and out of the State of Palestine without compromising Israel's security."[63] Where is the fallacy? It is that Palestinians already use these two ports for imports and exports, and this is a source of profit for Israel. Indeed, it is an artifact of the occupation. If Palestinians had been allowed to build a port in Gaza, they would not be using the ports of Haifa and Ashdod, though that would be a potential point of cooperation between two sovereign states. In other words, this is not a benefit given to the Palestinians pursuant to an agreement with Israel; it is part and parcel of the reality of occupation.

Third:

> Concerning the territorial issue, the text states that the "State of Israel and the United States do not believe the State of Israel is legally bound to provide the Palestinians with 100 percent of pre-1967 territory [i.e., the West Bank and the Gaza Strip] (a belief that is consistent with United Nations Security Council Resolution 242). This Vision is a fair compromise, and contemplates a Palestinian state that encompasses territory reasonably comparable in size to the territory of the West Bank and Gaza pre-1967."[64]

---

[63] Ibid., p. 12.

[64] Ibid., pp. 11–12. In this passage, the document suddenly shifts from the first person singular voice to the first person plural. This "slip of the pen" or "slip of the keyboard" is quite

The fallacy lies in the deceptive reference to less than 100 per cent of the territory occupied in 1967 as a fair compromise. Yet, for Palestinians, the territorial claim at issue is 100 per cent of all of Palestine, which came under a British Mandate after World War I and includes both the land occupied in 1948 and the remaining territory occupied in 1967. Accepting the 100 per cent of West Bank (including East Jerusalem) and the Gaza Strip as the sole territories of a Palestinian state is already a historical compromise, a significant political concession that meets Israel halfway. It consists of accepting an independent state with sovereignty over only 22 per cent of the land of Palestine.

Furthermore, according to the document, a peace treaty granting the Palestinians less than 100 per cent of the territories occupied in 1967 is consistent with Resolution 242, an assertion premised entirely on the Israeli reading of that resolution, which hinges on a distinction between "the territories" occupied in 1967 (implying all territories) and "territories" occupied in 1967 (implying some).[65] The precise wording in the English-language version of the resolution is *withdrawal of Israeli armed forces from territories occupied in the recent conflict*. In context, there was no need for the definite article ("the territories") to clarify that the entirety of the land was meant, because the territory in question is already defined by the phrase *in the recent conflict*, i.e., the 1967 war. This already differentiates these territories from other territories occupied in other conflicts and wars. Moreover, the French version of the resolution (as well as the Spanish, Russian and Chinese versions) uses the definite article.

Fourth: an additional fallacy appears in the same part of the document. The text says that the land swaps may include part of the Triangle, a region consisting of three areas with about fifteen villages and towns.[66] The Triangle was occupied in 1948 and under the 1949

---

revealing exposing the fact that the document is not the brainchild of the US alone, but a US-Israeli collaborative text.

[65] "Resolution 242 (1967) of 22 November 1967," *UN Security Council*, accessed at: http://bit.ly/38ThpCF

[66] There is no talk of returning the entire region, as parts of it are very close to Israel's major urban centres and the coast.

Armistice Agreement with Jordan and should have been returned to Amman, but Israel held on to it in violation of the armistice borders and granted the Arabs living there Israeli citizenship (today they number about 350,000). It is these communities that the text proposes to return to the Palestinian Authority, but the objective is not to return land per se, but to reduce the number of Arab citizens in Israel. In other words, what is envisioned is not a land swap, but a targeted population transfer of Arab residents in order to preserve Israel's Jewish character. Indeed, this is why some on the Israeli right like Avigdor Lieberman[67] have long advocated trading this area in a future peace treaty.

Fifth: according to the document, "Peace should not demand the uprooting of people—Arab or Jew—from their homes. Such a construct, which is more likely to lead to civil unrest, runs counter to the idea of co-existence."[68] But no political compromise has ever proposed expelling any Arabs from their homes. They were already expelled and displaced in 1948; many of them fled to the East Bank in Jordan after the 1967 war while others have continued to be expelled from their homes since then under the policy of house demolitions in Jerusalem and elsewhere.[69]

What is really meant, then, by the assertion that no one, Arab or Jew, should be uprooted from their homes is to preclude Israel's

---

[67] Avigdor Lieberman is a Soviet-born Israeli politician who immigrated with his parents to Israel at the age of 20. He is the leader of the nationalist right-wing political party Yisrael Beiteinu and served as Israel's Foreign Minister (2009–12; 2013–15) and Defence Minister (2016–18). A settler himself, Lieberman has rejected previous peace formulas, such as land for peace, and as part of a "Populated-Area Exchange Plan" has advocated transferring the Israeli Arab population to a Palestinian state, also known as the "Populated-Area Exchange Plan."

[68] "Part A: Political Framework," in: *Peace to Prosperity*, p. 8.

[69] According to B'Tselem, a Jerusalem-based non-profit organisation, from 2006 to 2021, 1,756 Palestinian-owned homes were demolished on the grounds of unlawful construction, leaving 7,492 Palestinians homeless. From 2004 to 2018, 1,883 homes were demolished for alleged military purposes, forcing 13,344 Palestinians out of their homes. Israel has also demolished 263 houses from 2004 to 2021 as punishment, leaving 1,288 Palestinians homeless. These figures apply to East Jerusalem, the West Bank and Gaza. See: "Database on Fatalities and House Demolitions," *B'Tselem: The Israeli Information Center for Human Rights in the Occupied Territories*, accessed at: https://bit.ly/3vZ6HpH

Map 7.1a, b & c: The Palestinian Triangle

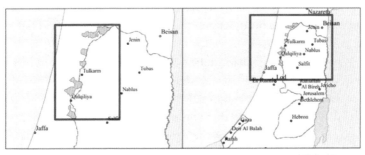

TRIANGLE:

An Arab-majority area of towns and villages adjacent to the Green Line Which Trump's vision proposed to be transferred to future Palestinian state. The Triangle is further divided into the "Northern Triangle" or Wadi Ara (around Kafr Qara, Ar'ara, Baqa al-Gharbiyye, Zemer and Umm al-Fahm) and the Southern Triangle (around Qalansawe, Tayibe, Kafr Qasim, Tira, Kafr Bara and Jaljulia).

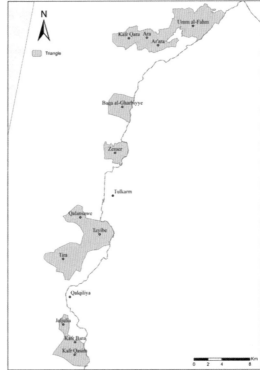

withdrawal from West Bank settlements. The language refers to both Jews and Arabs to make it appear as though letting settlers stay in their illegally acquired homes is somehow a just compromise. The text proposes equal status between settlers in "their homes" and Arabs whose land was occupied, establishing a false legal and moral equivalency between the occupier and the occupied, the armed robber and the robbery victim.

What this glaring fallacy indicates is that the deal does not foresee Israeli withdrawal from any settlement. In this respect, it goes further than even Sharon, whose 2005 unilateral withdrawal from Gaza forced settlers to leave "their homes" in the illegal settlements of the Gaza Strip, and one-ups the Zionism of most Israeli politicians, who have already recognised that withdrawal from "some settlements" will be part of a lasting negotiated solution. The document refers to "enclaves," i.e., settlements within Palestinian agglomerations, to distinguish them from the border settlement clusters previously mentioned.

The compromise mentioned in the text supposedly provides the Palestinians already uprooted from their homes—that is, refugees and their right to return—with solutions. the document states "The Israeli-Palestinian Peace Agreement shall provide for a complete end and release of any and all claims relating to refugee or immigration status. There shall be no right of return by, or absorption of, any Palestinian refugee into the State of Israel."[70] The language is categorical, definitively excluding the right of return from the agenda of negotiations. There is not even the barest attempt to pay lip service to refugees' rights along the line of proposals made in post-Oslo committee negotiations to allow the few thousand 1948 refugees still alive to return, but without their offspring. Regarding the Palestinian right of return to PA territories, the document limits it to Palestinian refugees without a permanent place of residence. These cases are to be brought before a joint Palestinian-Israeli committee, which shall review each application in light of Israeli security considerations and the ability of Palestine to absorb them (with both factors assessed

---

[70] "Part A: Political Framework," in: *Peace to Prosperity*, p. 32.

using Israeli-defined criteria). The document also envisions persuading Islamic countries to absorb 5,000 Palestinian refugees per year.[71]

On State and Sovereignty

The Trump-Netanyahu deal promises the Palestinians a state, but for the text's authors, this is a simple semantic issue: they merely christen the existing Palestinian Authority as a "state". This is reminiscent of Netanyahu's talk at Bar-Ilan University in 2009, soon after Obama first took office and after Netanyahu had to agree to use the term *Palestinian state*. He delivered a long speech informing his audience of this change, using language almost identical to that of Trump's document:

> "I told President Obama in Washington that if we could agree on the substance, then the terminology would not pose a problem. And here is the substance that I now state clearly: If we receive this guarantee regarding demilitarization and Israel's security needs, and if the Palestinians recognize Israel as the State of the Jewish people, then we will be ready in a future peace agreement to reach a solution where a demilitarized Palestinian state exists alongside the Jewish state."[72]

In other words, labels are unimportant (call it a state or whatever you want!) as long as the nature of this state meets Israel's conditions. A Palestinian state was acceptable to Netanyahu if it remained unarmed and allowed Israel to determine its borders, manage internal security and continue to protect the numerous Israeli settlement enclaves and all roads leading to them, according to the terms articulated in the Trump document.

Unlike Netanyahu, however, the document does not avoid controversial political terms. The authors thought it appropriate to theorise on the matter of sovereignty and share their thoughts:

> "Sovereignty is an amorphous concept that has evolved over time. With growing interdependence, each nation chooses to interact with other nations by entering into agreements that set parameters essential to each nation. The notion that sovereignty is a static and consis-

---

[71] Ibid., pp. 31–3.
[72] "Address by PM Netanyahu at Bar-Ilan University," *Israel Ministry of Foreign Affairs*, 14 June 2009, accessed at: https://bit.ly/3cn6c1g

tently defined term has been an unnecessary stumbling block in past negotiations. Pragmatic and operational concerns that effect security and prosperity are what is most important."[73]

This amateurish philosophising on the lack of the importance of sovereignty is not directed at Israel, of course—with the intention, for example, of encouraging it to alter its understanding of sovereignty to accommodate the idea of a state for all its citizens or a bi-national state, or to allow the international community to intervene in its nuclear weapons programme—but, obviously, at the Palestinians.

In asserting the amorphous nature of sovereignty, the document is effectively telling Palestinians not worry about such trifling matters. For these real estate developers, what should matter to the occupied Palestinians is work and prosperity. This vision of state-building encapsulates a real-estate mind-set *par excellence*. The authors cast themselves as hard-headed businessmen seeking to sway the population (who do not and should not care about politics) against the "extremists" preventing prosperity under occupation by insisting on invoking ideas like sovereignty, independence, liberation and other allegedly "static" and inflexible concepts.

In another passage on sovereignty, the document states,

"[T]he State of Israel will be responsible for security at all international crossings into the State of Palestine. With respect to the Rafah crossing, specific arrangements will be agreed upon between the Arab Republic of Egypt and the State of Israel to accomplish the security needs contemplated by this Vision. The State of Israel will continue to maintain control over the airspace and the electromagnetic spectrum west of the Jordan River."[74]

The document additionally grants Israel "static" and "inflexible" sovereignty over airspace and borders, saying, "The State of Israel will retain sovereignty over territorial waters, which are vital to Israel's security and which provides stability to the region."[75] It also gives Israel continued sovereignty over wells, which may not be dug with-

---

[73] "Part A: Political Framework," in: *Peace to Prosperity*, p. 9.

[74] "Appendix 2 C: Demilitarization Criteria and Other Security Arrangements," in: *Peace to Prosperity*, p. 49.

[75] "Part A: Political Framework," in: *Peace to Prosperity*, p. 13.

out Israeli authorisation because groundwater in the state of Palestine is a shared resource. Following a long paragraph, the document adds: "Additional funding will support the development of new wastewater treatment facilities in the West Bank and Gaza, putting an end to the ongoing public-health risk posed by untreated wastewater. This treated water will be reused, creating vast supplies of affordable water for agricultural and industrial use."[76] Israel's sovereignty, then, is not left undefined. It extends to the heavens and even to the water beneath the earth; in exchange, the lucky Palestinians will receive support for the development of wastewater treatment facilities.

While brimming with references to Israeli security, the document contains not a single reference to Palestinian security. The settlement enclaves (the brown spots on Map 7.2), which are mentioned in the document's appendices and labelled on the map as "enclave communities," are to be protected by the Israeli army even though they are located within the purported Palestinian state—as are all the roads identified on the map as "Israeli access roads," which lead to these settlements.

This deal amounts to nothing more than a formalisation of the status quo in the framework of a nominal "state". This is Israel's vision of a Palestinian state, with a bit of land thrown in to what are now the Palestinian-controlled Areas A and B.[77] In short, if you expand Areas A and B by 20–30 per cent, but retain Israeli sovereignty and settlement enclaves, then call the existing crossings along Israel's separation wall "borders"—then you've got yourself the "deal of the century."

Official Arab reactions to the vision were muted at best. Some Arab states openly supported the initiative,[78] setting the dangerous

---

[76] Ibid., p. 9.

[77] The Oslo Accords divided the West Bank into three administrative regions—Areas A, B and C—as a temporary measure pending a final agreement. These areas are non-contiguous and divided according to population areas and Israel's military needs. Area A falls under the civil and security control of the Palestinian Authority; Area B falls under Palestinian civil control and joint Israeli-Palestinian security control; and Area C falls under full Israeli civil and security control.

[78] A statement released by the Egyptian Ministry of Foreign Affairs professed Egypt's support for Trump's vision while underscoring principles that contradicted its very substance, stressing "the importance of reaching a compromise to resolve the Palestinian issue, in a

precedent of encouraging Israel to persist in its intransigence and diplomacy through fait accompli, which Trump had accepted. While European reactions varied, there was a clear difference between the critical responses of continental Europe and the opportunist position of the UK under Boris Johnson, whose support for the Trump-Netanyahu deal exemplified not only its persistent uncritical support of Israel, but also its unconditional submission to US foreign policy dictates, apparently having learned nothing from the Anglo-American invasion of Iraq.[79] The UK has not yet come to terms with its histori-

---

way that returns to the Palestinian people all their legitimate rights through the establish-ment of an independent Palestinian state with sovereignty over the Occupied Palestinian Territories, pursuant to international legitimacy and international decisions." The UAE ambassador to the US, who was present for the announcement of the deal, commented, "This plan is a serious initiative that addresses many issues raised over the years," adding that the plan "offers an important starting point for a return to negotiations." See: "Press Release," [Arabic] *Official Facebook Page of the Egyptian Ministry of Foreign Affairs*, 28 January 2020, accessed at: https://bit.ly/2WSItiz; "Ambassador Yousef Al Otaiba Statement on Peace Plan," *Embassy of the United Arab Emirates in Washington DC*, 28 January 2020, accessed at: https://bit.ly/3cpGcCd

[79] French President Emmanuel Macron expressed doubts about the feasibility of Trump's plan for peace, affirming that it could not be reached with just one side. His position aligned with that of Germany, as expressed by Minister of Foreign Affairs Heiko Maas, who said that the plan raised several questions and that a lasting peace between Israelis and Palestinians was not possible without a negotiated two-state solution. This position also aligned with that of the European Union; Josep Borrell, high representative of the European Union for Foreign Affairs and Security Policy, said in a statement that the plan did not adhere to "internationally agreed parameters." Borrell further expressed concern over statements floating the possible annexation of the Jordan Valley and other parts of the West Bank. In contrast, Boris Johnson stated, "No peace plan is perfect, but this has the merit of a two-state solution. It would ensure Jerusalem is both the capital of Israel and the Palestinian people." In response to criticism from opposition leader Jeremy Corbyn, Johnson said, "I would urge him rather than being so characteristically negative to reach out to his friend, my friend, our friends in the Palestinian authority, to Mahmoud Abbas—for whom I have the highest respect—and urge him for once to engage, to get talking rather than to leave a political vacuum." See: "Macron says believes in 'two sovereignties' between Israelis-Palestinians: Le Figaro," *Reuters*, 30 January 2020, accessed at: https://reut.rs/3h2wdpH; "EU rejects Trump Middle East peace plan, annexation," *Reuters*, 4 February 2020, accessed at: https://reut.rs/3vINRTm; "Germany, Europe react to Trump's Middle East peace plan," *DW*, 29 January 2020, accessed at: https://bit.

Map 7.2: Map of Palestine According to "Trump's Vision" with Settlement Enclaves Indicated

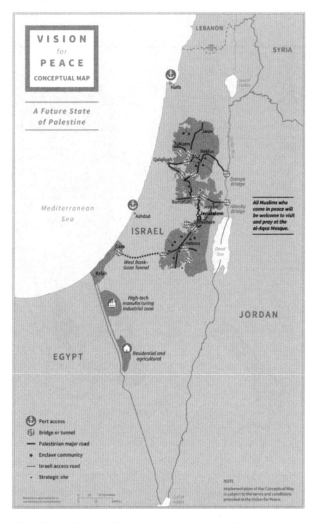

Source: The White House, "Peace to Prosperity: A Vision to Improve the Lives of the Palestinian and Israeli People (January 2020)", accessed at: https://bit.ly/2S6c3Rt

ly/3ursENo; "Boris Johnson praises Trump's Middle East peace plan at PMQs," *The Guardian*, 29 January 2020, accessed at: https://bit.ly/3ttmE5r; "EU Slams Trump's Middle East Peace Plan," *DW*, 4 February 2020, accessed at: http://bit.ly/2SXbMhl

Map 7.3: Map of Palestine According to Trump's Vision Compared to Areas A, B, and C as Delineated in the Post-Oslo Cairo Agreement

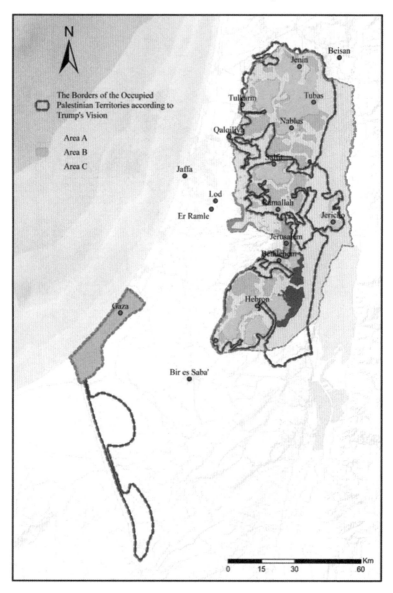

cal responsibility for the question of Palestine and certain other calamities of the Arab Mashreq. In any case, European official positions proved to have no real force and cannot be relied on until efforts succeed to establish a strong base of supporters of Palestinian rights among European publics.

Perhaps the one arguably positive aspect of Trump's initiative is that it conclusively dispelled the stubborn myth that the Oslo project represented a "peace" or "political" process. The initiative made it starkly evident that those with power want to impose their vision on the weaker side, which has no meaningful bargaining power or ability to resist. At least the weaker party is free to describe the conditions imposed upon them using any nomenclature it pleases—they can call it a state or even an empire if they wish!

For the Israeli right, the most important element of Trump's vision is its recognition that the reality on the ground has radically changed in the 53 years since the 1967 war; the deal neither denies this reality nor promotes the "illusion" that the clock can be turned back. This unusual American–Israeli candour could spur Palestinians to explore and articulate new strategies, and the changing position of the Palestinian cause in official Arab discourse and politics is another reason to think creatively about the future. Even if another US administration drops the Trump-Netanyahu deal, what incentives will it have to generate—and act on—ideas that are closer to justice, when some Arab regimes are normalising their relations with Israel? It seems clear that any real politics of liberation cannot rely on the influence of Arab regimes and will need to directly address public opinion in the US and elsewhere. This requires a justice-oriented discourse.

8

CHOICES AND ILLUSIONS

Israel and the Historic Choice

Even when nominally accepting a two-state solution, Israel did what it could to empty it of any meaningful content by maintaining its strategy of expansion through the de facto annexation of territories, systematic construction of settlements and denial of any notion of Palestinian sovereignty. Although a two-state solution would not have been entirely just, it would have met the minimum requirements of Arab consensus if it had included the return of Jerusalem, the withdrawal of Israel to the 1967 borders (in the West Bank and the Golan Heights) and the recognition of the right of return (with the vague phrase "a just settlement" of the refugee problem that became acceptable to the Palestinian official leadership).[1] But Israel rejected this option, and the policies it pursues—especially in and around Jerusalem,

---

[1] Speaking of the difference between acknowledging and implementing the right of return, Yasir Abed Rabbo, then a member of the PLO executive committee, said: "[At Taba] we asked for the principle of the right of return, but the implementation of it should be discussed in a very practical and even pragmatic way, without affecting or without—yes, without affecting—the Jewish nature of the state of Israel. We said it. This was our position." Tom Hill, "1948 after Oslo: truth and reconciliation in Palestinian discourse," *Mediterranean Politics*, vol. 13, no. 2 (2008), p. 159.

the settlements and the net of bypass roads—undermine any attempt at a two-state solution.

Negotiations on the two-state solution were reduced in scope and stripped of any content because the Palestinian national liberation movement lost the sources of power it once had: a reliance on popular struggle to change reality and influence Arab and global public opinion, coupled with political alignment with international blocs that no longer exist (the socialist bloc) or still exist in name only (the non-aligned movement). It relinquished its leverage, its informal power, without becoming a formal state and before full sovereignty had been guaranteed. Entirely consumed by peace negotiations, security coordination with Israel, the construction of internal security apparatuses and the daily needs of its population, the PA became dependent on American-Israeli good faith. Negotiations over the terms of a Palestinian state devolved into outright political extortion around the provision of basic needs of the population.

Consequently, the Occupied Territories under the PA has become one of the most heavily policed areas in the world. Its security apparatuses "are overstaffed and constitute a financial burden for Palestinian society." With a ratio of between 1:50 and 1:80 policemen per capita the PA scores one of the highest in the world.[2] Security consumes "more of its budget than the education, health, and agriculture sectors combined."[3] Furthermore, the security organisations have become the most important component of the social base of the PA.

---

[2] Roland Friedrich and Arnold Luethold, "Entry-Points to Palestinian Security Sector Reform," in: Roland Friedrich and Arnold Luethold (eds.), *Entry-Points to Palestinian Security Sector Reform* (Geneva: Geneva Centre for the Democratic Control of Armed Forces (DCAF), 2007), p. 154; Gal Luft, "The Palestinian Security Services: Between Police and Army," *Middle East Review of International Affairs (MERIA)*, vol. 3, no. 2 (June 1999).

[3] Omar Rahman, "From confusion to clarity: Three pillars for revitalizing the Palestinian national movement," *Policy Briefing*, Brookings Doha Center, December 2019, p. 6, accessed at: https://brook.gs/3pd9Y4c. See also: Ariella Azoulay and Adi Ophir, *The One-State Condition: Occupation and Democracy in Israel/Palestine* (Stanford: Stanford University Press, 2012), p. 86; "Mapping Palestinian Politics," *European Council on Foreign Relations*, accessed at: https://bit.ly/3BQHbWU; Alaa Tartir, "The Palestinian Authority Security Forces: Whose Security?" *Policy Brief*, al-Shabaka, 16 May 2017, accessed at: https://bit.ly/3aQ6AUJ

The idea that negotiations could be an alternative to, rather than result of, resistance gave birth to a new Palestinian leadership that is so bound up with the political process of negotiations that its very existence depends on the process continuing indefinitely. Israel knows this and has managed to replace political negotiation with demands that the PA make "good faith gestures" in order to reap some benefits from the peace process, while subjecting Palestinian forces choosing to remain on the path of resistance to a relentless campaign of repression and assassinations. Basic needs that were once the self-evident legal responsibility of the pre-Oslo occupying power—electricity, water, the right to travel abroad, work, food and medicine—are now used as cudgels to force continued good relations with the occupying power. The PA holds up its ability to secure such "concessions" as an achievement, contrasting itself with forces that "provoke" or "anger" Israel, exposing themselves and their community to a siege in Gaza with their refusal to renounce resistance.

During the national liberation period, Palestinians who were either appointed by Israel or who volunteered to be mediators with the occupying power, receiving travel permits, work opportunities, construction permits and other Israeli-bestowed advantages and perks as a result, were called collaborators with contempt. These collaborators organised under names like *rawabit al-qura* (village leagues or councils). Many Palestinians were imprisoned and even killed in the struggle against these local agents of the occupation and against any attempt to create "alternative leaderships" to the PLO. In a few cases, innocent people were also killed after being branded collaborators.

As defined by the occupier, a leader is merely someone capable of providing services and a semblance of self-rule, while those insisting on "static" ideas like sovereignty and national dignity are branded extremists and blamed for the blockades and other collective punishments inflicted by the occupier (for the authors of the Trump-Netanyahu deal, sovereignty is exclusively reserved for the occupier). Since the inception of the PA, this has been Israel's conception of Palestinian leadership, exemplifying an unequivocal rejection of Palestinian sovereignty.

The Palestinian bureaucracy that has grown up alongside the so-called peace process, along with Arab regimes desperate to abdicate responsibility for Palestine, are happy to help Israel pick and choose elements from the two-state solution to patch together something that, if you squint, looks like an independent Palestinian state.

Nonetheless, the question remains: would a negotiated settlement along the lines of a two-state solution not at least lead to peace, even if it is an *unjust* peace?

For about decade and a half before Trump, many policymakers in the US and Israel believed that merely establishing a polity and calling it a Palestinian state would be enough to produce peace in the region, even if that settlement demarcated borders falling short of the 1967 lines, excluded East Jerusalem as Palestine's capital and did not recognise the right of return. Israel and the US have expended considerable efforts to transform the demand for a Palestinian state into a politically vacuous, purely technocratic arrangement that entails the curtailment or elimination of all the national rights of the Palestinian people and allows Israel to maintain its total control of Palestine's borders, skies, subterranean water resources and overall economy.

Indeed, the proposed political entity resulting from a negotiated settlement, which is presented as a two-state solution, does not enjoy legitimacy in wider Arab public opinion, neither as a just political settlement nor as fair compensation for the injustices suffered by the Palestinian people.

Here it is worth considering what it meant when Yasser Arafat rejected just this sort of deal at Camp David (2000). It was more than just a stubborn refusal to compromise on the "non-negotiables," although that was surely part of it. It also reflected Arafat's clear understanding that such a solution would lack legitimacy among Arabs and Palestinians. Arafat had staked his personal and political life on the negotiations, but even after the Israelis effectively imprisoned him in his own Ramallah headquarters, he refused to accept an offer of this kind—and he paid the price for his resistance. His death (or more accurately, assassination by Israel) elicited a sigh of relief from Arab regimes and parts of the Palestinian leadership. They felt that they were burying a man whose insistence on a real state along the pre-June 1967 borders had been a constant impediment to the negotiating process he himself had initiated and that they could now continue that process unencumbered.

It may be argued that I am speaking in overbroad generalities. But the truth is that the salient issues (final status issues in the jargon of the Oslo accord) have practically been excluded from negotiations by Israeli fait accompli policies. For example, the only thing that any settlement will do for the refugees is to give them a new name. They will no longer be "refugees," but rather subjects of a formal Palestinian embassy in this or that country. Israel continues to build settlements around east Jerusalem, turning it to an Arab ghetto in a Jewish city. The Israeli state becomes ever more Jewish in nature, intensifying its religious-nationalist character and chauvinism towards its Arab citizens, who are expected to show their complete loyalty to Israel, a state that pointedly excludes them from its self-definition as the state of the Jews and does not grant them equal rights. This is the deal or the settlement as it stands now.

Israel will continue to be suspicious of democracy in the Arab world because it is afraid of the Arab majority, and of Arab public opinion and its vicissitudes. It does not relish the strategic uncertainty of annually waiting for election returns in another Arab country. Ideally, Arab countries should continue to obsessively calculate the implications of Israeli elections for themselves.

If the question is one of legitimacy, only the Palestinian people have the power to legitimise any agreement. Instead, the settlement currently on offer is being pushed through by pitting one Palestinian faction against others that have been excluded from or shunned negotiations[4] (one of which actually won elections in 2006). This kind of settlement is not only broadly illegitimate among Palestinians, but a source of internal strife. "Mobilising popular support" behind such an agreement means starving, bombing and exhausting segments of the

---

[4] Dana El Kurd thoroughly explains how the international reliance on Fatah and its subsidisation for its support of the "peace process" further polarised the Palestinian people. She shows how Palestinian decision-makers have become more removed from public accountability and identifies international intervention as a crucial decision-making factor. She also shows that excessive consideration of international donor/patron policy preference makes the PA more inclined to repression and less accountable. Dana El Kurd, *Polarized and Demobilized: Legacies of Authoritarianism in Palestine* (New York: Oxford University Press, 2020), pp. 45–66.

Palestinian population until they are no longer able to disagree. This coercive situation speaks of a lack of popular legitimacy.

In terms of regional politics, support for a negotiated two-state settlement is produced through American hegemony and the conflict between regional axes of power. One regional power bloc or another will waive the injustice of the settlement like a bloody shirt in its own battles.

The anaemic two-state settlement currently on the table has done little to change the Arab street's infamous aversion to the "peace process" or its lack of faith in Israel's claimed desire for a just peace or intention to relinquish the privileges it enjoys internationally. There is no doubt that Israel's casual brutality towards the Palestinian people, who are seen as fair game by Israel if that dissuades them from resistance and persuades them to accept Israeli conditions, has watered the seeds of animosity and heightened the sense that Arabs are being cheated, leading them to accuse supporters of this kind of settlement of collaboration with Israel and the US.

Settler Colonialism or Apartheid: Why Not Both?

Many of the first Zionist leaders would not have denied that their project was a colonial one, as "colonialism" was not a bad word in the nineteenth century. Being a colonialist meant being a part of Western civilisation in the East. Labour Zionism, however, which sanctified settlement and led the campaign for the conquest of land and labour, claimed to be the vanguard of a national movement, not only a colonial project. It wanted to be both and more, for example, a class movement if the struggle for leadership requires.

The Palestinians, on the other hand, considered themselves victims of colonialism. Indeed, in the postcolonial era, scholars such as the Palestinian Fayez al-Sayegh (1965) and the French historian Maxime Rodinson (1967) used the language of the postcolonial social sciences to show that Israel was a colonial settler state even before the 1967 occupation of the West Bank and Gaza.[5]

[5] See: Fayez Sayegh, *Zionist Colonialism in Palestine* [Arabic] (Beirut: Research Center, Palestine Liberation Organization, 1965); Maxime Rodinson, *Israel: A Colonial Settler-State?* (New

The PLO, along with Palestinian and many other Arab intellectuals, have been familiar with the concept of settler colonialism since the 1960s, when they began to employ the concept strategically to link Palestine to other liberation movements around the world and to present the Palestinian narrative to international anti-colonial audiences.[6]

This was not only an age of national liberation in the global south, but also an age in which nation-building through settler colonialism, which was taken for granted between the sixteenth and nineteenth century, was no longer acceptable. Israel was established at this very moment in history.

Sayegh identified the features of settler colonialism that apply to the Zionist project, but he also used the term 'apartheid' to describe the Israeli state's relationship with the Palestinians who remained in Israel after 1948 and were granted Israeli citizenship.[7] At the time that Sayegh wrote, Israel maintained two separate legal systems, a civil system for Jewish citizens and a military system that governed the native Palestinian Arabs remaining under its jurisdiction. Martial law for Palestinians was officially lifted in 1966, less than a year before the West Bank and Gaza were occupied and military rule was imposed on another part of the Palestinian people.

The major difference between these populations was that while the Arabs in Israel (approximately 150,000 in 1949) had been granted citizenship and acquired formal civil and political rights within a settler colonial ethnocracy, the Palestinians in the West

---

York: Monad Press, 1973). Rodinson's was originally published in French in 1967: Maxime Rodinson, "Is Israel a Colonial?," [French] *Les Temps Modernes, Le conflit israélo-arabe*, no. 253 (July 1967), pp. 17–88.

[6] See, for example: Fawwaz Tarabulsi, "The Palestine Problem: Zionism and Imperialism in the Middle East," *New Left Review*, vol. 1, no. 57 (September—October 1969); Georg Jabbour, *Settler Colonialism in Southern Africa and the Middle East* (Beirut: Palestine Liberation Organization Research Center, 1970); Ibrahim Abu-Lughod & Baha Abu-Laban (eds.), *Settler Regimes in Africa and the Arab World: The Illusion of Endurance* (Wilmette, IL: Medina University Press International, 1974); Elia Zureik, *Palestinians in Israel: A Study of Internal Colonialism* (London and Boston: Routledge/K. Paul, 1979). See also: Omar Jabary Salamanca et al., "Past is present: Settler colonialism in Palestine," *Settler Colonial Studies*, vol. 2, no. 1 (2012), p. 8.

[7] Sayegh, pp. 27–8.

Bank and Gaza were never granted Israeli citizenship and lived under direct military rule without civil or political rights after 1967. This difference cannot be ignored, as it produced different realities and different political strategies. Direct military occupation continued until the peace agreement with the PLO established self-rule under the PA (Bantustans, in South African terms).[8] So, Israeli settler colonialism first created an ethnocracy after mass Palestinian displacement in 1948, followed by a military occupation in 1967, which was later converted into an apartheid regime. Both sets of conditions are products of a settler colonial project.

It is interesting that the new generation of Palestinian researchers are reviving this earlier approach to Israel as settler colonialism, not in the literature of the PLO and the European radical left, but in peer-reviewed academic journals.[9]

Many of the scholars contributing to recent academic literature on settler colonialism refer to the works of Patrick Wolfe and Lorenzo Veracini. For Wolfe, the settler colonial concept "is premised on the securing—the obtaining and the maintaining—of territory."[10] This is also the impetus for the elimination of the natives. Territoriality is settler colonialism's specific, irreducible element.[11] Expulsion of the indigenous population provides a basis for the continuation of the settler colonial project; destruction is therefore closely linked to expansion and control of the land. It is "a structure rather than an event."[12] The settler colonial state is engaged in "an inclusive, land-

---

[8] Contrary to Sayegh's observations (Ibid., p. 28), Bantustans were never created for the Palestinian citizens of Israel after 1948.

[9] It is difficult to determine whether the normalisation and legitimation of this academic enterprise is an indication of the further liberalisation of Western academia, or a sign of hubristic confidence that the discussion of colonialism in academic journals is toothless or both. From the perspective of the struggle against ideological hegemony of Zionist discourse concerning the Palestinian issue and even the Middle East in general, it is an achievement.

[10] Patrick Wolfe, "Settler Colonialism and the Elimination of the Native," *Journal of Genocide Research*, vol. 8, no. 4 (2006), p. 402.

[11] Ibid., p. 388.

[12] Ibid., p. 390. At least one reservation to this reductionist description is that it excludes French settler colonialism in Algeria and its like.

centred project that coordinates a comprehensive range of agencies, from the metropolitan centre to the frontier encampment, with a view to eliminating indigenous societies."[13] One can only agree with this analytical description, and it corresponds with the analysis of the aforementioned scholars who described the Zionist project as settler colonialism long before Wolfe.

Veracini explained the main difference between classic and settler colonialism through the difference between two statements directed at the natives: "you, work for me" (classical colonisation) and "you, go away" (settler colonialism). The first derives from a "logic of exploitation" and the second from a "logic of elimination" that seeks to expel and replace the indigenous people.[14] This was clear to Palestinians long before Veracini's article, when they described Zionist colonialism as "replacement" or "substitutive" (*ihlali*) colonialism. The Zionist activists of the second *aliyah* (wave of Jewish immigration to Palestine) spoke loudly about the Judaisation of land and labour and, as discussed in part one, did not hesitate to use the Hebrew expressions *kibbush ha-adama* (conquest of land) and *kibbush ha-avuda* (conquest of labour).

Veracini subsequently elaborated:

"While a colonial society is successful only if the separation between colonizer and colonized is retained, a settler colonial project is ultimately successful only when it extinguishes itself—that is, when the settlers cease to be defined as such and become 'natives', and their position becomes normalized. To succeed, a settler project must emancipate itself from external supervision and control, establish local sovereign political and cultural forms, terminate substantive indigenous autonomies, and tame a landscape once perceived as intractably alien. In other words, a settler colonial project that has successfully run its course is no longer settler colonial."[15]

Veracini distinguished the successful Israeli settler colonialism between 1948 and 1967 from the failed project after 1967: "Israeli/

---

[13] Ibid., p. 393.

[14] Lorenzo Veracini, "Introducing Settler Colonial Studies," *Settler Colonial Studies*, vol. 1, no. 1 (2011), pp. 1–12.

[15] Lorenzo Veracini, "The Other Shift: Settler Colonialism, Israel and the Occupation," *Journal of Palestine Studies*, vol. 42, no. 2 (April 2013), p. 28.

Zionist settler colonialism was remarkably successful before 1967, and was largely unsuccessful thereafter. Indeed, if settler colonialism is about establishing legitimate claims to specific locations, Israel's occupation of the West Bank and Gaza ultimately has very little to show for after over forty years of unrestrained rule."[16] It may be right that Israel managed to "establish local sovereign political and cultural forms, terminate substantive indigenous autonomies, and tame a landscape once perceived as intractably alien"—it did after all succeed in building a nation, a Hebrew and Israeli *Sabra* culture, and a developed economy. But the Palestinians did not turn out to be the remnant community of an indigenous people (as a reminder, indigenous people make up 1 per cent of the US population)—instead, they sustained and even further developed their national character and aspirations. Furthermore, as explained previously, Israel did not nativise.

Moreover, Israel's relationship with the Palestinians who became its citizens was organised in accordance with settler colonial logic. According to the Israeli citizenship law (1952), Jewish citizens, including those born in Israel, obtain their citizenship by virtue of being Jews, as stated in the law of return (1950), which grants Israeli citizenship to every Jew in the world who immigrates to Israel. The law of return is not a regular statute, Ben-Gurion said when presenting it to the Knesset, but a foundational law of the state. He added that the Jewishness of the state does not stem from the fact of a Jewish-majority population, but rather from its status as the state of the Jews wherever they are.[17] In contrast, the citizenship of the Arab citizens of Israel is granted at the discretion of the Jewish state. Citizenship was only offered to non-Jews who remained in place and had lived uninterruptedly under Israeli sovereignty between May 1948 and the date of the enactment of the citizenship law (this covered the 150,000 Palestinians who remained in Israel).

[16] Ibid.

[17] David Ben-Gurion, "Speech in the Knesset Session for Discussing the Law of Return," *The Protocols of the Knesset*, vol. 7 (1950), pp. 2035–7. See also: Azmi Bishara, *From the Jewishness of the State to Sharon* [Arabic] (Cairo: Dar al-Shourouk, 2005), p. 38.

This means that Jewish citizenship is derived from the essential[18] nature of the state, which defines itself as a state for every Jew in the world regardless of their place of birth or residence, while Arab citizenship is of different, incidental quality; it is not derived from the nature of a state explicitly founded for the Jews.[19] The Palestinians who left during the war, even for a short time, and made it back to their homes[20] any time after May 1948, or were not present when the population census was held, were considered absentees despite being physically present. Such "present absentees" were denied citizenship and the state had the "right" to confiscate their land.

At issue here is not simply state discrimination against a minority, but a qualitative differentiation between two categories of citizenship, one superior and the other inferior. In this way, the settler colonial project was incorporated and inscribed in the state's legal edifice. This colonial core has been obscured by the granting of individual civil and political rights to Arab citizens (e.g., the right to vote), but it is readily observable in Israel's anti-Arab political culture, racist attitudes towards Arabs and daily discrimination in service provision (the focus of most parliamentary work of Arab Knesset members). It is plainly visible in the way the state deals with political protests by Arab citizens in Israel that express their Palestinian identity and in its land confiscation policies. In both of these cases, Israel treats its Arab citizens as adversaries, if not enemies. Here I am referring not to most appalling atrocities, like the 1956 massacre of Arab citizens in the

---

[18] Supreme Court Justice Dov Levin was definitive: "the essence of the state is that it is a Jewish state, while its system of rule is democratic." See: Dov Levin, in: "Yehoram Shalom and others vs. the Central Committee of Elections and the Progressive List for Peace," [Hebrew] *Judgements of the Supreme Court*, vol. 53, no. 4, p. 221. See also: Bishara, *From the Jewishness of the State to Sharon*, pp. 36, 82.

[19] On this fact and its ramifications, see: Azmi Bishara, "Zionism and Equal Citizenship: Essential and Incidental Citizenship in the Jewish State," in: Nadim Rouhana (ed.), *Israel and its Palestinian Citizens: Ethnic Privileges in the Jewish State* (Cambridge and New York: Cambridge University Press, 2017), pp. 137–55. Concerning discrimination against Arabs in law and in courts including by the Israeli Supreme Court in its liberal phase and its policy of legal activism, see: Nimer Sultani, "The Legal Structure of Subordination: the Palestinian Minority and the Israel Law," in: Rouhana (ed.), pp. 191–237.

[20] They were considered infiltrators according to the infiltration law discussed in Chapter 1.

village of Kafr Qasim,[21] which was akin to the massacres during the 1948 war, but of everyday repression like the use of live ammunition exclusively against demonstrations by Arab citizens.

Israel's land confiscation process is an area where tiered citizenship is readily observable. It is a deliberate process that employs different justifications of the public good to transfer land seized from Arab citizens to the state for the purpose of building Jewish settlements, with the declared goal of creating and maintaining a Jewish majority in every district—because a majority of Arab citizens in any district is considered a demographic and security threat and treated as such. This Judaisation policy is given the sterile name of "development" to make it more socially palatable. The mass confiscation of Arab land in the Galilee, the Negev and the Triangle[22] was the background for the original Land Day (30 March 1976), when Arab citizens declared a general strike and launched an unprecedented wave of protests.

---

[21] On the evening of 29 October 1956, forty-nine workers from the village of Kafr Qasim and another two from an adjacent village (Tirah) were killed in cold blood as they came home from work, for breaking a curfew they had not been apprised of. The most significant work on the massacre is a recent history written by an Israeli historian, which clearly connects the premeditated massacre (the order to kill without taking prisoners) with a prevailing anti-Arab mood, and plans to expel Arab citizens from the country and depopulate some villages in the Triangle. Adam Raz, *Kafr Qasim Massacre: a Political Biography* [Hebrew] (Jerusalem: Carmel Publication, 2018), pp. 84, 87.

[22] From 1948 to 1966, when Arab citizens of Israel lived under martial law, legal structures were created to organise the state appropriation of Arab lands and institutionalise native dispossession. This legal framework enabled Israel to confiscate vast tracts of Palestinian land and dispose of it in line with the state's ethnocratic agenda. The Planning and Construction Law of 1965, for example, which regulated aspects of statutory planning and development, established a hierarchy whereby the central government authorises national zoning plans, while the National Planning and Construction Board approves district plans, before local institutions outline detailed plans to implement them. Yosef Jabareen investigates Israeli national and district plans. See: Yosef Jabareen, "Controlling Land and Demography in Israel: The Obsession with Territorial and Geographical Dominance," in: Rouhana (ed.), pp. 238–65. On this issue, see also: Hussein Abu Hussein & Fiona McKay, *Access Denied: Palestinian Land Rights in Israel* (London and New York: Zed Books, 2003), Chapter 3 and Chapter 4; Mazen Masri, "Colonial Imprints: Settler-Colonialism as a Fundamental Feature of Israeli Constitutional Law," *International Journal of Law in Context*, vol. 13, no. 3 (2017), pp. 388–407.

A series of regressive laws emphasising the Jewishness of the state have been passed since the mid-1990s in response to Palestinian attempts to counter Israel's discriminatory land seizures and usage with a strategy that takes citizenship seriously and carries it to its logical conclusion. This strategy focused on making Israel a state of equal citizenship—a state of all its citizens—which is wholly inconsistent with Zionism and the so-called "essence" of the modern Israeli state. The wave of nationalist legislation culminated in 2018 in a new basic law (which in the Israeli system has the status of a constitutional law) titled "Israel the nation-state of the Jewish people."

The law is ideological and declarative but it also has some practical aspects. One of the declared aims of the framers of the law was to circumvent legal action by Arab citizens challenging discrimination on the basis of liberal rights upheld by the Supreme Court, which nevertheless adopts the discriminatory definition of Israel as a state of the Jews. The legislation sought to stem the extension of liberal rights and civil equality, and limit the interpretative latitude of the Supreme Court, especially after the enactment of the 1992 basic law on human dignity and liberty.

One way the Jewish nation-state law limits the application of liberal rights is by enshrining Jewish settlement as a basic state value. The seventh clause of the law states: "The state views Jewish settlement as a national value and will act to encourage and promote its establishment and development." In other words, the state is not only Jewish in character and in its "essential nature", but it also has the right to build and develop exclusively Jewish settlements inside the state—a state that lacks defined borders.[23]

I have previously written that

"At face value, there is nothing new about this provision. Zionism, since even before 1948, has followed a policy of settlement in all of Palestine, through institutions such as the Jewish National Fund, the Jewish Agency, and the Israeli State itself. This, however, was not enshrined in a basic law, despite the enactment of land confiscation laws, so settlements did not become a constitutionally fortified

---

[23] "Full text of Basic Law: Israel as the Nation State of the Jewish People," *The Knesset*, 19 July 2018, accessed at: https://bit.ly/3w1kkF8

value[...]. For example, settlement was often undertaken on miri (state) lands (which the Israeli state saw itself to have inherited from the former ruling powers); by purchasing land (even if fraudulently); or by confiscation in the name of the 'public good' (for closed military zones, streets, facilities, etc.), before diverting the land for settlements at a later date. In the new law, settlement itself has become the public good by definition; land can be confiscated for this purpose directly [...]. The legislation does not consider the idea of developing Arab communities from villages and cities and strengthening or expanding them in the same law."[24]

The nation-state law was also designed as a response to Arab citizens who applied for residence in Jewish settlements built on their village lands. Such applications were always rejected. One rejected applicant subsequently appealed to the Supreme Court, arguing that his rejection was indisputably flagrant discrimination, unjustified even in light of the proclaimed Jewishness of the state.[25] Jewish community settlements found various ways to deny Arab citizens residence regardless, but the Jewish nation-state law makes their efforts unnecessary insofar as it explicitly asserts the state's Jewish character and defends the right to discriminate. Shira Robinson and Mazen Masri are correct when they say that state policies and legislation towards Arab citizens should not be treated as an issue of discrimination against a minority, but should rather be viewed through the lens of settler colonialism.[26] Already in 1979, the Palestinian Canadian sociologist Elia Zureik studied the Israeli policies towards the Palestinian citizens as a case of "internal colonialism".[27]

[24] Azmi Bishara, "What does the 'Jewish Nation' Basic Law Mean?," *Arab Center for Research and Policy Studies*, 24 July 2018, accessed at: https://bit.ly/2S7fPKy

[25] Masri, p. 397. See also: Hassan Jabareen, "The Future of Arab Citizenship in Israel: Zionist Time in a Place with no Palestinian Memory," in: Daniel Levy & Yfaat Weiss (eds.), *Challenging Ethnic Citizenship: German and Israeli Perspectives on Immigration* (New York: Berghagen Books, 2002), p. 197.

[26] Shira Robinson, *Citizen Strangers: Palestinians and the Birth of Israeli Liberal Settler State* (Stanford: Stanford University Press, 2013), especially her conclusions in: pp. 194–8; Masri.

[27] Elia T. Zureik, *The Palestinians in Israel: A Study in Internal Colonialism*, International Library of Sociology (London: Routledge & Kegan Paul, 1979).

In the phase that theorists of settler colonialism considered a phase of nativisation before 1967, the nativisation was in fact a settler *Sabra* culture of obsessive attempts to belong to the place by negating both the character of the exilic Jew and the indigenous Arab through simultaneously dispossessing and acquiring elements of his native culture. In any case, the process of "normalising" the settler state (nativisation) had been underway for only 19 years when Israel occupied the rest of Palestine in 1967, an occupation that persists to this day. According to Veracini's concept of nativisation, Israel is a colonial state only in the West Bank and Gaza, but its insatiable urge to build settlements precludes its definition as a classical colonial state. Indeed, Israel's relentless colonisation of the West Bank is the extension of a process that began long before 1967 and so draws attention to the essentially colonial nature of the Israel state. The two-state solution, in imagining the end of the 1967 occupation, makes it necessary to normalise, or nativise, the pre-1967 Israeli state.

In the context of the anti-colonial struggle, Israel was always cast as a case of settler colonialism. This interpretive paradigm acquired greater currency within the burgeoning field of Palestine studies and is now commonly referenced in academic journals (special issues and articles), books and academic conferences. The breadth of these myriad contributions is striking, covering subjects as diverse as indigenous resistance and rights, decolonisation, environmental issues, international and transnational solidarity movements, settler colonialism and neoliberalism, settler colonialism and law, surveillance, and feminist and queer movements.[28] But despite the broad academic

---

[28] For example, see: Salamanca et al., "Settler Colonial Studies and Israel-Palestine," *Settler Colonial Studies*, vol. 5, no. 3 (2015); Yara Hawari, Sharri Plonski & Elian Weizman, "Settlers and Citizens: A Critical View of Israeli Society," *Settler Colonial Studies*, vol. 9, no. 1 (2019); "Special Issue: Settler Colonialism: The Palestinian/Israeli Case," *International Journal of Applied Psychoanalytic Studies*, vol. 17, no. 2 (2020); "Special Issue: Israeli Settler-Colonialism and the Palestinian Naqab Bedouin," *Journal of Holy Land and Palestine Studies*, vol. 15, no. 1 (May 2016); "Special Issue: Settler-Colonialism and Indigenous Rights in Al-Quds/Jerusalem," *Journal of Holy Land and Palestine Studies*, vol. 17, no. 1 (May 2018); "Environmental Justice, Settler Colonialism, and More-than-Humans in the Occupied West Bank," *Environment and Planning E: Nature and Space*, vol. 4, no. 1 (March 2021); "Special Issue: Settler Colonialism: United States, South Africa, Eritrea, and Palestine/

application of the settler colonialism model, it has attracted a substantial amount of criticism—Veracini has responded in detail to critiques[29]—including from some Palestinian academics.[30]

Needless to say, this conceptualisation of Israel has been dismissed by Israeli academia, where mainstream discourse views any criticism of Israel's colonial character as "tantamount to 'treason and self-hatred.'"[31] On the whole, Israeli academia remains committed to the belief that Zionism is at least an enlightened national movement, if not a national liberation movement, and that Israel is a liberal democratic nation state,[32] although some well-known Israeli academics have used the settler colonial paradigm in their research.[33]

Israel," *South Atlantic Quarterly*, vol. 107, no. 4 (2008). See also: Linda Tabar & Chandni Desai, "Decolonization is a Global Project: From Palestine to the Americas," *Decolonization: Indigeneity, Education & Society*, vol. 6, no. 1 (2017), pp. i–xix; Nadera Shalhoub-Kevorkian, *Security Theology, Surveillance and the Politics of Fear*, Cambridge Studies in Law and Society (Cambridge: Cambridge University Press, 2015), pp. 1–20; Nadera Shalhoub-Kevorkian & Sahar S. Huneidi, "Settler Colonialism, Surveillance, and Fear," in: Rouhana (ed.), pp. 336–66; Ahmad Sa'di, "Israel's settler-colonialism as a global security paradigm," *Race & Class* (April 2021); Elia Zureik, "Settler Colonialism, Neoliberalism and Cyber Surveillance: The Case of Israel," *Middle East Critique*, vol. 29, no. 2 (February 2020), pp. 219–35; Masri, pp. 388–407; Nadine Naber et al., "On Palestinian Studies And Queer Theory," *Journal Of Palestine Studies*, vol. 47, no. 3 (2018), pp. 62–71.

29 See: Lorenzo Veracini, "Is settler colonial studies even useful?," *Postcolonial Studies*, vol. 24, no. 2 (December 2020). See also: "Special Issue: New Directions in Settler Colonial Studies," *Postcolonial Studies*, vol. 23, no. 1 (2020).

30 For example, see: Nadia Hijab & Ingrid Jaradat Gassner, "Talking Palestine: What Frame of Analysis? Which Goals and Messages?," *Alshabaka*, 12 April 2017, accessed at: https://bit.ly/3bJuzFP; Rashid Khalidi, "Israel: 'A Failed Settler-Colonial Project'," *Institute for Palestine Studies*, 10 May 2018, accessed at: https://bit.ly/3bHckRv; Rana Barakat, "Writing/Righting Palestine Studies: Settler Colonialism, Indigenous Sovereignty and Resisting the Ghost(s) of History," *Settler Colonial Studies*, vol. 8, no. 3 (2018), pp. 349–63.

31 Elia Zureik, *Israel's Colonial Project in Palestine: Brutal Pursuit* (Abingdon, Oxon and New York: Routledge, 2016), pp. 69–70.

32 Ilan Pappé, "Shtetl Colonialism: First and Last Impressions of Indigeneity by Colonised Colonisers," *Settler Colonial Studies*, vol. 2, no. 1 (2012), p. 39.

33 Gershon Shafir, "Zionism and Colonialism: A Comparative Approach," in: Ilan Pappé (ed.), *The Israel/Palestine Question: Rewriting Histories* (London: Routledge, 1999), pp. 72–85; Gordon Neve & Moriel Ram, "Ethnic Cleansing and the Formation of Settler Colonial Geographies," *Political Geography*, vol. 53 (2016), pp. 20–9; Ilan Pappé, "Shtetl

Palestinian researcher Sabbagh-Khoury has argued that the,

"reemergence of the settler colonial paradigm in the social sciences and humanities in Israel can be ascribed in large part to political processes within Palestinian society in Israel in the mid-1990s, specifically the shift in political discourse from one that promotes a two-state solution to one that envisages a state for all citizens."[34]

She shows that this shift has been effected in part thanks to a rising political awareness advocating for the establishment of an inclusive state of equal citizens, the recognition of Palestinian identity and historical memory, and respect for the right of return and recognition of the Nakba, which entails full recognition of the expulsion and ethnic cleansing of Palestinians.

Academics who use the apartheid model to describe the nature of Israel's system of rule in Palestine tend to concur that it was established by settler colonialism, but, for them, this unnecessarily, and unhelpfully, conflates "apartheid" with "settler colonialism". Not every case of settler colonialism culminates in the establishment of an apartheid regime. But if such a regime does emerge, the process of dismantling it is tantamount to decolonisation.[35] Settler colonialism

---

Colonialism: First and Last Impressions of Indigeneity by Colonised Colonisers," *Settler Colonial Studies*, vol. 2, no. 1 (2012):, pp. 39–58; Ilan Pappé, "The Futility and Immorality of Partition in Palestine," in: Ilan Pappé & Noam Chomsky, *On Palestine* (UK: Penguin, 2015), pp. 167–80; Arnon Yehuda Degani, "The Decline and Fall of the Israeli Military Government, 1948–1966: A Case of Settler-Colonial Consolidation?," *Settler Colonial Studies*, vol. 5, no. 1 (2015), pp. 84–99.

[34] Areej Sabbagh-Khoury, "Tracing Settler Colonialism: A Genealogy of a Paradigm in the Sociology of Knowledge Production in Israel," *Politics & Society* (March 2021), p. 2. See also: Azmi Bishara, "Palestinian Minority in Israel: a proposed new vision," [Arabic] *Journal of Palestine studies*, vol. 3, no. 11 (Summer 1992), pp. 1–30; Azmi Bishara, *The Ruptured Political Discourse and Other Studies*, [Arabic] 2nd ed. (Ramallah: Muwatin-The Palestinian Institute for the Study of Democracy, 2002). For more about Zionist movement as a settler colonial movement that established a settler colonial state, see: Azmi Bishara, "One Hundred Years of Zionism, from the Dialectic of Existence to the Dialectic of Substance," [Arabic] *al-Carmel Journal* (1997), pp. 11–20; Bishara, *From the Jewishness of the State to Sharon*.

[35] I agree here with Mamdani who calls overthrowing the apartheid regime in South Africa "the decolonization of the political." Mahmood Mamdani, *Neither Settler nor Native: the*

may sometimes be acknowledged out of hubris in the way that some Israeli academics acknowledge and justify the Nakba. It may also be reassuring; why not join the club of the US, Canada, New Zealand and Australia? Well, settler colonialism is not a "normal" way of nation-building in the twentieth century, certainly not if, in contrast to the US, Canada and Australia, the indigenous people survive as a coherent nationality; the state established on their ruins remains exclusive to one religio-ethnicity rather than a state for all its citizens; and it is surrounded by people sharing the same ethnicity with the displaced and occupied natives.[36]

Calling for a state for all its citizens inside the Green Line 30 years ago, I used the term apartheid to describe the reality of the occupation in the West Bank and Gaza. My argument was that the Oslo Accords would produce Bantustans and not a state.[37] Today, we have multiple Bantustans, the only difference between them and those of South Africa being that "our" Bantustans refuse to acknowledge their painful reality. This outcome was an obvious possibility after the 1993 signing of the Oslo Declaration of Principles, but the unwarranted enthusiasm that followed Israel's recognition of the PLO and the return of some of its leadership to their homeland meant that opinions in opposition to Oslo outside the context of factional infighting were rarely given a hearing.

The apartheid character of Israeli rule became more obvious after the Oslo Accords for two reasons: first, the ethnic hierarchy inherent

---

Making and Unmaking of Permanent Minorities (Cambridge, MA and London: Belknap Press of Harvard University Press, 2020), p. 18.

[36] Here is where I disagree with Mehran Kamrava, although I agree with his presentation of the meaning of the term indigenous people: "These indigenous civilizations were conquered by industrially more advanced intruders who brought with them superior organization." This is in contrast to cases like Tibet and Poland, where indigenous people "did not completely die out, nor were they altogether reborn." This is similar to the case of the Palestinians. Mehran Kamrava, *The Impossibility of Palestine: History, Geography and the Road Ahead* (New Haven and London: Yale University Press, 2016), p. 219. It seems, then, that there is more than one model between vanished indigenous peoples and those completely reborn in a nation state. The Palestinian case is different to the case of the indigenous people in North America and Australia, although they are all victims of settler colonialism.

[37] See: Graham Usher, "Bantustanisation or Bi-nationalism?: An Interview with Azmi Bishara," *Race and Class*, vol. 37, no. 2 (1995).

in the occupation became apparent, and second, the notion that this was a case of classic colonialism that would end with an Israeli withdrawal and the emergence of a new state was gradually exposed as an illusion to many Palestinians after the creation of the PA (which assumed the form of a Bantustan) and the intensification of Jewish settlement construction.

In Israel, the Palestinian Arab minority's status of national and cultural alienation and second-class citizenship is the result of settler colonialism, which also produced the refugee issue. Without the expulsion of the refugees, the Palestinians would not have become a minority and strangers in their own land. The settler colonialism's policies in the part of Palestine occupied in 1967 produced an apartheid regime.

From Ethnocracy to Apartheid

The apartheid regime in South Africa was itself originally created by the Dutch settler-colonialists who first constructed the modern state of South Africa. It was actually established by the national party that won the elections in 1948.[38]

---

[38] The National Party won elections in South Africa in the year Israel was established. In the 1948 war, South Africa sent over 1000 volunteers to fight with the Israeli army. In 1953, Daniel F. Malan, the then South African Prime Minister visited Israel and became the first head of state to do so. In the aftermath of the 1967 war, South African whites were inspired by the Israeli victory in the war, which raised the potential for future cooperation. South African Jews transferred currency to Israel worth $20.5 million to help the war effort. Along with spare aircraft and military equipment, volunteers were also sent to Israel, and some joined military units. Cooperation markedly increased with South Africa. Shimon Peres, David Ben-Gurion, and General Chaim Herzog visited South Africa. Since the 1970s and until the dismantling of the apartheid regime, every defence minister in Israel and some senior officers and intelligence officials visited South Africa. During those visits, besides the declared fundraising purposes, they met with their South African counterparts to discuss arms sales and other cooperation. During the October 1973 war, South African volunteers also flew to Israel. In addition, currency transfers to Israel were facilitated. Benjamin M. Joseph, *Besieged Bedfellows: Israel and the Land of Apartheid* (New York: Greenwood Press, 1988), p. 10; James Adams, *The Unnatural Alliance* (London: Quartet Books, 1984), pp. 5, 12–14, 17, 43–4; Naomi Chazan, "The Fallacies of Pragmatism: Israeli Foreign Policy towards South Africa," *African Affairs*, vol. 82, no. 327 (April 1983),

Although "apartheid" is used to describe several other settler colonial regimes, South African apartheid remains historically unique. A model can be constructed capturing some of its features—for example, racial separation, racial hierarchy and official legal discrimination—and by extending the term "racial" to include ethnic and other identity groups. Accounting for the specificities of the South African apartheid regime's racial doctrine, this model can be used to analyse other cases, which may then be considered apartheid.

When we describe the Israeli system as apartheid, it is important to bear in mind the differences between apartheid as an analytical concept and the use of the term in a political strategy of struggle. Taking it in the latter sense, an anti-apartheid campaign is possible and Israel can be considered an apartheid system under international conventions, which do not classify apartheid as a uniquely South African system.

The International Convention on the Suppression and Punishment of the Crime of Apartheid considers apartheid a crime against humanity and declares as "criminal those organisations, institutions and individuals committing the crime of apartheid."[39] Article II enumerates several practices used to preserve this system. Most of them, like murder, torture and forced labour, are already deemed criminal with or without apartheid, but these may also define the crime of apartheid itself, "which shall include similar policies and practices of racial segregation and discrimination as practised in southern Africa."[40] The convention goes into more detail in Articles II (b), (c) and (d): "deliberate imposition on a racial group or groups of living conditions calculated to cause its or their physical destruction in whole or in part;" and:

> "any legislative measures and other measures calculated to prevent
> a racial group or groups from participation in the political, social,

---

p. 172; Rosalyne Ainslee, "Israel and South Africa: An Unlikely Alliance?," *Report no. 81–18876*, United Nations Department of Political Security Affairs, Center Against Apartheid, 1981, p. 6; Michael Brecher, *The Foreign Policy System of Israel* (New Haven: Yale University Press, 1974), p. 173.

[39] "International Convention on the Suppression and Punishment of the Crime of *Apartheid*, Adopted by the General Assembly of the United Nations on 30 November 1973," *United Nations*, p. 245, accessed at: https://bit.ly/3uYbp61. Italics in the original.

[40] Ibid.

economic and cultural life of the country and the deliberate creation
of conditions preventing the full development of such a group or
groups, in particular by denying to members of a racial group or
groups basic human rights and freedoms, including the right to
work, the right to form recognised trade unions, the right to education, the right to leave and to return to their country, the right to a
nationality, the right to freedom of movement and residence, the
right to freedom of opinion and expression, and the right to freedom of peaceful assembly and association; [and] Any measures
including legislative measures, designed to divide the population
along racial lines by the creation of separate reserves and ghettos for
the members of a racial group or groups, the prohibition of mixed
marriages among members of various racial groups, the expropriation of landed property belonging to a racial group or groups or to
members thereof."[41]

Parenthetically, Israel did not sign the 1973 United Nations
International Convention on the Suppression and Punishment of the
Crime of Apartheid and South Africa did not call for Israeli withdrawal from 1967 occupied territories. By January 1978, "fourteen
new United Nations General Assembly resolutions against apartheid
have gone on the books without the participation of Israel in any of
the votes on grounds of 'hypocrisy of Third World sponsors'."[42]

In 1972, South Africa opened its first diplomatic mission in Tel Aviv
and the Israeli Consulate in South Africa was upgraded to an embassy
in 1974. The Israeli South-African Chamber of Commerce that published the *Israel-South Africa Trade Journal* was founded that year in Tel
Aviv. In 1975, South Africa reciprocated the embassy move.[43]

In December 1977, an embargo stricter than the 1963 international arms embargo on the military of South Africa occurred when
the Security Council issued Resolution 418, which stated that the
"acquisition of arms by South Africa constituted a threat to international security." As a result, it became an obligation that members
of the United Nations "stop the supply of weapons, ammunition,

---

[41] Ibid., pp. 245–6.

[42] Joseph, pp. 22–3.

[43] Deon Geldenhuys, *Some Foreign Policy Implications of South Africa's Total National Strategy*
(Braamfontein: South African Institute of International Affairs, 1979), p. 3; Joseph, p. 22.

and equipment" to South Africa.[44] Days after, Moshe Dayan announced that South Africa was a "good friend" and that Israel would not "leave her to the mercy of fate."[45] Nonetheless, Israel announced that it would abide by the embargo. However, its observation of the embargo would be "subject to Israeli reading of the document and certainly excluding commitments made before the United Nations resolution."[46]

The International Court of Justice included the crime of apartheid in its elaboration of the elements of crimes against humanity in Article 7 (1) (j).[47] The UN Convention on the Elimination of All Forms of Racial Discrimination has additionally explained what is meant by racial discrimination, classifying it as:

> "any distinction, exclusion, restriction or preference based on race, colour, descent, or national or ethnic origin which has the purpose or effect of nullifying or impairing the recognition, enjoyment or exercise, on an equal footing, of human rights and fundamental freedoms in the political, economic, social, cultural or any other field of public life."[48]

Israel's system of rule over the West Bank and Gaza and its explicit Judaisation policy in Jerusalem, which is codified in law, meets most of the definitional criteria of the crime of apartheid. For example, attempts to reduce the number of Arab residents in Jerusalem rely on immigration and residency laws that consider native Palestinians born in the city as newly arrived immigrants who were granted residency when Israel occupied the city in 1967. Palestinian Jerusalemites may lose their residency status if they leave for three consecutive years, in order to work abroad, for example, or if they move to one of the villages around the city after being priced out by high urban rents.

---

[44] Joseph, p. 44.

[45] Olusola Ojo, "Israeli-South African Connections and Afro-Israeli Relations," *International Studies*, vol. 21, no. 1 (January–March 1982), p. 46.

[46] Joseph, p. 45. Joseph and other researchers give a detailed record of the military cooperation between both countries, see: Adams pp. 38–71, 80, 179; Joseph, pp. 47–53.

[47] See: "Article 7 (1) (j): Crime against humanity of apartheid," in: *Elements of Crimes* (The Hague: International Criminal Court, 2013), p. 8, accessed at: https://bit.ly/3z6e00Y

[48] "International Convention on the Elimination of All of Racial Discrimination," *United Nations*, 7 March 1966, accessed at: https://bit.ly/3g8lGHk

Even the South African apartheid regime was not so creative in its discriminatory policymaking as to treat the natives as strangers and the strangers as landlords.[49]

The question of whether the colonised want to free themselves from this regime by struggling for equal citizenship in one state or self-rule in a separate state is irrelevant to the question of whether the political system of governance is an apartheid system.

Equally irrelevant is the government's justification for the measures, whether they are instituted to ensure the security of the ruling ethnicity or secure its superiority. Parts of the ruling coalitions in Israel speak frankly of the need to take all necessary measures to ensure Jewish superiority in the "land of Israel" between the river and the sea; others justify crimes of apartheid by citing security considerations for the Israeli government regime in the West Bank and Gaza, which allows limited Palestinian self-rule in isolated ghettos behind walls, checkpoints and other technologies of separation to limit their freedom.

The Israeli system thus meets the core definitional elements of ethnicity-based rule within a constructed hierarchy of superior and inferior ethnicities, subjugating two peoples to one system of power and one economy while preserving legal separation via two distinct systems of rights. Since the term "apartheid" was first coined in Afrikaans, the language of the settlers in South Africa, it seems fitting that the settler colonialist system in Israel, which combines conquest, displacement, expropriation and the requisition of land and space, be

---

[49] Personal note: When I was representing the National Democratic Assembly (Balad) in the Knesset, I was responsible for a campaign against what we then called "the confiscation of Jerusalemites' blue identity cards," i.e., the termination of their residency in their own city. While raising the issue of some young academics whose residency was revoked because they worked abroad and were unable to come back to visit their families for three consecutive years, I met with Anatoly Sharansky, who served then as interior minister (1999–2000). Sharansky, a Soviet dissident, was a Zionist activist persecuted by the KGB who arrived in Israel in 1986. So, I found myself trying to convince a man who arrived in the country in 1986 and had already served twice as minister not to revoke the residencies of native Jerusalemites who came from families that had lived in the city for centuries. He showed no understanding of their plight, much less compassion. This was just one of many strange things I experienced in that thankless capacity.

known by its Hebrew terms: a system of *kibbush* and *nishul* (understood in Hebrew to mean direct occupation and other forms of conquest; confiscation of land which includes the displacement of natives; forced settlement; the negation of the identity of places; Judaisation).

In seeking to establish the settler colonial character of the Israeli state and the creation of an apartheid-like system, it is essential to first recognise its distinct features and even to acknowledge its exceptionalism. The distinction will be briefly examined here and illustrated through comparison with South Africa and French colonialism in Algeria.

First, there is no sense in denying the success of the construction of a Jewish Israeli nationality that does not include the native people. The French settlers in Algeria didn't engage in such a project while the South African whites became a part of one South African nation. Arabs who are convinced of this realistic position will be surprised to discover that this nationality is denied by Israel itself, which insists it is the embodiment of a global Jewish Nation.

Second, as in the case of Algeria and South Africa, the native population did not become an indigenous people asking for cultural rights and compensation, but instead continued to develop their national character and national aspirations as Palestinian Arabs.

Third, unlike apartheid South Africa, the Palestinian population in the occupied territories is not separated from Jews within the framework of one citizenship. That is, they do not share Israeli citizenship and, although they live under the same regime, are not considered part of the state. In contrast, South African blacks were citizens, separated from white citizens by different systems of rights and duties.[50] Moreover, international and Arab approaches to the West Bank and Gaza Strip treat them as occupied areas. However, unlike the case of the French in occupied Algeria, total separation and Palestinian sovereignty is made impossible by aggressive settlement construction and other integration measures, i.e., by settler colonialism itself. In addition, the settlers in Palestine have no mother country to return to, unless we consider the 1967 occupation as the only settler colonial

---

[50] On the other hand, the Oslo agreement produced a political structure which is similar to the Bantustans in South African apartheid.

project and Israel "proper" (within its 1949 borders) to be the set-tlers' mother country, forgetting that 1949 Israel was already a settler state. This is the approach of the two-state solution, which Israel has rejected and made impossible.

Fourth, the geographical proximity between coloniser and colo-nised in the West Bank and the Gaza Strip is more reminiscent of South African apartheid than an overseas colony. At the same time, the *kibbush* regime is a system of racist separation characterised by two separate legal systems under the same Israeli sovereignty.

Fifth, like Israel, French settler colonialism settlement policies in Algeria were extensive. But whereas France tried to impose the French language on Algeria and the Algerians, Israel did not try to impose the Hebrew language or to Judaise the Palestinians ("just" their land and its history). Nor did Israel legally annex the occupied territories, with the exception of Jerusalem and the Golan Heights, though it continues to build Jewish settlements everywhere.

Zionist colonialism thus inhabits a space between the two extinct models provided by the Dutch in South Africa and French colonial practices in Algeria. It blends some of the main features of each. The Israeli system is a settler colonial, apartheid-like regime and the Palestinian struggle for justice can certainly invoke the internationally recognised convention against apartheid mentioned above.

More and more human rights organisations, including American and Israeli groups, are in fact using the term apartheid to describe Israeli rule over the Palestinians in the West Bank and Gaza.[51]

---

[51] In this context, there were three important developments in 2021. In early March, the International Criminal Court prosecutors announced that a formal investigation into the situation in Palestine had begun. See: "Statement of ICC Prosecutor, Fatou Bensouda, respecting an investigation of the Situation in Palestine," *International Criminal Court*, 3 March 2021, accessed at: https://bit.ly/3w1pUHp. Second, a Human Rights Watch report drew attention to Israeli racial discrimination and "apartheid" practices both inside and outside Israel: Human Rights Watch, *A Threshold Crossed: Israeli Authorities and the Crimes of Apartheid and Prosecution* (United States: April 2021), accessed at: https://bit.ly/3wXE9go. Third, B'Tselem, the Israeli human rights organisation, published a report that described the regime of Jewish supremacy that extends from the Jordan River to the Mediterranean as "apartheid." See: "A regime of Jewish supremacy from the Jordan River to the Mediterranean Sea: This is apartheid," *Position Paper*, B'Tselem, The Israeli

Former US President Jimmy Carter also used the term to describe the Israeli occupation in the West Bank and Gaza in the absence of a two-state solution.[52] With the prospect of a sovereign Palestinian state along the 1967 borders growing ever dimmer, it will not be long before this nomenclature prevails worldwide. Israel will be unable to maintain the existing system without accepting this term and its connotations.

Whether Israel's regime qualifies as settler colonialism or apartheid, or both, it is important to keep in mind that this is an interpretative diagnosis of a dominant structure and the process that created it. As such, it neither indicates nor necessitates any particular political "solution," but may lead to different endpoints.

Veracini is right to observe that "settler colonisation, a colonising act where settlers envisage no return, still tells a story of either total victory or total failure."[53] I essentially agree with Nadim Rouhana that settler colonialism in Palestine is an ongoing project, the end of which is not determined yet.[54] Nevertheless, just because Israel is a settler colonial structure and has failed to nativise does not necessarily mean that it will be dismantled. Political outcomes or so-called solutions are not determined solely by the diagnosis of the structure. Many other factors intervene and must be taken into consideration, some of which were discussed in the first part of this book.

One-State Solution?

The option of a single state for all its citizens, both Arab and Jewish, was never seriously considered after 1948. When the state of Israel was declared, the Arabs viewed Zionism as a colonial movement that

Information Center for Human Rights in the Occupied Territories, 12 January 2021, accessed at: https://bit.ly/3uTiip6

[52] Jimmy Carter, *Palestine: Peace Not Apartheid* (New York: Simon and Shuster, 2006).

[53] Lorenzo Veracini, *Settler Colonialism: A Theoretical Overview* (London: Palgrave Macmillan, 2010), p. 115.

[54] Nadim N. Rouhana, "Homeland Nationalism and Guarding Dignity in a Settler Colonial Context: The Palestinian Citizens of Israel Reclaim Their Homeland," *Borderland e-Journal*, vol. 14, no. 1 (Spring 2015), pp. 1–2.

aimed to establish a state in a land inhabited by another people. The Balfour Declaration was not a secret. Although Zionist plans to establish a Jewish state were initially obscured by the term "homeland for Jews," their true meaning was hidden from no one but the wilfully ignorant. The goal of a Jewish state that would also be a state for all Jews everywhere, not just those Jews already in Palestine, precluded—and still precludes—any serious discussion of shared equal citizenship.

The Zionist movement has persistently framed the idea of a Jewish state in Palestine as the only conceivable solution to the Jewish question. In the movement's own view, this is the historical justification for the existence of Zionism itself. A Jewish state was the *raison d'être* of the Zionist movement since its inception in the diaspora, when the Balfour Declaration and the settlement project itself were still no more than a distant dream. Zionism never formulated a programme for a political entity in which Arabs and Jews would live side by side, with two brief exceptions. The first was articulated by thinkers influenced by the cultural Zionism of Asher Ginsberg (1856–1927), known by his Hebrew name Ahad Ha'am, who took the distinction between homeland and state seriously. The second grew out of movements like Hashomer Hatzair in the 1930s, which was a socialist Zionist movement that was both deeply involved in the colonial settlement project in Palestine and practiced socialism in the *kibbutzim*.

With the consolidation of the state of Israel, it is foolish to believe that Zionism or any of its strands—or Israel and any of its major political social movements—will accept a single democratic state for both people as a framework for a solution today. Yet equal citizenship is the key to coexistence in one state without Zionist hegemony, and it also offers an alternative to the Jewish population, who will need to be convinced that there is no need for an exclusivist Jewish state. What I am talking about here is legitimising the Jewish presence and Jewish polity in Palestine through shared equal citizenship and the recognition of the national character of the Jewish population in Israel. This is necessary not only as a message of coexistence, but, more importantly, for the self-understanding of any Palestinian liberation movement and for a better understanding of Israel.

When the single state framework was briefly proposed in the past, for example by Fatah at the end of the 1960s,[55] it was perceived by Israelis as the latest iteration of the call for Israel's demise. A one-state solution was floated again by the PLO as a programme for "a democratic secular state" that would guarantee total equality of rights between the inhabitants of the country: Muslims, Christians and Jews (Only religious and not national affiliations were named). Unfortunately, no path was articulated to enable Jewish-Arab collaboration to transform the idea into a practical political programme. Rather, the democratic state was envisaged as being a corollary result of Palestine's liberation. In any case, the idea soon lost popular currency.

The PLO proposal differed from the bi-national state envisioned long ago by others. The Hashomer Hatzair model, for example, provided for the recognition of two national communities in Palestine, each forming a distinct entity within one state. This proposal accommodated the idea of a national homeland for the Jews without requiring a nation state; the resulting entity could serve as a bi-national state and homeland for Arab and Jews in Palestine, allowing both to exercise national self-determination. This idea had its roots in the thought

---

[55] According to Salah Khalaf, the first Fatah proposal supporting a single democratic state in historic Palestine dates to 10 October 1968, when he stated in a press conference that Fatah's strategic objective was to "work toward the creation of a democratic state in which Arabs and Jews would live together harmoniously as fully equal citizens in the whole historic Palestine." Salah Khalaf & Eric Rouleau, *My Home, My Land: A Narrative of the Palestinian Struggle*, Linda Butler Koseoglu (trans.) (New York: Times Books, 1981), p. 139. However, Khalaf said that this proposal "triggered a storm of protest both within the ranks of the Resistance." Ibid. Later, in the sixth session of the Palestinian National Council (September 1969), the council discussed the adoption of a new document stipulating the following: "The Palestinian armed struggle aims to terminate the Zionist entity in Palestine, ensure the return of the Palestinian people [the refugees to their homeland], and establish a democratic state on the whole of Palestinian soil, absent all forms of racial discrimination or religious fanaticism." Faisal Hourani, *Palestinian Political Thought (1964–1976): A study of PLO Basic Documents* [Arabic] (Beirut: PLO's Research Center, 1980), p. 164. However, after careful deliberation, the statement was replaced by another stipulating that "the armed struggle aims to liberate all Palestine [to become] a society where all citizens coexist with equal rights and duties in [a manner consistent with] Arab aspirations for unity and progress." Ibid., p. 167.

of Jewish intellectuals who believed in a special Jewish link to Palestine, but also believed it need not be actualised in a Jewish state. From the 1920s to 1960s, a handful of political groups advocated the establishment of a bi-national state. In addition to Hashomer Hatzair, the Palestinian Communist party—an anti-Zionist Jewish party by then—promoted a bi-national state for Arabs and Jews on the eve of Israel's establishment. But it quickly changed its position after the Soviet Union declared support for the partition of Palestine, becoming an enthusiastic supporter of a Jewish state and participating in the so-called war of independence.

There was also the humanist-oriented Brit Shalom (Covenant of Peace), which did not believe that the uniqueness of the Jewish people justified realising their aspirations for self-determination in a Jewish state that would do injustice to the native Palestinian majority. Brit Shalom included political and academic figures such as Arthur Ruppin, Hugo Bergmann and Martin Buber, who sought "to arrive at an understanding between Jews and Arabs as to the form of their mutual social relations in Palestine on the basis of absolute political equality of two culturally autonomous peoples."[56] Brit Shalom suggested creating a legislative council for Jewish–Arab parity that would administer the bi-national state on the basis of equal rights, irrespective of the size of either group at any given time.[57] The organisation argued that bi-nationalism would liberate Zionism from imperial influence and enable Jews to integrate into the surrounding Arab world.[58]

Ihud (Union) was a bi-national movement that emerged in 1942 and continued until the mid-1960s. A successor to Brit Shalom, it was led by the president of the Hebrew University, Judah Magnes, and the philosopher Martin Buber. Ihud advocated a form of government "based upon equal political rights for both peoples" and proposed a federal union between Palestine and neighbouring countries that

---

[56] Ran Greenstein, *Zionism and Its Discontents: A Century of Radical Dissent in Israel/Palestine*) (London: Pluto Press, 2014), p. 11.

[57] Tamar Hermann, "The Bi-national Idea in Israel/Palestine: Past and Present," *Nations and Nationalism*, vol. 11, no. 3 (2005), p. 385.

[58] Maor Zohar, "Moderation from Right to Left: The Hidden Roots of Brit Shalom," *Jewish Social Studies*, vol. 19, no. 2 (2013), p. 80.

would "guarantee the national rights of all the people within it," along with a covenant between it and "an Anglo-American Union which is to be part of the future Union of the free peoples."[59]

These ideas were marginalised by mainstream Zionists on the left and right alike before they even reached the Palestinians, who in any case would not have accepted them at that point given their dismissal of the Zionist project as a whole.

In Israel, the Matzpen (Compass) radical leftist movement revived the idea of one state in the 1960s, couching it in Marxist terms. Although the socialist, anti-Zionist political group only had a few dozen members (most were Jews, but it also included Arabs), it was very active during the 1960s surge of radical left youth and student movements in the West, which otherwise did not extend to Israel. The boldest expression of this radicalism in Israel, Matzpen made no compromises with Zionism. After the 1967 war, it called for an immediate end to the occupation and expressed solidarity with Palestinian resistance organisations. In this, it concurred with the Israeli Communist Party, but Matzpen went further to call for the "de-Zionisation" of Israel, including the abolition of all institutionalised forms of Jewish political supremacy, advocating for one socialist state within which Arabs and Jews would live together. Matzpen spread bold, revolutionary ideas in a nationalist, militarist society, but it remained a small, marginal group prone to factionalism.

I myself returned to the idea of a bi-national state in an interview with *Race and Class* in 1995, as it was clear for me that the Oslo agreement would not lead to a meaningful two-state solution but to "Bantustanisation" instead.[60]

---

[59] Greenstein, p. 47.

[60] Graham Usher, pp. 43–8. See also: "Bridging the Green Line: The PA, Israeli Arabs, and Final Status. An Interview with Azmi Bishara," *Journal of Palestine Studies*, vol. 26, no. 3 (Spring 1997), pp. 67–80. See also Uri Avnery's response to that article: Uri Avnery, "A Binational State? God Forbid: A Response to Azmi Bishara," *Journal of Palestine Studies*, vol. 28, no. 4 (1999), pp. 55–60. A debate about the bi-national state took place on the margins of Israeli political discourse during the second Intifada when journalist Ari Shavit published in August 2003 an article entitled "Cry, the Beloved Two-State Solution" in the Israeli daily newspaper, *Haaretz*. The article included a joint interview with Meron Benvenisti and Haim Hanegbi in which they advocated for the establishment of a single,

A spate of recent academic books and articles[61] addressing the subject of the bi-national state in Palestine have triggered a lively debate, and new grassroots activism on the issue has also emerged, for example the One Democratic State Campaign,[62] Association for One Democratic State in Israel/Palestine[63] and the One State Foundation.[64] There is also a new talk of political confederation.[65]

In the aftermath of apartheid, South Africans rejected the idea of distinct "nations" in favour of a multicultural, multilingual, multi-religious and multi-ethnic nation-state with undifferentiated citizenship. In Palestine, there are already two distinct national communities with different national aspirations. While bi-nationalism may therefore seem closer to the status quo, it is not politically realistic given the current balance of power within Palestine, in the sense that it is not perceived as a possible solution in current negotiations.

In South Africa, the African National Congress (ANC) made equal citizenship within a multicultural state a central plank of its political platform. The ANC represented a majority of the population, which had been systematically deprived of civil and political rights within one state and was largely without separatist national aspirations. In contrast, the Palestinian national liberation movement was primarily a movement of refugees; when the PLO was established, most Palestinians did not live under the rule of the colonising state. It did not recognise the state of Israel, let alone demand equal rights within

---

democratic state for two peoples and for the complete abandonment of the two-state solution. See: Ari Shavit, "Cry, the Beloved Two-state Solution," *Haaretz*, 6 August 2003, accessed at: https://bit.ly/2Qxqm0R

[61] See: Jeff Halper & Nadia Naser-Najjab, *Decolonizing Israel, Liberating Palestine: Zionism, Settler Colonialism, and the Case for One Democratic State* (London: Pluto Press, 2021); Ariella Azoulay & Adi Ophir, *The One-State Condition: Occupation and Democracy in Israel/Palestine* (Stanford: Stanford University Press, 2012); Benny Morris, *One State, Two States: Resolving the Israel/Palestine Conflict* (New Haven and London: Yale University Press, 2009).

[62] See the main website: *One Democratic State Campaign*, accessed at: https://bit.ly/2PycFhr.

[63] See the main website: *The Association for One Democratic State in Israel/Palestine*, accessed at: https://bit.ly/3aNUFak

[64] See the main website: *One State Foundation*, accessed at: https://bit.ly/3nDnDyP

[65] Sam Bahour & Bernard Avishai, "Want Israeli-Palestinian Peace? Try Confederation," *The New York Times*, 12 February 2021, accessed at: https://nyti.ms/3psouDf

it. Whereas the PLO initially called for the full liberation of Palestine from that occupying state, since the mid-1970s, it has gradually orientated itself towards the idea of a specifically Palestinian nation state in the parts of Palestine occupied in 1967.

The first and second Intifadas in Gaza and the West Bank were uprisings or revolts against occupation, not demonstrations for equal civil and political rights in one state, and the same is true of the May 2021 protests against occupation policies and settler activity in Jerusalem. No serious Palestinian political force has adopted as its aim the establishment of a single state incorporating both Jewish-Israeli and Palestinian-Arab nationalities. Even if it had, Israel is unlikely to entertain such a proposal today in negotiations, which remain the sole focus of the Palestinian leadership's political strategy.

Notwithstanding other disagreements, groups across the entire Palestinian political spectrum—left, right, Islamist, nationalist—favour an independent Palestinian state. Even so, the fact that a bi-national state has only recently been suggested by Palestinian democrats does not make it any less serious or unworthy of discussion. Quite the opposite. Moreover, I see no great ideological or structural obstacles to such a solution among Palestinians. It is in the interest of the Palestinian people to put forward a democratic programme that includes the right of return and retains other inalienable Palestinian rights, while also providing a rational and just alternative to Jewish Israelis.

If Palestinians themselves endorse the idea, there will be no serious obstacles from the Arab world as well. People's actual behaviour indicates acceptance of a struggle for equal rights under a single regime, though the discourse among activists with various political factions remains dogmatic.

The real problem is that Israel has never accepted this hypothetical position, and no Israeli political or social force has ever endorsed a bi-national paradigm. This is the main obstacle to its adoption by the Palestinian political elite, who see peace negotiations as their only option—that is, negotiations with Israel as it exists today with the current power imbalance. The bi-national model cannot conceivably be posited as a negotiated "solution" in the context of existing power dynamics, but then neither will be an acceptable version of the two-state solution.

The discourse, slogans and strategies of those Palestinian forces that endorse various forms of armed struggle for the liberation of Palestine (although what they do is at best armed resistance), fly in the face of bi-nationalism and the spirit of the one-state approach. In the case of the Islamists, they are incompatible with the very idea of democratic citizenship in a secular state.

There is clearly no point in waiting for a major segment of Israeli society to warm up to such a proposal. The powerful do not relinquish their privileges willingly, and the one-state solution would most certainly entail relinquishing privileges. This is even truer for a single secular democratic state based solely on equal citizenship regardless of nationality than a bi-national state, which, though it may also be secular and democratic, is predicated on the recognition of two nations in the manner of a federal union (in contrast, the confederation model is simply another iteration of the two-state model).

On the other side, there is neither a significant Arab democracy in the region presenting an attractive alternative political model nor an Arab state dedicated to the welfare of all its citizens regardless of their religious or ethnic origins. The sole example so far is Tunisia, which is a relatively homogenous country in ethnicity and religion, and yet still shows signs of instability.

One organised Arab political force presenting a programme striving for a state of equal citizenship and collective rights for the Palestinian citizens of Israel is the National Democratic Assembly (Balad), an Arab party in Israel. In response to Balad's efforts, Israel did everything it could, including enacting legislation, to undermine its programme, emphasise the Jewishness of the state and counter its democratic aspiration.

Those who have come to support a one-state solution in recent years have done so largely because they believe that the two-state solution along the 1967 borders is a "failed paradigm", or because they have realised that the two-state solution as envisaged cannot include the right of return. This change of heart is not rooted in any conviction that the one-state solution has a better chance of success. The failure of the two-state solution does not in itself imply success for the one-state model. But if we are speaking only theoretically, then a single democratic bi-national state is the model that best fulfils

Palestinian national and civil rights while offering a democratic vision for Jewish Israelis.

The single most important reason that the one-state model is making no discernible political inroads is that Israel, both the state and the public, dismisses it, and there is no serious Jewish movement that can argue for it in the arena of public opinion. On the contrary, liberal and leftist Zionist forces make apocalyptic warnings about the possible consequences of retaining control of areas like Gaza that are densely packed with Palestinians. In this framing, a one-state solution is portrayed as a grave danger and a threat, which can only be averted by swallowing the bitter pill of the two-state solution. This type of rhetoric on the so-called Zionist left is not exactly a ringing endorsement of one state. Officially, fearing that natural developments on the ground will lead inexorably to an apartheid-like, one-state reality,[66] Israel favours a nominal two-state solution—the official position since the Sharon government, despite several attempts by Netanyahu (and currently Naftali Bennet) to drop even the idea of a nominal Palestinian state.

In short, one democratic state is not currently a viable alternative to a negotiated two-state solution, nor is it made inevitable by the failure of the two-state solution. In fact, Israel accepts neither a two-state solution nor one bi-national state for Jews and Arabs, preferring to maintain and consolidate its apartheid-like model of settler colonialism in Palestine.[67]

It is impossible to ignore that Israel is unwilling to integrate into the region through just compromises, preferring instead to prevail by force. This state of affairs invites a comparison between the present Arab-Israeli context and that of the Crusader states in the Arab region. Of course, no structural analogy can be drawn between the

---

[66] Sharon's plan to disengage from Gaza included the annexation of the Jordan Valley and settlement blocs. Ehud Olmert explained it clearly as "withdrawal to lines we chose" in order to avoid the South African model, though we had already begun to point to South Africa to describe realities in Palestine. See: David Landau, "Maximum Jews minimum Palestinians: Ehud Olmert speaks out," *Haaretz*, 13 November 2003, accessed at: https://bit.ly/3fOQQ6D

[67] In this sense, I agree with Mehran Kamrava that the prospects for a just solution in the foreseeable future are grim. Kamrava, pp. 216–23.

two: although Israel's emergence as a state was the fruit of a colonial project, ethnic cleansing and imperialist support, it became a modern nation state in a modern global order; the Crusaders formed feudal religious kingdoms in an age before nationalism. Israel built an advanced economy and modern army, developed nuclear weapons and enjoys not only the support of the US, but also its unconditional commitment to Israeli-defined security; the Crusader kingdoms did not enjoy such superiority. The comparison hinges on only one shared feature: the sense of being an illegitimate alien entity in the region and acting as such.

Even after the Arabs had officially proposed multiple settlements and peace initiatives, Israel chose not to integrate in the region. In its view, it is the region that should accommodate Israel's needs and change accordingly, not vice versa. The fact that Israel has concluded numerous bilateral settlements and agreements with states in the region in not a relevant counterpoint. The Crusader states would never have survived if their only assets had been military prowess and the skilful construction of citadels. At least one of the four Crusader kingdoms survived for 190 years by signing several accords with various neighbouring principalities and sultanates, and by exploiting the divisions among rival forces to sow discord. Yet, these agreements never established a genuine peace. The Crusader kingdoms continued to be regional anomalies, both culturally and politically, rejected by the local populace and existing only insofar as contemporaneous Muslim leaders were unable to defeat them in a fight. Indeed, the Crusader states failed despite all their agreements and truces and despite their military campaigns and massacres.

I draw this comparison in order to provoke thought on the options that Israel has rejected and the choice it has made to be a Jewish apartheid state, a choice inimical to both the two-state and one-state solutions. In short, after establishing itself through violent aggression, Israel has chosen to continue its existence as an isolated settler colonial outpost, never genuinely engaging with its surroundings apart from relationships with Arab authoritarian regimes at odds with their own populations. It lives by the sword, by temporary agreements and truces, and by exploiting regional rivalries and divisions to its advantage. No matter how much time passes, it gains no legitimacy in the eyes of those who surround it—and it will never gain legitimacy so long as it refuses to acknowledge the injustices inflicted on the Palestinians and reach a just settlement with them.

By refusing any agreement that provides what many Palestinians and Arabs consider a just and legitimate solution, Israel has committed itself to perpetual conflict. Whether or not it can ultimately impose an unjust solution, it has historically chosen permanent warfare and so remained without legitimacy in the eyes of its neighbours.

I will not belabour the comparison between the contemporary conflict and the Crusader campaigns. It is not the point of this chapter, and the historical contexts are completely different. We could support the analogy by pointing to the many alliances concluded between the Crusader states and their neighbours, such as the pact with the northern emirates that allowed the Crusaders of Antioch to make way to Jerusalem. We could cite the justifications proffered for the Crusades, like the decision by the mentally disturbed Fatimid Caliph al-Hakim to burn down the Church of the Holy Sepulchre. We could even delve into how religion was exploited to mobilise fighters. But ultimately, we will face the legitimate objections that the contemporary international system is qualitatively different from the prevailing order in the era of the Crusader kingdoms; that modern states are essentially different from political entities and principalities of that age; that the role of religion differs; that the relationship between Israel and the West is much closer and more efficient than that of the Crusader kingdoms to Europe (Pope Urban II, who died a full fortnight after the fall of Jerusalem, nonetheless did not live to hear the news). And, of course, there is the role of technology and science. The point is that in the past this region saw kingdoms alienated from their surroundings, established by conquest and settled not by integrating in the region, but by ensconcing themselves in isolated citadels and exploiting rivalries between local political entities. The point of the comparison is not to naively imagine Israel meeting an end similar to the Crusader kingdoms. Crusader kingdoms could neither change nor integrate in an age in which religion was the major component of culture. Israel and the Arab region can change and can be changed. The factors that support the consolidation of the Israeli apartheid model may be used to change it.

By rejecting all potential solutions with any legitimacy, Israel has chosen to remain behind its walls, surviving by means of coercive deterrence and by taking advantage of intra-Arab disputes, both between regimes and between despotic regimes and their peoples.

This might be a permanent situation. Even today, this choice is deeply entrenched among the Israeli public. It relies on the position of strength provided by Israel's unhealthy relationship with the United States, a bilateral relationship without parallel in modern times. Israel thus seems unlikely to accept either a one- or two-state solution any time soon. And while the Palestinians will keep rejecting unjust settlements, they will also need to propose a solid democratic programme for Jews and Arabs. This is a form of resistance that will achieve partial but important gains and prevent further normalisation of this apartheid settler colonialism. To do this, Palestinians need a long-term resistance strategy that includes democratic forces inside and outside the region.

This is a long struggle that must be managed correctly. Time is not necessarily on Israel's side. One of the most important lessons of the past 70 years is that time is on the side of whoever makes the best use of it.

9

CONCLUDING REMARKS

The Palestine issue is the just cause of a people who fell victim to an organised settler colonialist project that sought to establish a Jewish state through conquest and by forcibly changing the demographic structure of Palestine; the result was the Nakba of 1948. The regime of the settler colonialist state that emerged took first the shape of an ethnocracy and then, after Israel occupied the rest of Palestine in 1967 and came to rule directly over the Palestinian people in the West Bank and Gaza, the shape of an apartheid-like system of *Kibbush* and *Nishul*, that can be called in short an Israeli apartheid regime.

The Palestinians already possessed a national consciousness, aspirations, and a national leadership while the Zionist movement was working as a settler colonial project in Palestine to realise its own self-described national ambition of a Jewish state in Palestine. This project could not be implemented without ethnic cleansing and committing a sociocide/politicide against the Palestinians, entailing atrocities such as massacres and looting; an armed robbery in the middle of the twentieth century. The self-justification, cognitive dissonance, amnesia and mythology needed to maintain the sanity of a "civilised society" after the commission of such acts have been constituent components of the settler society culture in the new state, which effectively pursued the task of nation-building.

This clear instance of settler colonialism, which took root in Palestine during the age of decolonisation, has been particularly complicated and vexatious due to the conjuncture of the Jewish question and the Arab question, and the imperialist partition of the Arab Levant. Both issues and their impact were discussed at length in the first part of this book. It may not be fair that the Palestinians, the people of a small Arab country on the eastern Mediterranean coast, have had to endure the consequences of complex European, American and Arab histories, ideologies and regime interests, but history is neither fair nor unfair. This is the reality that has heretofore hindered the imposition of a just, or relatively just, solution on Israel, and it is incumbent upon Israel to face this fact.

Victims of colonialism are not the good guys in a movie, nor is the colonialist society made up of bad guys. The victims should not be expected to always do the right thing or consistently take the moral high ground, as some intellectuals seem to believe or expect them to do. Nevertheless, Palestinian elites, especially the political leadership, are required to maintain a liberation ethos while also adopting a democratic programme. Other colonised nations gained their independence without having to incessantly account for the words and deeds of their leadership, but, unfortunately, due to the aforementioned complexities, the Palestinians do not have this luxury.

In no phases of the conflict were Zionism and Israel the victims; additionally, they were never "the few" against "the many". The occupier's monopolisation of victimhood—and the collusion of the major Western major powers, especially successive US administrations, with this deception—is just one of the discursive dimensions upholding and continually reproducing the settler colonial status quo.

The Palestinian calamity began in 1948, when the Palestinians were expelled from their homeland by organised settler militias that perceived themselves to be a national movement and tried to change the demography of Palestine and establish a Jewish state. This is similarly the origin of the Arab-Israeli conflict. Disingenuous attempts to start the debate from the occupation of 1967 deliberately distort history for political ends.

The memory of Palestine before 1948 is important not only on the level of personal identity, but also politically. Acknowledgement of

CONCLUDING REMARKS

this memory is what makes the acceptance of a Palestinian state in the West Bank (including East Jerusalem) and Gaza, or the acceptance of equality in a bi-national state in Palestine, historical compromises. Moreover, we are no longer talking solely about an intangible Palestinian collective memory. By refuting dominant Israeli myths about the Nakba and (re)writing the history of Palestine before 1948 to describe and document the ethnic cleansing of its people, Palestinian and Israeli critical historians have proven that writing history, even in an academic framework, is no longer the sole privilege of the victor.

Most Palestinians became refugees; Israel refused to implement the right of return according to UN Resolution 194, and the West Bank fell under Jordanian and Gaza under Egyptian administrations. The few Palestinians who managed to remain in their homeland became Israeli citizens and lived under martial law until 1966. The state defined itself as a Jewish state—and a state for Jews—treating its Arab citizens as if they were foreigners in their own country. This definition of the nation and the state is the root of the many contradictions inherent in the conception of Israel as an exclusivist democracy for the Jews, many of whom are not citizens of Israel and belong to other, mostly democratic, nations. Over time, it has led to a unique confluence between extremist nationalism and religious fundamentalism in a militarised Israeli society, despite seeming to be independent, and even antagonistic, ideological positions at Zionism's outset.

Initially a product of the interaction between Palestinian initiatives and the Arab order under the leadership of the pan-Arab camp, the PLO succeeded in building an institutional national entity and becoming the recognised representative of the Palestinian people as a liberation movement, especially after 1967, when the factions engaged in armed struggle controlled the organisation.

The 1967 war was not a defensive war; it was an aggressive war. Israel planned to defeat the pan-Arab regimes building modern states and armies, especially Nasserite Egypt. It also intended to annex territories in the West Bank and to use the occupied territories in Sinai and the Golan Heights as a bargaining chip, in order to conclude an unconditional peace with Egypt and Syria without resolving the question of Palestine. For the Arab regimes, this meant capitulation after a military defeat.

East Jerusalem was annexed and the settlement project in the newly occupied territories was launched. After the 1967 war, the secular modern settler colonial state came to be increasingly identified with the mythical biblical land of Israel (*Eretz Yisrael*). The religious component in Zionism, inherent in the definition of the nation and its connection to Palestine, expressed itself through a religious-nationalist ideology that gave birth to a new colonialist settler project in the West Bank. This ideology gradually moved to the mainstream of Israeli society.

The bilateral peace between Egypt and Israel (1979) demonstrated Israel's perception of the Palestinian issue as independent of the Arab-Israeli conflict. It facilitated Israel's 1967 war goal of forcing Arab countries to accept peace agreements with Israel in exchange for the territories occupied in 1967 but without justice for the Palestinians. Bilateralism as a way to retrieve the occupied territories proved to be an exclusive Egyptian-Israeli model that did not apply for other Arab countries and the PLO after the Oslo Accords; once Egypt was removed from the conflict, threats of war by neighbouring Arab states immediately lost all credibility and Israel had no motivation to return any of the territories occupied in 1967. Any ostensible future threat to Israeli security would come from armed resistance movements.

Egypt's separate peace lent a new significance to the Arab official recognition of the PLO as the sole legitimate representative of the Palestinians, changing the way Arab regimes, which see peace with Israel as the key to America's heart, viewed the conflict. In a nutshell, the Palestine question became the problem of the Palestinians. Arab regimes might (or might not) offer assistance and support, but it was no longer their shared responsibility. This position not only distorts history, but also flies in the face of prevailing Arab public opinion.[1]

The first Palestinian Intifada forced Israel to address the Palestinian question and sit down with the PLO, which was experiencing a profound crisis after the war for Kuwait (1991) and the collapse of the Arab order and the Soviet Union. In exchange for recognition, the PLO was ready to give up its hard-won status as a national liberation movement and become a subordinate authority under Israeli sovereignty.

---

[1] See the Appendix: "Arab Public Opinion on the Palestinian Issue."

CONCLUDING REMARKS

That was the actual substance of the Oslo Accords, which were not based on the mutual acceptance of key principles as peace negotiations typically are. Instead, the peace process consolidated the unequal balance of power between coloniser and colonised, unfolding in line with the pro-Israel bias of the US and Israeli domestic consensus. That consensus currently rejects withdrawal to the pre-June 1967 borders (including East Jerusalem), the dismantlement of settlements and a just solution to the refugee issue (the three Israeli No's explained in Chapter 4). An increasingly right-wing Israeli society treats the Palestinians only as a demographic problem; at best, it may agree to jettison the most heavily Arab-populated centres while keeping the rest. The formula is a disclosed secret: maximum land, minimum Arabs.

The Oslo Accords cleared the way for many countries in the Global South to develop relations with Israel. The agreement was not the actual reason for the normalisation of bilateral relations, but it provided a handy excuse: if the Palestinians did it, so can everyone else.

The second Intifada, the US need for Arab allies in the war on Iraq (2003), and the US desire to refute accusations of double standards forced Israel's hand. Acting to pre-empt an American roadmap for peace, it chose to withdraw from the most populated part of the occupied territories (the Gaza Strip) and intensify the settler colonial project in the West Bank (including East Jerusalem).

The effective thwarting of a Palestinian state, the aggressive expansion of settlements, and Israel's separation policies (including the construction of a separation wall) are the key features of the apartheid system instituted in Palestine. This system is an extension of settler colonialism, and not merely an occupation by a "normal state" (e.g., a nativised settler colonial state) of the land of another state (the occupied state of Palestine, which is a member of the UN). An anti-apartheid campaign is therefore justified by the nature of this regime.

The US did not pressure Israel to reenergise the peace process because of its close strategic alignment with Israel, the influence of the Israeli lobby in Washington and domestic politics, and the absence of Arab official pressure.

In the Trump era, this close alignment turned into a total identification with the positions and ideology of the Israeli nationalist religious right. The intersection between the distinct Biblical theology of Evangelical Christian Zionism and the extreme Israeli right produced a new US policy position on Palestine. The Trump-Netanyahu peace initiative, the so-called "deal of the century," not only accentuated the US pro-Israel alignment, but also managed to assemble in a single text all the shibboleths about Palestine found in Israeli propaganda and Zionist religious-nationalist narratives.

These developments have raised profound questions about the usefulness of a Palestinian strategy based solely on US-sponsored peace negotiations. Chapter 7, which discussed this issue, provided an opportunity to refute the unfounded myth of Arab rejectionism and show that, to the contrary, Israel has spurned peace initiatives as a consistent policy. It also offered the chance for a close textual analysis of the persistent myths and fallacies of Israeli propaganda that found their way into an official American peace proposal.

The Way Forward

Look for Strategies Not Solutions!:

The path ahead requires engaging in a democratic national struggle for justice and equality. The specific political model under which justice and equality will be realised will only crystallise over the course of the struggle and through long dialogue once certain principles have been accepted. The political system may eventually take the form of a single bi-national state or two states. In both cases, the system should be an inclusive state for all its citizens, with the Palestinian state maintaining its Arab character and the Israeli state maintaining its Jewish character. Both models can address the issues of refugees and citizenship, and neither will arise from current negotiations.

Nevertheless, this book does not approach the discussion from the perspective of solutions because colonialism and apartheid are not dilemmas requiring creative remedies. They are unjust institutionalised regimes that must be resisted, and no realistic, viable and just solution is imaginable under prevailing conditions, whether premised on a one-state or two-state solution. A political reorientation may be necessary, to move away from the existing negotiations, towards a long-term struggle to achieve justice for the Palestinian people. There are no negotiations on the horizon promising a "one-state solution" in place of the "two-state solution" that negotiations have failed to construct. Hence, I am not discussing solutions here, but instead emphasising the struggle for justice in all of Palestine.

After the Nakba, the Palestinian national liberation movement quickly gained a foothold in the diaspora, in refugee camps and among educated middle-class Palestinians abroad, becoming the movement of the Palestinian people as a whole. When it was reduced to a truncated political entity in the West Bank and Gaza, it triggered a process of fragmentation that soon split it into two different parts: one in the West Bank and the other in the Gaza Strip, each with its own political agenda and interest in maintaining power. This is not a strategy, unless reproducing the status quo is the goal.

Currently, each Palestinian constituency deploys different forms of resistance against the same occupying regime. Resistance will inevitably continue given the relentless struggle of living in an apartheid-like system of occupation, but a nationally coordinated strategy could revolutionise the impact of such everyday resistance. The question of strategy, however, is one for the various factions and parties, and the leaders of the two Palestinian authorities. Although the latter seem uninterested in leading a liberation movement—and likely incapable of it—leaders should nevertheless have answers about future programmes, paths for engaging in the struggle, and prospective strategies. This is not a theoretical matter, but is directly relevant to political organisation.

In the case of the Palestinian people, the duty of resistance is of special importance whether liberation takes the form of a Palestinian state (coupled with other provisions for the Palestinian people outside the West Bank and the Gaza Strip), or a bi-national Arab-Jewish state or a two-state confederation. The Palestinian people would accept any one of these models provided it promises at least some degree of justice. But the Palestinian people cannot choose it unilaterally, and the apartheid regime has not seriously engaged with solutions.

As such, the answer to the question "what is to be done?" is this: there can be no strategy without an actor or clarity about the roles of the leadership. There is no such a thing as a theoretical political strategy absent of political organisation. Analytical studies like this one can describe trends, but they cannot prescribe strategies, unless they are directed towards a specific organisation that has already defined its goals.

Repeating clichés and slogans detached from the current political moment that only serve to preserve the identity of one particular faction or party is not an answer.

How can a liberation organisation develop a liberation strategy when it has been subordinated to a constrained authority with its own strategy, one that effectively incapacitates and obviates the role of the liberation organisation itself?

While the Israeli settlement project has continued in the West Bank throughout the so-called peace process, the PA's political efforts have been channelled into two tracks. The first is fundraising (with its political supplements and accessories), which guarantees the survival of the PA and its ability to provide services to Palestinians living under its authority. These efforts have been hindered by repeated Israeli attempts to exercise control by exerting financial pressure whenever a conflict with the PA arises. Meanwhile, the PA has continued to carry out its vital security functions for Israel. Indeed, the Palestinian leadership has flaunted their achievements in security coordination to the Israeli public and the Western media, much to the astonishment of Arab and Palestinian audiences. The second track of Palestinian political activity has focused on efforts to join formal international bodies, in order to consolidate the international status of a state.

While there has been much talk of peaceful resistance, it is rarely acted upon, aside from local initiatives in villages and towns subject to land confiscations and settler attacks, or those directly impacted by the illegal separation wall. In Jerusalem, civil resistance has increased given the intensified Judaisation and the residents' direct contact with the occupation and the absence of the PA and its security obligations. The stagnation of the so-called peace process, the weakening of the PA by successive Israeli right-wing governments and the entrenched competition between Hamas and Fatah have increased the possibility of protests spreading to the West Bank.

The more dangerous development since 2007 is the internal Palestinian conflict. Power struggles erupted before a Palestinian state has even been established, and this has absorbed the energy of those involved in Palestinian politics, not just locally but in the Arab region and across the globe. When Fatah learned of Trump's deal, it was preoccupied with the question of who would succeed Abbas as PA president and with its ongoing conflict with Hamas. Fatah's internal conflicts and the changing political alliances they engender, the intricacies of which are beyond the average citizen, have become a topic of everyday conversation in the West Bank, distracting Palestinians from the struggle against occupation. The Hamas authority, on the other hand, has survived the Gaza siege and gained experience in deterring Israeli attacks. But it does not present an alternative, neither for a strategy of struggle against the Israeli apartheid system nor for the administration of Palestinian societal affairs.

Not only did the reality of the PA and the demands of its work undermine the PLO as an instrument in the international struggle for Palestine, but it also marginalised popular solidarity movements that once supported the Palestinian struggle for liberation. The PA put all its eggs in one basket, relying exclusively on the White House as the primary mediator in negotiations. Only in Trump's term did it realise that it cannot depend on the good intentions of the US to lead the negotiations to a just peace. But instead of reviving the popular struggle against an undeniably apartheid regime, it called for the Quartet to mediate the negotiations because the US was not an "honest broker".

Meanwhile, solidarity movements shifted their attention to the siege of the Gaza Strip. The PLO's decline as a national liberation movement and the rise of Hamas gave the PLO's internal rivals an opportunity to Islamise the Palestine cause. This has adversely influenced public opinion in many countries and buttressed the erroneous conception of the conflict as a religious one, which is to the benefit of Israel since it has a clear interest in portraying the question of Palestine as a primarily religious conflict.

Moreover, the political polarisation of the two rival "authorities" in the West Bank and Gaza has significantly undercut the symbolic valence of the Palestinian liberation movement in the Global South, formerly a major source of political support. The PA, preoccupied with the conflict between the two authorities and heavily reliant on the decisions of US administrations, has gradually distanced itself from the global democratic movement of solidarity with Palestine.

At the same time, however, the global solidarity movement with Palestine has been revived in recent years by courageous Palestinian civil initiatives that continue the peaceful struggle against apartheid and settlers in Jerusalem and various villages in the West Bank, and by an assertive Palestinian diaspora youth generation capitalising on democratic liberal and leftist reactions against Trump's populism and his total identification with the Israeli right.

Waiting for Israeli Elections

A strategy that hinges on the centre left one day replacing the far right in Israeli government is a lethal illusion. The Israeli Zionist left is all but extinct in mainstream politics and no longer holds any meaningful political clout. Moreover, it should be remembered that during the Nakba and the 1967 war Israel was led by the Zionist labour movement, and the two Intifadas took place when the Labour Party was in power. Things did change, but nostalgia for that era is effectively a yearning for endless, futile negotiations.

The real struggle for power in Israel is between the section of the right that allies itself with orthodox religious parties and the section of the right that refuses to do so because of conflicting views about rights and duties in citizenship and about religious strictures by religious parties in ruling coalitions. There are no significant or substantive differences between them on Palestine. Regardless of the coalition in government, public consensus in Israel clings to the three No's discussed earlier. But Israeli public opinion can be changed by other means: a resistance struggle that prevents the normalisation of apartheid and extracts a price from the Israeli economy, a global anti-apartheid campaign that espouses a discourse of democratic justice, and international pressure, especially American. The latter method requires strategies that do not rely on official Arab assistance, but on American civil society and alignments with progressive social movements, African American lobbies, Muslim American lobbies, progressive Jewish movements, etc.

The votes of Arab Palestinian citizens of Israel in national elections could be significant if the goal is to organise Arabs in Israel as citizens and as an ethnic national group fighting for their rights and the preservation of their Palestinian Arab identity. But any strategy that hinges on their votes to determine issues of war and peace or Israeli policy towards Palestine is doomed to fail, because it assumes that Israeli government approval for a settlement with the Palestinians would rely on a Jewish Knesset minority joined by Arab votes to outweigh the nationalist-religious bloc. This fantasy underestimates the centrality of Zionism and the Jewishness of the state and overestimates Israeli democracy. It also encourages the "Israelisation" of Arabs in a country that explicitly defines itself as a Jewish state.

In tandem with Palestinisation, Arab citizens are also undergoing a process of Israelisation, manifested in Arab citizens' everyday lives through the exercise of various dimensions of citizenship, such as paying taxes and expecting state services; demanding access to public service, basic civil rights, appropriate school curricula and university education; and being exposed to Hebrew media and culture. These parallel processes produce cultural hybrids and raise both Palestinian national and Israeli civic consciousness and expectations. This is an inevitable organic process. Palestinians in Israel would thus marginalise any national movement that ignores the significance of their everyday demands for civil rights. Israelisation beyond these pragmatic requirements, however, risks distorting both equal citizenship and national identity. The only form of assimilation that Arab politics in Israel can embrace without giving up their Palestinian identity is one based on a programme aspiring to make the state one for all its citizens that also recognises the national identity of its Palestinian citizens. Such a programme grants Arabs individual civil rights as equal citizens, while preserving collective rights for Palestinian Arabs inside Israel, and it is compatible with both an acceptable, relatively just two-state solution and the model of one bi-national state.[2] Any other assimilationist project would ultimately compel Arab Palestinians in a Jewish

---

[2] This was the central thesis in my article: Azmi Bishara, "'The Israel Arab': A Reading in a Ruptured Political Discourse," [Arabic] *Majallat al-Dirasat al-Filastiniyya*, vol. 6, no. 4 (Autumn 1995), pp. 1–30.

state to live as half-Arabs and half-Israelis instead of wholly Palestinian Arabs and full citizens.[3]

The PA's tendency to encourage a subgroup of Palestinians (Arab citizens of Israel) to support the Zionist centre-left is a grave mistake because it is based on a warped understanding of Israel. The Arab citizens of Israel can contribute to the liberation struggle by holding fast to their people's just cause, maintaining their identity as Palestinians and persisting in their civil struggle for equal rights as citizens in a citizenship-based state, which by definition contradicts Zionism. Moreover, experience has shown that, in Israel as it exists today, a Jewish majority is necessary for any important national policy decision to be considered legitimate.[4]

---

[3] This was the political and cultural project of national struggle that I previously advocated for the Palestinian citizens of the state of Israel and to Israeli non-Zionist democrats. This model does not include the Palestinians in the West Bank and Gaza because it was conceived as a programme for the struggle of Palestinians inside Israel and, although I opposed the Oslo Accords, I did not want to contradict the PLO and the Palestinian consensus on the issue of the Palestinian state. However, even in 1995, I was explicit that this programme could be extended to a bi-national state that comprised the Palestinian population in the West Bank and Gaza. I did not then and do not see now a contradiction between bi-nationalism and a state of all its citizens in which collective national rights are also recognised, a programme that contradicts Zionism. Outside of this context, from the beginning of my first term in the Knesset, I consistently criticised the demand of equality in a Jewish state as a demand for equality with the oppressors of the Palestinians in the West Bank and Gaza. The legislations I suggested combined recognition of the national collective rights of the Palestinian minority in the framework of a state of all its citizens. This was probably not understood by Mahmood Mamdani, as he conveyed in his book, perhaps because he insists exclusively on the South-African model and cannot perceive a democratic programme that combines civil individual and national collective rights in one state, or because he does not read Arabic nor Hebrew and could not read my writings and interviews on the issue: Mahmood Mamdani, *Neither Settler nor Native: the Making and Unmaking of Permanent Minorities* (Cambridge, MA and London: Belknap Press of Harvard University Press, 2020), pp. 312–17.

[4] The political assassination of Rabin, who dared to rely on five Arab votes in the Knesset to pass a decision to return land to Arabs, and the Israeli coalition crisis of 2020–1, when radical right-wingers refused to join a coalition with Netanyahu because it was supported by four Arab MKs and Haim Ganz hesitated to form a coalition against Netanyahu with similar Arab support, provide enough evidence of this point. In the final reading of this book before it was forwarded for publication, an Israeli coalition of fifty-eight MKs from the far right, the centre right and the left was formed in order to topple Netanyahu. It required

CONCLUDING REMARKS

Long-Term Resistance Strategy

In the occupied territories, an effective resistance movement needs a long-term plan. The PA's role is to competently administer and organise the daily affairs of Palestinians living in the regions it oversees. Given that the PA has devolved mostly into a security apparatus whose main function is to protect Israel and a service provider without sovereignty and basic rights—not even freedom of movement for its own officials—it is no surprise that many advocate for its dissolution. Not only has the PA imposed agreements on the Palestinian people that are now widely recognised as disastrous, but it has also freed the occupying power of all its responsibilities for civil governance without freeing its own people from the occupation. However, the dissolution of the PA would spark a civil war, which would destroy any remaining gains and likely end with the PA's security apparatus taking direct control with Israeli support.

There is an additional dimension to consider: the PA's historical role, as distinct from its political positions. The Palestinian people cannot be left without economic, educational, health, social and police institutions. Any people striving for collective liberation must sustain their ability to self-organise and care for their daily needs. The Palestinian people cannot survive, endure and develop without basic institutions and organs with the power to administer society. These institutions could be those of the existing PA, which has achieved some progress in the civil sphere, provided it can bear the consequences of ending security coordination, even if it means repeated Israeli incursions into its territories or the sanction of PA leaders.

Acceptance of the PA's continued existence—to carry out critical domestic functions, build institutions, and contribute to human development—will allow for the establishment of political institutions with new horizons and the articulation of programmes that face the hard reality on the ground, in turn strengthening the struggle

---

the support of an Arab list of four members, but this coalition will not make any decisions on settlements or occupied territories relying on these Arab votes. Nor do the four Arab MKs (who agreed to be in the government of the occupation) expect that. Their demands are focused exclusively on services to the Arab population inside Israel.

against apartheid on different fronts. The concerns of Palestinians in Jerusalem, the West Bank, the Gaza Strip and Israel (inside the Green Line) are inseparable, given that they all pertain to a single people all living under Israeli sovereignty. The May 2021 protests in solidarity with Jerusalem and Gaza united Palestinian protesters on both sides of the Green Line, but it did not alter the different realities they returned to after the protests subsided.

Building economic, educational and health institutions; strengthening structures vital for continued resilience and livelihoods in the West Bank (including Jerusalem), the Gaza Strip, Israel, the Arab world and the diaspora; and coordinating these vital elements under the guidance of a political system—all of this is part of the long-term struggle against Israel's apartheid system.

Abbas's threat to dissolve the PA in his 1 February 2020 speech to the Arab League after the announcement of the Trump-Netanyahu deal did not represent a new way of thinking or a constructive strategy. It was empty rhetoric of the type that Abbas himself once criticised the Palestinian armed factions for using. In his speech, Abbas said that he had called on the occupation to reassume its responsibilities from the PA.[5] What exactly does that mean? In any case, it was already obvious that Israel would decline his "invitation".

The real question centres on the role of the PA and the potential political options still available to it in the framework of a coherent liberation strategy (which the current leadership is unable to devise while caught in a convoluted network of subordination to Israel). The PA could continue to operate under such a coherent strategy, but only as a central administrative power facilitating Palestinian autonomy, with local authorities or municipalities managing the population's affairs and providing local police services, absent of any security coordination with Israel, then challenge Israel to dissolve the PA and reoccupy the West Bank! It will not; instead, Israel will try to influence the PA, and meddle and interfere in its internal affairs through intrigue, threat of punishment and promise of reward.

---

[5] "President Abbas: I will never accept annexing Jerusalem to Israel," *Wafa*, 1 February 2020, accessed at: https://bit.ly/3iqQo0Y

CONCLUDING REMARKS

This sort of confrontation needs the combative political spirit of a political elite who recognise that collaboration with Israel will not persuade it to withdraw from the West Bank and grant the PA independence and sovereignty; it will simply reproduce the Bantustan pattern. To face such challenges, a national liberation movement must be well organised and united.

The dissolution of the PA will only lead to the rule of a security apparatus in the West Bank and another in the Gaza Strip without a Palestinian state. However, although the PA's service provision is indispensable, it is not the political leader of the Palestinian people. So while it is necessary to cast aside the notion that the main remit of the PA is to protect the security and stability of Israel, it is also essential to revive the PLO as the representative of the Palestinian collective. This revival can be real and genuine if it happens as a result of adopting a new vision and includes the new forces in the Palestinian society. If not, it will be a nominal and performative act.

I remind the reader that this is a political choice; it can be adopted or rejected. It is neither a theoretical conclusion nor a historical necessity.

There are thousands of young activists in Palestine and the diaspora, with no connection to the PA and PLO factions, who are searching for meaningful opportunities to contribute to the liberation struggle. They are engaged in grassroots initiatives of all sorts, but there is no national framework in place to integrate them.

Since the signing of the Oslo Accords and to the present day, the PLO has been systematically hollowed out and stripped of its essence, structure and powers (or perhaps unsystematically, as the unintentional result of the PA's growing importance). It is as though the mission of the organisation was to fertilise the seed that culminated in the birth of Oslo, after which it could be discarded. Moreover, it seems that it was for this reason alone that Israel recognised the PLO at Oslo. The goal was to exploit the PLO's legitimacy to obtain the settlement and make it amend its Charter,[6] before forcing it to surrender the stage to the PA.

---

[6] The Palestinian National Council (PNC), the parliament in exile of the Palestinian people, held its twenty-first session in Gaza City on 22–25 April 1996 (the first session to be held

A reconciliation between Fatah and Hamas via Arab mediation will not be enough to rebuild the PLO; this can only be done by involving a much broader range of actors. The PLO is the framework necessary to undertake urgent tasks, such as integrating the efforts of the young political and civil activists in Palestine and the diaspora into the struggle.

Whatever form the next Palestinian National Council (PNC) takes, and accounting for structural developments since Oslo, it must incorporate the PA's elected Legislative Council and other elected delegates from the diaspora. The various factions, militant parties, unions and civil society organisations should all be brought into the fold.

The first task of the new PNC is to learn the political lessons of the failure of the Oslo Accords. No time need be wasted arguing about terminating previously signed agreements because, for all practical purposes, Israel has already annulled them. Any clear-eyed assessment of the current conditions of the Palestinian people requires internalising the fact that there is no negotiated settlement on the horizon.

The Palestinian national movement ought to recognise the situation for what it is: an unresolved colonial condition that has taken the form of an apartheid regime. Palestine's visceral symbolic value to Arabs and those in the Global South derives from the Israeli regime's militarised settler colonial character. Different Arab people face their own hardships in the form of oppressive regimes and refugee problems, but the Palestinian cause continues to strike a chord with them because it is a colonial issue that impacts the entirety of the Arab region and continues to play a significant role in today's changing

---

after the signing the Oslo Accords). In an extraordinary session, it decided that the "Palestine National Charter is hereby amended by cancelling the articles that are contrary to the letters exchanged between the P.L.O and the Government of Israel on 9–10 September 1993." The new amendments removed all articles that call for armed struggle, deny the legitimacy of Israel and condemn Zionism as a racist, imperialist and colonialist political movement that must be eliminated. See: "Letter from President Yasser Arafat to President Clinton," *Miftah, The Palestinian Initiative for the Promotion of Global Dialogue and Democracy*, 13 January 1998, accessed at: https://bit.ly/3xjJHTu.

geopolitical context, as well as the link between Israel and the authoritarian Arab regimes that rule over them.

Is the Palestinian cause a primary issue for Arabs in the wider region? For Arabs as a whole, certainly, but not necessarily for each and every Arab society. For example, it is not a priority for Syrians involved in their own national struggle against despotism to preserve their country. The same can be said of Iraqis confronting sectarianism, corruption and foreign intervention, Egyptians facing military authoritarianism and poverty, the Sudanese, Libyans, Yemenis—the list goes on. But while Arab peoples face their own national difficulties and have their own priorities, Arabs as a group continue to identify Palestine as a priority, making support for the cause a component of Arab identity.[7]

Israel threatens the sovereignty of each Arab country through regional interventions that fuel domestic conflicts or by interfering with Arab countries' bilateral relations with their neighbours in Africa and Asia. The region is expected to adhere to conditions determined by Israeli foreign policy and security needs, just as it is continually shaped and divided into "extremists" and "moderates" based on Israel's standards.

As has been demonstrated in Egypt, Jordan and South Sudan, normalisation with Israel does not solve domestic economic or social problems, and the same is true for countries being extorted to normalise their ties with Israel, like Sudan and Morocco. On the contrary, normalisation is often the source of social and political crises. Socioeconomic problems are resolved only by democratic processes that not only protect political rights, but also address social justice and human development.

It is only natural for any new Palestinian leadership to mobilise support for the Palestinian cause through diplomatic engagement with as many Arab and non-Arab countries as possible—but it cannot neglect public opinion nor appear uninterested in Arab public concerns. Adopting a democratic discourse in the struggle against the Israeli colonial apartheid regime will enable the liberation struggle to reclaim its global credibility.

---

[7] See the Appendix: "Arab Public Opinion on the Palestinian Issue."

A Democratic Discourse of Justice

Trying to strike a pragmatic pose, Arab regimes normalising their relations with Israel say, as if it were a shocking revelation, that Israel is a fait accompli. Israel has been an established fact for a long time, much like the Palestinian people and the apartheid regime they face. Those, too, are established facts.

One cannot be a true activist for liberation from occupation in the twenty-first century while also dismissing the suffering of Arab peoples under dictatorship, just as one cannot oppose despotism while dismissing the struggle against racism and the occupation of Arab land. Those who choose not to express a clear position against despotism in the Arab world can at least remain silent.

A national liberation movement aligns, at least indirectly through its discourse and goals, with larger public trends demanding democratisation in Arab countries. If the Palestinian struggle focuses on fighting apartheid structures produced by the settler colonial system in Palestine, then its demands are inherently democratic, just as the ANC's struggle against apartheid in South Africa was inherently based on democratic principles.

The PA wants to become a state through negotiations, but without struggling against the Israeli apartheid system on the ground and in regional and international politics. This strategy cannot be a democratic national liberation framework that unites Palestinians. Moreover, although some may disagree, I insist that the Palestinian state that could have hypothetically emerged from the Oslo path is largely what already exists today, with some modifications plus the purely ceremonial state appellation. A relatively just two-state solution cannot be achieved through negotiation in the absence of struggle. But struggle will not necessarily culminate in a state; other forms of justice or outcomes may emerge due to Israeli intransigence, American collusion and irreversible exogenous developments. Those who have fetishized the idea of a state gained through negotiations are unable to perceive this reality.

The Palestinian cause is liberation from occupation, racial discrimination and displacement, as well as liberation from Palestinian fragmentation. Only a discourse of democratic justice can combine them and lead a struggle that could change the conditions of the negotiations.

CONCLUDING REMARKS

Palestine as a demographic and territorial space is subjected to varying degrees of land confiscation, the usurpation of national character, and systems of surveillance and control by a single Israeli authority. Palestinians in the West Bank and Gaza Strip, Israel, and Jerusalem all strain under the same regime. But their respective circumstances are different, as are their forms of resistance. The refugee issue is part and parcel of this same settler colonial apartheid reality. In 1948, the colonial project enforced ethnic separation through expulsion and displacement, to turn a Jewish minority into a majority, establish a Jewish state and "inherit" not only the land, but also the natives' possessions. Today, it takes the form of occupation and ethnic discrimination. It is no longer possible to envision or implement a "solution" to the Palestinian question that includes only one subgroup of the Palestinian people. The abject failure of negotiations aiming for just such a solution has demonstrated the monumental absurdity of this ambition.

This new strategy requires all Palestinians to engage in the struggle against the Israeli apartheid regime. In turn, this requires a high degree of organisation and coordination, without disregarding the specific context and characteristics of each Palestinian subgroup and their forms of resistance. Different Palestinian constituencies do not need to follow the agenda of a single authority, but they do need to struggle under one umbrella organisation. It is important to have local leaders who each independently manage the affairs of their own constituency and citizenry, while simultaneously working towards an inclusive national liberation.

Palestinian young people, often representing the third generation in the diaspora, have proved to be modern, engaged, adept, connected and effective in their host societies. If they were to attempt to establish a political organisation, they would immediately be accused of seeking to supplant the PLO. This same dilemma confronts all the political factions now mired in a political impasse.

Diaspora initiatives are important because they influence public opinion around the world and demonstrate that the Palestinian collective continues to be involved in the struggle despite the crisis of political leadership. These initiatives, however, will not be effective in the long term because they are unconnected to a coordinated movement capable of influencing Palestinian politics. It is critical for these fragmented initiatives to unite under a common framework if they are to gain greater political leverage.

The One-State Solution and Armed Struggle

The alternative to negotiations as an exclusive strategy is not a return to old strategies. The Arab reality that once gave rise to armed organisations along the Arab-Israeli borders has changed radically and irrevocably. Current organised armed resistance in the Gaza Strip and Lebanon has made clear in both word and deed that it is merely an organised form of defence and deterrence. This resistance has assumed an institutional form in the Gaza Strip, but it does not constitute a liberation strategy; rather, it is a strategy to defend Gaza and protect the political achievements of its ruling authority. In May 2021, Hamas tried to extend its deterrence to Jerusalem, mainly to prevent Israel from changing the status of al-Aqsa Mosque and displacing Palestinian residents of Jerusalem to illegally transfer their homes to Jewish settlers. Hamas's capacity to endure Israeli attacks and respond with missiles to Israeli cities boosted its popularity among Palestinians and Arabs and enhanced its regional and international status. Nevertheless, it neither changed the realities in Jerusalem, nor became a liberation strategy. It sent a message that the occupation will not continue with its infringements scot-free.

Slogans and rhetoric aside, neither Hamas nor Hezbollah really believe in their own ability to destroy Israel. Neither started as a national liberation movement and neither developed into one over time. They both began as armed resistance movements against occupation, in Palestine and south Lebanon respectively, before evolving into political powers whose most important feature is their purported ability to defend their respective populations against Israeli aggression. The strategy of Hamas and the Islamic Jihad is that of deterrence. When they declare victory after each war with Israel, they are actually asserting their persistence and better deterrence. After each armed confrontation with Israel, they win popularity among Palestinian and Arab audiences due to public admiration for any force that "finally" forces Israel to pay for its crimes in any way, even if the human costs are higher for the Palestinian or Lebanese side than for Israel.

The organised armed struggle of the Palestinian liberation movement in the 1960s and 1970s, as embodied by the PLO, kept alive the unresolved issue of colonialism, expressed a national presence and popular aspirations, and fostered the emergence of a politically conscious and active youth generation in the refugee camps. However, it did not come anywhere near liberating Palestine, and this must be acknowledged. It forced the question of Palestine onto the agenda but did not receive an answer. In its decadent phase, the armed struggle against Israel was consumed by the deleterious dynamics of armed factional competition and political showmanship.

The new reality must be faced, despite the inevitable nostalgia for the days of armed resistance, which warms the hearts of those veterans that struggled loyally and made personal sacrifices despite their mistakes and illusions. It is over. And it cannot be compared to the individual instances of armed activity in the West Bank that hamper the normalisation of the occupation, nor to the deterrence forces of Hamas and other movements in Gaza. These are new phenomena that have arisen in a very different context. The idea of abandoning the two-state solution for a return to the strategy of liberation through armed resistance is therefore a fantasy. Furthermore, it strips the one-state model of any resonance among Arabs and Jews. A single state for all citizens in historical Palestine is not possible without the support of a majority of its Jewish and Arab citizens—it cannot be coercively imposed. Conditions will need to be created to drive the majority towards support for this outcome. While Israel can be forced to withdraw to the borders of 1967 by a combination of factors, Jews and Arabs cannot be forced to live together as equal citizens in one state. That is a different dynamic.

Given the current situation in the Arab world, dismantling the Israeli apartheid is a long-term process requiring patience, organisation and the democratisation of the discourse. And because the road is so long, it should not simply be a road of sacrifice, but also achievement, marked by the construction of vibrant institutions everywhere Palestinians are found. We are speaking of the life of a people, after all, not the Via Dolorosa.

A unified state would not be a democratic, secular, assimilationist state as some people might want to believe. The Palestinian people is a politicised national collective that has developed political aspirations linked to a distinct identity—combining Arab and Palestinian identity—over more than a century. Palestinians have made costly sacrifices for the sake of a homeland and a sovereign entity, and they will continue to preserve their identity, historical narrative and national symbols. By the same token, the colonial Zionist movement managed to establish state institutions, a national economy and a national language. That is, an Israeli-Jewish religio-ethnic nationality has been established in Palestine with its own Hebrew language and culture. This developed at the expense of the Palestinian people as part of a colonial programme that was initially based on a quasi-state during the British Mandate in Palestine and subsequently state-based after the end of the Mandate. The state aimed to produce a Jewish nation, but it actually shaped and reproduced a Jewish-Israeli nationality that Zionist Israel does not recognise. Israel has a developed economy, a high standard of living and a political system that is indeed democratic for Jews. Of course, the system continues to embody profound contradictions: between the democratic and Jewish character of the state; between a secular lifestyle and religiously defined nationality; between civic participation and colonialism within the same sovereign system; and, most fundamentally, between a privileged occupier and an occupied people without rights.

A just compromise in the future will need to recognise the existence of these two distinct national characters and aspirations. The thrust of the one-state solution is that the two ethnic groups are no longer separable in practice and cannot live in two separate states, so they must find a way to coexist equally in one. Both Palestinians and Jewish Israelis need to be convinced of this, and that requires persistent struggle. Although the primary purpose of the struggle is to achieve justice for the Palestinian people, who have been stripped of their homeland and subjugated to apartheid, it will require a credible approach to democratic liberation to convince both peoples that justice and equality are in their shared interest. Israeli public opinion is unfortunately moving in the opposite direction. Broader segments of the Israeli public must be addressed to identify more Jewish people ready to cooperate in a struggle that anchors coexistence in justice. This is fundamentally different from current "peace dialogues."

Palestinian elites should not become fixated on a single-state utopia, as though that were the only alternative solution, and thereby infer that the challenge is to demonstrate the failure of the two-state solution. Neither argument is true: It is not the only alternative, and the failure of the two-state solution does not make it inevitable. The more pressing task is to devise a framework for struggle against a settler colonial apartheid system. To achieve justice through national action driven by a democratic programme, this framework should be addressed to both Jews and Arabs. While it should be inclusive, it should not whitewash past colonial injustices.

Can a political leadership representing the Palestinian liberation movement, superordinate to the two authorities in the West Bank and Gaza Strip, succeed in uniting the Palestinians around such a framework? In the current circumstances, negotiations cannot bring Hamas and Fatah together because neither will give up its limited authority over people and security forces, or its separate international interests, which dictate either direct or mediated negotiations with Israel. This is the trap of non-sovereign authority: the narrow-minded conflict between parties and factions takes precedence over the wider struggle for sovereignty and self-determination. The only path to unity is to redefine the mission of the Palestinian authorities and turn them into institutions that recognise a common political leadership. As I said earlier, there is no historical necessity here; it is a matter of human choice. But if this does not happen, the status quo may persist despite occasional revolts and cyclical crises, leaving the two authorities more deeply entrenched after each cycle. Then there will be neither a two-state nor one-state solution, but rather one Israeli state and two Palestinian Authorities ruling over an archipelago of Bantustans.

I have spoken at length about weaknesses, but what about strengths? The Palestinian cause's main asset is the Palestinian people's presence on their land, their refusal to surrender to the occupation and Israel's inability to either swallow the Palestinians whole or spit them out entirely. The continued struggle and the ongoing process of institution building in the West Bank and Gaza are two vital paths to (re)organise the Palestinian people and strengthen their resilience. The Arab and international solidarity with Palestine demonstrated during the May 2021 protests is proof that the Palestinian cause remains pivotal and continues to provoke regional anger and protests. Additionally, public opinion in Western countries has shifted significantly in favour of justice in Palestine in recent years. As stated in the introduction, this is in part due to the rise of a new generation that places principled moral values above political ideologies and takes a critical stance on global issues. It is also a response to resurgent far-right populism around the world.

APPENDIX

ARAB PUBLIC OPINION ON THE PALESTINIAN ISSUE

The regional valence of the Palestinian issue has qualitatively shifted in recent years, particularly for Arab regimes, which today either have peace agreements with Israel or are devising ways to normalise bilateral relations with it. Only a few Arab regimes are opposed in principle to normalisation with Israel without a just solution in Palestine. At the same time, Israel has completely failed to make any inroads among Arab peoples; for them, it remains illegitimate and alien. Palestine is still invoked as a political symbol of suffering and open colonial wounds, and an exemplar of Western states' double standards on human rights. It is true that in condemning human rights violations in the occupied territories, dictatorial regimes in the Arab region and third world may be evincing some double standards themselves, but this does not make their recognition of the specifically colonial nature of these abuses any less salient. In any case, when such dictatorships normalise relations with Israel, this censure tends to abate in favour of mutual toleration of each other's human rights abuses.

This is indicative of the widening gap between the position of the peoples of the Arab region and that of their rulers. Even when revolutions and popular uprisings erupted in 2010 and 2011, Arab regimes did not make so much as a rhetorical effort to bridge this gap, as they used to do in the past. According to testimonies I collected during research for my book on the Egyptian revolution, the Mubarak regime's collusion with Israel in its war on Gaza was clearly an important motivation for the activists organising politically against the regime from 2009–11.[1]

The announcement of the Trump-Netanyahu deal, in a ceremony attended by ambassadors from three Arab countries, again made the attitudes of Arab states and peoples towards the Palestinian issue a focus of discussion. This debate tends to heat up whenever Palestine can be used to support the position of one or another bloc of rival Arab states. Arab politicians and media figures aligned with these rival blocs quickly air their disagreements about any new initiative under consideration, giving the impression of a genuine divide in Arab public opinion on the Palestinian issue. The debate itself is often initiated at the behest of political authorities or governments, whereupon the media, politicians, political analysts and intellectuals join in. Though the discussion is confined to a narrow segment of people with their own agendas, it is portrayed as a broad, representative debate. Often sweeping generalisations are heard during these debates: "There has been a radical change in public opinion"; "People in the Arab world are complaining about the burden of the Palestinian issue"; "Citizens of this country have no problem with Israel"; "Citizens of that country want to focus on their own affairs."

Such crude claims cast the Palestinian cause as a matter of personal preference, or seem to suggest that all Arabs dropped everything after 1948 to station themselves along the Israeli border and fight unceasingly until they finally exhausted themselves. In fact, the proponents of these opinions favour normalisation with Israel and are not reflecting Arab public opinion so much as looking for a legitimate justification that could persuade Arab publics. In other words, what appears to be a trend in Arabic public opinion is, in reality, an elite-led attempt *to create such a trend.*

For their part, pro-Israel lobbyists in the US applaud normalisation as confirmation of their thesis that Arab regimes care solely about their own national interests, not about Palestine, with the goal of convincing the American administration that Arab rhetoric on

---

[1] See: Azmi Bishara, *Egypt's Revolution*, vol. 2 (Beirut and Doha: Arab Center for Research and Policy Studies, 2014), pp. 240–8, 276–82.

APPENDIX

Palestine is insincere and so it need not pressure Israel to make concessions. (In fact, Arab regimes do not actually care about Palestine, and those that do are uninterested in pleasing the US.) In 2009, Dennis Ross and David Makovsky co-authored a book titled *Myths, Illusions and Peace*, in which they blamed the US' consistent failure to achieve its strategic goals in the Middle East on its foreign policy approach, which they argued heavily relies on some common misperceptions about the nature and motivations of Middle East countries. The "core mythology"—"mother of all myths"—which the authors sought to debunk is that all Middle Eastern issues are linked to the Israeli-Palestinian conflict. According to Ross and Makovsky, this is a fiction; Arab leaders do not follow this logic in their foreign policy decisions, they say, which are usually based on their own interests, not the Palestinian issue:

> "We show that at historical junctures dating back to the middle of the twentieth century, Arab rhetoric on linkage has not been followed by action. [...] The irony is that Arab regimes—with few notable exceptions—have largely shaped their foreign policy around their own priorities, independent of both US ties to Israel and the Arab-Israeli conflict. [...] With few exceptions, Arab regimes have pursued their national interests instead of developing policy based on the Palestinian conflict. [...] there were times when the United States responded to Arab rhetoric by pushing Israel to make concessions [...] In short, the argument of linkage has profoundly misled US policy makers who embraced its logic and the assumptions that underpinned it."[2]

Commenting on the normalisation of relations between the UAE, Bahrain and Israel without a prior peace agreement between Israel and the Palestinians, and on what these agreements "tell us about how the region is changing," Ross penned an opinion piece in *The Washington Post* restating his argument:

> "The Palestinian issue has become far less of a priority for most Arab states. Their preoccupation is not with the Palestinians but with threats from Iran and the Muslim Brotherhood, and they see Israel as a bulwark against both. They see benefits from cooperation with Israel

[2] David Makovsky & Dennis Ross, *Myths, Illusions, and Peace: Finding a New Direction for America in the Middle East* (New York: Viking, 2009), pp. 14–15.

on security [...] Like the UAE and Bahrain, others in the region are going to be driven by their own national interests. The risk for the Palestinians is that they will be left behind."[3]

There is nothing new about this diagnosis. Indeed, many opposition forces in the Arab world asserted the same thing long before pro-Israel lobbyists, with the essential difference that the former did not believe that the public interest was ever a priority for self-interested Arab regimes obsessed with maintaining their own power. Importantly, however, while Israeli lobbyists praise this purportedly newfound attitude on the part of Arab regimes, Arab publics generally criticise it, seeing no contradiction between the interests of Arab countries and a just solution for Palestine. The lobbyists tend to overlook that Arab peoples, including the Palestinians, reject the superpower's strategic reliance on collusion between Arab authoritarian regimes and Israel, which disregards not only Palestinian rights, but Arab peoples' rights.

In this context, a review of contemporary public opinion polling on this topic can be useful to distinguish citizens' opinions from the claims of some political and media elites. In order to assess trends in public opinion with regard to the Arab-Israeli conflict and the Palestinian cause, we included several questions in the Arab Opinion Index[4] questionnaire to gauge respondents' attitudes towards various aspects of the issue.

---

[3] Dennis Ross, "Opinion: The Middle East is changing. Will Palestinians be left behind?," *The Washington Post*, 14 September 2020, accessed at: https://wapo.st/3u0bo1Q

[4] The Arab Opinion Index is a series of surveys conducted by the Arab Center for Research and Policy Studies since 2011 on a periodic basis to gauge Arab public opinion on a number of political, cultural and social issues relevant to the Arab world. The results are based on the findings of face-to-face interviews, with respondents chosen based on a sampling methodology that uses a randomised, stratified, multi-stage, self-weighted clustered approach, giving an overall margin of error between +/− 2% and 3% for the individual country samples. The overall samples guarantee probability-proportional-to-size (PPS), ensuring fairness in the representation of various population segments. The AOI remains the largest public opinion survey carried out in the Arab world in terms of sample size, number of countries covered, number of variables tested and the volume of data collected. For more information, see: "Arab Opinion Index 2019/2020," *Index*, Arab Center for Research and Policy Studies, accessed at: https://bit.ly/3pylEwL

Arab Opinion Index (AOI) data from 2011 to 2020 indicates that Arab public opinion generally perceives the Palestinian issue as an Arab cause, not just a Palestinian one. This is the opinion of the overwhelming majority of citizens in the societies surveyed by the AOI: more than 75 per cent (and up to 84 per cent) of all respondents indicated that the Palestinian issue is a cause shared by all Arabs, not just Palestinians. Some 8–18 per cent of respondents thought that the issue is solely a Palestinian one and that Palestinians alone need to resolve it (see Figure 10.1). These percentages have remained more or less constant over time, with no significant change in respondents' opinions when asked the same question in repeated polls over the past decade. This data decisively refutes claims made by supporters of normalisation that Arabs have grown weary of Palestine or that public opinion has already shifted. In fact, Arab regimes and pro-Israel supporters are manufacturing public opinion out of thin air.

In every country included in the AOI, public opinion is near unanimous that Palestine is an Arab concern. The highest positive response

Figure 10.1: Is Palestine a Pan-Arab Issue or an Exclusively Palestinian Issue?[5]

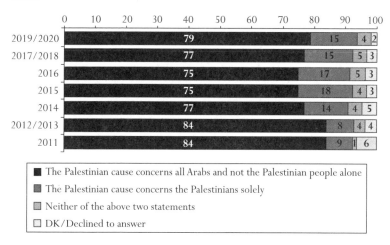

- ■ The Palestinian cause concerns all Arabs and not the Palestinian people alone
- ■ The Palestinian cause concerns the Palestinians solely
- ◧ Neither of the above two statements
- ☐ DK/Declined to answer

[5] The following communities were polled: Algeria, Egypt, Iraq, Jordan, Kuwait, Lebanon, Libya, Mauritania, Morocco, Palestine, Qatar, Saudi Arabia, Sudan, Tunisia, Yemen and Syrian refugees.

rates in the latest round of the AOI (2019/2020) came from Algeria, Jordan, Qatar, Tunisia, Saudi Arabia and Mauritania, where over 80 per cent of respondents agreed that Palestine is a pan-Arab issue. Ironically, the lowest rate (66 per cent) came from Palestine, where more than a quarter (29 per cent) of respondents indicated that the issue only concerns Palestinians. This is attributable to multiple factors, most importantly that one of the foundational goals of the Palestinian national project launched in the mid-1960s was the establishment of a Palestinian entity through legitimate representation and independent decision-making. I believe it also speaks to respondents' frustration with the inability of Arab regimes to confront Israel and their unbridled instrumentalisation of the Palestinian cause, whether in their relations with the US or other international powers, or in intra-Arab conflicts. In other words, the 29 per cent of Palestinians who said that Palestine was their cause alone were not so much reflecting Arab public opinion as expressing their bitter disappointment in Arab regimes.

In order to flesh out public opinion trends on the Palestinian issue and the Arab-Israeli conflict, a question was included about the recognition of Israel. Given the near unanimous opinion that the Palestinian cause is a shared pan-Arab issue, the question was designed as a practical way to test the limits of this unanimity and the Arab popular consensus on the non-recognition of Israel. It is also an indicator of the degree to which Arab citizens would support their governments if they decided to recognise Israel and normalise bilateral relations (including in the countries whose regimes have already normalised relations and signed agreements with Israel). Results indicated that respondents overwhelmingly opposed recognition of Israel, at rates that have remained nearly constant from the first AOI poll in 2011 to 2020. The highest rate was around 88 per cent opposed, compared to only 9 per cent in favour of their countries recognising Israel. This correlated with a rejection of the separate peace treaties between Israel and Arab regimes, and the perception that Israel is the country posing the largest threat to the security of the Arab world. This correlation was found in every one of the surveyed countries. Significantly, when asked about a specific Israeli threat to their own countries, respondents gave different answers, indicating that Israel is perceived first and foremost as a threat to Arabs collectively. In addition, a majority of respondents from countries whose governments have signed peace treaties or normalisation agreements with Israel—Egypt, Palestine, Jordan and recently Sudan and Morocco[6]—rejected their countries' recognition of Israel at rates close to the general average and as high as 93 per cent (Jordan).

In other words, even among those who see the Palestine issue as a problem solely for the Palestinians, there is a significant percentage opposed to the recognition of Israel, let alone normalisation with it.

This question taps into a very deep aspect of the Arab consciousness: the legitimacy of Israel's presence in the region. Yet, we should not draw too many conclusions from it about Arabs' readiness to act against the recognition of Israel or the normalisation of ties, or the persistence of these attitudes in the future. The reader should also be reminded that what this poll captures is not the same as public opinion in democracies, which can safely express itself through elections, lobbies or other channels to influence the decision-making process. Public opinion under authoritarian regimes expresses itself through different channels; it can also be suppressed and manipulated by the rulers and is shaped by the survival strategies of the ruled. All we can infer from the data is that Arab public opinion opposes the idea of Arabs granting legitimacy to Israel and rejects normalisation of relations under prevailing conditions and in the absence of a just solution for Palestine, though this may be the opinion of the silent majority in some countries.

Since 2014, the AOI has sought to identify respondents' reasons for their position on the recognition of Israel. An open-ended question was included to allow respondents to express their reasons in their own words and to avoid the potential drawbacks of multiple-choice questions, whose predetermined responses might be misleading.

Respondents to the open-ended question gave a variety of reasons for opposition to normalisation with Israel. Around one-third of respondents cited the fact that "it is a settler colonialist state and occupies Palestine." The second most common reason (9 per cent) was "because it is an expansionist state that wants to dominate or occupy

---

[6] The AOI surveys were not conducted in Bahrain or the UAE.

Figure 10.2: Do You Support Your Country Recognising Israel?

Year	Support	Oppose	DK/Declined
2019/2020	6	88	6
2017/2018	8	87	5
2016	9	86	5
2015	9	85	6
2014	6	87	7
2012/2013	6	87	6
2011	9	84	7

■ Support ■ Oppose ☐ DK/Declined to answer

other Arab countries and take possession of their resources," followed by "it is a terrorist country that supports terrorism" (8 per cent). The fourth most common reason (7 per cent) was that Israel had displaced the Palestinians and continued to persecute them. Religious reasons came in fifth (7 per cent), while the sixth most common reason (6 percent) was that "it is an entity that deals with Arabs in a hateful and racist way." The seventh most common response (5 per cent) was that recognition of Israel would mean invalidating Palestinians and their rights, and legitimising Israel's actions against the Palestinian people. The latter reason focused on historical dimensions; for these respondents, Israel is not legitimate because it robbed the Palestinians of their homeland and displaced them.

Other reasons named by respondents include that Israel is hostile towards "our country in particular and Arabs in general" (4 per cent), that it posed a threat to the security and stability of the region in general (4 per cent) and that it did not honour agreements and treaties (2 per cent).

Overall, the responses reveal that Arab citizens share a common perception of Israel's policy, its role in the region, its history, what it represents, and whether it poses a threat. Part of the consensus also stems from Israel's historic and current actions against Palestinians. Opposition to the recognition of Israel does not arise, then, from hostility towards Jews qua Jews, or from a cultural clash or a religious conflict between Muslims and Jews or Islam and Judaism. The percentage of respondents opposed to recognition of Israel for religious reasons has remained stable over the years, within a range of 3–7 per cent.

A large percentage of respondents used the terms *colonialism* and *occupation*, described Israel as having a racist character and cast the Palestinian cause as one of national liberation and justice. Any PR campaigns designed to shift Arab public opinion on Israel using religiously inflected cultural, media or educational programmes are thus based on a misapprehension of the situation and doomed to fail. If governments deploy religious figures and preachers to justify normalising relations with Israel, they will be addressing only a small segment of Arab societies. The data suggests that Arab public opinion is not likely to change before the reality on the ground does.

Table 10.1: Reasons for Opposing Recognition of Israel (in % of Total Respondents)

Reasons Given by Respondents Opposed to the Recognition of Israel	2019/ 2020	2017/ 2018	2016	2015	2014
Because it is a settler colonialist state and occupies Palestine	33.7	31.7	27.0	24.5	23.4
Because it is an expansionist state that wants to dominate or occupy other Arab countries	9.4	10.1	13.0	13.0	2.4
Because it is a terrorist country that supports terrorism	7.6	7.4	7.6	10.4	1.2
Because the state arose by ethnically cleansing Palestinians and continues to persecute them	6.8	8.3	8.1	6.9	5.5
Oppose for religious reasons	6.7	6.6	5.2	3.3	4.9
Because it is an entity that deals with Arabs in a hateful and racist way	5.9	6.3	8.2	10.3	12.2
Because it opposes Palestinian rights and continues to legitimise what it did to the Palestinian people	4.8	5.3	5.8	5.6	7.5
Because it is an enemy to our country in particular and to the Arabs more generally	4.1	3.4	3.3	4.7	11.5

Because it threatens the stability and security of the region	3.6	3.4	3.2	3.4	2.5
It does not respect peace agreements	1.6	1.6	2.1	2.4	2.3
I do not agree with the existence of the state of Israel	2.0	1.1	0.6	0.3	3.4
No reasons were given for opposing the recognition of Israel	1.8	1.6	1.8	0.6	10.2
Total respondents opposed to recognition of Israel	**88.4**	**86.8**	**85.9**	**85.4**	**87.0**
Total respondents in favour of recognition of Israel	**6.2**	**7.9**	**9.5**	**8.9**	**6.0**
I do not know/Declined to answer (% of the total respondents)	**5.6**	**5.3**	**4.6**	**5.7**	**7.0**
Total	**100.0**	**100.0**	**100.0**	**100.0**	**100.0**

Respondents favouring recognition of Israel by their countries (6.2 per cent of total respondents) gave many different reasons, the most common of which were that Israel is an established political reality (1.2 per cent) and that Israel is a recognised country with peace treaties with some Arab countries (1.1 per cent). Some respondents (1.0 per cent) indicated that they were motivated by a desire for peace and stability in the region, while 0.5 per cent said that Israel was a country like any other and that Israelis should have a country of their own. Some 0.5 per cent of respondents would only support recognition of Israel if it recognised a fully sovereign state of Palestine, while another 0.5 per cent supported recognition of Israel on the grounds that it would make the establishment of a Palestinian state more likely. Another 0.4 per cent said that Israel is a powerful country that Arabs could not contend with, while 0.4 per cent cited common interests and a desire to strengthen their relationships and 0.2 per cent stated admiration of Israel's level of advancement and development as their reason. Finally, just 0.1 per cent cited religious reasons for supporting recognition of Israel.

APPENDIX

All in all, supporters of recognising Israel constitute a small percentage of Arab public opinion. They can be divided into three main groups: those motivated by their support for Palestinian rights; those critical of the question itself (about 1.2 per cent of the total) who argued that recognition is the de facto state of affairs since Israel exists and peace treaties have been signed with it; and those who support recognition of Israel based on principle and conviction (representing just 1 per cent of the total).

A comparison of the 2019/2020 responses with those of previous years shows no significant changes over time, and support for recognition of Israel remains the position of a narrow minority.

Table 10.2: Reasons for Supporting Recognition of Israel (% of Total Respondents)

Reasons Given by Respondents Supporting the Recognition of Israel	2019/ 2020	2017/ 2018	2016	2015	2014
It exists inevitably	1.2	1.8	2.5	2.0	1.6
Recognition has already happened and peace agreements have been signed	1.1	1.7	2.6	2.2	0.5
In order to achieve peace and stability in the region	1.0	0.8	0.9	1.5	1.4
Because it is a state like any other with the right to be a state	0.5	0.4	0.5	0.3	0.4
Provided it recognises a fully sovereign Palestinian state	0.5	1.0	0.7	0.9	0.4
It could lead to a Palestinian state	0.5	0.9	1.0	0.9	0.1
Because it is a strong state that we are unable to combat	0.4	0.4	0.5	0.5	0.5

Because of common interests and to strengthen relationships	0.4	0.4	0.3	0.4	0.6
Because of its progress and development	0.2	0.1	0.2	0.1	0.1
Religious reasons	0.1	0.0	0.1	0.1	0.1
Other reasons	0.1	0.0	–	0.0	0.2
No reasons were given for favouring the recognition of Israel	0.2	0.4	0.2	0.0	0.1
Total respondents in favour of recognition of Israel	**6.2**	**7.9**	**9.5**	**8.9**	**6.0**
Total respondents opposed to recognition of Israel	**88.4**	**86.8**	**85.9**	**85.4**	**87.0**
I do not know/ Declined to answer (% of the total respondents)	**5.6**	**5.3**	**4.6**	**5.7**	**7.0**
Total	**100.0**	**100.0**	**100.0**	**100.0**	**100.0**

I said earlier that the citizens of every Arab country are concerned with the issues specific to their country and everyday life there. These concerns have intensified with ongoing struggles for democracy, and it is only natural for this struggle to heighten public interest in domestic affairs and underscore the population's common interests as citizens of a particular state. I have no doubt that the emergence of Arab democracies will strengthen political pluralism on the national level, and this may come partially at the expense of Arab ethnic identity. On the other hand, democracy will allow public opinion to be expressed more honestly, which is in the interest of the Palestinian cause and, in the long run, the interest of the unity of democratic

Arab countries. Arab citizens should not be restricted to the false choice of supporting the Palestinian issue as a just cause or struggling to improve socioeconomic conditions and achieve political and civil rights in their own countries. The two are not mutually exclusive. Forcing such a choice, in addition to being fundamentally immoral, reflects a shallow dismissal of the complexity of human beings and their choices.

AOI polls from 2011 to 2020 have indicated that Arab publics prefer democratic governance to other political systems and that the most significant challenges facing Arab countries today are economic (unemployment, poverty and a declining standard of living) or the lack of political stability or security. That same Arab public continues to support Palestinians, embrace the Palestinian issue as its own and oppose recognition of Israel as an occupying state.

An analysis based on a cross-tabulation of the data on respondents' positions on recognition of Israel and their positions on areas that they considered priority concerns sheds more light on these overlapping sympathies.

When we cross-tabulated respondent positions on recognition of Israel with household income, we observed that lower household incomes correlated with higher rates of opposing recognition of Israel. This clearly demonstrates falseness of the claim that Arabs have wearied of the Palestinian issue and are willing to abandon it to attend to their own immediate economic conditions. In any case, the association between economic conditions in Arab countries and the conflict with Israel is itself questionable; otherwise, how is it that Israel continues to develop economically amidst chronic conflicts with Arab countries? But even assuming such an association for the sake of argument demonstrates that the claim does not hold water.

If the claim had any merit, the data should show an increasing trend favouring recognition of Israel. Instead, when we cross-tabulated respondents' priorities with their positions on recognition of Israel, we found that an emphasis on domestic economic problems and everyday life in their own countries correlated with opposition to recognition of Israel.

Table 10.3: Position on Recognition of Israel Cross-Tabulated with Household Income (in %)

Would you agree with your home country recognising the state of Israel?	Please indicate which of the following expressions most accurately describes your household income		
	Our household income meets our basic requirements and we are able to save	Our household income meets our basic requirements but we are unable to save	Our household income does not cover our basic requirements and we have difficulty meeting our needs
Support	9	8	7
Oppose	91	92	93
Total	100	100	100

What is striking—but to me not surprising—is that Arab citizens who named their top priorities in their countries to be government policy, external threats, social problems, political unrest and the threat of terrorism or provincial and sectarian divisions also remained strongly opposed to recognition. Indeed, the respondents most interested in democratisation and who cited faltering economies, lack of security and political instability as priority domestic concerns, were more opposed to recognition of Israel. In addition, a correlation was found between opposition to recognition of Israel and support for democratic governance.

Table 10.4: Position on Recognition of Israel Cross-Tabulated with Stated National Priorities (in %)

In your opinion, what is the most important challenge facing your home country today?	Would you agree with your home country recognising the state of Israel?		
	Support	Oppose	Total
Transition to democracy	5	95	100
Weak social services	6	94	100

Lack of security and safety	8	92	100
Economic problems (unemployment, poverty)	8	92	100
Lack of political stability	8	92	100
Refugees	9	91	100
Administrative and fiscal corruption	10	90	100
Regional/sectarian/ethnic/tribal divisions	11	89	100
Governmental policy	13	87	100
Social Issues	15	85	100
External intervention	18	82	100

Table 10.5: Position on Recognition of Israel Cross-Tabulated with Position on Democratic Governance (in %)

Would you agree with your home country recognising the state of Israel?	Democracy has its own problems but remains better than other systems	
	Agree	Disagree
Support	8	9
Oppose	92	91
Total	**100**	**100**

BIBLIOGRAPHY

Books

Abbasi, Mustafa. *Safad During the British Mandate Period, 1917–1948: A Social and Political Study* [Arabic]. Beirut and Ramallah: The Institute for Palestine Studies, 2019.

Abdul-Hamid, Issa. *Six Years of the Open Bridges Policy* [Arabic]. Beirut: PLO Research Centre, 1973.

Abu ʿAmr, Ziad. *The Islamic Movement in the West Bank and Gaza Strip* [Arabic]. Acre: Dār al-Aswār, 1989.

Abu Hussein, Hussein & Fiona McKay. *Access Denied: Palestinian Land Rights in Israel*. London and New York: Zed Books, 2003.

Abu-Lughod, Ibrahim & Baha Abu-Laban (eds.). *Settler Regimes in Africa and the Arab World: The Illusion of Endurance*. Wilmette, IL: Medina University Press International, 1974.

Adams, James. *The Unnatural Alliance*. London: Quartet Books, 1984.

Ajami, Fouad. *The Arab Predicament*. Cambridge: Cambridge University Press, 1981.

Al Hout, Bayan Nuwayhid. *The Political Leadership and Institutions in Palestine, (1917–1948)* [Arabic]. Beirut: Institute of Palestine Studies, 1986.

Albanese, Francesca P. & Lex Takkenberg. *Palestinian Refugees in International Law*. Oxford: Oxford University Press, 2020.

al-Ghazali, Mohammad. *Jihad call home between internal deficit and external conspiracy* [Arabic]. Cairo, Dar al-Sahwa, 1998.

al-Hashemi, Taha. *Diaries of Taha al-Hashemi 1942–1955: Iraq-Syria-the Palestinian Cause* [Arabic]. Khaldun Satiʿ al-Husri (ed. and intro.). vol. 2. Beirut: Dar aṭ-Ṭaliʿa lil-Ṭibāʿa wal-Nashr, 1978.

Aljubouri, Saleh Saeb. *The Plight of Palestine and its Political and Military Secrets* [Arabic]. Beirut: Arab Center for Research and Policy Studies, 2014.

al-Kayal, Nizar. *A Study in the Contemporary Political History of Syria 1920–1950* [Arabic]. Damascus: Dar Tlass, 1997.

al-Kayyali, Abd al-Wahhab. *Documents on the Palestinian Arab Resistance to the British Mandate and Zionism (1918–1939)* [Arabic]. 2nd ed. Beirut: The Institute for Palestine Studies, 1988.

305

BIBLIOGRAPHY

al-Mu'allim, Walid. *Syria 1916–1946: The Way to Freedom* [Arabic]. Damascus: Dar Tlass, 1988.

al-Qaradawi, Yusuf. *Lesson on the Second Nakba, Why We Were Defeated and How We Can Win* [Arabic]. [n.p], 1968.

Alroey, Gur. *An Unpromising Land: Jewish Migration to Palestine in the Early Twentieth Century*. Stanford, CA: Stanford University Press, 2014.

Amnesty International. *Uncovering the Iceberg: The Digital Surveillance Crisis Wrought by States and the Private Sector*. London: Amnesty International Ltd, 2021.

Aronson, Shlomo. *Sadat's Initiative and Israel's Response: The Strategy of Peace and the Strategy of Strategy*. n. 14. Los Angeles, CA: Center for Arms Control and International Security, UCLA, 1978.

Arslan, Adil. *Prince Adil Arslan: The Recanted Diaries 1948* [Arabic]. Youssef Abish (ed.). al-Mukhtara [Lebanon]: ad-Dar at-Taqadumiyya, 2009.

Azoulay, Ariella & Adi Ophir. *The One-State Condition: Occupation and Democracy in Israel/ Palestine*. Stanford: Stanford University Press, 2012.

Baconi, Tareq. *Hamas Contained: The Rise and Pacification of Palestinian Resistance*. Stanford: Stanford University Press, 2018.

Barghouti, Iyad. *Islamization and Politics in the Palestinian Occupied Territories* [Arabic]. Jerusalem: Al-Zahra' Center for Studies and Research, 1990.

Barr, James. *A Line in the Sand: The Anglo-French Struggle for the Middle East, 1914–1948*. London and New York: Simon & Schuster, 2012.

Batatu, Hanna. *The Old Social Classes and the Revolutionary Movements of Iraq: A Study of Iraq's Old Landed and Commercial Classes and of its Communists, Ba'thists, and Free Officers*. Princeton: Princeton University Press, 1978.

Ben-Guryon, Dayid. *The War of Independence: Ben-Gurion's Diary 1948–1949* [Hebrew]. Gershon Rivlin & Elḥanan Oren (eds.). vol. 1. [Tel Aviv]: ha-Ḥevrah le-hafatsat mishnato shel Dayid Ben-Guryon; Miśrad ha-biṭaḥon, 1984.

Benite, Zvi Ben-Dor et al. (ed.). *The Scaffolding of Sovereignty: Global and Aesthetic Perspectives on the History of a Concept*. New York: Columbia University Press, 2017.

Benvenisti, Eyal. *The International Law of Occupation*. Princeton, NJ: Princeton University Press, 2004.

Biale, David. *Power & Powerlessness in Jewish History*. New York: Schocken, 1986.

―――. "Palestinian Minority in Israel: a proposed new vision." [Arabic] *Journal of Palestine studies*. vol. 3. no. 11 (Summer 1992).

―――. "The Vortex of Religion and State in Israel." *Majallat al-Dirasat al-Filastiniyya*. no. 3 (Summer 1990).

in "Journals" section (p. 301).

―――. "'The Israel Arab': A Reading in a Ruptured Political Discourse." [Arabic] *Majallat al-Dirasat al-Filastiniyya*. vol. 6. no. 4 (Autumn 1995).

Bishara, Azmi. *Civil Society: A Critical Study* [Arabic]. Beirut: Center of Arab Unity Studies, 1996.

―――. *Egypt's Revolution*. vol. 2. Beirut and Doha: Arab Center for Research and Policy Studies, 2014.

BIBLIOGRAPHY

————. *From the Jewishness of the State to Sharon*. [Arabic] Cairo: Dar al-Shourouk, 2005.

————. *On the Arab Question: An Introduction to an Arab Democratic Manifesto* [Arabic]. Beirut: Center for Arab Unity Studies, 2007.

————. *The Ruptured Political Discourse and Other Studies*. [Arabic] 2nd ed. Ramallah: Muwatin-The Palestinian Institute for the Study of Democracy, 2002.

Bou Nassif, Hicham. *Endgames: Military Response to Protest in Arab Autocracies*. Cambridge: Cambridge University Press, 2021.

Bradshaw, Samuel Alexander. *Tract for the Times, Being a Plea for the Jews*. London: Edwards and Hughes/Ave Maria Lane, 1844.

Brecher, Michael. *The Foreign Policy System of Israel*. New Haven: Yale University Press, 1974.

Bunton, Martin. *Colonial Land Policies in Palestine 1917–1936*. Oxford: Oxford University Press, 2007.

Burrell, Robert Michael & Abbas Kelidar. *Egypt: The Dilemmas of a Nation*. Beverly Hills, CA: Sage Publications, 1977.

Butenschon, Nils A., Uri Davis & Manuel Hassassian (eds.). *Citizenship and the State in the Middle East: Approaches and Applications*. Syracuse: Syracuse University Press, 2000.

Carter, Jimmy. *Palestine: Peace Not Apartheid*. New York: Simon and Shuster, 2006.

Chomsky, Noam. *Fateful Triangle: The United States, Israel, and the Palestinians*. Edward W. Said (Foreword). 3rd ed. Cambridge, MA: South End Press, 1999.

Cohen, Hillel. *The Present Absentees: The Palestinian Refugees in Israel since 1948* [Arabic]. Beirut: Institute for Palestine studies, 2003.

Dayan, Moshe. *Moshe Dayan: Story of My Life*. Jerusalem: Steimatzky's, 1976.

Doumani, Beshara. *Rediscovering Palestine: Merchants and Peasants in Jabal Nablus, 1700–1900*. Berkeley: University of California Press, 1995.

Dugdale, Blanche E. C. *Arthur James Balfour: First Earl of Balfour, K.G., O.M., F.R.S., Etc.* vol. 1. London: Hutchinson & Co., [1936].

El Kurd, Dana. *Polarized and Demobilized: Legacies of Authoritarianism in Palestine*. New York: Oxford University Press, 2020.

Findley, Pual. *They Dare to Speak Out: People and Institutions Confront Israel's Lobby*. New York: Lawrence Hill Books, 1989.

Flapan, Simha. *The Birth of Israel: Myths and Realities*. New York: Pantheon Books, 1987.

Friedrich, Roland & Arnold Luethold (eds.). *Entry-Points to Palestinian Security Sector Reform*. Geneva: Geneva Centre for the Democratic Control of Armed Forces (DCAF), 2007.

Gazit, Shlomo. *At Key Points of Time* [Hebrew]. [Tel Aviv]: Miskal-Yedioth Ahronoth Books/Chemed Books, 2016.

Geldenhuys, Deon. *Some Foreign Policy Implications of South Africa's Total National Strategy*. Braamfontein: South African Institute of International Affairs, 1979.

Gitelman, Zvi (ed.). *The New Jewish Diaspora: Russian-Speaking Immigrants in the United States, Israel, and Germany*. New Brunswick, New Jersey, and London: Rutgers University Press, 2016.

Greenstein, Ran. *Zionism and Its Discontents: A Century of Radical Dissent in Israel/Palestine*. London: Pluto Press, 2014.

BIBLIOGRAPHY

Guinness, Henry Grattan. *Light for the Last Days: A Study Historic and Prophetic.* 2nd ed. London: Hodder and Stoughton, [1888].

Halper, Jeff & Nadia Naser-Najjab. *Decolonizing Israel, Liberating Palestine: Zionism, Settler Colonialism, and the Case for One Democratic State.* London: Pluto Press, 2021.

Heikal, Mohamed Hassanein. *Thrones and Armies: The Crisis of Thrones, the Shock of Armies* [Arabic]. Cairo: Dar ash-Shurūq lil-Nashr wal-Tawzīʿ, 2009.

Herzl, Theodor. *A Jewish State: An Attempt at a Modern Solution of the Jewish Question.* Sylvie D'Avigdor (trans.). Jacob de Haas (ed.). 3rd ed. New York: Federation of American Zionists, 1917 [1896].

Hourani, Faisal. *Palestinian Political Thought (1964–1976): A Study of P.L.O Basic Documents* [Arabic]. Beirut: PLO's Research Center, 1980.

Hroub, Khaled. *Hamas: Political Thought and Practice.* Washington, D.C: Institute for Palestine Studies, 2000.

Huneidi, Sahar. *A broken Trust: Herbert Samuel, Zionism and the Palestinians, 1920–1925.* New York: I.B. Tauris, 2001.

———. *The Hidden History of the Balfour Declaration.* New York: OR Books, 2019.

Hussein, Ahmed (ed.). *The June 1967 War: Paths and Implications.* Doha and Beirut: The Arab Center for Research and Policy Studies, 2020.

Huweidi, Amin. *Lost Chances* [Arabic]. Beirut: Sharikat al-Matbuʿat, 1992.

'Iyad, Khalid Hammad. *The United States and the Peace Process in the Middle East (1973–2013).* Amman: Alaan Publishers & Distributors, 2017.

Jabbour, George. *Settler Colonialism in Southern Africa and the Middle East.* Beirut: Palestine Liberation Organization Research Center, 1970.

Jansen, Michael. *The United States and the Palestinian People.* Beirut: The Institute of Palestine Studies, 1970.

Jawhariyah, Wasif, Salim Tamari & Issam Nassar (eds.). *The Storyteller of Jerusalem: The Life and Times of Wasif Jawhariyyeh, 1904–1948.* Northampton and Massachusetts: Olive Branch Press, 2014.

Joseph, Benjamin M. *Besieged Bedfellows: Israel and the Land of Apartheid.* New York: Greenwood Press, 1988.

Judis, John B. *Genesis: Truman, American Jews and the Origins of the Arab/Israeli Conflict.* New York: Farrar, Straus and Giroux, 2014.

Kadish, Alon (ed.). *Independence War 1948–1949, Renewed Discussion*, part 1 [Hebrew]. [Tel-Aviv]: Ministry of Defence, 2004.

Kadish, Alone & Benjamin Z. Kedar (eds.). *The Few Against the Many, Studies on the Balance of Forces in the Battles of Judas Maccabaeus and Israel's War of Independence* [Hebrew], Jerusalem: The Hebrew University Magnes Press, 2005.

Kamrava, Mehran. *The Impossibility of Palestine: History, Geography and the Road Ahead.* New Haven and London: Yale University Press, 2016.

Kedourie, Elie & Sylvia G. Haim (eds.). *Zionism and Arabism in Palestine and Israel.* London: Frank Cass, 1982.

Khalaf, Salah & Eric Rouleau. *My Home, My Land: A Narrative of the Palestinian Struggle.* Linda Butler Koseoglu (trans.). New York: Times Books, 1981.

BIBLIOGRAPHY

Khalidi, Rashid. *The Hundred Years' War on Palestine: A History of Settler Colonial Conquest and Resistance, 1917–2017*. New York: Metropolitan Books, 2020.

———. *The Iron Cage: The Story of the Palestinian Struggle for Statehood*. Boston: Beacon Press, 2006.

Khalidi, Rashid. *Palestinian Identity: The Construction of Modern National Consciousness*. New York: Columbia University Press, 2010.

Khalidi, Walid. *All That Remains: The Palestinian Villages Occupied and Depopulated by Israel in 1948*. Beirut: Institute for Palestine Studies, 1992.

———. *Fifty Years since the Partition of Palestine (1947–1997)* [Arabic]. Beirut: Dar al-Nahar, 2002.

———. *Fifty Years since the War of 1948 and the Zionist Arab Wars* [Arabic]. Beirut: Dar al-Nahar, 1998.

Khoury, Yousef (ed.). *The Arab Unity Projects 1913–1989*. 2nd ed. Beirut: Center for Arab Unity Studies, 1990.

Kimmerling, Baruch & Joel S. Migdal. *The Palestinian People: A History*. Cambridge, A: Harvard University Press, 2003.

Kobler, Franz. *The Vision Was There: A History of the British Movement for the Restoration of the Jews to Palestine. The World Jewish Congress, British Section*. London: Lincolns-Praeger, 1956.

Laron, Guy. *The Six-Day War: the Breaking of the Middle East*. New Haven and London: Yale University Press, 2017.

Le More, Anne. *International Assistance to the Palestinians After Oslo: Political Guilt, Wasted Money*. London and New York: Routledge, 2008.

Levenberg, Haim. *The Military Preparations of the Arab Community in Palestine, 1945–1948*. London: Frank Cass, 1993.

Levy, Daniel & Yfaat Weiss (eds.). *Challenging Ethnic Citizenship: German and Israeli Perspectives on Immigration*. New York: Berghagen Books, 2002.

Litvak, Meir (ed.). *Palestinian Collective Memory and National Identity*. New York: Palgrave Macmillan, 2009.

Makovsky, Ross & David Makovsky. *Myths, Illusions, and Peace: Finding a New Direction for America in the Middle East*. New York: Viking, 2009.

Mamdani, Mahmood. *Neither Settler nor Native: the Making and Unmaking of Permanent Minorities*. Cambridge, MA and London: Belknap Press of Harvard University Press, 2020.

Manna', Adel. *Nakba and Survival: The Story of the Palestinians who Remained in Haifa and the Galilee (1948–1956)*. Beirut: Institute for Palestine studies, 2016.

Markovitzky, Yacov. *The Fighting Cinder: Recruitment Abroad during the War of Indepedence* [Hebrew]. [Tel Aviv]: Ministry of Defence, 1995.

Masalha, Nur (ed.). *Catastrophe Remembered: Palestine, Israel and the Internal Refugees*. London: Zed Books, 2005.

———. *Expulsion of the Palestinians: The Concept of "Transfer" in Zionist Political Thought 1882–1948*. Washington, D.C.: Institute of Palestinian Studies, 1992.

———. *The Politics of Denial: Israel and the Palestinian Refugee Problem*. London: Pluto Press, 2003.

BIBLIOGRAPHY

Massad, Joseph A. *Colonial Effects: The Making of National Identity in Jordan*. New York: Columbia University Press, 2001.

Mearsheimer, John & Stephen Walt. *The Israel Lobby and U.S. Foreign Policy*. New York: Farrar, Straus and Giroux, 2007.

Melamn, Yossi & Daniel Raviv. *Hostile Partnership: The Secret Contacts between Jordan and Israel* [Hebrew]. [Tel Aviv]: Mitam, 1987.

Merkley, Paul Charles. *The Politics of Christian Zionism 1891–1948*. London and New York: Routledge, 1998.

Migdal, Joel S. (ed.). *Palestinian Society and Politics*. Princeton University Press, 2014.

Miron, Guy. *The Waning of Emancipation: Jewish History, Memory, and the Rise of Fascism in Germany, France, and Hungary*. Detroit: Wayne State University Press, 2011.

Morris, Benny. *1948: A History of the First Arab-Israeli War*. London: Yale University Press, 2008.

————. *Israel's Border Wars, 1949–1956: Arab Infiltration, Israeli Retaliation, and the Countdown to the Suez War*. Oxford: Clarendon Press, 1993.

————. *One State, Two States: Resolving the Israel/Palestine Conflict*. New Haven and London: Yale University Press, 2009.

————. *Righteous Victims: A History of the Zionist-Arab Conflict, 1881–2001*. New York: Vintage Books, 2001.

————. *The Birth of the Palestinian Refugee Problem Revisited*. Cambridge: Cambridge University Press, 2004.

Moughrabi, Fouad & Munirakash (eds.). *The Open Veins of Jerusalem*. Maryland: Jusoor Books, 1997/1998.

Muasher, Marwan. *A Decade of Struggling Reform Efforts in Jordan: The Resilience of the Rentier System*. Washington, D.C: Carnegie Endowment for International Peace, 2011.

————. *The Arab Center: The Promise of Moderation*. New Haven: Yale University Press, 2008.

Muhammad, Naktal 'Abd al-Hadi 'Abd al-Karim. *The Positions of the United States towards the Palestinian Issue* [Arabic]. Amman: Dar al-Mu'taz, 2016.

Muslih, Muhammad Y. *The Origins of Palestinian Nationalism*. New York: Columbia University Press, 1988.

Myers, David N. & David B. Ruderman (eds.). *The Jewish Past Revisited: Reflections on Modern Jewish Historians*. New Haven and London: Yale University Press, 1998.

Naor, Moshe. *Social Mobilization in the Arab–Israeli War of 1948 on the Israeli Home Front*. Shaul Vardi (trans.). New York: Routledge, 2013.

Obama, Barack. *A Promised Land*. New York: Viking/Penguin Books, 2020.

Oroub, El-Abed. *Unprotected: Palestinians in Egypt since 1948*. Washington, D.C: Institute for Palestine Studies/International Development Research Centre, 2009.

Pappé, Ilan & Noam Chomsky. *On Palestine*. UK: Penguin, 2015.

Pappé, Ilan (ed.). *The Israel/Palestine Question: Rewriting Histories*. London: Routledge, 1999.

Pappé, Ilan. *The Ethnic Cleansing of Palestine*. Oxford: Oneworld Publications, 2006.

————. *The Rise and Fall of a Palestinian Dynasty: The Husaynis, 1700–1948*. Berkeley, C A: University of California Press, 2010.

BIBLIOGRAPHY

Peres, Shimon. *No Room for Small Dreams* [Hebrew]. Rishon LeZion: Yediot Ahronot & Hemed, 2018.

Piterberg, Gabriel. *The Returns of Zionism: Myths, Politics and Scholarship in Israel*. London: Verso, 2008.

Pollack, Kenneth M. *Armies of Sand: The Past, Present and Future of Arab Military Effectiveness*. New York: Oxford University Press, 2019.

Porath, Yehoshua. *The Emergence of the Palestinian-Arab National Movement, 1918–1929*. London: Frank Cass, 1974.

Rabin, Yitzhak. *The Rabin Memoirs*. Berkeley and Los Angeles: University of California Press, 1979.

Ranta, Ronald. *Political Decision Making and Non-Decisions: The Case of Israel and the Occupied Territories*. New York: Springer, 2015.

Raz, Adam. *Kafr Qasim Massacre: A Political Biography* [Hebrew]. Jerusalem: Carmel Publication, 2018.

Renton, James. *The Zionist Masquerade: The Birth of the Anglo-Zionist Alliance, 1914–1918*. New York: Palgrave Macmillan, 2007.

Rigby, Andrew. *The Palestinian Intifada Revisited*. Sparsnäs, Sweden: Irene Publishing, 2015.

Robinson, Shira. *Citizen Strangers: Palestinians and the Birth of Israeli Liberal Settler State*. Stanford: Stanford University Press, 2013.

Rodinson, Maxime. *Israel: A Colonial Settler-State?*. New York: Monad Press, 1973.

Rouhana, Nadim N. (ed.). *Israel and Its Palestinian Citizens: Ethnic Privileges in the Jewish State*. Cambridge: Cambridge University Press, 2017.

Rouhana, Nadim N. & Nadera Shalhoub-Kevorkian (eds.). *When Politics Are Sacralized: Comparative Perspectives on Religious Claims and Nationalism*. Cambridge: Cambridge University Press, 2021.

Sayegh, Fayez. *Zionist Colonialism in Palestine* [Arabic]. Beirut: Research Center, Palestine Liberation Organization, 1965.

Sayigh, Yezid. *Armed Struggle and the Search for State: The Palestinian National Movement, 1949–1993*. New York: Oxford University Press, 1997.

Segev, Tom. *A State at all Costs: The Life of David Ben Gurion* [Hebrew]. Ben Shemen: Keter Sfarim, 2005.

———. *One Palestine, Complete: Jews and Arabs under the British Mandate*. Haim Watzman (trans.). New York: Metropolitan Books, 2000.

———. *The Seventh Million: The Israelis and the Holocaust*. Haim Watzman (trans.). New York: Macmillan, 2000.

Seikaly, May. *Haifa: Transformation of an Arab Society, 1918–1939*. Walid Khalidi (Foreword). London: IB Tauris, 2002.

Seikaly, Sherene. *Men of Capital: Scarcity and Economy in Mandate Palestine*. Stanford, C A: Stanford University Press, 2015.

Shalash, Bilal. *Jaffa, Blood on Stone: The Jaffa Garrison and its Military Action; Study and Documents* [Arabic]. vol. 1. Beirut: ACRPS, 2019.

Shalhoub-Kevorkian, Nadera. *Security Theology, Surveillance and the Politics of Fear*. Cambridge Studies in Law and Society. Cambridge: Cambridge University Press, 2015.

BIBLIOGRAPHY

Shlaim, Avi & Eugene L. Rogan (eds.). *The War for Palestine: Rewriting the History of 1948*. Cambridge: Cambridge University Press, 2001.

Shlaim, Avi. *Lion of Jordan: The Life of King Hussein in War and Peace*. NewYork: Vintage Books, 2007.

Stein, Rebecca L. & Ted Swedenburg (eds.). *Palestine, Israel, and the Politics of Popular Culture*. Durham, N.C: Duke University Press, 2005.

Tamari, Salim. *Mountain against the Sea: Essays on Palestinian Society and Culture*. Berkeley, Los Angeles, and London: University of California Press, 2009.

Thrall, Nathan. *The Only Language They Understand: Forcing Compromise in Israel and Palestine*. New York: Metropolitan Books, 2017.

Tuchman, Barbara W. *Bible and Sword: England and Palestine from the Bronze Age to Balfour*. New York: Ballantine Books, 1984.

United Nations. *The Status of Jerusalem: Prepared for, and under the Guidance of, the Committee on the Exercise of the Inalienable Rights of the Palestinian People*. New York: United Nations, 1997.

Veracini, Lorenzo. *Settler Colonialism: A Theoretical Overview*. London: Palgrave Macmillan, 2010.

Vickery, Matthew. *Employing the Enemy: The Story of Palestinian Labourers on Israeli Settlements*. London: Zed Books, 2017.

Victor, Kattan. *From Coexistence to Conquest: International Law and the Origins of the Arab-Israeli Conflict, 1891–1949*. London and New York: Pluto Press, 2009.

Wiktorowicz, Quintan (ed.). *Islamic Activism: A Social Movement Theory Approach*. a: Indiana University Press, 2004.

Willcox, Walter F. (ed.). *International Migrations. vol. 2: Interpretations*. Cambridge, M A: National Bureau of Economic Research, 1931.

Wilmer, Franke. *Breaking Cycles of Violence in Israel and Palestine: Empathy and Peacemaking in the Middle East*. Lanham and London: Lexington Books, 2021.

Yiftahel, Oren. *Ethnocracy: Land and Identity Politics in Israel/Palestine*. Philadelphia: University of Pennsylvania Press, 2006.

Zureik, Elia T. *Israel's Colonial Project in Palestine: Brutal Pursuit*. Abingdon, Oxon and New York: Routledge, 2016.

————. *The Palestinians in Israel: A Study of Internal Colonialism*. London and Boston: Routledge/ K. Paul, 1979.

Journals

Abbasi, Mustafa. "The Battle for Safad in the War of 1948: A Revised Study." *International Journal of Middle East Studies*. vol. 36. no. 1 (February 2004).

————. "The Fall of Acre in the 1948 Palestine War." *Journal of Palestine Studies*. vol. XXXIX. no. 4 (Summer 2010).

————. "The War on the Mixed Cities: the Depopulation of Arab Tiberias and the Destruction of Its Old, 'sacred' City (1948–9)." *Journal of Holy Land and Palestine Studies*. vol. 7. no. 1 (May 2008).

BIBLIOGRAPHY

Abrams, Elliott. "The Settlement Obsession: Both Israel and the United States Miss the Obstacles to Peace." *Foreign Affairs*. vol. 99. no. 2 (July/August 2011).

"Annual General Meeting of the Palestine Exploration Fund." *Palestine Exploration Fund: Quarterly Statement for 1875*. vol. 7. no. 3 (1875).

Aronson, Geoffrey. "Israel's Policy of Military Occupation." *Journal of Palestine Studies*. vol. 7. no. 4 (Summer, 1978).

"A Speech by President Mahmoud Abbas on the Fourth Commemoration of the Martyrdom of Yasser Arafat." [Arabic] *Journal of Palestine Studies*. vol. 19. no. 76 (Fall 2008).

Avnery, Uri. "A Binational State? God Forbid: A Response to Azmi Bishara." *Palestine Studies*. vol. 28. no. 4 (1999).

Awwad, Hani. "Understanding Hamas: Remarks on Three Different and Interrelated Theoretical Approaches." [Arabic] *Siyasat Arabiya*. vol. 45 (July 2020).

Barakat, Rana. "Writing/righting Palestine studies: settler colonialism, indigenous sovereignty and resisting the ghost(s) of history." *Settler Colonial Studies*. vol. 8. no. 3 (2018).

Baram, Amatzia. "Territorial Nationalism in the Middle East." *Middle Eastern Studies*. vol. 26. no. 4 (October 1990).

Bar-Or, Amir. "The Evolution of the Army's Role in Israeli Strategic Planning: A Documentary Record." *Israel Studies*. vol. 1. no. 2 (1996).

Barout, Mohammad Jamal. "The Fall of Safad: The Beginning of the fall of Galilee." [Arabic] *al-Karmel*. no. 57 (October 1998).

Bar-Yosef, Eitan. "Christian Zionism and Victorian Culture." *Israeli Studies*. vol. 8. no. 2 (Summer 2003).

Baumgarten, Helga. "The Three Faces/Phases of Palestinian Nationalism, 1948–2005." *Journal of Palestine Studies*. vol. 34. no. 4 (2005).

Bendman, Yona. "British Military Efforts to Prevent the Fall of Jaffa, April 1948." [Hebrew] *Iyunim Bitkumat Israel*. vol. 2 (1992).

Ben-Gurion, David. "Speech in the Knesset Session for Discussing the Law of Return." *The Protocols of the Knesset*. vol. 7 (1950).

Bishara, Azmi. "One Hundred Years of Zionism, from the Dialectic of Existence to the Dialectic of Substance." [Arabic] *al-Carmel Journal* (1997).

———. "Palestinian Minority in Israel: a proposed new vision." [Arabic] *Journal of Palestine studies*. vol. 3. no. 11 (Summer 1992).

———. "The Vortex of Religion and State in Israel." *Majallat al-Dirasat al-Filastiniyya*. no. 3 (Summer 1990).

"Bridging the Green Line: The PA, Israeli Arabs, and Final Status: An Interview with Azmi Bishara." *Journal of Palestine Studies*. vol. 26. no. 3 (Spring 1997).

Brownlee, Jason. "Peace Before Freedom: Diplomacy and Repression in Sadat's Egypt." *Political Science Quarterly*. vol. 126. no. 4 (Winter 2011–12).

Chazan, Naomi. "The Fallacies of Pragmatism: Israeli Foreign Policy towards South Africa." *African Affairs*. vol. 82. no. 327 (April 1983).

Cohen, Hillel. "The Internal Refugees in the State of Israel: Israeli Citizens, Palestinian Refugees." *Palestine-Israel Journal*. vol. 9. no. 2 (2002).

Degani, Arnon Yehuda. "The Decline and Fall of the Israeli Military Government, 1948–

BIBLIOGRAPHY

1966: A Case of Settler-Colonial Consolidation?." *Settler Colonial Studies*. vol. 5. no. 1 (2015).

Dessus, Sébastien. "A Palestinian Growth History, 1968–2000." *Journal of Economic Integration*. vol. 19. no. 3 (September 2004).

Doumani, Beshara. "Archiving Palestine and the Palestinians: The Patrimony of Ihsan Nimr." *Jerusalem Quarterly*. vol. 36. no. 3–12 (2009).

Eldar, Eran. "David Ben-Gurion and Golda Meir: from partnership to enmity." *Israel Affairs*. vol. 26. no. 2 (2020).

"Environmental justice, settler colonialism, and more-than-humans in the occupied West Bank." *Environment and Planning E: Nature and Space*. vol. 4. no. 1 (March 2021).

Frank, Haggai, Zdeněk Klíma & Yossi Goldstein. "The First Israeli Weapons Procurement Behind the Iron Curtain: The Decisive Impact on the War of Independence." *Israel Studies*. vol. 22. no. 3 (Fall 2017).

Friedman, Isaiah. "Theodor Herzl: Political Activity and Achievements." *Israel Studies*. vol. 9. no. 3 (Fall 2004).

Friesel, Ofra. "Israel's 1967 Governmental Debate about the Annexation of East Jerusalem: The Nascent Alliance with the United States, Overshadowed by "United Jerusalem"." *Law and History Review*. vol. 34. no. 2 (May 2016).

Gabriel, Judith. "The Economic Side of the Intifadah." *Journal of Palestine Studies*. vol. 18. no. 1. Special Issue: Palestine 1948 (Autumn 1988).

Golan, Arnon. "The Battle for Jaffa, 1948." *Middle Eastern Studies*. vol. 48. no. 6 (November 2012).

Golani, Motti. "The 'Haifa Turning Point': The British Administration and the Civil War in Palestine, December 1947-May 1948." *Middle Eastern Studies*. vol. 37. no. 2 (April 2001).

Hansell, Herbert J. "United States Letter of the State Department Legal Adviser Concerning the Legality of Israeli Settlements in the Occupied Territories." *International Legal Materials*. vol. 17. no. 3 (May 1978).

Hasan, Manar. "Palestine's Absent Cities: Gender, Memoricide and the Silencing of Urban Palestinian Memory." *Journal of Holy Land and Palestine Studies*. vol. 18. no. 1 (2019).

Hawari, Yara, Sharri Plonski & Elian Weizman. "Settlers and Citizens: A Critical View of Israeli Society." *Settler Colonial Studies*. vol. 9. no. 1 (2019).

Hermann, Tamar. "The Bi-national Idea in Israel/Palestine: Past and Present." *Nations and Nationalism*. vol. 11. no. 3 (2005).

Hersh, Jacque. "Inconvenient Truths about 'Real Existing' Zionism." *Monthly Review*. vol. 61. no. 1 (May 2009).

Hill, Tom. "1948 after Oslo: truth and reconciliation in Palestinian discourse." *Mediterranean Politics*. vol. 13. no. 2 (2008).

Hillel, Maayan. "Constructing modern identity–new patterns of leisure and recreation in mandatory Palestine." *Contemporary Levant*. vol. 4. no. 1 (2019).

Hyamson, Albert M. "British Projects for the Restoration of Jews to Palestine." *Publications of the American Jewish Historical Society*. no. 26 (1918).

Inbar, Efraim. "The 'no choice war' debate in Israel." *The Journal of Strategic Studies*. vol. 12. no. 1 (1989).

BIBLIOGRAPHY

Israeli, Raphael. "Sadat between Arabism and Africanism." *Middle East Review*. vol. 11. no. 3 (Spring 1979).

Karawan, Ibrahim A. "Sadat and the Egyptian-Israeli Peace Revisited." *International Journal of Middle East Studies*. vol. 26. no. 2 (May 1994).

Khalaf, Issa. "The Effect of Socioeconomic Change on Arab Societal Collapse in Mandate Palestine." *International Journal of Middle East Studies*. vol. 29. no. 1 (1997).

Khalidi, Tarif. "Palestinian Historiography: 1900–1948." *Journal of Palestine studies*. vol. 10. no. 3 (1981).

Khalidi, Walid. "Plan Dalet: Master Plan for the Conquest of Palestine." *Journal of Palestine Studies*. vol. 18. no. 1 (1988).

———. "Revisiting the UNGA Partition Resolution." *Journal of Palestine Studies*. vol. 27. no. 1 (1997).

———. "The Fall of Haifa Revisited." *Journal of Palestine Studies*. vol. 37. no. 3 (Spring 2008).

———. "Why Did the Palestinians Leave, Revisited." *Journal of Palestinian Studies*. vol. 34. no. 2 (Winter 2005).

Kurtulus, Ersun N. "The Notion of a 'pre-emptive War:' the Six Day War Revisited." *The Middle East Journal*. vol. 61. no. 2 (2007).

Luft, Gal. "The Palestinian Security Services: Between Police and Army." *Middle East Review of International Affairs* (MERIA). vol. 3, no. 2 (June 1999).

Masri, Mazen. "Colonial Imprints: Settler-Colonialism As a Fundamental Feature of Israeli Constitutional Law." *International Journal of Law in Context*. vol. 13. no. 3 (2017).

Mathew, William M. "The Balfour Declaration and the Palestine Mandate, 1917–1923: British Imperialist Imperatives." *British Journal of Middle Eastern Studies*. vol. 40. no. 3 (2013).

Muharib, Mahmoud. "From Negotiations to Infiltration: The Relationship between the Jewish Agency and the Syrian National Bloc and the Shahbandar." [Arabic] *Ostour Journal for Historical Studies*. no. 5 (January 2017).

———. "The Negotiations between the Jewish Agency and the Syrian National Bloc." [Arabic] *Ostour Journal for Historical Studies* . no. 1 (January 2015).

———. "The Zionist Intelligence: the Beginnings of Spying on Arabs." [Arabic] *Al Mustaqbal al-Arabi*. Year 31. no. 357 (November 2008).

Naber, Nadine et al. "On Palestinian Studies And Queer Theory." *Journal Of Palestine Studies*. vol. 47. no. 3 (2018).

Neve, Gordon & Moriel Ram. "Ethnic Cleansing and the Formation of Settler Colonial Geographies." *Political Geography*. vol. 53 (2016).

Ojo, Olusola. "Israeli-South African Connections and Afro-Israeli Relations." *International Studies*. vol. 21. no. 1 (January–March 1982).

O'Neill, Patrick Howell. "Pegasus Unbound." *MIT Technology Review*. vol. 123. no. 5 (September/October 2020).

Pappé, Ilan. "Shtetl Colonialism: First and Last Impressions of Indigeneity by Colonised Colonisers." *Settler Colonial Studies*. vol. 2. no. 1 (2012).

BIBLIOGRAPHY

Pappé, Ilan. "The 1948 Ethnic Cleansing of Palestine." *Journal of Palestine Studies*. vol. 36. no. 1 (2006).

Peled. Yoav. "Ethnic Democracy and the Legal Construction of Citizenship: Arab Citizens of the Jewish state." *American Political Science Review*. vol. 86. no. 2 (1992).

Popp, Roland. "Stumbling decidedly into the six-day war." *The Middle East Journal*. vol. 60. no. 2 (2006).

Radai, Itamar. "Jaffa, 1948: The fall of a city." *The Journal of Israeli History*. vol. 30. no. 1 (March 2011).

————. "The rise and fall of the Palestinian-Arab middle class under the British mandate, 1920–39." *Journal of Contemporary History*. vol. 51. no. 3 (2016).

Ram, Uri. "Zionist historiography and the invention of modern Jewish nationhood: The case of Ben Zion Dinur." *History and Memory*. vol. 7. no. 1 (1995).

Raz, Avi. "The Generous Peace Offer that was Never Offered: The Israeli Cabinet Resolution of June 19, 1967." *Diplomatic History*. vol. 37. no. 1 (January 2013).

Rempel, Terry. "Resolution 194 (III), A Retrospective." *al-Majdal*. no. 39–40 (Autumn 2008-Winter 2009).

Rempel, Terry. "The Right to Return: Drafting Paragraph 11 of General Assembly Resolution 194 (III), December 11, 1948." *The Palestine Yearbook of International Law Online*. vol. 21. no. 1 (2020).

Robarge, David. "Getting it Right: CIA Analysis of the 1967 Arab-Israeli War." *Studies in Intelligence*. vol. 62. no. 2 (June 2018).

Rodinson, Maxime. "Is Israel a Colonial?." [French] *Les Temps Modernes, Le conflit israélo-arabe. no.* 253 (July 1967).

Rouhana, Nadim N. & Areej Sabbagh-Khoury. "Memory and the Return of History in a Settler-colonial Context: The Case of the Palestinians in Israel." *Interventions*. vol. 21. no. 4 (2019).

Rouhana, Nadim N. "Homeland Nationalism and Guarding Dignity in a Settler Colonial Context: The Palestinian Citizens of Israel Reclaim Their Homeland." *Borderland e-Journal*. vol. 14. no. 1 (Spring 2015).

Ryan, Sheila. "Constructing a New Imperialism: Israel and the West Bank." *MERIP Reports*. no. 9 (May–June 1972).

Sa'di, Ahmad. "Israel's settler-colonialism as a global security paradigm." *Race & Class* (April 2021).

Sabbagh-Khoury, Areej. "Tracing Settler Colonialism: A Genealogy of a Paradigm in the Sociology of Knowledge Production in Israel." *Politics & Society* (March 2021).

Salamanca, Omar Jabary et al. "Past is present: Settler colonialism in Palestine." *Settler Colonial Studies*. vol. 2. no. 1 (2012).

————. "Settler Colonial Studies and Israel-Palestine." *Settler Colonial Studies*. vol. 5. no. 3 (2015).

Shemesh, Moshe. "The Founding of the PLO 1964." *Middle Eastern Studies*. vol. 20. no. 4 (1984).

Shlaim, Avi. "The Debate About 1948." *International Journal of Middle East Studies*. vol. 27. no. 3 (1995).

BIBLIOGRAPHY

Slater, Jerome. "The Superpowers and an Arab-Israeli Political Settlement: The Cold War Years." *Political Science Quarterly*. vol. 105. no. 4 (Winter 1990–1991).

"Special Issue: Israeli Settler-Colonialism and the Palestinian Naqab Bedouin." *Journal of Holy Land and Palestine Studies*. vol. 15. no. 1 (May 2016).

"Special Issue: New Directions in Settler Colonial Studies." *Postcolonial Studies*. vol. 23. no. 1 (2020).

"Special Issue: Settler-Colonialism and Indigenous Rights in Al-Quds/Jerusalem." *Journal of Holy Land and Palestine Studies*. vol. 17. no. 1 (May 2018).

"Special Issue: Settler Colonialism: The Palestinian/Israeli Case." *International Journal of Applied Psychoanalytic Studies*. vol. 17. no. 2 (2020).

"Special Issue: Settler Colonialism: United States, South Africa, Eritrea, and Palestine/Israel." *South Atlantic Quarterly*. vol. 107. no. 4 (2008).

"Statistics of Jews." *The American Jewish Year Book*. vol. 42 (October 3, 1940 to September 21, 1941 / 5701).

Tabar, Linda & Chandni Desai. "Decolonization is a global project: From Palestine to the Americas." *Decolonization: Indigeneity, Education & Society*. vol. 6. no. 1 (2017).

Tarabulsi, Fawwaz. "The Palestine Problem: Zionism and Imperialism in the Middle East." *New Left Review*. vol. 1. no. 57 (September—October 1969).

Terrill, W. Andrew. "The political mythology of the Battle of Karameh." *The Middle East Journal*. vol. 55. no. 1 (2001).

Troen, S. Ilan & Zaki Shalom. "Ben-Gurion's Diary for the 1967 Six-Day War: [Introduction and Diary Excerpts]." *Israel Studies*. vol. 4. no. 2 (1999).

Usher, Graham. "Bantustanisation or Bi-nationalism?: An Interview with Azmi Bishara." *Race and Class*. vol. 37. no. 2 (1995).

Veracini, Lorenzo. "The Other Shift: Settler Colonialism, Israel and The Occupation." *Journal of Palestine Studies*. vol. 42. no. 2 (April 2013).

———. "Introducing Settler Colonial Studies." *Settler Colonial Studies*. vol. 1. no. 1 (2011).

———. "Is settler colonial studies even useful?." *Postcolonial Studies*. vol. 24. no. 2 (December 2020).

Vereté, Mayir. "The Balfour Declaration and its makers." *Middle Eastern Studies*. vol. 6. no. 1 (1970).

Wakim, Wakim. "The Internal Refugees in their homeland: present absentee in Israel." [Arabic] *Palestine Studies Journal*. vol. 45/46 (Winter 2001).

Weitz, Yechiam. "Taking Leave of the 'Founding Father' Ben-Gurion's Resignation as Prime Minister in 1963." *Middle Eastern Studies*. vol. 37. no. 2 (April 2001).

Wolfe, Patrick. "Settler Colonialism and the Elimination of the Native." *Journal of Genocide Research*. vol. 8. no. 4 (2006).

Yazbek, Mahmoud. "Jaffa Before the Nakba." [Arabic] *Journal of Palestine Studies*. vol. 93 (Winter 2013).

"Yehoram Shalom and others vs. the Central Committee of Elections and the Progressive List for Peace." [Hebrew] *Judgements of the Supreme Court*. vol. 53. no. 4.

Zohar, Maor. "Moderation from Right to Left: The Hidden Roots of Brit Shalom." *Jewish Social Studies*. vol. 19. no. 2 (2013).

BIBLIOGRAPHY

Zureik, Elia. "Settler Colonialism, Neoliberalism and Cyber Surveillance: The Case of Israel." *Middle East Critique*. vol. 29. no. 2 (February 2020).

Reports, Studies, Documents, and Speeches

"194 (III). Palestine—Progress Report of the United Nations Mediator A/RES/194 (III)." *Progress Report*. UN General Assembly. 11 December 1948. Accessed at: https://bit.ly/3aBHJnZ.

"A regime of Jewish supremacy from the Jordan River to the Mediterranean Sea: This is apartheid." *Position Paper*. B'Tselem, The Israeli Information Center for Human Rights in the Occupied Territories. 12 January 2021. Accessed at: https://bit.ly/3uTiip6.

"Absentees' Property Law, 5710–1950." *The Knesset*. Accessed at: https://bit.ly/3uDJJD2.

"Address by PM Netanyahu at Bar-Ilan University." *Israel Ministry of Foreign Affairs*. 14 June 2009. Accessed at: https://bit.ly/3cn6c1g.

"Address to the Nation on United States Policy for Peace in the Middle East, 1 September 1982." *United Nations*. Accessed at: https://bit.ly/3wXCR5l.

"Advisory opinion of the International Court of Justice on the Legal Consequences of the Construction of a Wall in the Occupied Palestinian Territory." *United Nations*. Accessed at: https://bit.ly/32IOVdD.

Ainslee, Rosalyne. "Israel and South Africa: An Unlikely Alliance?." *Report no. 81–18876*. United Nations Department of Political Security Affairs, Center Against Apartheid. 1981.

"Ambassador Yousef Al Otaiba Statement on Peace Plan." *Embassy of the United Arab Emirates in Washington DC*. 28 January 2020. Accessed at: https://bit.ly/3cpGcCd.

"Arab Opinion Index 2019/2020." *Index*. Arab Center for Research and Policy Studies. Accessed at: https://bit.ly/3pylEwL.

Arafeh, Nur, Samia al-Botmeh & Leila Farsakh. "How Israeli Settlements Stifle Palestine's Economy." *Policy Brief*. al-Shabaka. December 15, 2015. Accessed at: https://bit.ly/3p8zxS0.

————. "Long Overdue: Alternatives to the Paris Protocol." *Policy Brief*. al-Shabaka. February 27, 2018. Accessed at: https://bit.ly/3uEptRS.

Bishara, Azmi. "Is Anti-Zionism a Form of Anti-Semitism?." *Case Analysis*. Arab Center for Research and Policy Studies. 3 March 2019. Accessed at: https://bit.ly/3g376AX.

————. "Trump-Netanyahu Deal ... The American-Israeli Right-wing Plan to End the Palestinian Cause in a Historical Context." *Arab Center for Research and Policy Studies YouTube channel*. 6 February 2020. Accessed at: http://bit.ly/2HOR7Wj.

————. "What does the 'Jewish Nation' Basic Law Mean?." *Arab Center for Research and Policy Studies*. 24 July 2018. Accessed at: https://bit.ly/2S7fPKy.

"Camp David Accords—17 Sep 1978." *Israel Ministry of Foreign Affairs*. Accessed at: https://bit.ly/3eCnvvm.

Dana, Tariq. "The Palestinian Capitalists That Have Gone Too Far." *Policy Brief*. al-Shabaka. January 14, 2014. Accessed at: https://bit.ly/3uCz0c3.

"Database on Fatalities and House Demolitions." *B'Tselem: The Israeli Information Center for Human Rights in the Occupied Territories*. Accessed at: https://bit.ly/3vZ6HpH.

BIBLIOGRAPHY

El-Atrash, Ahmad. "Israel's Stranglehold on Area C: Development as Resistance." *Commentary*. al-Shabaka. September 27, 2018. Accessed at: https://bit.ly/3g3kkgS.

Elements of Crimes. The Hague: International Criminal Court, 2013. Accessed at: https://bit.ly/3z6e00Y.

"Estimated Population in Palestine Mid-Year by Governorate,1997–2021." *Database*. The Palestinian Central Bureau of Statistics. Accessed at: https://bit.ly/2SaWbgE.

"Forced Population Transfer: The Case of Palestine—Denial of Reparations." *Working Paper no. 22*. BADIL Resource Center for Palestinian Residency and Refugee Rights. October 2018. Accessed at: https://bit.ly/32Se9pH.

"Full text of Basic Law: Israel as the Nation State of the Jewish People." *The Knesset*. 19 July 2018. Accessed at: https://bit.ly/3w1kkF8.

Harel, Tal Orian et al. "The Partnership Index among Youth in Israel in 2020." *Index*. aChord, the Hebrew University of Jerusalem. April 2021. Accessed at: https://bit.ly/3teHpSm.

Hawari, Yara. "The Revival of People-to-People Projects: Relinquishing Israeli Accountability." *Policy Brief*. al-Shabaka. April 6, 2021. Accessed at: https://bit.ly/3i8fJgb.

Hijab, Nadia & Ingrid Jaradat Gassner. "Talking Palestine: What Frame of Analysis? Which Goals and Messages?." *Alshabaka*. 12 April 2017. Accessed at: https://bit.ly/3bJuzFP.

Human Rights Watch. *A Threshold Crossed: Israeli Authorities and the Crimes of Apartheid and Prosecution*. United States: April 2021. Accessed at: https://bit.ly/3wXE9go.

"International Convention on the Elimination of All of Racial Discrimination." United Nations. 7 March 1966. Accessed at: https://bit.ly/3g8lGHk.

"International Convention on the Suppression and Punishment of the Crime of *Apartheid*, Adopted by the General Assembly of the United Nations on 30 November 1973." *United Nations*. Accessed at: https://bit.ly/3uYbp61.

International Labour Organization. *The situation of workers of the occupied Arab territories*. International Labour Conference: 109th Session, 2021. Accessed at: https://bit.ly/3hKFfXF.

"Israel's Settlements Have No Legal Validity, Constitute Flagrant Violation of International Law, Security Council Reaffirms." *UN Security Council*. 23 December 2016. Accessed at: http://bit.ly/2T97x0V.

"Israeli Settlements in the Occupied Palestinian Territory, Including East Jerusalem, and the Occupied Syrian Golan." *Report of the Secretary-General A/HRC/37/43*. UN General Assembly. March 6, 2018. Accessed at: https://bit.ly/3gJRAM2.

Kerry, John. "Restoring Leadership in the Middle East: A Regional Approach to Peace." Martin Indyk (intro.). *The Brookings Institution (Washington, DC)*. March 4, 2009. Accessed at: https://brook.gs/32d5hd6.

"Letter from President Yasser Arafat to President Clinton." *Miftah. The Palestinian Initiative for the Promotion of Global Dialogue and Democracy*. 13 January 1998. Accessed at: https://bit.ly/3xjJHTu.

MACRO: The Center for Political Economics. *Work Conditions of the Palestinian Paid-Workers in Israel* [Arabic]. [Tel Aviv]: February 2017.

Mearsheimer, John J. & Stephen M. Walt. "The Israel Lobby and US Foreign Policy."

BIBLIOGRAPHY

Working Papers Series No. RWP06–011. Harvard University: John F. Kennedy School of Government, Faculty Research. 15 March 2006. Accessed at: https://bit.ly/3xyYVo2.

"Moshe Dayan's Eulogy for Roi Rutenberg—April 19, 1956." *Eulogy*. Jewish Virtual Library. Accessed at: https://bit.ly/2Q2gvj3.

Nakhleh, Khalil. "Oslo: Replacing Liberation with Economic Neo-Colonialism." *Commentary*. al-Shabaka. April 10, 2014. Accessed at: https://bit.ly/3uEGdlI.

"Nationality Law, 5712–1952." *The Knesset*. Accessed at: https://bit.ly/34wDerl.

"PHROC Nakba Statement: Stop the Ongoing Nakba: Protect Palestinian Refugees." *Statement*. BADIL Resource Center for Palestinian Residency and Refugee Rights. May 2019. Accessed at: https://bit.ly/32eMyPm.

"PM Netanyahu addresses the 2016 AIPAC Policy Conference." *Israel Ministry of Foreign Affairs*. 22 March 2016. Accessed at: https://bit.ly/3x3NC6W.

Public Papers of the President of the United States: George Bush, 1990. Book I—January 1 to June 30, 1990. Washington, D.C.: United States Government Printing Office, 1991.

Rahman, Omar. "From confusion to clarity: Three pillars for revitalizing the Palestinian national movement." *Policy Briefing*. Brookings Doha Center. December 2019. Accessed at: https://brook.gs/3pd9Y4c.

"Remarks by the President at Cairo University, 6–04–09." *The White House: Office of the Press Secretary*. 4 June 2009. Accessed at: http://bit.ly/39Q7XQy.

"Remarks on Middle East Peace." *US Department of State*. 28 December 2016. Accessed at: http://bit.ly/2SODUDn.

"Resolution 2334 (2016)." *UN Security Council*. 23 December 2016. Accessed at: http://bit.ly/2wGIOtt.

"Resolution 242 (1967) of 22 November 1967." *UN Security Council*. Accessed at: http://bit.ly/38ThpCF.

"Resolution 446 (1979) of 22 March 1979." *UN Security Council*. Accessed at: http://bit.ly/2uniqUJ.

Rosner, Shmuel, Noah Slepkov & Camil Fuchs. "The 2021 Israel Pluralism Index: Consensus and Disagreements." *The Jewish People Policy Institute*. 8 April 2021. Accessed at: https://bit.ly/2PHLYH9.

"S.1322—Jerusalem Embassy Act of 1995." Congress.Gov. Accessed at: http://bit.ly/2HOShRO.

Sharp, Jeremy M. "U.S. Foreign Aid to Israel." *Report*. Congressional Research Service. 22 December 2016. Accessed at: https://bit.ly/2QUTuiy.

———. "US Foreign Aid to Israel." *Report*. Congressional Research Service. 16 November 2020. Accessed at: https://bit.ly/3tTw0II.

Shikaki, Ibrahim & Joanna Springer. "Building a Failed State: Palestine's Governance and Economy Delinked." *Policy Brief*. al-Shabaka. April 21, 2015. Accessed at: https://bit.ly/2RaGyVT.

"Silencing: DSDE's Concealment of Documents in Archives." *Report*. Akevot Institute for Israeli-Palestinian Conflict Research. July 2019. Accessed at: https://bit.ly/3tnNGw7.

"Sixty-Eighth Congress: Sec. I. Chs. 185, 190, 1924." *Act*. GovTrack.us. May 1924. Accessed at: https://bit.ly/3fgbkWF.

BIBLIOGRAPHY

"Sixty-Seventh Congress: Sec. I. Ch. 8, 1921." *Act*. GovTrack.us. May 1921. Accessed at: https://bit.ly/3hUTv1f.

"Statement by Middle East Quartet." *United Nations*. 23 September 2011. Accessed at: http://bit.ly/2uXJhXT.

"Statement of ICC Prosecutor, Fatou Bensouda, respecting an investigation of the Situation in Palestine." *International Criminal Court*. 3 March 2021. Accessed at: https://bit.ly/3w1pUHp.

"Statement to the Knesset by Prime Minister Eshkol, 12 June 1967." *Israel Ministry of Foreign Affairs*. Accessed at: https://bit.ly/3bFL2eg.

"Survey of Palestinian Refugees and Internally Displaced Persons 2016–2018: Volume IX." *Survey*. BADIL Resource Center for Palestinian Residency and Refugee Rights. November 2019. Accessed at: https://bit.ly/3tn6Kuq.

Swirski, Shlomo. "The Cost of Occupation: The Burden of the Israeli–Palestinian Conflict 2010 Report." *Adva Center*. June 2010.

Tartir, Alaa. "The Palestinian Authority Security Forces: Whose Security?" *Policy Brief*. al-Shabaka. May 16, 2017. Accessed at: https://bit.ly/3aQ6AUJ.

"The Law of Return 5710 (1950)." *The Knesset*. Accessed at: https://bit.ly/3vCJREt.

Tartir, Alaa, Sam Bahour & Samer Abdelnour. "Defeating Dependency, Creating a Resistance Economy." *Policy Brief*. al-Shabaka. February 13, 2012. Accessed at: https://bit.ly/3vKy6M8.

The Quest for Peace: Principal United States Public Statements and Related Documents on the Arab-Israeli Peace Process 1967–1983. Washington, D.C.: US Department of State, 1984.

The White House. *Peace to Prosperity: A Vision to Improve the Lives of the Palestinian and Israeli People*. January 2020. Accessed at: https://bit.ly/2S6c3Rt.

UN Department of Public Information. *The Question of Palestine and the United Nations*. New York: 2008. Accessed at: https://bit.ly/3dMKkgz.

UN General Assembly. *Special report of the Director and Advisory Commission of the United Nations Relief and Works Agency for Palestine Refugees in the Near East*. Official Records: Sixth Session Supplement No. 16 A (A/1905/Add. 1). Paris: 1951. Accessed at: https://bit.ly/2PjX1pN.

United Nations Special Committee on Palestine. *Official Records of the Second Session of the General Assembly, Supplement No. 11, Report to The General Assembly*. vol. 1 (A/364). New York: 1947. Accessed at: https://bit.ly/3nkDT7H.

United Nations Conference on Trade and Development. "UNCTAD assistance to the Palestinian people: Developments in the economy of the Occupied Palestinian Territory." *Report*. Sixty-seventh session (2–3 July, 7–9 September and 28 September–2 October 2020). Accessed at: https://bit.ly/2Z2PvnT.

United Nations Department of Public Information. *Yearbook of the United Nations 1948–49*. New York: 1949. Accessed at: https://bit.ly/3sUe6Ep.

United Nations General Assembly Official Records. "186 (S-2). Appointment and terms of reference of a United Nations Mediator in Palestine." *Resolution A/RES/186 (S-2)*. May 14, 1948. Accessed at: https://bit.ly/3sQvx8U.

———. *Progress Report of the UN Mediator for Palestine submitted to the secretary-general for*

BIBLIOGRAPHY

transmission to the members of the United Nations, 16 September 1948. Third session supplement no. 11 (A/648). Paris: 1948. Accessed at: https://bit.ly/3tRSidZ.

United Nations Security Council. *Calling for a cessation of hostilities in Palestine*, Resolution S/RES/50(1948). May 29, 1948. Accessed at: https://bit.ly/3hb66Ml.

————. *Question of Palestine/Majority plan (Partition), Minority plan (Federal State)—UN Special Committee on Palestine (UNSCOP)—Report.* New York: 1947. Accessed at: https://bit.ly/2QsMPfa.

United Nations. *Resolutions and Decisions of the Secretary Council 1967: Security Council Official Records Twenty-Second Year.* New York: 1968. Accessed at: http://bit.ly/31DlKas.

Wildeman, Jeremy & Alaa Tartir. "Can Oslo's Failed Aid Model Be Laid to Rest?." *Policy Brief.* al-Shabaka. September 18, 2013. Accessed at: https://bit.ly/3yUnBYI.

News Websites

Al Jazeera: The online website for Arabic language channels of Al Jazeera Media Network.

Al-Ahram Weekly: The website of an English-language weekly broadsheet printed by the Al-Ahram Publishing House in Cairo, Egypt.

Al-Araby al-Jadeed: The online website of a pan-Arab media outlet headquartered in London.

Axios: An American news website based in Arlington County, Virginia. It was founded in 2016 and launched the following year by former Politico journalists Jim VandeHei, Mike Allen and Roy Schwartz.

BBC News: The online website for an operational business division of the British Broadcasting Corporation responsible for the gathering and broadcasting of news and current affairs.

Brookings: The website of an American research group.

DW: The online website for a German public state-owned international broadcaster funded by the German federal tax budget.

Encyclopaedia Palestina: An online website which offers a comprehensive reference that presents Palestine's history, land, people, cause and jihad.

European Council on Foreign Relations (ECFR): An international think-tank that aims to conduct cutting-edge independent research on European foreign and security policy.

Facebook: American online social media and social networking service based in Menlo Park, California. It was founded by Mark Zuckerberg.

Government of Iraq. *Report of the Parliamentary Committee of Enquiry into the Palestine Question* [Arabic]. Baghdad: 1949.

Haaretz: The online website for an Israeli newspaper.

HuffPost: The online website for an American news aggregator and blog, with localised and international editions.

Institute for Palestine Studies: The online website for the oldest independent non-profit public service research institute in the Arab world.

Israel State Archives: The online website for the national archive of Israel.

NSO Group: The online website of an Israeli technology firm.

One Democratic State Campaign: The online website for a Palestinian-led initiative that calls

BIBLIOGRAPHY

for the end of the colonial Zionist regime and strives for the establishment of a single democratic state in historic Palestine, based on political, social, economic and cultural justice, in which Palestinians and Israeli Jews live in equality.

One State Foundation: The online website for a foundation that aims to provide full transparency on its agenda and its finances and in this framework will also publish its annual financial reports online.

Politico: The online website for a political journalism company based in Arlington County, Virginia, that covers politics and policy in the United States and internationally.

Reuters: The online website of an international news organisation owned by Thomson Reuters.

SIPRI: The website of an independent international institute dedicated to research into conflict, armaments, arms control and disarmament.

Slate. The online website for a progressive online magazine that covers current affairs, politics, and culture in the United States.

Smithsonaian: The website of an institution of learning which is known as the world's largest museum, education, and research complex.

The Association for One Democratic State in Israel/Palestine: The online website for a non-governmental organisation incorporated according to the Swiss association law.

The Guardian: The online website for a British news and media website owned by the Guardian Media Group.

The Independent: A British online newspaper that was established in 1986 as a national morning printed paper.

The Knesset: The online website for the unicameral national legislature of Israel.

The Middle East Research and Information Project (MERIP): A non-profit independent research group established in 1971, that has released reports and position papers on various Middle East conflicts.

The New York Times: The online website for an American daily newspaper based in New York City with a worldwide readership.

The Spectator: The online website for a weekly British magazine on politics, culture, and current affairs.

The Washington Post: The online website for an American daily newspaper published in Washington, D.C.

The White House: The online website for the official residence and workplace of the president of the United States.

The World Bank: The official website for an international financial institution that provides loans and grants to the governments of low-and middle-income countries for the purpose of pursuing capital projects.

UCLA-EDI: The website of The Office of Equity, Diversity and Inclusion, dedicated to leading and advancing campus strategies for enhancing equity, diversity and inclusion, combating discrimination.

UN Department of Public Information: The online website page for the UN Department of Public Information that is dedicated to communicating the ideals and work of the UN to the world.

BIBLIOGRAPHY

UN News: The online website page for the UN news.

UN Relief and Works Agency for Palestine Refugees (UNRWA): The online website page for the UNRWA.

Vanity Fair: The online website for a monthly magazine of popular culture, fashion, and current affairs published by Condé Nast in the United States.

Wafa: The Palestine News Agency is the news agency of the Palestinian National Authority, and was "the P.L.O.'s news agency" in the years before the formation of the PA.

World Development Indicators: The website of the World Bank's premier compilation of cross-country comparable data on development.

Youtube: Online video platform owned by Google.

INDEX

Note: Page numbers followed by "*n*" refer to footnotes, "*f*" refer to figures and "*t*" refer to tables.

Abbas, Mahmoud, 131, 142, 175, 197, 204
  Arab League speech, 278
  Hamas and, 143–4
  as PA president, 273
Abdullah (Crown Prince of Saudi Arabia), 149–50
Abdullah (King of Jordan), 44, 45, 50
Abdullah II (King of Jordan), 92–3
Absentees' Property Law (1950), 47
The aChord Center, 207–8
African National Congress (ANC), 257, 282
Afrikaans, 249
Afula, 172
agriculture settlements, 213
AIPAC (*American Israel Public Affairs Committee*), 199
Al-Aqsa (Mosque), 173, 174, 210
Albanese, Francesca P., 50
Algeria, 7, 250
Allon, Yigal, 37, 122–3, 122–3*n*44

Amer, Abdul Hakim, 111
American civil society, 274
American Israel Public Affairs Committee (AIPAC), 134
Amman, 53, 139, 216
ANC. *See* African National Congress (ANC)
Anglo-American Union, 256
Anglo-American, invasion of, 222
Anglo-Egyptian treaty (1936), 44
Annual General Meeting of the Palestine Exploration Fund (1875), 82
anti-colonialism, 233, 241
anti-Zionist, 255, 256
  See also Matzpen (Compass); Palestinian Communist party
apartheid regime, 234, 243
  constitution models approach, 271
  South Africa, 245–6, 249
apartheid system/term/model, 170, 233, 243, 244–5, 249
  crimes of, 246–7, 249
  features of, 269

International Convention on, 246–7
UN Assembly for, 247
US usage of, 251
Aqsa Mosque (Jerusalem), 5, 284
Arab armies, 41, 43, 90, 114, 116–17
truce agreements with Israel, 95–6
Arab citizens, 231, 233n22, 248
citizenship in Palestinian state, 236, 259, 267
as protester, 237–8, 239, 240
under Israelisation process, 275–6
votes of, 274–5
Arab elites (Palestine), 65–6, 80, 97
Arab evacuation order, 35
Arab ghetto, 231
Arab Higher Committee, 55
Arab League Council, 39
Arab League, 198, 214, 278
Beirut Summit (2002), 149, 214
Military Committee, 39
Rabat Summit (1974), 128
Arab Mashreq, 87, 87n20, 225
Arab Nationalist movement, 54, 69
Arab Palestinian Congress I (1919), 60, 60n5
Arab Peace Initiative, 149–57
Arab peoples/Arab community, 8, 37, 49, 280
as group to expose issue, 281
hostility of, 9
See also Arabs (Palestine)
Arab question, 77, 88–9, 266
Arab regimes, 5, 6, 91, 102, 131–2, 148, 155, 225, 229–30, 281

dispelling Israeli anxieties, 152
Israel defeat plan to, 267
Israel engagement with, 261–2
Israel normalisation conditions of, 282
rivalry between, 88–9
US attention, need for, 268
Arab residents. See Arab citizens
Arab revolt (1936–9), 51
Arab Spring/uprising (2011), 4, 5, 6, 100, 103–4
Arab states/Arab world (Arab country), 9, 31, 39, 53, 55, 68n22, 79, 115, 148, 149, 189, 214, 231
against UN Resolution, 32–3
alliance against Iraq, 165
bilateral alliances, 6, 10, 281
commemorations of Nakba, 69
democracy, struggle for, 105
democratic concept projection, 282
Israel rejections, 214, 227
Israel threatens to, 281
joined anti-Iraqi coalition, 193
Kushner on, 200
myth about, 198
nations building, failure of, 88
Palestinian cause, support for, 100–1
Palestinian resistance activity banned in, 137–8
partition plan, response to, 188, 212
PLO's position in, 140
reaction to Israel vision, 221–2
reactions to Egypt peace, 268
and Trump administration, 4–5, 200–1
US mediator, 187, 190, 214
war declaration, 42–3
war on Israel, 212
youth against, 208

INDEX

Arab troops, 39–40, 42, 45

Arab-Israeli conflict, 1, 9, 88, 107–8, 193, 266, 268

Arab-Israeli war (1967), 116, 119, 120–1, 189, 190, 211–12, 267, 268

  Israeli occupation during, 108–110

  as an Israeli war of choice, 115–17

Arab-Israeli War (1973), 117, 118, 125–6

Arabs (Palestine), 8, 60, 81, 133, 155, 250

  against partition plan, 188

  Arab-Israeli war defeat, response to, 120–1

  armed resistance to Israel, 284

  favour to Israel, 231

  Israel military rule, 233

  misguiding about Trump-Netanyahu document, 215–16, 218

  tensions between Israel and, 113–14

  as victims of racism, 78

  on Zionism, 252–3

  See also Arab citizens

Arab revolt (1936–9), 51

Arab summit I (Cairo, 13–17 Jan 1964), 53

Arafat, Yasser, 142, 148, 153, 167, 173–4, 175

  assassination of, 196, 230

  during Kuwait crisis, 194

  after Madrid Conference (1991), 130–1

  as PLO leader, 144

Area A (West Bank), 170, 221, 221n77

Area B (West Bank), 170, 221, 221n77

Area C (West Bank), 170, 221, 221n77

Area H-1 (Hebron), 170

Area H-2 (Hebron), 170

Argentina, 17

Ariel, 198

armed resistance movement, 284–5

Armistice Agreements (1949), 34, 38, 196, 216

Ashdod, 214

Association for One Democratic State in Israel/Palestine, 257

Auschwitz, 115

Avigdor Lieberman, 216n67

B'Tselem, 216n69

Bahrain, 93, 153

Baker, James, 128, 184n3, 193

Balfour Declaration, 28, 59–60n4, 79, 84, 86, 87n20, 88n23, 253

Balfour, Arthur, 84, 86–7

Bank of Israel, 163

Bantustans, 234, 244, 245, 279

Barak, Ehud, 170, 173, 174

Bar-Ilan University, 219

Basel, 62

basic law/Jewish nation-state law (1992), 239

Bayet Aravi (an Arab house), 34

Bayt Nuba (village), 109, 109n4

Begin, Menachem, 112, 115, 191, 192

  and Reagan, 191–2n15, 202–3

Beirut Summit (2002), 149, 214

Beirut, 53, 192

Ben-Gurion, David, 36, 40, 113–14, 116, 236

Bennett, Naftali, 10, 260

Beqaa Valley, 152

Bergmann, Hugo, 255

Berkowitz, Avi, 200n33

INDEX

Berlin Wall, 189
Bernadotte, Folke, 45–6
Biale, David, 112–13
Biblical theology. *See* US policy
bi-national movement (Ihud), 255–6
bi-national state, 255, 256–7, 270, 271
    Hatzair about, 254–5
    Palestinian encouragement, 258
    single democratic model, 259–6
    See also one-state solution/ model; two-state solution
The Birth of Israel: Myths and Realities (Flapan), 36
Black Lives Matter (BLM), 4
Bolsheviks, 87
Bradshaw, Samuel Alexander, 83
Brit Shalom, 255
British army, 51, 96
British Mandate, 17, 28–9, 31, 51–2, 60, 81, 143, 286
    beginning of, 65
    Palestinian identities before, 67
    Zionist movement, helping to, 87
British, 28, 34, 42, 44, 51, 83, 96
    colonialism, 76
British-Iraqi agreement (1933), 44
British-Jordanian agreement (1946), 44
Brzezinski, Zbigniew, 190
Bush, George H. W., 151, 153, 165, 203
    loan to Israel, 184, 184–5n3
    as peacemaker, 192, 195, 196

Cairo, 53–4, 131, 169
Cairo summit (13–17 Jan 1964), 53
Cairo University, 196

Camp David Agreement (1978–9), 124–5, 127
Camp David II (2000), 170, 174, 230
Camp David, 173, 190
Canada, 134
Carter, Jimmy, 190, 202, 252
Central Bureau of Statistics (2021), 34
Childers, Erskine, 35
Chomsky, Avram Noam, 133–5, 212
Christian Zionist core, 205
    See also Trump-Netanyahu deal (2020)
CIA (Central Intelligence Agency), 115
Clinton, Bill, 173
Clinton–Barak alliance, 174
Cold War, 4
colonial project/settler colonial project (1948), 234
    Zionist movement as, 265, 283
    Israel occupation (1967); *See also* Nakba war (1948); war (1967)
colonialism state, victims of, 159, 211, 232, 265, 266
    See also Palestinians
colonised people, 203, 207
Congress (Israel), 201
Congress (US), 184, 184n2, 193
Construction Law, 238n22
corpus separatum, 31
Crusader kingdoms/states, 260, 261, 262
Crusaders, 261, 262
Czechoslovakia, 41, 42

Damascus, 45, 59
Dayan, Moshe, 111, 113, 123–5, 123n45, 248

Dayton, Keith, 175
"deal of the Century". *See* Trump-
  Netanyahu deal (2020)
Democratic Party (US), 174
diaspora Jews, 22, 113, 118, 278
  of Israel, 253
  of Palestinians youth, 274, 280,
    283
  of Palestinians, 271
Dugdale, Blanche E. C., 84
Dutch settler-colonialists, 245

East Jerusalem, 2, 152, 168,
  184–5n3, 230
  during occupation (1967), 140,
    146
  Israel settlements, 203, 231
  Obama activities, 181, 197
Eban, Abba, 111, 114, 122–3
Egypt, 53, 128, 152, 189, 190,
  267
  Anglo-Egyptian treaty (1936),
    44
  face struggles of, 281
  and Israel peace agreement,
    191, 214, 268
  Joint Defence Treaty (1950),
    112
  liberal era, end of, 68
  military coup (1952), 90
  Nasser's action on military of,
    110–11
  during October War (1973),
    125–6
  during Sadat presidential
    period, 91–2
  Trump vision, support for,
    221–2n78
  "UN Resolution 194", 267
  war (1956), 211
Egyptian army, 44
Egyptian-Israeli model, 268

Egypt–Israel peace treaty, 126
El Kurd, Dana, 231n4
"elitist populism", 4
Eretz Israel. *See Eretz Yisrael* (Land
  of Israel)
Eretz Yisrael (Land of Israel), 23,
  268
Eshkol, Levi, 111, 112, 114
  Egypt and Syria, peace settle-
    ment with, 119–20
Etzion bloc, 123
Europe, 17, 26, 41, 80, 129
  antisemitism in, 78–9, 85–6
  Arab Peace Initiative welcomed
    in, 151
  Zionism in, 62–3
European Jews, 16, 62, 78, 81
European Union, 195
Evangelical Christian Zionism,
  270
Evangelical churches, 81, 85
extremists, 220, 229

Faisal (king), 59
Farouq (King of Egypt), 44–5
Fatah, 54, 71, 144–6, 148, 181,
  273
  and Hamas, 180, 272–3, 280
  on Intifada II, 174
fedayeen fighters, 74, 74n29, 76,
  117
Flapan, Simha, 36
foreign direct investment (FDI),
  of Israel, 162, 163, 164, 166f
France, 7, 42, 62, 87, 134, 250
Friedman, David, 200
Friedman, Thomas, 149–50

Galilee (lake), 173
Galilee, 238
Galili, Yisrael, 123–4, 123n45
Gawler, George, 82–3

INDEX

Gaza Strip, 2, 5–6, 29, 38, 50, 85, 141, 146n3, 166, 191, 236, 241, 250, 258, 267
  agreement on, 169
  Arab armed resistance, 284
  blockade of, 131, 144, 148
  Brzezinski action, 190
  Bush letter, 196, 197
  as an enormous refugee camp, 146–9
  Hamas in, 180
  Hamas seized power in, 144
  Israel apartheid in, 251, 271
  Israel bombing attack, 71
  Israel direct military rule, 233, 234
  Israel settlement evaluation, 265, 271
  Israel water territories control, 221
  Israel withdrawal from, 195
  Palestinians sufferings in, 125
  protest (May 2021), 278
  siege in, 229, 273
  wars on, 148
Germany, 62, 86, 134
geulat ha-adama (redemption of the land), 28
Ginsberg, Asher (1856–1927), 253
global Jewish question. *See* Jewish question
Global South, 233, 273, 280
Golan Heights (Israel legal settlements), 110, 156, 173, 214, 251
  as bargaining chip, 267
Goldstein, Baruch, 172
Great Britain, 81, 82
Greater Syria, 45, 60
Green Line/1967 border, 69, 69n23, 136, 174, 197, 244, 278, 227

Greenblatt, 200n32
Gregorian calendar, 16
gross domestic product (GDP), of Israel, 162, 163, 164, 165f
gross national income (GNI), of Israel, 162, 163, 164
Guinness, Henry Grattan, 84
Gulf states, 6, 53, 200–1
Gulf war I, 128, 135, 195
Gulf War II, 192
Gush Emunim movement, 133
Gush Etzion, 198

Ha'am, Ahad, 253
Haganah (armed forces), 33, 39, 42, 43, 96
Hague, 156
Haifa, 39, 59, 75, 214
al-Hakim, Fatimid Caliph, 262
Hamas, 5, 71, 71–2n26, 170, 171, 180, 194, 280
  after elected in Israel, 143–5
  competition with Fatah/Fateh, 272–3
  deterrence of, 284
  Israeli apartheid system, strategy lacking of, 273
  and PA on Intifada II, 174
  resistance against Israel occupation, 147–8
  as solo leader in Gaza, 180
  suicide bombings, 172, 174
Hansell Memorandum, 202n38, 202–3
Haredi, 208
Hashemite Kingdom, 54
haskalah (culture), 62–3
Hatzair, Hashomer, 253, 254
Hebrew (language), 1, 8, 34, 212, 236
  apartheid, defined, 249–50
  as Israeli-Jewish spoken language, 8, 251

Hebrew calendar, 15–16
Hebrew media, 275
Hebrew University (Jerusalem),
    64, 207–8
Hebron Protocol, 170
Hebron, 173
Hechler, William Henry, 83
Hersch, Liebmann, 17
Herzl, Theodor, 26, 83
Hezbollah, 284
Holocaust Memorial Day, 16
Holocaust, 16–17, 24, 78–9,
    112–13
Holy Sepulchre, 262
homeland (Palestine)
    for Israeli Jews, 253, 254
    Palestinians expelled from, 266
    See also Palestinian refugees
Horn of Africa, 93
Hungary, 62
al-Husayni, Hajj Amin, 51–2
al-Husayni, Musa Kazim, 51
Hussein (King of Jordan), 54, 112

Ibrahimi Mosque (Hebron), 172
IDF (Israeli Defence Forces), 42,
    48
Ihud (bi-national movement),
    255–6
Immigration Act (US, 1924), 17
'Imwas (village), 109, 109n4
industrial settlements, 213
International Court of Justice,
    156, 156n13, 248
international law (West Bank),
    202, 203
Intifada I, 71, 71–2n26, 80, 129,
    135, 140, 159, 160–1t, 176
    damage to Israel, 161–3, 164–5
    impact of, 194–5, 268
    Oslo cause, 194
Intifada II, 142, 163, 269

reason for, 174–5, 180
Iran, 6, 90, 149, 192
    nuclear agreement with US,
        196
Iraq, 4, 45, 68, 165, 192, 281
    anti-Iraqi coalition, 193
    British-Iraqi agreement (1933),
        44
    civil war (2008), 72
    joined Joint Defence Treaty
        (1950), 112
    military coup (1958), 90
Iraqi army, 45
Islamic Jihad, 172, 174, 284
Islamist militant groups, 172
Islamists, 259
Israel military, 190
    agreement with Beirut, 167
    Gaza under, 233, 234
    during Intifada I, 161, 162
    Palestinian security forces,
        confrontation with, 174
    Palestinians expelled by, 266
Israel occupation (1967), 189,
    241, 250–1, 266
    on Gaza through direct military
        rule, 233, 234
Israel regime, 252, 265
Israel security forces (Palestine),
    174, 175, 221
Israel, 1, 2, 6–7, 28, 41, 47–8,
    61, 75, 116, 132–3, 135–6,
    171
    Arab land occupation, 190,
        238, 282
    Arab Peace Initiative, rejection
        of, 154–5
    Arab region, emergence in, 90
    Arab states normalised relation-
        ships with, 150
    bi-national paradigm, lack of
        support to, 258

Crusaders and, 260–1, 262
as custodian to Palestine, 206
domination on basic needs,
    221, 229, 232
economy, 99–100
Egypt peace with, 91–2, 126
existence and unity, 97–8
Hamas deterrence, 284–5
independence, 15–31
indication on Israeli-Jewish
    racism, 207, 231
Israeli Jews, 7, 8, 173, 188,
    236
Jordan peace agreement, 168
and Jordan peace deal, 131
land confiscation process of,
    238
Lebanon air strikes, 172–3
nation-building process, 29–30,
    30n28
neighbours relation, 261–2
occupied territories, with-
    drawal from, 213–14
PA threat to, 277, 278
Palestinian autonomy, rejection
    to, 191, 191–2n15, 197
peace between PLO and, 141
PLO, recognition of, 144–5,
    152
religious conditions in, 210
Trump administration and, 5,
    10, 200, 210
Trump-Netanyahu document
    fallacies advantage to,
    215–16, 218, 219
UN Resolutions refusal, 121,
    267
US and, 174, 175, 189–90,
    191, 196, 198
See also East Jerusalem; Gaza
    Strip; Jerusalem; Oslo
    Accords/Agreements;

Palestinians; West Bank;
    Zionist movement/project/
    colonialism (Palestine)
Israeli academia, 242, 243–4
one religio-ethnicity concept,
    244
Israeli apartheid system, 246, 249,
    251, 260, 265, 273
features of, 269
long term struggles against,
    278, 282
Israeli army/forces, 5, 28, 41,
    42–3, 47–8, 117, 159, 169–70,
    172, 174, 192, 221
on Intifada I, 159
See also Oslo Accords/
    Agreements
"Israeli Cabinet Resolution 563",
    120
Israeli citizenship law (1952), 236
Israeli Consulate (South Africa),
    247
Israeli Defence Forces (IDF), 42,
    48
Israeli foreign policy, 193–4n18,
    281
Israeli Labour Party, 167, 174,
    194
Israeli law, 203
Israeli leaders, 6, 195–6n19
Israeli lobby, 184, 193, 196
Israeli policy, 202, 275
Israeli publics
    Lebanon attack, reaction to,
        172–3
    towards extremist religious
        nationalism, 175
Israeli settlers, 7–8, 169, 177–9f,
    250–1
    Palestinian Muslim worshippers
        attack, 172
    PLO opposition to, 176, 180

INDEX

Sharon forced, 218
Israeli society, 159, 167, 208, 259
Israeli South-African Chamber of
  Commerce, 247
Israeli TV, 204
Israeli-Jewish, 231, 233, 236–7
  Israel polls indication, 207
  language of, 8
  youth of, 208
Israeli-Palestinian peace negotia-
  tions, 181, 203
Israeli-Palestinian conflict, 9, 53,
  62, 69, 80, 89, 90–1, 109, 122,
  131–2, 168
  before Israeli settlements, 233
  loss power on Palestinian State,
    228, 230
  on one-state solution, 254
  See also Israel; Oslo Accords/
    Agreements
Israel-South Africa Trade Journal,
  247

Jaffa, 32, 39, 44, 75
Japan, 134
Jericho, 169
Jerusalem, 1, 5, 6, 31, 54, 71,
  147, 156, 174, 184, 204, 251
  Arab residents issue, 248, 272
  Bernadotte assassination in, 46
  conditions of, 209–10
  Hamas deterrence to, 284
  Knesset legislative acts on,
    121–2
  Palestinians on, 283
  protest (May 2021), 258, 278
Jesus Christ, 81, 83
Jewish Agency, 32n30, 44,
  102–3n32
Jewish Israeli culture. See sabra
  culture
Jewish movement. See Zionist

movement/project/colonialism
  (Palestine)
Jewish question, 26, 52, 77, 253,
  266
  Palestine and, 78–87
Jewish settlement. See Jewish state
Jewish state
  Arab land confiscation, 238
  democracy of, 28–9, 97
  establishment of, 3, 5, 16, 22,
    31, 36, 113, 208, 232, 233,
    236, 239, 266, 267, 283
  goal of, 253, 265, 271
  partition plan (1947), 188
Jewish troops, 40
Jews (Palestine), 8, 17, 22, 29,
  62–3, 85–6
  British protection for, 82
  immigration from Soviet
    Union, 162–3
  immigration to Palestine, 17,
    18–21t
  Kerry actions for, 198
  return to Palestine, 81, 83
  See also Jewish state
Johnson, Boris, 222
Johnson, Lyndon B., 114, 118n33
"Jordan First" campaign, 92–3
Jordan Valley, 121, 123, 128
Jordan, 3, 38, 45, 50, 123, 128,
  138–9, 216
  Armistice Agreement with
    Israel, 196, 216
  assistance to PA, 206
  British-Jordanian agreement
    (1946), 44
  joined Joint Defence Treaty,
    112
  Palestinians welcomed by,
    49–50
  permanent peace treaty with
    Israel, 139

INDEX

PLO contribution, 168
UN resolution acceptance, 190, 267
Judaisation policy, 238, 248
Judea, 212
June war. *See* Arab-Israeli war (1967)

Kafr Qasim, 237–8, 238n21
Karameh, Battle of, 117
Kerry, John, 151, 197–8
Khalidi, Rashid, 52, 65
Khalidi, Tarif, 66
Khalidi, Walid, 35
Khartoum Resolution (29 Aug 1967), 120–1
Kibbush, 250, 251
Kimmerling, Baruch, 40, 65
Knesset (Israel), 47, 120, 121–3, 209, 236, 275
kufiyya, 74, 74n30
Kurtulus, Ersun N., 112
Kushner, Charles, 199–200, 199n30
Kushner, Jared, 199–200, 199n30, 205
Kuwait war, 166, 268
Kuwait, 53, 165, 189, 192, 194
    Iraqi occupation of, 126, 140, 193

Labour Party (Lebanon), 115, 122–3, 124
Labour Zionism, 232
Land Day (30 Mar 1976), 238
Laron, Guy, 114
Law and Administration Ordinance (1948), 121–2
Law of Return (1950), 47, 236
Lebanon War (1982), 115–16, 138, 148
Lebanon, 4, 38, 45, 50, 115, 140, 166, 194, 212

Israeli occupation, 167
    Operation "Grapes of Wrath", 172–3
Lehi (Zionist terrorist group), 46
Letters on Egypt, Edom and the Holy Land, 82
Levant, 49, 68, 88, 101
Libya, 93
Light for the Last Days: A Study Historic and Prophetic (Guinness), 84
Likud (party/government), 167
Lindsay, Lord, 82
Litvak, Meir, 66
Lord Shaftesbury (the seventh Earl of Shaftesbury), 82

Ma'ale Adumim, 198
Madrid Conference (1991), 128, 130–1, 165–6, 168, 184, 193
Madrid, 144–5
Magnes, Judah, 255
Manama, 183
Mandatory Palestine, 34, 38, 39
martial law, 233, 267
Martin, Buber, 255
Masalha, Nur, 38
Masri, Mazen, 240
Matzpen (Compass), 256
May, Theresa, 79
Mecca Agreement (Feb 2007), 144, 148
Mecca, 210
Meir, Golda, 85
Middle East, 191, 200, 204–5
Migdal, Joel S., 40, 65
Mizrahi (Oriental Jews), 16, 118–19
Morris, Benny, 36, 48
Muhammad, Prophet, 210
Muslih, Muhammad, 65–6
Muslims, 210, 213, 254, 296

INDEX

Myers, David, 63

Nakba (1948), 2, 10, 16, 31–9, 48–9, 101–2, 211, 243, 265
  aftermath of, 97
  causes of, 105
  commemorations of, 69–73
  Palestinians after, 271
al-Nashashibi, Raghib, 51
Nasser, Gamal Abdel, 53, 91, 110–11
  Arab coalition, 115
  Rogers Plan acceptance, 121
National Democratic Assembly (Balad), 259
Nationality Law (1952), 47
Nazism, 63, 78–9
"Negation of Exile" (*shlilat hahgula*), 23
Negev, 238
Netanyahu, Benjamin, 10, 134, 143, 173, 181, 200, 204, 260
  on AIPAC conference, 198
  Palestinian State term usage, 219
  White House meeting, 197, 205
  See also Trump-Netanyahu deal (2020)
the Netherlands, 82
new basic law/nation-state law, 239
9/11 attacks (2001), 149–50
Nishul, 250
North Africa, 101
Norway, 169
nuclear agreement, 196

Obama, Barack, 80, 134, 151, 181, 185n4, 219
  on Jewish state establishment, 85
  as peacemaker, 196–7, 197–8n24, 203, 204

October War (1973). *See* Arab-Israeli War (1973)
One Democratic State Campaign, 257
One State Foundation, 257
one-state solution/model, 252, 254, 285
  Balad support to, 259
  Palestinian approach to, 259
  See also two-state solution
Only Language They Understand, The (Thrall), 198
Operation "Grapes of Wrath", 172
Oslo Accord I, 70, 73, 91, 141, 143, 152, 154, 169, 172
Oslo Accord II, 169, 171, 172, 180
Oslo Accords/Agreements, 163, 163–4, 176, 202, 204, 221n77, 256
  emergence of, 194
  impact of, 268, 269, 279
  issues of, 231, 244
  PLO and, 167–8
  See also Trump-Netanyahu deal (2020); United States (US)
Oslo, 128, 144–5

PA. *See* Palestinian Authority (PA)
Palestine Liberation Organization. *See* PLO (Palestine Liberation Organization)
Palestine National Congress (PNC), 54
Palestine
  before 1948, 101–2, 266–7
  history, 2–5, 286
  and Israel, 7, 9–10
  occupation history of, 33t, 215, 241, 286
  under British, 214, 286
  Zionism, 10

Palestinian Authority (PA), 9–10,
    10n2, 66, 71, 94, 131–2, 141,
    143, 175–6, 195, 228, 271
  Europe and US relations with,
    147–8
  Hamas joined, 144–5
  and Hamas on Intifada II, 174
  Israel against actions to, 197
  Israel domination on, 176, 181,
    206–7, 216, 229
  Israel local authority transfer to,
    169
  Kushner warning, 205
  myth about, 198
  Occupied Territories under,
    228
  after Oslo Accords, 171–2, 180
  PLO actions, undermining, 273
  role under Israeli Jewish state,
    271, 277–8, 279, 280, 282
  Sharon invasion, 196
  transformation from PLO to,
    98, 168, 234, 268, 279
  on West Bank, 170
  See also Oslo Accords/
    Agreements; PLO (Palestine
    Liberation Organization)
Palestinian autonomy, 191–2n15
  US proposal, 190, 191
Palestinian calamity, 266
  See also Nakba (1948); war
    (1948)
"Palestinian Catastrophe". See
  Nakba (1948)
Palestinian cause/question/issues/
  struggles, 1, 2, 4, 5, 6, 9, 15,
    57, 69, 70, 72, 90, 103, 119,
    125, 155, 273, 280, 280–1
  as Arab cause, 169
  Arab regimes and, 91
  Arab support for, 100–1
  Bush contribution, 193

  democratic discourse for
    justice, 282–4
  Egypt's separate peace impact
    on, 268
  Fatah distraction to, 273
  history of, 88–9
  Israel struggle for power, 274,
    276n3
  Israel's rejection, 7, 198
  long-term struggles, 277–81
  after Nakba, 139–40
  struggles for justice, 270–1
  Trump four-person team,
    199–200, 204
  Trump's vision impact on, 225
Palestinian Communist party, 255
Palestinian Congress III, 59–60
Palestinian constituency, 271
Palestinian entity/entitativity. See
  PLO (Palestine Liberation
  Organization)
Palestinian forces, 259
Palestinian Jerusalemites, 248
Palestinian leadership/leaders
  Arab country engagement, 281
  after Arafat death, 230
  Israel diplomatic recognition
    on, 191, 229, 258
  among PA, 175, 176, 287
  political activities of, 272
  roadmap acceptance, 195
Palestinian Legislative Council
  elections, 171
Palestinian Muslim worshippers,
  172
Palestinian National Authority
  (PNA). See Palestinian
  Authority (PA)
Palestinian National Council
  (PNC), 279–80n6, 280
Palestinian National Council
  elections, 170

Palestinian National Covenant, 195

Palestinian national movement/ national liberation movement, 28, 102, 127, 140, 141–2, 266, 275, 282
  Global South support, need for, 273
  after Nakba, 271
  PLO contribution to, 257–8
  See also bi-national movement; Intifada I; Intifada II

Palestinian people. See Palestinians

Palestinian political elites, 258, 287

Palestinian refugees, 29, 45–50, 71, 73, 121, 138, 201, 218
  issue of (1948), 189, 234, 237, 267, 283
  national liberation movement, 257, 258

Palestinian society, 30, 40

Palestinian State, 10, 33n37, 128, 141–2, 149, 267, 270
  citizenship of, 236–7
  during national liberation period, 229
  emergence of, 219
  international community intervention on sovereignty, 219
  Israel sovereignty on water territories, 220–1
  legitimacy of, 231–2
  Martial law, 233
  Palestinian embassy of, 231
  Palestinians conditions, 233–4
  PLO power loss, 228
  regional politics of, 232
  See also Area A (West bank); Area B (West bank); Area C (West bank); West bank; Gaza strip

Palestinian-Israeli conflict, 168–9, 198

Palestinian-Israeli negotiations, 198
  Trump-Netanyahu document basis for, 209

Palestinian–Jordanian delegation, 168

Palestinians, 263, 266
  Arab states blamed, 10
  delegation at Madrid negotiations, 194
  democratic programme, 258, 266, 287
  demographic threat of, 198, 229, 238
  diversity of, 2–3, 8
  during Zionist project, 8, 204–5, 206
  emigration from Lebanon, 138
  expelled from Levant, 49
  Fatah distracting, 273
  forced relocation to Tunisia, 140
  Hamas deterrence, belief on, 284
  on Intifada I, 161–2
  Israel rule over, 24
  Israeli colonial settlement, 233–4, 248, 249, 277
  Jordanian vs., 139
  land rights, 57–64
  modern identity, 65–8
  national liberation movement, 257, 258, 271, 282
  as "present absentees", 237
  protest (May 2021), 278
  resistance to Israel, 229, 271
  strength of, 287–8
  suicide attacks, 172
  UN partition resolution, rejection of, 95

as victims, 159, 211, 232, 265, 266

in West Bank and Gaza Strip, 283

See also Arab citizens; Arabs (Palestine); Palestinian refugees

pan-Arab camp, 267

Pappé, Ilan, 38

Paris, 164, 169

Pasha, Ibrahim, 65

"Peace to Prosperity". *See* Trump-Netanyahu deal (2020)

Peasants' revolt (1834), 65, 65n16

Peled, Yoav, 29

Pentagon, 115

Peres, Shimon, 115–16, 172, 194

"Permanent Status Agreement". *See* Oslo Accord II

"permanent status issues". *See* Palestinian cause/question/issues/struggles

Philistines, 61

'Plan Dalet' (Plan D), 37, 38

PLO (Palestine Liberation Organization), 9, 53–5, 67, 89, 98, 124, 126–8, 140–3, 159, 166, 184n3, 257, 279

against Israeli settlement, 176, 180

agreed partition plan, 189

clashed with Jordan, 128, 139

departure from Lebanon, 137

emergence as representatives of Palestinian people, 125, 267

error of, 168

financial support loss, 195

Gaza strip siege, declining, 273

Madrid negotiations delegation of, 193, 194

Oslo Accords impact on, 279

after Oslo Accords, 170–1, 244, 268

and Oslo negotiations with Israel, 70, 167–9, 194

PLO-PA, 131–2, 168, 234, 268, 279

security coordination with Israel, 195, 227

sidelining of, 94

under supervision, 167

warning to South Africa, 247–8

PNC. *See* Palestinian National Council (PNC)

Pollack, Kenneth, 114

Pompeo, Mike, 202, 204

Popp, Roland, 110

Porath, Yehoshua, 65

post-Gulf War (1991), 80

Prevention of Infiltration Law (1954), 48

protest (May 2021), 258, 278, 288

Protestant monarchs, 82

Prussia, 82

Qalandia airport, 121

Qalqilya (city), 109, 109n5

Qana, 173

"Quartet", 195, 197, 273

quasi-state, 285

Qur'an, 209–10

Rabat Summit (1974), 130

Rabat, 128

Rabbo, Yasir Abed, 227n1

Rabin, Yitzhak (1992–5), 167, 170–1, 184

election victory, 194

murder of, 172, 173, 276–7n4

Race and Class, 256

Rafah, 131

Ramallah, 109n4, 121, 147, 174, 196, 230

rawabit al-qura, 229

Reagan, Ronald, 191, 191–2n15
    and Israel settlements, 202–3
Resolution 181 (II). *See* United
    Nations Partition Resolution
    (1947)
*Restoration of the Jews to Palestine
    according to the Prophets, The*, 83
roadmap (US Peace initiatives),
    195, 196, 269
    See also United States (US)
Robinson, Shira, 240
Rodinson, Maxime, 232
Rogers, William P., 189, 189–
    90n9, 190
Ross, Dennis, 173, 193,
    193–4n18
Rouhana, Nadim, 252
Ruppin, Arthur, 255
Russia, 22, 86, 195

Sabbagh-Khoury, Areej, 243
Sabra culture, 31, 236, 241
Sadat, Anwar, 91–2, 127
el-Sadat, Muhammad Anwar,
    190–1
Safad, 39
Safwat, Ismail, 39
Samaria, 212
San Remo conference (1920), 59
Sapir, Pinchas, 122–3
Saudi Arabia, 149–50
al-Sayegh, Fayez, 232, 233
separation wall, 221, 249, 263,
    269, 272
Sephardi Jews, 100, 118–19
Shamir, Yitzhak, 184, 194
Sharett, Moshe, 36
Sharm el-Sheikh Summit (2005),
    175
Sharm el-Sheikh, 153, 153n10
Sharon, Ariel, 115, 146, 153,
    174, 192, 197

    and Abbas meeting, 175
    diplomatic action in Gaza Strip,
        195–6, 218
Sheikh Jarrah, 5
Shlaim, Avi, 40
shtahim muhzakim (captured or
    seized territories), 212
al-Shuqayri, Ahmad, 53–4
Silwan, 5
Sinai, 110–11, 126, 131
    Israel attitude during war
        (1967), 267
    Israel withdrawal from, 214
single state solution. *See* one-state
    solution/model
Six-Day War (1967). *See* Arab-
    Israeli war (1967)
solidarity movements, 273, 274
South Africa, 11, 244, 245–6n38
    acquisition of arms by, 247–8
    against apartheid, 257, 282
    citizens of, 250
    Israel embassy, opening of, 247
South African blacks, 250
South African whites, 250
South Africans, 257
Soviet Union, 32, 41n67, 42, 114
    break-up of, 164–5, 195, 268
    collapse of, 140
    Jews of, 162–3
    Palestine partition declaration,
        255
Spectator, The (magazine), 35
"The State and Prospects of the
    Jews" (article), 82
Sudan, 281
Suez Crisis (1956), 111
superpower, 193, 205, 210–11
Supreme Court, 239, 240
Supreme Muslim Council, 51
Switzerland, 82
Syria, 38, 45, 50, 68, 126, 140,
    173, 189

draft resolution (A/C.1/402)
   submission, 46–7
Joint Defence Treaty (1950),
   112
military coup (1949), 90
national struggles of, 281
peace negotiations with Israel,
   138
unconditional Israel peace with,
   267

Taba, 169
Takkenberg, Lex, 50
Tehran, 6
Tel Aviv, 6, 184
   during Oslo negotiation, 194
   Israel embassy in, 247
   US embassy relocation, 201
Third World sponsors, 247
Thrall, Nathan, 198–9
Tiberias, 39
Times, The (newspaper), 82
Torah, 208, 209, 210, 211, 213
*Tract for the Times, Being a Plea for
   the Jews* (Bradshaw), 83
Transjordan, 44
Triangle (region), 215–16, 217,
   238
Trump, Donald, 6
   administration of, 5, 10, 80,
      143, 204–5, 210, 269–70
   four-person team, creation of,
      199–200, 204
   Oslo Accords withdrawal, 180
   as peacemaker, 183
   Trump vision, 187, 205,
      223–4, 225
   See also Trump-Netanyahu deal
      (2020)
Trump-Netanyahu deal (2020), 1,
   10, 12, 135, 180, 185n4, 189,
   201, 205, 270, 273

Abbas reward from, 175
document of, 208–13
emergence of, 183–4
fallacies of, 213–19
language of, 207
nature of, 205–7
on state and sovereignty,
   219–26, 229
world leaders on, 222n79
See also Netanyahu, Benjamin;
   Oslo Accords/Agreements
Tuchman, Barbara, 84
Tunis, 195
Tunisia, 140, 259
Tunnel Uprising (1996), 173
Turkey, 192
two-state settlement, 232
two-state solution, 198, 222n79,
   227, 230, 259, 270, 285
   failure of, 287
   Intifada I, 195
   Israeli favours about, 260
   Israeli settlements, end of, 241
   See also bi-national state;
      one-state solution/model

Umayyad Caliphate, 210
umbrella organisation, 283
UN Convention on the
   Elimination of All Forms of
   Racial Discrimination, 248
UN General Assembly, 31–2, 46,
   150
UN partition plan (1947), 188,
   212
UN Relief and Works Agency
   (UNRWA), 38, 50
UN Resolution (194/1948),
   46–8, 201, 267
UN Security Council, 146, 150,
   204, 247
   Israel rejections, 189–90

INDEX

Israeli reading of, 215
"Resolution 242", 146
Resolutions, 169, 189, 193, 202
unemployment rate (Israel), 162, 163, 164, 167f
UNESCO (United Nations Educational, Scientific and Cultural Organization), 197
UNGA Resolution. See UN partition plan (1947)
United Arab Emirates (UAE), 93, 150, 201
United Kingdom (UK), 46, 134, 222, 225
United Nations (UN), 45, 79, 120, 173
International Convention on apartheid, 247
PLO and, 159
on Quartet, 195
refugee problem and, 45–6
United Nations Conciliation Commission for Palestine (UNCCP), 47
United Nations International Convention (1973), 247
United Nations Partition Resolution (1947), 7, 31–2, 36, 38, 44, 73, 95
United Nations Special Committee on Palestine (UNSCOP), 31, 32
United Nations Trusteeship Council, 32
United States (US), 6, 46, 80, 97–8, 102, 114, 118n33, 141, 173, 222, 225, 232
alliances with Israel, 10, 79, 133–5, 230, 263, 266, 269
apartheid usage, 251
Arab Peace Initiative welcomed in, 151

Arafat and, 174
depicting PLO as terrorist organization, 127
foreign policy, 132, 133–4
Immigration Act (1924), 17
on Israel, 118
Israel's hegemony in, 153
Jewish immigration to, 16–17, 18–21t, 22
as "mediator", 187–201, 273
need Arab help on Iraq war, 269
"obstacle to peace" consideration on Israeli settlements, 197, 202, 203
real estate character of, 205, 208, 213, 220
UNRWA financial cutting, 201
as a "virgin land", 81
See also Trump, Donald; Trump-Netanyahu deal (2020)
UNRWA (United Nations Relief and Works Agency), 201
uprising (2019), 4
Urban II, Pope, 262
US policy, 193–4n18, 199, 270

Veracini, Lorenzo, 234, 235–6, 241, 242, 252
Vienna, 83

war (1948), 212, 237, 238
war (1956), 211
War Diaries (Ben-Gurion), 40
War of Attrition, 117
"War of Independence" (1948), 16, 22, 68
Ward, William, 175
Washington, D.C., 6, 94, 111, 128, 130, 169, 201
Israeli lobby in, 184, 269

Weizmann, Chaim, 86
West Bank, 1, 2, 29, 49–50n94,
    85, 123, 132, 139n1, 174, 205,
    236, 250, 258, 267, 268
    apartheid crime, meeting of,
        248, 251
    authorities of, 273
    blockade lifting, 145–6
    Brzezinski plan, 190
    Fatah seized power in, 144
    Hamas and Fatah competition,
        272–3
    Israel and Palestine administra-
        tive areas, 170
    Israel regime on, 249
    Israel settlements, 170, 177–9f,
        241, 265, 271, 272
    Israeli withdrawal from, 121
    Jordan's annexation of, 139
    Obama administration actions,
        181, 197, 203, 204
    Palestinian autonomy establish-
        ment, 191, 197
    Palestinian in, 125, 213
    Pompeo declaration, 202, 204
    representatives in Madrid Peace
        Conference, 166
    waste water treatment funding,
        221
    See also Gaza Strip; Israeli
        leaders; Palestinians
West Jerusalem, 122
Western academia, 234n9
Western media, 168, 272
Western powers, 10
White House, 184, 211, 273
    Kerry-Abbas-Netanyahu
        meeting, 197, 205
    See also Washington, D.C.
Wolfe, Patrick, 234, 235
World Bank, 162
World War I, 17, 65, 214
World War II, 63, 78, 96

Wye River Memorandum, 170

Yalu (village), 109, 109n4
Yemen, 93
Yeshuv, 22n13, 42, 61, 95–6
Yishuv leadership, 188
Yom Kippur War. See Arab-Israeli
    War (1973)
youth solidarity campaign, 4
youth, 4
    Hebrew University study on,
        208
    Palestine young activists, 279,
        283

Zionism, 10, 16, 23, 27, 62,
    63–4, 102, 218. See Zionist
    movement/project/colonialism
    (Palestine)
"Zionist band". See "Zionist entity"
Zionist Congress I (Basel,
    29–31 Aug 1897), 62
"Zionist entity", 68
Zionist ideology, 23–4, 26–7,
    30–1, 36, 113
Zionist militias, 30, 33, 36, 42
Zionist movement/project/
    colonialism (Palestine), 2, 7, 8,
    16, 23n14, 26, 33, 51, 95–6,
    218, 233, 235, 239
    framed idea 'Jewish state', 253,
        256, 265
    from colonial project (1948),
        265, 283
    history of, 286
    independence declaration
        (15 May 1948), 31
    Israeli academia concept, 242
    South Africa and French
        colonial practices, compari-
        son with, 251
    after war (1967), 268
Zureik, Elia, 240